# Beyond Mestizaje

# Beyond Mestizaje

CONTEMPORARY DEBATES
ON RACE IN MEXICO

Edited by
Tania Islas Weinstein
and Milena Ang

Amherst
College
Press

Each essay of this work was subjected to two rounds of a fully closed ("double-blind") review process by the Editorial Board. For more information, visit https://acpress.amherst.edu/peerreview/.

Cover image: "Paraíso Perdido" by Julián Islas Madero. Used with permission.

Published in the United States of America by Amherst College Press
Manufactured in the United States of America

Library of Congress Control Number: 2023948421
DOI: https://doi.org/10.3998/mpub.14369172

ISBN 978-1-943208-67-8 (Print)
ISBN 978-1-943208-68-5 (OA)

# Contents

# Note on the Translations

## Ellen Jones

There are two questions identified in the introduction to this book that have important implications for its translation: how are people in Mexico racially classified and categorized, both officially and colloquially, and in what ways are Mexicans' experiences with racism similar to (or different from) those of their US counterparts?

The first of these questions involves paying attention to the use of specific vocabulary in Spanish: to the official and colloquial terms used to classify and categorize Mexicans racially in different contexts and at different points in time. When it comes to translating such terms, my strategy has usually been to retain them in Spanish but to accompany them with a gloss or explanation in English wherever necessary. This includes racial terms such as "prieto," "güero," and "moreno" (as Alejandra Leal points out in her contribution to this volume, "prieto does not easily translate as brown and güero is not equivalent to white"), but also extends to terms for aspects of Indigenous culture, such as "gabanes," "huipil," and "calenda," and terms to do with land tenancy, such as "campesino," "hacienda," and "ejido." It also includes the term "mestizaje" (which has variously been translated by others as "miscegenation," "mixing," or "mixed racial descent"), as its meaning is so crucial to all of the discussions in this book as to warrant being retained in all its specificity. This is despite awkward neologisms such as "mestizofication" (from "amestizamiento"), which I believe are worth enduring for the particular meaning the term "mestizaje" brings to the discussion. Also worth mentioning are the terms used in Eugenia Iturriaga's chapter, which relies extensively on Bolívar Echeverría's concepts "blancura," "blanquitud," and "blanqueamiento" from his book *Modernidad y blanquitud* (Echeverría 2010). In Rodrigo Ferreira's

2019 translation of this volume, blancura is rendered as whiteness while blanquitud becomes "whiteness," in inverted commas. Rather than replicate this decision, I have preferred to keep blanquitud in Spanish throughout, in part because it makes it easier for readers to distinguish between two concepts it is crucial to hold apart, and in part because blanquitud contains an echo of the term of négritude, a neologism coined by francophone intellectuals, writers, and politicians of the African diaspora that is rarely, if ever, translated as "blackness." By leaving these Spanish terms in my English translations it is hoped that the subtle ethno-racial and class distinctions they denote might become more widely understood in the English-speaking world, thus helping to nuance the conversation about racial dynamics in Mexico and Latin America beyond the Black/white binary.

Relatedly, I have chosen not to italicize "non-English" words in my translations. Khairani Barokka articulates the motivation for this decision particularly eloquently when she describes the practice of italicizing such words as "a form of linguistic gatekeeping" that marks a boundary between words that are "exotic," "other," or "foreign" and those that have a rightful place in an English language text (Barokka 2020). Spanish words are foreign neither to the contributors to this book nor to the cultural contexts it discusses, so I see no reason to estrange them visually in my translations—to do so would be to reinforce anglophone cultural dominance. Barokka also points out that the decision to italicize or not is a question of assumed audience. If I italicize the word moreno, for instance, I am assuming a lack of familiarity with the term, thus alienating any US-based reader who does have knowledge of Spanish, and for whom we might anticipate this book to have special relevance and resonance.

This decision is complicated by the fact that Spanish is, of course, not the only language spoken in Mexico. Several contributions to this volume were written by Indigenous scholars and activists whose personal and professional lives sometimes take place in languages other than Spanish. Ariadna Solis, for instance, conducted her research in Zapotec, communicating with elderly women in the community of Yalálag, Oaxaca, through an interpreter. When she first published her research, Solis was already making decisions about how to translate Zapotec objects and ideas into Spanish; indeed, in some instances, she signals her belief that they are not translatable at all. Her Spanish-language article presented Zapotec terms in italics, which had the effect of highlighting the specificity and lack of transferability of certain key community concepts (a *xtap* is not the same as a refajo or underskirt, for instance). However, I think the change of language and context implied by this English edition warrants a different approach here: in my translation I have chosen to include both Spanish and Zapotec terms in regular font in order to avoid othering or exoticizing an Indigenous language in relation to two European ones, or indeed alienating any Indigenous readers who may find this book in their hands.

The second question posed in the Introduction that is relevant to my own work as translator—"In what ways are Mexicans' experiences with racism similar to (and different) from those of their US counterparts?"—is explored extensively in the third section of this volume. The chapters by Alejandra Leal and Eugenia Iturriaga are particularly insightful when it comes to thinking about the language we use to discuss racialization and racism, particularly how English terms have been adopted into Spanish-speaking contexts and have therefore influenced the framing of the debate there. Incidentally, the term "whitexican" strikes me as particularly telling in this regard: it appends a suffix derived from an English word ("-xican") to an Anglo-American racial concept with limited currency in Mexico ("white") and yet does not follow any established rules of English pronunciation (counter-intuitively, for English speakers who see the word for the first time, it's a two-syllable "white-xican," not a three-syllable "whitexican" with a short "i"). It thus simultaneously critiques both the "whiteness" of elite sectors of Mexican society and their habitual use of English as a prestige marker (or as a means of achieving a "whitening" effect). I hope other scholars and translators continue to nuance and develop this conversation in future publications. It will be interesting to see, for instance, whether the capitalization of the words "Black" and "Indigenous" (as readers will see used here when in direct reference to a person or people) will at some point become the norm in Mexico and Latin America too. In the English-speaking world it is customary to capitalize these terms as a sign of respect for the political and historical communities they denote (in the same way that the terms "German" or "Asian" are capitalized), but it is not currently the convention to capitalize "negro" or "indígena" in Spanish.

One Spanish word whose usage varies considerably is "indio," both as an adjective and a noun. The authors in this book use it widely when discussing historical contexts, particularly the colonial period up to independence, and often interchangeably with the term "indígena." In these instances, I have rendered "indio" as "Indian." However, Itza Amanda Varela Huerta, for instance, uses the term in her chapter about present-day Black Afro-Mexican communities on the Costa Chica. In these instances, I have preferred to translate "indio" as "Indigenous person" because "indio" can sometimes be pejorative, depending on the speaker and the context. The Real Academia Española notes that it is used across much of Central and South America as a synonym for "inculto"—uncultured or ignorant (although, to be clear, the term is evidently not used in this way in Varela Huerta's chapter). Moreover, in English, of course, Indian more commonly refers to a person from India, while the term "American Indian" is steadily being replaced in many contexts by "Native American," which is often considered both to be more accurate and to avoid stereotypes associated with the "Wild West."

Finally, it is worth noting that all contributions to this volume originally written and published in Spanish appear here in my English translation, and I am grateful to their authors for their input when certain ideas or terms were thrown into doubt by the movement between languages. However, the volume's introduction was conceived and written in English, as were the contributions by Alejandra Leal, Alice Krozer, and Metzli Yoalli Rodríguez Aguilera. Unless otherwise noted, all translations of quotations from Spanish into English are my own.

## References

Barokka, Khairani. 2020. "The Case Against Italicizing 'Foreign' Words." *Catapult*, February 11, 2020. https://tinyurl.com/4xy8ewzj.

Echeverría, Bolívar. 2010. *Modernidad y blanquitud*. Mexico City: Era.

# INTRODUCTION: UN LUGAR DE ENCUENTRO

## Milena Ang and Tania Islas Weinstein

In the last decade, race and racism have become important topics of discussion in Mexico's public and academic spheres. A growing number of articles, monographs, edited volumes, and special issues that tackle the intersections between race and class, the relationship between phenotypical traits and racialization, and anti-racist efforts, to name a few, have been published in recent years both in the popular press and in academic outlets.[1] These publications have been accompanied by university courses, research groups, workshops, and conferences in and outside academia.[2] Scholars and experts on the topic are increasingly seeking venues to share their work with non-academic publics, including through the use of social media.[3] Racism is also being discussed in unprecedented ways on television and in radio shows, films,[4] art exhibitions,[5] media campaigns, and social media posts,[6] as well as in public conversations with artists, actors, public intellectuals, and members of the lay public. In the last ten years, several organizations that work specifically to combat racism have also been created, including RacismoMx,[7] Colectivo Copera (Colectivo para Eliminar el Racismo),[8] Colectiva Muafro (mujeres afromexicanas),[9] México Negro AC,[10] Censo MX,[11] and Basta Racismo MX,[12] to name a few. Politicians also constantly bring up the topic of racism, even if they often do so in co-optative and tokenistic ways (Islas Weinstein and Ang 2021). Their words, together with a small but rising number of legal cases that challenge racial discrimination and the criminalization of racialized individuals, have an important symbolic dimension that is helping to change existing narratives about racism and racial justice (Moreno Parra 2022).

This book seeks to introduce readers outside of Mexico to these unprecedented and timely conversations. Some of the questions that are addressed by this book's contributors—who are either from Mexico or who work and reside in Mexico—include the following: How is race currently perceived in Mexico? How is racism experienced? How are people in the country officially and colloquially racially classified and categorized? What are the different ways in which racism is currently being documented, measured, and denounced in Mexico? What are the upsides (and drawbacks) of mapping race onto biological phenotypes rather than onto cultural attributes? In what ways are Mexicans' experience with racism similar (and different) from those of their US counterparts? In addressing these questions, this book shows how public conversations have led to difficult—but necessary—discussions, disagreements, and debates between activists, scholars, public intellectuals, and the public at large.

As will quickly become evident to the reader, all the authors in the book agree that there is no such thing as race or ethnicity outside of the social conditions that make these concepts meaningful ones. In other words, they consider race to be an "ontologically empty social construct" (Sánchez Contreras in this book) that results from a series of complex processes of identification, distinction, and differentiation between human beings. In Mexico, these processes take into account a wide range of factors that can include phenotypical traits, as well as cultural ones like everyday practices and worldviews, descent and ancestry, location of birth or residency, attire, and language. But while all the texts presented here acknowledge that race is a socially constructed category, there are also important disagreements between them. Some authors included here have conflicting views on how race can (and should) be observed and studied and, relatedly, how race and racial categories relate to socioeconomic stratification. And while all authors understand racism as a process that marks differences between people in relation to hierarchical discourses in ways that become naturalized, some authors also disagree on whether or not racism is internal to, and even constitutive of, a capitalist social order. Rather than seeing these disagreements as conflicts that need to be resolved, we believe that they reveal the trade-offs and illuminate the stakes that come with analyzing racism in different ways.

One of the main disagreements that has come to the fore in Mexico in recent years and that is prominently featured in the book is the way in which race can (and should) be studied and measured. Specifically, authors disagree on the role phenotypical characteristics such as skin color or hair type play in racialization and, therefore, also disagree on how to observe and measure race, racialization, and racism. While all authors in this book recognize that skin color and other phenotypical traits matter when distinguishing individuals based on their identities, some authors argue that physical traits can be objectively observed and measured using various instruments, the most important of which is the use of a color palette that is compared against an individual's skin.[13] Studies that use these tools have consistently found that, compared to light-skinned individuals, darker-skinned ones score lower in a variety of socioeconomic indicators, such as income and education. But other authors in this book argue, instead, that physical characteristics are not always the most prominent traits at stake when analyzing processes of racialization and contend that racial categorization and stratification are substantially determined by socioeconomic characteristics.[14] Following the old adage that says that "Money whitens," these authors contend that, as people climb the socioeconomic ladder, they are more likely to be perceived as white. As we argue later in the introduction, these disagreements have crucial implications for how we study and understand not only racial categories and processes of racialization, but also the relationship between race and social class, and between racism and economic structures like capitalism.

In addition, some of the contributions in this book invite the reader to reflect on the processes and effects of racialization of black and indigenous people.[15] Some of the authors rely on first-hand experiences to show how capitalist practices, policies, and institutions have impacted everything from the material conditions of their communities to their own individual identities.[16] Overall, these contributions not only denounce the profound racism that permeates the political and socio-economic environment in contemporary Mexico, but also provide ideas about the kinds of actions that can be taken to prevent and dismantle such racism. One of the recurrent propositions raised by many of these authors is that a world without racism is only possible if current economic structures are dismantled.

In short, the chapters in this book focus on the meaning and experiences of race and racism—including the relationship between race and class—in Mexico in the aftermath of the market reforms implemented in the late twentieth century. In this sense, rather than theorize about socioeconomic classification or social class more broadly, the chapters here help us think through the socioeconomic and political institutions and processes that construct and shape racial identities, hierarchies, and forms of stratification, as well as their consequences. While some chapters are written by scholars coming from different academic disciplines, others are authored by activists, practitioners, and public intellectuals with very different backgrounds, experiences, and perspectives on these issues. Thus, another main contribution of this book is to bring together different—and sometimes even conflicting—understandings of the interaction between race and class in Mexico.

Each of the ten chapters and seven interludes can be read as stand-alone articles, but the book can also be regarded as a meeting place—or, as per the title of this introduction, as a "lugar de encuentro"[17]—where scholars, activists, and public intellectuals gather to discuss and debate their views about race and class. As a meeting place, this book is unique because it brings together voices that coexist in the country's public sphere but that tend to talk past each other because of their ontological, epistemological, and methodological differences. In short, this is the first book to bring together dissenting views about race and racism in contemporary Mexico, and it does so by acknowledging these very different voices while seeking to put them in conversation with one another. By the time readers reach the end of the book, they will have a clear idea of the different perspectives about racism that prevail in Mexico's academic and public spheres. This Introduction seeks to clarify both the nature of these different perspectives and explain the political stakes that ground these disagreements.

This introduction is divided into five main sections. First, we historically contextualize the concept of mestizaje (i.e., Mexico's national ideology and state project of racial mixing) because, as the different chapters show, while it is losing its unifying force and authoritative power as both an ideology and a state project, it continues to shape the way that many Mexican citizens understand and navigate race. The second section presents some of the main ideas and debates featured in the book, including, in particular, the attempts to isolate the effects of skin color on socioeconomic opportunities and the discussions on the intersections between structural racism and the capitalist social order. In this section we also discuss the relationship between the production of knowledge on issues about race and the existing and potential political and public-policy effects of these recent discussions. The third section centers around the topic of translation and discusses some of the main promises and risks—literally and substantively—of translating these debates from Spanish for an English-speaking public. The fourth section is a preview of the book, presenting its layout and explaining the conceptual differences between chapters and interludes. In this section we also offer a brief comment on our positionality as editors. The fifth and last section of the introduction presents the limitations of the book, including the insufficient discussion on the intersections between race, class, gender, and sex, and points to references and sources that readers might want to consult to fill in these gaps.

## Mestizaje, Then and Now

The Spanish colonial rule of the territory that would eventually become Mexico (1521–1821) created a highly stratified society along ethnic lines. Spanish settlers were located at the top followed by different categories (or *castas*) of individuals based on the intermixing of what were considered ostensibly different yet relatively homogenous race groups: Spanish settlers, indigenous residents, and African slaves. The largest category at the time was made up of members of different indigenous groups, who constituted over 60% (Gall 2021). Following Mexican Independence, the complex racial dynamics of the colonial period were simplified "into a bipolar model (Indian/whites) with an intermediate class of '*mestizos*'" (Lomnitz-Adler 1993). At the time, people's skin color was an important signifier, but individuals could "redefine themselves into a whiter category based on their level of education and wealth" (Villareal 2010). By migrating to urban areas and adopting certain cultural markers, such as speaking Spanish rather than an indigenous language, indigenous people began to be portrayed as mestizos.

Following the Mexican Revolution (1910–1921), which took the lives of over 10% of the population, the newly established state—headed by the Revolutionary National Party or PNR (1929–1938), which later became the Revolutionary Institutional Party or PRI (1938–2000)—sought to rebuild, unify, and modernize the country. A crucial part of these state building efforts was the material and discursive incorporation into the nation of the masses that had fought in the armed struggle. This included the creation of party and state structures that led to the implementation of mass social programs and that foregrounded the narrative of a politically and racially unified national mestizo community (Leal in this book). It was at this time that being Mexican became synonymous with being mestizo. As a result, the boundaries between racial categories were further blurred as mestizaje became the official discourse that sought to describe an ideal (racial) nation-state, one in which Mexicans were considered to be the product of the miscegenation between Europeans and indigenous people (Alonso 2004, 462). The post-revolutionary mestizaje project enabled a certain level of socioeconomic equality via strong public investments in education, health, and infrastructure that helped to do away with many "racist barriers" that privileged the political and economic elites (Zollá 2022).

But the equalizing effects of mestizaje's ideology had its shortcomings and limits. While mestizaje portrayed Mexico's indigenous past as a glorious one that Mexicans were taught and expected to be proud of,[18] it simultaneously framed indigenous peoples as needing to be civilized if they were to be incorporated into the national project. The indigenous subject was, in other words, placed in a position of "intimate alterity," meaning that it was considered as constitutive of the national mestizo subject yet racialized as backward and inferior and in need of education by a paternalistic state, through public education and other top-down measures that included, among others, enforcing Spanish as the primary language, eliminating traditional medical practices, and redefining the way that communal land tenure was organized (López Caballero 2021, 136).[19] Therefore, there is a foundational tension at the heart of mestizaje: it is an ideology that ostensibly unifies people of European and indigenous descent into a single, equal Mexican subject while constitutively regarding indigenous people as racially inferior and in need of "civilization" and "modernization" to become more European. Ultimately, the project of mestizaje was unable to eradicate forms of discrimination and violence against indigenous communities, all while doing very little to eliminate racial violence within and amongst indigenous communities (López Caballero 2020).

The mestizo project, moreover, focused on the European and indigenous roots of the nation, and it radically disavowed black and Asian populations from the country's national project. Black populations were absent from official narratives. For instance, during the colonial period, more African slaves entered the country than Spaniards, yet they were unmentioned in textbooks or official discourse (Cunin 2018). Even historical details such as the fact that Mexico's first president, Guadalupe Victoria, was of African descent, were rarely brought up during national commemorations (Moreno Figueroa and Saldívar Tanaka 2016, 7). In turn, Asian populations, particularly Chinese immigrants who came to Mexico to work on plantations, railroads, and other industries during Porfirio Díaz's regime (1884–1911), were persecuted by the postrevolutionary regime, especially in the northern states.[20] Yet, in the new social imagination of the ideal citizenry championed by the mestizaje ideologues, neither black nor Asian people figured, and black and Asian anti-racism was considered irrelevant for Mexico's nationalist project (Sue

2013; Moreno Figueroa 2013; Moreno Figueroa and Saldívar Tanaka 2016). Notwithstanding countless historical examples of everyday invisibilization and racism, the official rhetoric of Mexican mestizaje was able to position itself in opposition to Anglo-American racial ideologies. Rather than leading to the enslavement or extermination of racialized populations, mestizaje allegedly sought to "liberate" them from oppression by integrating them into a unified and racially mixed country.

But even as racial mixing is foregrounded in the ideology of mestizaje, the post-revolutionary state and its new institutions did not conceive of "race" as a series of phenotypical and epidermal traits and, instead, favored cultural practices as racial markers (Gall 2004; Sue and Golash-Boza 2013; Sue 2013). Categories such as skin color (for example, black, white, brown, yellow, etc.) were not recognized by the state, be it in the census, birth certificates, medical records, legal acts, or any other official documents, nor did these matter when making public policies (Wade 2010, also Ceron-Anaya in this book). Instead, the state's census recorded characteristics such as the language spoken at home and people's country of origin.[21] Mestizaje, in other words, entailed the incorporation of the masses into the modern state, a process that did not mean transforming the phenotypical features of the population but instead involved transforming people's everyday worldviews and practices in ways that undermined certain views and values that were considered by the state ideologues to be incompatible with the Western ethos.

Given that phenotypes and other biological attributes did not neatly map onto racial categories, there was flexibility when reading phenotypical characteristics as racial categories in everyday interactions. The corollary of race not being treated as a fixed biological condition was that people could be "racially" read in different ways depending on their socioeconomic position, the way they dressed, the language they spoke, their level of education, their everyday habits, and so on, depending on the context. And, as anthropologist Rihan Yeh has argued, mestizaje also organizes social hierarchies at the international level: being mestizo in the southern part of the country can be a radically different experience from being so in a place like the northern border city of Tijuana where racial (and social) status often depends on holding, or not, a US visa (Yeh 2015).

Throughout the twentieth century, mestizaje ideology was so deeply ingrained that discussions of racism among politicians, scholars, activists, and even the mestizo majority were almost non-existent. The academy, particularly before the 1980s, focused almost exclusively on discrimination of indigenous people, but mestizaje was rarely considered the root of the problem.[22] The idea that mestizaje was inclusive and equalizing, and therefore an anti-racist ideology, was so taken for granted that even critical scholars proposed tackling racism by deploying the same state corporatist tactics and institutions that had been enabled by the ideology of mestizaje.[23]

While the ideology of mestizaje continues to prevail in Mexico,[24] the socioeconomic and political transformations of the late twentieth century have transformed existing racial imaginaries, narratives, and discourses in ways that have only recently begun to be assessed. First, the country underwent a formal electoral transition which put an end to the PRI's 70-year near monopoly in power. With their ousting, the party that had championed mestizaje could not access the public institutions and resources that they had deployed to incorporate the masses—including that of racialized groups like black populations[25]—into the project. Secondly, following the 1982 oil crisis, a series of neoliberal economic reforms led to the unprecedented privatization of public assets and to the elimination of publicly funded projects, many of which targeted indigenous populations. These changes further impacted the state's ability to function as a corporate structure and implement policies that could incorporate and continue to "modernize" the population.

The market reforms implemented at the end of the twentieth century also led to an unprecedented increase in economic inequality. By 2014, the richest 10% owned over 64.4% of Mexico's total income (Esquivel Hernández 2015). Tellingly, while the number of multimillionaires in the country has not necessarily increased over the last few decades, the magnitude of their wealth has grown at a rate much higher than the GDP. As economist Gerardo Esquivel notes, in 2002 the wealth of the top 15 millionaires represented 2% of the country's GDP but 12 years later this number had risen to 9%. Meanwhile, in the last 25 years, over 40% of the population has continued to live in poverty and close to 10% do so in extreme poverty (CONEVAL 2014). Income disparities and poverty rates within the country vary significantly, with southern states—including Chiapas, Oaxaca, and Guerrero—consistently presenting the highest poverty rates in the country (over 60% of their population lives in poverty) and those in the north—including Nuevo León and Coahuila—and

Mexico City presenting the lowest (less than 30% of their population lives in poverty).[26]

The country's adoption of market reforms that led to this increase in economic inequality was accompanied by a turn to multiculturalism, which entailed a legal and discursive acknowledgement that nations are conformed by a variety of ethnic and cultural groups. A 1992 constitutional reform, for instance, recognized the country as a pluricultural state and acknowledged indigenous communities' right to self-determination (International Labour Organization 1996). Despite specific rights being granted to these communities,[27] it was not always clear who belonged to these categories and enjoyed such rights, or even what these rights actually entailed or how they could be enforced.[28] These changes, moreover, meant very little to the country's black and Asian populations. While the censuses from 2000 and 2010 included a question on self-identification for indigenous peoples, it was not until 2015 that activists lobbied for the modification of the census to include a category for Afro-Mexicans which finally appeared in 2020.[29] A year earlier, Article 2 of the constitution had finally recognized Afro-Mexicans as part of the pluricultural composition of the nation, marking a crucial departure from the traditional mestizaje narrative that had prevailed throughout the twentieth century.

The modifications that the state and economic apparatuses experienced in the turn of the twenty-first century have profoundly transformed national narratives, discourses, and practices, including the ideology of mestizaje. The chapters in this book are a window into these transformations and the debates that have ensued in response.

## Debates: Race, Class, Skin Color, and Dispossession

Recent years have seen an increased interest in questions of race and its relationship to class and capitalism.[30] Although most literature on this subject has addressed these questions in the United States, Canada, and Western Europe, there has been an interest in how these issues appear in different Latin American contexts.[31] Given the region's unique set of racial and economic dynamics—for example, Mexico's mestizaje ideology, or Brazil's racial democracy—the relationship between race and class operates in distinct and particularly complex ways and it is only in recent years that such complexity is being examined more closely, including by scholars and experts in the region.

Much of the literature written on this topic is rooted in cultural anthropology, qualitative sociology, and history.[32] Consistent with their disciplinary roots, these studies tend to share a strong commitment to interpretive epistemologies and deploy research methods that include ethnography, long-term participant-observation, and archival research. The chapters by Iturriaga and Forssell Méndez help us better understand these approaches, showing how racial and socioeconomic stratification are intertwined. In her chapter, Iturriaga anchors an insightful discussion on race in the category of whiteness (blanquitud). Following Marxist philosopher Bolivar Echevarría, Iturriaga explains that whiteness as a racial term is not merely a description of fixed phenotypical characteristics but also encompasses a capitalistic ethos with associated behaviors that can explain one's belonging to the elite.[33] In turn, Forssell Méndez's chapter provides a different exploration along these lines: in his reading, the Mexican post-revolutionary State deployed the ideology of mestizaje to erase racial differences, create a proletariat class, and enforce capitalistic modes of ownership. In this view, racialization is not completely unrelated to phenotypical traits, but it is created and enforced simultaneously with social class. In this view, empirically separating race and class is impossible and, to a certain degree, analytically fruitless.

In the past couple of decades, scholars coming from more positivist-oriented disciplines like quantitative sociology, economics, and development studies have approached the link between race and class in a different way. Mainly, these scholars have focused on studying the role phenotypical characteristics—including, in particular, skin color—play in determining material outcomes related to socioeconomic class, such as income, education, or job opportunities. These approaches, showcased in this book in the chapters by Solís and Güémez, and Jaramillo-Molina, rely on large surveys that capture individual physical characteristics.[34] These are then treated as observable and quantifiable racial markers that can be correlated to socioeconomic features such as income or education.

To be clear, these approaches rarely claim that skin color—or any similar phenotypical characteristic—is synonymous with race. Their approach instead aims at understanding the different ways in which individual socioeconomic classification comes about, focusing, in large part, on phenotypical determinants of this classification. Solís and Güémez, for example, analyze a nationally-representative survey and report that people with lighter-colored skin—and other physical racial markers such as eye color or hair characteristics—are more likely to reach higher income quintiles. Jaramillo-Molina, in turn, relies on a combination of social media posts and a survey on social mobility to study how narratives about economic success reify racial distinctions and economic inequality. These findings are consistent with other studies that use a similar approach and have found that skin color has a *systematic* effect on people's material conditions (Woo-Mora 2022; Monroy-Gómez-Franco, Vélez-Grajales, and Yalonetzky 2022; Cruz 2017; s-Vázquez and Rivas Herrera 2019). More specifically, these studies show how dark-skinned individuals are, on average, less economically and educationally privileged than individuals with lighter skin. Even within a large mestizo population like Mexico's, these findings show that darker skinned mestizos are more likely to suffer from lack of employment and education compared to those with lighter-skin tones. The corollary of these findings is that cultural traits, such as speaking an indigenous language or dressing in specific ways, are not the only reasons why individuals are racially discriminated. Instead, these findings show that structural racism in Mexico encompasses phenotypical elements that are analytically distinct and that can be empirically isolated from cultural practices and measured accordingly.

These seemingly small theoretical differences have had relevant consequences, of which we want to highlight two. First, some have criticized the use of color scales, warning that focusing on biological traits can lead to essentializing and naturalizing people's identities.[35] After all, it is hard to reconcile that skin color is a fixed trait that can be objectively measured with the idea that race is a social construct. To reiterate, scholars who rely on these surveys recognize that skin tone is not synonymous with race, but it does seem that their arguments and findings can be misread as a case for why race should be treated as a fixed identity that exists prior to the outcomes that they seek to explain, such as the lack of economic opportunities for dark-skinned people. As Mara Loveman argued decades ago, surveys present as "given" the categories of "black," "white," or "prieto," but theories of race making should precisely explain how these categories are understood by respondents, and how resulting statistics come to be seen as indicators of "race relations" in a particular location (Loveman 1999, 909).

To illuminate some of these discussions, the contributions by Ceron-Anaya and Krozer explicitly address the complexity between skin color, class, and its relation to racialization. In their studies of Mexican elites, their chapters show how race and racism are discussed and reproduced among wealthy

Mexicans. Drawing from his fieldwork at golf clubs in Mexico, Ceron-Anaya argues that, among elites, lighter skin color becomes a more prominent stratifying characteristic than money: the rich all have money, but not all have fair skin. Krozer, on the other hand, draws from interviews with the Mexican elite to illustrate how the wealthiest 1% in Mexico incorporate racial elements to explain or justify socioeconomic inequality. The rich empirical data presented in these two chapters helps us understand the complexity of these issues. Among other things, these chapters problematize claims like the ones recently made by Mónica G. Moreno Figueroa and Peter Wade in their 2022 book *Against Racism* where they argue that in Latin America the intermingling of racism and classism has led to a "racially aware class consciousness," in which people's sense of suffering and injustice is shaped both by perceptions of the distribution of wealth and by an underlying sense of their racialized condition (Moreno Figueroa and Wade 2022, 6). While Moreno Figueroa and Wade are right in highlighting the inextricable links between racism and classism, what the work of Ceron-Anaya and Krozer shows is that such links are neither perceptible to everyone, nor do they exist homogenously across space and time. For instance, they demonstrate that when the elites talk about class they allude to racial differences, but this does not necessarily hold the other way around.

Our goal in presenting these divergent views in a single volume goes beyond simply introducing conceptual disagreements and scholarly debates: we want to show how different approaches generate different kinds of solidarities that help mobilize communities to fight and dismantle systemic racism. Approaches that focus on phenotypes as fixed and measurable data center around a specific and pervasive type of racism, one that is based on phenotypically visible traits. The possibility of clearly and quickly showing how skin color has systematic discriminatory effects helps explain why surveys and quantitative studies have been enthusiastically embraced by anti-racist activists, scholars, and organizations.

These studies have also gained popularity in the eyes of the state, which often funds them and uses them to create and evaluate social policies.[36] Perhaps surprisingly, this acceptance by the state is one of the main reasons why many of these scholars and activists have come to embrace them. While they are aware of the ways in which states use data generated by these kinds of studies to police, identify, and even silence critical voices, they maintain that, in this case, the potential benefits exceed the risks. Ultimately, the data generated by these surveys and studies can help mobilize social groups to demand better living conditions and access to social programs.[37] This has been the case, for example, with black and Afro-descendants, populations that were ignored by the state in Latin America (De la Fuente and Reid Andrews 2018). Starting in the 1990s, some national governments began efforts to visibilize Afro-descendants by, first, counting them, and second, by enacting policies that would address their material conditions.[38] International organizations such as the World Bank have also appropriated racial discourses for distributive purposes. For example, they have published several reports that show how Afro-descendants face exclusion and discrimination because of their race.[39] The Inter-American Development Bank (IADB), in turn, has stated that "The Bank works to address Africa descendant's exclusion due to origin, racial, or ethnic status" (IADB 2022). These institutions deploy novel racial categories that change the outreach of their policies even when in doing so they reproduce economic logics that some of the authors in this book, such as Sánchez Contreras and Koyoc Kú, denounce as being the culprits of racism and inequality.

These new approaches—and the identities they help visibilize—have fostered the emergence of movements that focus on people's phenotypical traits. In this book, two chapters allude to such movements: the Afro-Mexican women movement in the Costa Chica analyzed by Varela Huerta and the #PoderPrieto movement critiqued by Leal in her chapter. Both of these contributions show that academic knowledge can shape new social identities into being, create new forms of solidarity between individuals and communities, mobilize and organize them, and, in some ideal cases, help the state craft public policies that are directed to these populations and which help address specific forms of racial oppression.[40] Of course, activists and scholars are aware that visibilizing populations by creating new categories that identify them as such is not enough to combat racism, but it can be a very useful first step.

But these new forms of solidarity can be limited in other ways. Scholars and activists who critique anti-racist efforts that focus mainly or exclusively on epidermal traits argue that these approaches refrain from discussing the class component that is, in their view, central to racial discrimination. Some authors in the book go as far as to contend that the recent wave of quantitative surveys and studies might help generate awareness about the broad social patterns that exist between skin color and income, but in doing so they invisibilize—even if unwittingly—other salient forms of oppression that have to do with class and economic inequality. This invisibilization entrenches the prevailing neoliberal ideologies that assess poverty as a problem that should be solved at the individual level. For example, arguing that people are not offered jobs because of the color of their skin can underscore the existence of individual-level racism while obscuring the myriad institutions and practices that concentrate capital and allow systematic exploitation and dispossession of large populations.

Along these lines, the chapter by Alejandra Leal in this volume presents a poignant critique of the studies that foreground the role played by skin color by carefully dissecting how these can be used to build social movements that call out individual racism without challenging racist structures. One of the consequences of focusing on skin color, Leal argues, is that wealthy Mexicans can position themselves as "victims of racialized oppression together—and seemingly at the same level—with indigenous and afro-Mexican populations, effectively erasing class differences and the severe historical and contemporary marginalization of those populations. And it is in this same context that other historically racialized groups, like the urban poor, are excluded from discussions about racism" (Leal in this book). Similarly, the chapter by Forssell Méndez draws from thinkers such as Stuart Hall and Judith Butler to argue that foregrounding critiques of mestizaje on skin color can limit the construction of solidarities because political action is constrained to (allegedly) biological groups predicated on "sameness without an internal difference" (Forssell Méndez in this book). These arguments echo those of anthropologist Emiliano Zollá Márquez who has claimed that trying to do away with racism through increasing the representation of racialized populations in films and advertisements will not change the country's racial structure or the violence suffered by its racialized population, as has been demonstrated in the case of the United States (Zollá 2022).[41]

In her short but poignant chapter, Mixe linguist and activist Yásnaya Elena A. Gil provides a slightly different word of caution against recent anti-racists efforts that focus on skin color. While these efforts might help dark-skinned individuals be recognized by existing institutions and benefit from certain social programs, she contends that they nonetheless fall short of dismantling racism. Prioritizing representative forms of inclusion that focus on phenotypical traits diversifies the dominant class but leaves the oppressive capitalist system untouched and can even reinforce it. Social class, Gil argues, "is also racialized: structurally, poverty has been assigned a skin color, and the fact that some people can escape the class to which the system confines them does not imply the destruction of the structures that racialize class" (Gil in this book). These criticisms send a similar message: it simply is not possible to fight racism without fighting existing economic structures.

Discussions about how racist forms of oppression (and antiracist struggles) are deeply intertwined with capitalist ones (and anticapitalist ones) is another major topic that runs across the different chapters of this book. It is perhaps not a coincidence that most of the chapters that theorize racism as a form of economic dispossession, displacement, and extractivism are written by a generation of young indigenous activists and scholars, including Díaz Robles, Gil, Koyoc Kú, Sánchez Contreras, and Solis. These chapters highlight the devastation and plunder of racialized populations' land, wealth, and knowledge by private corporations, transnational organizations, and foreign governments, as well as by the Mexican state itself. Although discussions of racism have always highlighted the lack of access to state services and redistribution of wealth, recent discussions also tend to include topics such as cultural appropriation (Díaz Robles and Solis), ecological racism (Koyoc Kú, Sánchez Contreras, Rodríguez Aguilera), and racialized regimes of labor (Gil and Valero).

The authors who bring up these issues are explicit about the way that race, racism, and processes of racialization interact with political and economic structures, agreeing that structural racism and the capitalist order cannot be disentangled from one another. While not necessarily in dialogue with or interested in the recent wave of discussions regarding racial capitalism that have been happening in the United States and Europe, these thinkers seem to agree with Cedric Robinson's famous claim that capitalism *is* racial capitalism and that processes of racialization and capitalism cannot be separated from one another.[42] The contributors to this book are less concerned with getting into historical debates about whether it was capitalism or a racist system which preceded the other. Instead, their concerns are much more focused on the present moment. Through case studies often of their own communities—ranging from the construction of wind farms in the Itsmo de Tehuantepec (Sánchez Contreras), agricultural techniques and pig farms in Yucatán (Koyoc Kú), and the commercialization of the huipil (Solís and Díaz Robles)—these authors demonstrate and denounce the ways in which capitalist accumulation is rooted in excessive violence against racially subordinate populations.

## Translation

Many of the most important debates and conversations currently taking place in Latin America on the topic of race and racism are absent from Anglosphere scholarship quite simply because they have yet to be translated into English.[43] This book takes some of these conversations that are occurring in Mexico and presents them for an English-speaking audience. In doing so, we aim to decenter the production of knowledge about the imbrications between race and capitalism from the United States and Europe. Presenting these debates for an English-speaking audience, however, has its own intellectual and political limitations. First, Spanish is not the only language spoken in Mexico, which means that this book overlooks some of the work that has been written on race and racism in different languages. This shortcoming is a result of both editors' language limitations (we only speak English and Spanish), as well as of the existing racism in the editorial industry. Books about racism in indigenous languages are not widely available and the search engines provide no translation for these languages.[44] Relatedly, we only include work that was presented in a written format, but we are aware that many indigenous languages—and, therefore, forms of knowledge production—are based on oral rather than written traditions. Most importantly, we want to acknowledge that there are racial and political overtones to the relationship between Spanish and indigenous languages. As was discussed earlier, central to mestizaje ideology was the incorporation of indigenous peoples into the "modern" Mexican state including the adoption of Spanish as a primary language.[45] Despite these limitations, we are convinced that translating the debates that are happening in Mexico's (Spanish-speaking) public and academic spheres is key to enriching the conversation on racism that is currently happening in the United States and Europe.

Secondly, one of the criticisms that has been voiced about the emerging conversations about racism in Mexico's public and academic spheres is that they are sparked not by a genuine concern to understand and combat racism in the country, but merely in response to protests and discussions about racism occurring in the United States.[46] Gil makes this very argument in her chapter,

> The idea that we have only begun to talk about racism in Mexico in the wake of recent antiracist protests in the United States implies that the discussion is only relevant when it reaches those elite members of society

who pay careful attention to our northern neighbors despite systematically ignoring the voices of community members racialized as inferior who have been talking about this for years.[47]

This critique is in many ways relevant to the work that we are doing in this book and invites us to think seriously about the reasons for conducting this translation. After all, the Black Lives Matter protests and other racially-motivated demonstrations have certainly enabled ideas, concepts, and categories, such as whiteness and blackness, to travel much more quickly than they would have otherwise. Despite the constant flux and globalization of the academic world, ideas concerning race and racialization generated in the United States and Europe tend to travel to places like Mexico and other Latin American countries much more frequently and forcefully than the other way around. The fact that scholars in non-English speaking countries are expected to read (and publish) in English whereas those in the English-speaking setting are not, partly helps explain this phenomenon but so do other factors that scholars around the world have denounced for decades.

In the late 1990s, for instance, French sociologists Pierre Bourdieu and Loïc Wacquant denounced American and US-based scholars who research race and identity in other parts of the world of being cultural imperialists because they imposed the US experience and applied racial categories that are particular to US history to situations elsewhere in the world: "[T]he American tradition superimposes on an infinitely more complex social reality a rigid dichotomy between whites and blacks."[48] One of the main consequences of doing so, they maintained, is that the concept of racism stops being an analytical tool and becomes a mere instrument of accusation. These academics, Bourdieu and Wacquant further argued, are aided by a wide range of organizations, philanthropic foundations, think tanks, and academic publishing venues that have the means and resources to communicate and impose these ideas in foreign contexts. Among those accused was political scientist Michael Hanchard who defended himself by claiming that the critiques voiced against him and others rely "on presumptions and critical analytical methods which privilege the nation-state and 'national' culture as the sole object for comparative analysis" (Hanchard 2003, 6). Hanchard invites scholars to analyze social movements and the ideas that circulate around them not as national-territorial and entirely self-referential but as transnational phenomena.[49] Although we are aware that racial demonstrations in the United States (and the scholarship that these have produced) have influenced the debates in Mexico, it is in the spirit of Hanchard's defense that we seek to translate these debates. More recently, sociologists Jonathan Warren and Christina Sue also made the argument that concepts and theories "generated in one region may prove useful in another part of the world, especially when applied with a learned sensitivity of the particularities of the place, both from which the lessons were generated and to which they are being applied" (Warren and Sue 2011, 33). In their 2011 piece, they discuss some of the main findings on the topics of race and ethnic studies in Latin America that might prove useful for anti-racist struggles in the United States. We see this book as building on their piece and actualizing some of the findings based on recent discussions on these topics happening in the public sphere in Mexico.

As all the chapters in this book demonstrate, the discussions and conversations that have been happening in Mexico regarding race, racism, and racialization do not mindlessly borrow or mimic US-based racial paradigms and campaigns. The scholars and activists included in this volume show how activists, scholars, and social movements can learn from, adopt, and adapt to their own context ideas about race and racialization from abroad. As Mónica G. Moreno Figueroa argues in her chapter about blackness in Mexico, comparing the kind of racism that happens in the United States and the kind that happens in Mexico is like comparing apples to pears, but that does not mean that anti-black racism is absent in Mexico. Thus, the claim that debates from the United States should not travel to Mexico arbitrarily silences conversations about racism in Mexico by, for instance, fostering the idea that there are no black people or racism in Mexico.

Another point made by Hanchard in his response to Bourdieu and Wacquant's critiques is that their argument precludes "the possibility that US-based funding institutions would actually be in a position to enhance, rather than pervert national and/or local activism" (Hanchard 2003, 12). Crucial to this renewed conversation about race in Mexico is the emphasis (and funds) that international organizations have placed on race and discrimination issues. Institutions such as the World Bank or Article 19 have conducted studies to document racist practices and institutions, and the Ford Foundation funded a USD15m project to address racial-based inequality in the classroom using affirmative action policies.[50] It is entirely plausible that these organizations have shaped racial discourses by emphasizing their own concerns regarding race and discrimination.[51] As antiracist activist and scholar Gisela Carlos Fregoso has argued, the efforts spearheaded by these organizations have certainly enabled members of indigenous communities to enroll and obtain university degrees, but this experience has, in many cases, entailed a process of whitening, including leaving their communities and abandoning or reneging their language (Carlos Fregoso 2022). Thus, further studies must be conducted to understand the impact that these programs have had on these individuals and their communities.

Given the subject matter and scope of this book, translation is not limited to the literal translation between languages: it also involves rendering concepts, meanings, and practices legible to different societal and political contexts, as well as translating ideas from academic settings to the public sphere (and vice versa). One of the key lessons learnt while conducting this exercise is that it is impossible to neatly separate the acts of theorizing, analyzing, and translating theoretical constructs and ideas. Concepts like "blancura" (white), "blanquitud" (whiteness), and "blanqueamiento" (whitening)—which were themselves recently popularized after being translated from English into Spanish[52]—are readily deployed by authors in the book as analytic categories and used in public campaigns, surveys, and everyday conversations.[53] But while some use these words to describe epidermal schemes, others maintain that they stand as "habitus of (western) modernity" (Forssell Méndez in this book) or as an "ethos of capitalism (…) which has to do with social class and with cultural and social capital" (Iturriaga in this book). To put it differently, even as words that directly allude to color are used to theorize about race and racism, it is not always clear if they are referencing skin color, class, or both. Therefore, it is not always clear how exactly to translate certain words and concepts, or which theoretical framework is being referred to and what the contributions are to the debate.[54] The book's translator, Ellen C. Jones, reflects more deeply on this process in the essay preceding this introduction.

## Layout

The book consists of 17 contributions that show different ways in which the topics of race and racism—and their relationship to class and classism—occur in contemporary Mexico. Ten of the contributions—which we refer to as chapters (Iturriaga, Valero, Solís & Güémez, Jaramillo-Molina, Leal, Forssell Méndez, Ceron-Anaya, Krozer, Sánchez Contreras, Solis)—read like traditional academic texts, meaning that they engage with established academic scholarship, and follow established disciplinary rules when laying out arguments and presenting evidence. The remaining seven contributions—which we call interludes (Ogata-Aguilar, Moreno-Figueroa, Gil, Varela Huerta, Koyoc Kú, Díaz Robles, Meztli Yoalli Rodríguez Aguilera)—are less concerned with contributing to bodies of scholarly literature, and more with illustrating particular phenomena related to race, racism, and capitalism. These interludes provide case-specific examples of the larger theoretical points developed in the chapters, or address issues that are relevant to the study of race and racism in Mexico via beautifully written auto-ethnographies. In combining these different types of texts, the book acknowledges that crucial debates and knowledge production about race and its intersection with class are occurring outside academia.

The structure of the book also responds to the racial dynamics in academia. Racialized populations are systematically excluded from entering the academy as students, professors, and researchers. Furthermore, academia privileges specific types of knowledge-making from being considered as meaningful contributions (see Solis' chapter in this book).[55] In an attempt to slightly overcome these exclusions, we opted to include articles that were written for the popular press and especially for non-academic audiences by authors who work outside academic circles.[56]

Finally, we also want to acknowledge the way in which the different contributors in the book—including ourselves—have dealt with disclosures of racial identification. As the readers might notice, not all authors disclose their racial identity and those who do tend to be members of racialized communities who are writing about their first-hand experience. Why might this be the case? One possible explanation is related to sources of authority. That is, most academics reflect and write on topics on which they are considered experts, and their expertise is generally derived from their academic training. Activists and members of racialized communities, on the other hand, derive their authority and expertise from their lived experience. This is not to say that activists do not engage with theoretical debates, nor that many academics are drawn to their research topics because of their lived experience. Our point is simply to note that in academia, racial identification of authors is not a norm in large part because academic credentials, rather than other aspects of people's identities, are a much more important source of authority.

Another possible explanation as to why some authors avoid self-disclosing their racial identity might have to do with the fluidity of some racial categories.

Throughout the process of editing and working on this volume, we (the editors) have incessantly reflected on our position as Mexican assistant professors based at US/Catalunya and Canadian public universities. One of the main issues that we have reflected on stems from the fact that we have been exposed to different ways of forming and understanding racial categories. As we move across different countries, and even different contexts within countries, our racial identities tend to shift. We are aware that not everyone experiences such shifts and that such experience often conveys immense privilege.[57] In fact, it was in large part as a result of these reflections and discussions about race and class that we decided to work on a book that featured the voices of different racialized populations located in Mexico.

## Pending Questions and Future Research Avenues

This book aims at introducing readers to unresolved debates about race that are taking place in the Mexican academic and public sphere. By way of concluding this introduction, we want to acknowledge that, despite the wide range of debates and conversations included in this book, and summarized in this introduction, it is by no means all-encompassing or representative of the whole range of relevant topics on race and racism in Mexico, and we would be remiss not to mention three key topics that are crucial to understanding race and racism that are absent from the book. First, even as none of the chapters explicitly engages with immigration, Mexico's location between the United States and Central America shapes racial imaginaries of the over two million migrants living in or passing through Mexico (Yeh 2017; Lomnitz-Adler 1993; Yankelevich 2015, 2020; Gall 2018). This is a topic that has become increasingly salient and in need of further study, largely due to the fact that the Mexican Armed Forces have recently acquired new responsibilities, including to police migration of South and Central Americans. Secondly, with the important exceptions of Solis's, Varela Huerta's, and Sánchez Contreras's chapters, which explicitly foreground the topic of gender, the intersection between race, class, *and* gender is mostly absent from the analyses in this book.[58] Finally, even as the book has ample examples of the racism and classism that affect indigenous and black populations, it barely mentions racial discrimination of other racialized groups like the Asian community (Augustine-Adams 2015; Gómez Izquierdo 1992), the Middle Eastern populations (Ramírez Carrillo 2018; Yankelevich 2020), and those who belong to the Jewish community (Gall 2016; Yankelevich 2009; Lomnitz 2010).

We acknowledge these absences and hope that this book will open new research avenues and foster conversations that will incorporate these and other issues both to improve our understanding of race in contemporary Mexico and to strengthen existing anti-racist efforts and struggles.

## Notes

1 Three particularly poignant examples of literature on the topic of racism that have circulated widely in the public sphere include the special issues published on the topic by the *Revista de la Universidad de México* (2020) and Chilango (2018) as well as the weekly column published by Mixe linguist Yásnaya Elena A. Gil in *El País* newspaper which, at times more overtly than others, addresses issues related to racism (Gil n.d.).

2 For example, the permanent seminar "Anthropology and History of Racisms, Discriminations, and Inequalities" organized by the National Coordination of Anthropology of the National Institute of Anthropology and History (INAH), which organizes public discussions with scholars and experts on the effects of racism on issues that include the environment, education, and transphobia. Short videos showcasing these lectures can be found on their channel (DEAS-TV n.d.) Another example of a research group that focuses on ethnic-racial discrimination and socio-economic inequalities in Mexico is the Proyecto sobre Discriminación Étnico-Racial en México (PRODER). Based in the Colegio de México, this project conducts surveys, oversees publications, organizes a permanent seminar and a workshop, and raises social awareness via short videos which are disseminated on their webpage and in the digital medium Animal Político (Colmex 2019).

3 For example, social scientists, bioloüists, archeologists, and artists coordinated by Federico Navarrete, a history professor at the Instituto de Investigaciones Históricas at Mexico's National University (UNAM), run the project Noticonquista which narrates Mexico's "conquest" in a colloquial and comic manner (https://www.noticonquista.unam.mx/main). Although not explicitly an anti-racist project, Noticonquista—which has its own website and also operates on Twitter, Instagram and Facebook—seeks to dismantle taken-for-granted racist tropes and myths embedded in the official narratives about the formation of the Mexican nation. In addition to appearing regularly in television and radio shows to speak about everyday forms of racism, Navarrete has published two of the most widely read books on racism in Mexico (Navarrete 2016, 2017) which are written in accessible and colloquial language.

4 Films that tackle the topic of racism do not necessarily do so didactically or explicitly and have, in some cases, generated heated debates about whether they reproduce racist tropes. Two of the most popular and controversial films around issues of racism are *Roma* by Alfonso Cuarón (2018) which starred the Mixteca school teacher

Yalitza Aparicio and the 2020 film *Nuevo Orden* by Michel Franco (Frías Gamez 2023; Solís Hernández and Salazar Cortés 2019; Spyer Dulci and Nava Sánchez 2020).

5   For instance, in 2014 Mexico's National University Museum of Contemporary Art (MUAC) organized the exhibition *Theory of Color* (2014) which brought together artists from different generations and countries who deal with the issue of racism through the lenses of nationalism, scientism, homogenization, exoticization, and colonization (https://muac.unam.mx/exposicion/teoria-del-color). In 2016, the Museo de la Ciudad de México opened the exhibition *Imágenes para verte. Una exhibición del racismo en México*, which not only included works of art but also photographs, scientific documents, and a wide range of objects that sought to demonstrate the ways racism is perpetuated in the country. An online version of this exhibition is organized by César Carrillo Trueba, the curator of the exhibition, here: https://www.exhibirelracismo.mx/es/.

6   Two of the most prominent hashtags include: #PoderPrieto and #Donde hay prietura hay sabrosura.

7   See https://racismo.mx/

8   See https://colectivocopera.org/

9   See Muafro (2020).

10  See https://www.facebook.com/MexicoNegroAc/?locale=es_LA

11  See https://censomx.wordpress.com/

12  See https://linktr.ee/bastaracismomx

13  See, for instance, the chapters by Solís and Güémez and Jaramillo-Molina in this book.

14  See, for instance, the chapters by Iturriaga, Ceron-Anaya, Forssell Méndez, Krozer, and Leal in this book.

15  See, for instance, the chapters by Díaz Robles, Gil, Moreno Figueroa, Sánchez Contreras, and Varela Huerta in this book.

16  See, for instance, the chapters by Ogata-Aguilar, Koyoc Kú, and Solís in this book.

17  "Un lugar de encuentro" can be translated as "a meeting place." This phrase was used by Judith Bautista to describe the set of chapters that make up this book in one of the virtual workshops that we held in July 2021 in preparation for the book.

18  This movement became known as indigenismo. See Lomnitz-Adler (1992, esp. 277).

19  For a statement on the principles that anchored public education for indigenous communities, see Beltran (1954).

20  Anti-Chinese racism is noticeably absent from academic discourses on racism in Mexico. For a comprehensive treatment of this topic in the late 19th and early 20th centuries, see Chang (2017).

21  See Loveman (2014, especially 135 and 181). In 1921, the Mexican census included a question about race, but it only reported Indigenous, mixed, white, other/uncertain, and foreigners.

22  For an insightful analysis of the consequences of the lack of research on Black Mexican populations see Hoffmann (2006).

23   For example, in the 1940s, a series of academics, most notably archeologist Antonio Caso, created an anthropology and an ethnology program for rural workers that "articulated the demands of the indigenous communities with the government programs" (Medina Hernández 2018, 96).

24   See Martínez-Casas, Saldívar, and Sue (2014, 52).

25   For an analysis of how the Revolutionary Institutional Party (PRI co-opted the "afro" movement in Mexico see Hoffmann and Gloria (2016).

26   See Langner (2015).

27   The turn to multiculturalism in Latin America acknowledged Indigenous and Black communities. In Mexico, however, multiculturalism first included Indigenous peoples and until recently Afro-Mexicans were not included.

28   See the introduction in Sieder (2002).

29   In 2013–2014, after activists pushed to include Afro-Mexicans in the official national counts (Thompson-Hernández 2015), the national institute in charge of census and statistics (INEGI) met with activists and academics to discuss the inclusion of race questions in the 2015 inter-censal surveys, as well as to pilot some possible wordings. The question that was ultimately included asked if the respondents identified themselves as Afro-Mexicans instead of Black, because the latter wording was considered racist. However, respondents did not seem to understand the question because they did not know what Afro-Mexican meant (EI 2015). See also #AfroCensoMX at https://colectivocopera.org/afrocensomx/.

30   See, for example: Byrd, Goldstein, Melamed and Reddy (2018); Dawson (2016); Fraser (2016); Melamed (2015); Jenkins and Leroy (2021).

31   See, for example: Aguiló (2018); Ramos-Zayas (2020); Viveros Vigoya (2015); Ceron-Anaya, de Santana Pinho, and Ramos-Zayas (2022).

32   For poignant examples that pertain specifically to Mexico see: Ceron-Anaya (2019); Córdoba Azcárate (2020); Echeverria (2019).

33   For a discussion on the distinction between race and ethnicity and how these map onto phenotype and cultural and social characteristics see Martínez-Casas, Saldívar Tanaka, Sue and Flores (2014). See also Solís and Güémez in this volume.

34   See, for example, PERLA (see Tellez, 2014); Encuesta Intercensal (INEGI 2015); Módulo de Movilidad Social (INEGI 2016); Encuesta Nacional de Viviendas y Hogares (ENVHI 2018); Encuesta sobre discriminación (INEGI 2017; Leite & Meza Holguín 2018); PRODER (2019).

35   Other types of research can also lead to essentializing people's identities. For a poignant critique of how ethnography can essentialize identities but also how it can be used to problematize such essentialization, see Martínez-Casas, Saldívar Tanaka, Sue, and Flores (2014).

36   For example, the most recent census conducted by INEGI (2020) included a color palette to classify respondents.

37   Two recent examples of anthropologists and literary scholars who were historically unfamiliar with statistics but now champion these surveys include "Seminario

Racialidad: Activismo Estadístico" (Ciencias Antropológicas 2021); "Coloquio Nacional ¿Cómo queremos llamarnos?" (Puic Unam and UC-Santa Barbara 2017)

38  In Colombia, for example, the 1993 law (Ley 70) granted communal land rights to Afro-Colombians (Gómez Giraldo 2010).

39  See, for example, Banco Mundial (2018).

40  For example, the inclusion of Afro-Mexicans in the census, or the symbolic reparations for the killings of Chinese in Sonora and Torreon (Osorio 2021)

41  See also Dawson and Francis (2016).

42  With the exception of Perla Valero, who centers her chapter around a discussion of Robinson's oeuvre in Latin America.

43  For an incisive critique of how knowledge produced in Spanish and Portuguese is rarely taken seriously in US academia—in part because these works are not translated and many anglophone scholars do not speak these languages—see Tenorio-Trillo (2020).

44  For an excellent critique on how Spanish language dominates writing, see the interviews with Yásnaya Elena Gil in El País and Letras Libres (Osorio 2020; Sánchez 2021).

45  Recently it was reported that all indigenous languages were at risk of disappearing (Instituto Nacional de Lenguas Indígenas 2019).

46  The police killings of unarmed Black individuals in the United States inspired protests in Mexico against (racialized) abuses of the state, helping to visibilize the presence of Black communities in Mexico. For example, in January 2020 in Tijuana, a Haitian man who was panhandling was beaten by the police. According to witnesses, while he was being assaulted, he said he was asthmatic and could not breathe (NTX 2020). Later that year, after the murder of George Floyd by a police officer in Minnesota, Mexican activists and the Tijuana Black migrant community organized a protest where they had signs that read "Black Lives Matter" and "I can't breathe" (Olvera Cáñez, Bailey, and Meyer 2020). The fact that the protests occurred after the murder of George Floyd—six months after the murder of the Haitian man—suggest that the former inspired the latter.

47  Gil in this book.

48  While none of the chapters in this book make the types of accusations echoed by Bourdieu and Wacquant, these accusations are constantly made in social media. See Bourdieu and Wacquant (1999).

49  For a compelling discussion of how discussions about race travel across the Mexican-US border see Vaughn and Vinson III's analysis of the 2005 controversy over the Black Mexican comic book character Memín Pinguin (Vaughn and Vinson III 2008)

50  See, for example, Banco Mundial (2018); Friedrich Naumann Stiftung and Article19 (2020); Fregoso (2017).

51  This argument mirrors Megan Ming Francis's analysis of that of the National Association for the Advancement of Colored People (NAACP). In her study she shows that fundraising constantly risks "movement capture," meaning that funders will use financial leverage to redirect the agenda of movements or organizations away

from, or towards, specific issues (Francis 2019). In this way, Ming Francis shows the gap between funders and activists, a crucial issue to keep in mind when writing and translating work written by activists, including many of the ones included in this book.

52 For a helpful overview of the literature on how, until recently, "whiteness" in Latin America has been rendered peripheral or absent see Ceron-Anaya, de Santana Pinho, and Ramos-Zayas (2022). Note particularly the list of scholars working on whiteness in the region on page 5.

53 For an insightful discussion of different processes of whitening—including social, cultural, and intergenerational whitening—in Latin America, see Golash-Boza (2010).

54 The same is true for concepts like "moreno," "güero," or "prieto."

55 For discussions about the standardization of academic publishing and its consequences see Santos Herceg (2015; Garcés Mascareñas (2013); Moscoso Rosero and Várela-Huerta (2021).

56 These authors include Tajëëw B. Díaz Robles, Yásnaya Elena A. Gil, José Ángel Koyoc Kú, and Jumko Ogata-Aguilar.

57 For an insightful argument—based on ethnographic and historical examples from Mexico and Latin America—about the volatility and mutability of racial and ethnic identifications, see López Caballero (2021).

58 Compelling works on the intersections between race and gender include Segato (2016) and Cumes (2012). Recent works on the connection between gender and whiteness are from García Blizzard (2022) and Ceron-Anaya (2019). For a summary of recent literature on this topic, see Mora (2022). For a discussion of the need to recognize the crossover between systems of oppression of gender and race in Latin America, see Viveros Vigoya and Moreno Figueroa (2022).

## References

Aguiló, Ignacio. 2018. *The Darkening Nation: Race, Neoliberalism and Crisis in Argentina*. Iberian and Latin American Studies. University of Wales Press. https://press.uchicago.edu/ucp/books/book/distributed/D/bo29574457.html.

Alonso, Ana María. 2004. "Conforming Disconformity." *Cultural Anthropology* 19 (4): 459–90. https://doi.org/10.1525/can.2004.19.4.459.

Augustine-Adams, Kif. 2015. "Hacer a México: La Nacionalidad, Los Chinos y El Censo de Población de 1930." In *Inmigracion y Racismo: Contribuciones a la Historia de los Extranjeros en Mexico*, edited by Pablo Yankelevich. Mexico, D.F.: El Colegio de Mexico.

Banco Mundial. 2018. "Afrodescendientes En Latinoamérica: Hacia Un Marco de Inclusión." Washington, DC: World Bank.

Beltrán, Gonzalo Aguirre. 1954. "Teoría y Práctica de La Educación Indígena." *Revista Mexicana de Sociología* 16 (2): 225–34. https://doi.org/10.2307/3537537.

Bourdieu, Pierre, and Loïc Wacquant. 1999. "On the Cunning of Imperialist Reason." *Theory, Culture & Society* 16 (1): 41–58. https://doi.org/10.1177/026327699016001003.

Byrd, Jodi A., Alyosha Goldstein, Jodi Melamed, and Chandan Reddy. 2018. "Predatory Value: Economies of Dispossession and Disturbed Relationalities." *Social Text* 36 (2): 1–18. https://doi.org/10.1215/01642472-4362325.

Campos-Vázquez, Raymundo M., and Carolina Rivas Herrera. 2019. "Documento de trabajo 2: El color de piel de los representantes de elección popular en México." Mexico: PRODER y El Colegio de México. https://discriminacion.colmex.mx/?p=3893.

Carlos Fregoso, Gisela. 2022. "Upward Mobility, Professionalization, and Anti-Racism." In *Against Racism: Organizing for Social Change in Latin America*, edited by Peter Wade and Mónica G. Moreno Figueroa, 123–44. University of Pittsburgh Press.

Ceron-Anaya, Hugo. 2019. *Privilege at Play*. Global and Comparative Ethnography. Oxford, New York: Oxford University Press.

Ceron-Anaya, Hugo, Patricia de Santana Pinho, and Ana Ramos-Zayas. 2022. "A Conceptual Roadmap for the Study of Whiteness in Latin America." *Latin American and Caribbean Ethnic Studies* 18 (2): 1-23. https://doi.org/10.1080/17442222.2022.2121110.

Chang, Jason Oliver. 2017. *Chino: Anti-Chinese Racism in Mexico, 1880–1940*. University of Illinois Press.

Chilango. 2018. "Racismo." Chilango. February 1, 2018. https://www.chilango.com/racismo/.

Ciencias Antropológicas, dir. 2021. *Seminario Racialidad: Activismo Estadístico*. https://www.youtube.com/watch?v=F_4-gDNXn2s.

Colmex, Colegio de México. 2019. "Discriminación Étnico-Racial En México (PRODER)." https://discriminacion.colmex.mx/.

CONEVAL. 2014. "Pobreza En México." 2014. https://www.coneval.org.mx/Medicion/MP/Paginas/Pobreza_2014.aspx.

Córdoba Azcárate, Matilde. 2020. *Stuck with Tourism: Space, Power, and Labor in Contemporary Yucatan*. University of California Press. https://www.ucpress.edu/book/9780520344495/stuck-with-tourism.

Cruz, Mónica. 2017. "Así se ven los tonos de piel de 500 diputados mexicanos a partir de sus fotos en internet." *Verne | ElPaís* (blog). Ediciones El País. June 23, 2017. https://verne.elpais.com/verne/2017/06/22/mexico/149816 4985_265368.html.

Cumes, Aura Estela. 2012. "Mujeres indígenas patriarcado y colonialismo: un desafío a la segregación comprensiva de las formas de dominio." *Anuario de Hojas de Warmi* 17: 1–16. https://revistas.um.es/hojasdewarmi/article/ view/180291.

Cunin, Elisabeth. 2018. *Administrar los extranjeros: raza, mestizaje, nación: Migraciones afrobeliceñas en el territorio de Quintana Roo, 1902–1940*. Collection D'Amerique Latine, translated by Silvia Kiczkovsky. Marseille: IRD Éditions. http://books.openedition.org/irdeditions/17600.

Dawson, Michael C. 2016. "Hidden in Plain Sight: A Note on Legitimation Crises and the Racial Order." *Critical Historical Studies* 3 (1): 143–61. https://doi.org/10.1086/685540.

Dawson, Michael C., and Megan Ming Francis. 2016. "Black Politics and the Neoliberal Racial Order." *Public Culture* 28 (1): 23–62. https://doi.org/ 10.1215/08992363-3325004.

De la Fuente, Alejandro, and George Reid Andrews. 2018. "The Making of a Field: Afro-Latin American Studies." In *Afro-Latin American Studies: An Introduction*, edited by Alejandro De la Fuente and George Reid Andrews, 1–26. Cambridge University Press.

DEAS-TV. n.d. "Cápsulas Contra El Racismo." YouTube. Accessed February 18, 2023. https://www.youtube.com/playlist?list=PLHkNH_ tG5jXxoAIbEWN0wUSdmyteKshO8.

Echeverría, Bolivar. 2019. *Modernity and "Whiteness."* Translated by Rodrigo Ferreira. 1st edition. Cambridge, UK; Medford, MA: Polity.

Esquivel Hernández, Gerardo. 2015. "Desigualdad Extrema En México. Concentración Del Poder Económico y Político." *OXFAM México*. https:// dds.cepal.org/redesoc/publicacion?id=4045.

Francis, Megan Ming. 2019. "The Price of Civil Rights: Black Lives, White Funding, and Movement Capture." *Law & Society Review* 53 (1): 275–309. https://doi.org/10.1111/lasr.12384.

Fraser, Nancy. 2016. "Expropriation and Exploitation in Racialized Capitalism: A Reply to Michael Dawson." *Critical Historical Studies* 3 (1): 163–78. https://doi.org/10.1086/685814.

Fregoso, Gisela Carlos. 2017. "Diferencia y racismo en las políticas de educación superior: el caso de la Universidad de Guadalajara, Jalisco, México." *Voces y silencios. Revista Latinoamericana de Educación* 5 (2): 172–205. https://doi.org/10.18175/vys5.2.2014.05.

Frías Gamez, Luis Gerardo. 2023. "Conservadurismo, clasismo y racismo: Nuevo orden (2020) un análisis ideológico." *Anuario Electrónico de Estudios en Comunicación Social "Disertaciones"* 16 (1):1–20. https://doi.org/10.12804/revistas.urosario.edu.co/disertaciones/a.12299.

Friedrich Naumann Stiftung, and Article19. 2020. "Las Narrativas Estigmatizantes y Discriminatorias Alrededor de la Afromexicanidad, Mujeres y Pueblos Indígenas, Personas Migrantes e Identidades Sexogenéricas." Mexico City: Friedrich Naumann Stiftung.

Gall, Olivia. 2004. "Identidad, exclusión y racismo: reflexiones teóricas y sobre México." *Revista mexicana de sociología* 66 (2): 221–59.

Gall, Olivia. 2016. "Discursos de odio antisemita en la historia contemporánea y el presente de México." *Desacatos* 51 (August): 70–91.

Gall, Olivia. 2018. "Racismos y xenofobias mexicanos frente a los migrantes: 1910–2018." *REMHU: Revista Interdisciplinar da Mobilidade Humana* 26 (August): 115–34. https://doi.org/10.1590/1980-85852503880005308.

Gall, Olivia. 2021. "Mestizaje y Racismo En México | Nueva Sociedad." *Nueva Sociedad | Democracia y Política en América Latina* 292 (April): 53–64. https://nuso.org/articulo/mestizaje-y-racismo-en-mexico/.

Garcés Mascareñas, Marina. 2013. "La estandarización de la escritura. La asfixia del pensamiento filosófico en la academia actual." *Athenea Digital. Revista de pensamiento e investigación social* 13 (1): 29–41. https://doi.org/10.5565/rev/athenead/v13n1.1039.

García Blizzard, Mónica. 2022. *The White Indians of Mexican Cinema*. SUNY Press. https://sunypress.edu/Books/T/The-White-Indians-of-Mexican-Cinema.

Gil, Yásnaya Elena A. n.d. "Artículos Escritos Por Yásnaya Elena A. Gil en *El País*." *El País*. Accessed February 18, 2023. https://elpais.com/autor/yasnaya-elena-aguilar-gil/.

Golash-Boza, Tanya. 2010. "Does Whitening Happen? Distinguishing between Race and Color Labels in an African-Descended Community in Peru." *Social Problems* 57 (1): 138–56. https://doi.org/10.1525/sp.2010.57.1.138.

Gómez Giraldo, Lucella. 2010. "El territorio en la Ley 70 de 1993 y la política pública para la población afroantioqueña." *Diálogos de Derecho y Política* 5: 1–26.

Gómez Izquierdo, José Jorge. 1992. *El movimiento antichino en México (1871–1934): Problemas del racismo y del nacionalismo durante la Revolución Mexicana*. INAH. https://estudioshistoricos.inah.gob.mx/?p=2111.

Hanchard, Michael. 2003. "Acts of Misrecognition: Transnational Black Politics, Anti-Imperialism and the Ethnocentrisms of Pierre Bourdieu and Loïc Wacquant." *Theory, Culture & Society* 20 (4): 5–29. https://doi.org/10.1177/02632764030204002.

Hoffmann, Odile. 2006. "Negros y afromestizos en México: viejas y nuevas lecturas de un mundo olvidado." *Revista mexicana de sociología* 68 (1): 103–35.

Hoffmann, Odile, and Lara Gloria. 2016. "Reivindicación Afromexicana: Formas de Organización de la Movilización Negra en México." In *Las Poblaciones Afrodescendientes de América Latina y el Caribe. Pasado, Presente y Perspectivas Desde el Siglo XXI*. Universidad Nacional de Tres de Febrero, Universidad Nacional de Córdoba, CIECS.

INEGI [Instituto Nacional de Estadística y Geografía]. 2015. *Encuesta Intercensal*. Mexico: INEGI. www.inegi.org.mx/programas/intercensal/2015/.

INEGI [Instituto Nacional de Estadística y Geografía]. 2016. *Módulo de Movilidad Social Intergeneracional*. Mexico: INEGI. www.inegi.org.mx/programas/mmsi/2016/.

INEGI Instituto Nacional de Estadística y Geografía. 2017. *Encuesta Nacional sobre Discriminación*. Mexico: INEGI. www.inegi.org.mx/programas/enadis/2017/.

Inter-American Development Bank (IADB). 2022. "Afro-Descendants." InterAmerican World Bank: Gender and Diversity. 2022. https://www.iadb.org/en/gender-and-diversity/afro-descendants.

International Labour Organization. 1996. "Acuerdos de San Andrés Larraínzar." https://www.ilo.org/public/spanish/region/ampro/mdtsanjose/indigenous/propuest.htm.

Instituto Nacional de Lenguas Indígenas. 2019. "Lenguas En Riesgo." *INALI-Secretaría de Cultura* (blog). February 21, 2019. https://site.inali.gob.mx/Micrositios/DILM2019/lenguas_riesgo.html.

Islas Weinstein, Tania, and Milena Ang. 2021. "A Tren to Nowhere: Statist Development and Co-Optation of Racial Justice in AMLO's Mexico" (unpublished manuscript).

Jenkins, Destin, and Justin Leroy, eds. 2021. *Histories of Racial Capitalism*. Columbia University Press.

Langner, Ana. 2015. "Niveles de pobreza en México sin cambios en últimos 20 años: OCDE." *El Economista*, July 27, 2015, sec. Política. https://www.eleconomista.com.mx/politica/Niveles-de-pobreza-en-Mexico-sin-cambios-en-ultimos-20-anos-OCDE-20150726-0099.html.

Leite, Paula and Adrián Meza Holguín (coords). 2018. *Encuesta Nacional sobre Discriminación 2017. Prontuario de Resultados*. Mexico: Consejo Nacional para Prevenir la Discriminación.

Lomnitz, Claudio. 2010. *El antisemitismo y la ideología de la Revolución mexicana*. Mexico: Fondo de Cultura Económica.

Lomnitz-Adler, Claudio. 1993. *Exits from the Labyrinth*. University of California Press.

López Caballero, Paula. 2020. "¿Identidades subversivas?" *Revista Común* (blog). November. https://revistacomun.com/blog/identidades-subversivas/.

López Caballero, Paula. 2021. "Inhabiting Identities." *The Journal of Latin American and Caribbean Anthropology* 26 (1): 124–46. https://doi.org/10.1111/jlca.12535.

Loveman, Mara. 1999. "Making 'Race' and Nation in the United States, South Africa, and Brazil: Taking 'Making' Seriously." *Theory and Society* 28 (6): 903–27.

Loveman, Mara. 2014. *National Colors: Racial Classification and the State in Latin America*. Oxford: Oxford University Press.

Martínez-Casas, Regina, Emiko Saldívar Tanaka, Christina A. Sue, and René D. Flores. 2014. "The Different Faces of Mestizaje: Ethnicity and Race in Mexico." In *Pigmentocracies: Ethnicity, Race, and Color in Latin America*, edited by Edward Telles, 36–80. University of North Carolina Press.

Medina Hernández, Antonio. 2018. "Diálogos y Confrontaciones: La Antopología y La Política Indigenista En El Siglo XX Mexicano." In *Las Ciencias Sociales y El Estado Nacional En México*, edited by Óscar F. Contreras and Cristina Puga. Mexico City: Fondo de Cultura Económica.

Melamed, Jodi. 2015. "Racial Capitalism." *Critical Ethnic Studies* 1 (1): 76–85. https://doi.org/10.5749/jcritethnstud.1.1.0076.

Monroy-Gómez-Franco, L., R. Vélez-Grajales, and G. Yalonetzky. 2022. "Layers of Inequality: Unequal Opportunities and Skin Color in Mexico." *The Review of Black Political Economy* 49 (3): 230–250. https://doi.org/10.1177/00346446211044149.

Mora, Mariana. 2022. "Agendas feministas anti-racistas y descoloniales, la búsqueda del locus de enunciación del ser mestiza." *Estudios Sociológicos de El Colegio de México* 40 (special issue): 193–227.

Moreno Figueroa, Mónica G. 2013. "Displaced Looks: The Lived Experience of Beauty and Racism." *Feminist Theory* 14 (2): 137–51. https://doi.org/10.1177/1464700113483241.

Moreno Figueroa, Mónica G., and Emiko Saldívar Tanaka. 2016. "'We Are Not Racists, We Are Mexicans.'" *Critical Sociology* 42 (4–5): 515–33. https://doi.org/10.1177/0896920515591296.

Moreno Parra, María. 2022. "Giving Meaning to Racial Justice: Symbolic Uses of Law in Anti-Racist Struggles." In Mónica G. Moreno Figueroa and Peter Wade (Eds.), *Against Racism: Organizing for Social Change in Latin America* (145–166). University of Pittsburgh Press. https://doi.org/10.2307/j.ctv270ktsp.10.

Moscoso Rosero, María Fernanda, and Amarela Várela-Huerta. 2021. "El 'Paper' Como un Campo de Batalla: Conversaciones Académicas Deslenguadas." *Perífrasis. Revista de Literatura, Teoría y Crítica* 12 (24): 204–22. https://doi.org/10.25025/perifrasis202112.24.11.

Muafro. 2020. "Muafro." Mujeres afromexicanas. 2020. https://afromexicanas.mx/.

Navarrete, Federico. 2016. *México racista: Una denuncia*. Mexico: Grijalbo.

Navarrete, Federico. 2017. *Alfabeto Del Racismo Mexicano*. MALPASO. https://hchlibrary.org/Hoopla/14479106.

NTX. 2020. "Muere haitiano, al parecer, golpeado por policías de Tijuana." *El Informador*, January 9, 2020. https://www.informador.mx/mexico/Muere-haitiano-al-parecer-golpeado-por-policias-de-Tijuana-20200109-0152.html.

s2020. "Commentary: 'No Puedo Respirar.' The Black Lives Matter Movement Is Growing in Tijuana." *San Diego Union-Tribune*, June 25. https://www.sandiegouniontribune.com/opinion/commentary/story/2020-06-25/commentary-no-puedo-respirar-the-black-lives-matter-movement-is-growing-in-tijuana.

Osorio, Camila. 2020. "Yásnaya Elena A. Gil: 'La literatura mexicana tiene que ser multilingüe o no puede ser llamada mexicana.'" *El País México*, December 31, 2020, sec. México. https://elpais.com/mexico/2020-12-31/yasnaya-elena-a-gil-la-literatura-mexicana-tiene-que-ser-multilingue-o-no-puede-ser-llamada-mexicana.html.

Osorio, Camila. 2021. "La disculpa diplomática de López Obrador por la masacre de chinos en 1911." *El País México*, May 17, 2021, sec. México. https://elpais.com/mexico/2021-05-17/la-disculpa-diplomatica-de-lopez-obrador-a-china.html.

PRODER Proyecto sobre Discriminación Étnico-Racial en México. 2019. *Ficha técnica PRODER 2019*. Mexico: El Colegio de México. https://discriminacion.colmex.mx/?page_id=4389.

PUIC-UNAM, and University of California, Santa Barbara, dirs. 2017. *Coloquio Nacional ¿Cómo Queremos Llamarnos? Horizonte INEGI 2020: Dra Emiko Saldívar Tanaka*. https://www.youtube.com/watch?v=elaYc1h-RJs.

Ramírez Carrillo, Luis Alfonso. 2018. "Identidad Persistente Y Nepotismo Étnico: Movilidad Social De Inmigrantes Libaneses En México: Persistent Identity and Ethnic Nepotism: Social Mobility of Lebanese Immigrants in Mexico." *Nueva Antropología: Revista de Ciencias Sociales* 31 (89): 9–23.

Ramos-Zayas, Ana Y. 2020. *Parenting Empires: Class, Whiteness, and the Moral Economy of Privilege in Latin America*. Durham, NC: Duke University Press.

Salazar Cortés, Arantxa, and María Edita Solís Hernández. 2019. "La blanquitud e industria cinematográfica 'incluyente': el caso de Yalitza Aparicio." *La Aljaba* 23 (2): 191–201.

Sánchez, Karla. 2021. "Entrevista a Yásnaya Elena A. Gil. 'La lengua tiene una carga política.'" *Letras Libres* (blog). March 1, 2021. https://letraslibres.com/revista/entrevista-a-yasnaya-elena-a-gil-la-lengua-tiene-una-carga-politica/.

Santos Herceg, José. 2015. "Saberes académicos: de la producción textual a la creación de conocimiento." *Literatura: Teoría, Historia, Crítica* 17 (2): 97–112. https://doi.org/10.15446/lthc.v17n2.51276.

Segato, Rita. L. 2016. *La guerra contra las mujeres*. Madrid: Traficantes de sueños. https://traficantes.net/libros/la-guerra-contra-las-mujeres.

Sieder, Rachel, ed. 2002. *Multiculturalism in Latin America: Indigenous Rights, Diversity and Democracy*. Institute of Latin American Studies. Palgrave Macmillan UK. https://doi.org/10.1057/9781403937827.

Solís Hernández, Maria Edita, and Aranxa Salazar Cortés. 2019. "La blanquitud e industria cinematográfica 'incluyente': el caso de Yalitza Aparicio." *La Aljaba. Segunda Época. Revista de Estudios de la Mujer* 23 (December): 191–201. https://doi.org/10.19137/aljaba-2019-230110.

Spyer Dulci, Tereza María, and Alfredo Nava Sánchez. 2020. "Una Discusión Sobre El Racismo y El Trabajo Doméstico En Roma, de Alfonso Cuarón." *Diálogo* 23 (1): 55–67. https://doi.org/10.1353/dlg.2020.0006.

Sue, Christina A. 2013. *Land of the Cosmic Race: Race Mixture, Racism, and Blackness in Mexico*. Illustrated edition. Oxford; New York: Oxford University Press.

Sue, Christina A., and Tanya Golash-Boza. 2013. "'It Was Only a Joke': How Racial Humour Fuels Colour-Blind Ideologies in Mexico and Peru." *Ethnic and Racial Studies* 36 (10): 1582–98. https://doi.org/10.1080/01419870.2013.783929.

Telles, Edward. 2014. *Pigmentocracies. Ethnicity, Race, and Color in Latin America*. Chapel Hill: The University of North Carolina Press.

Tenorio-Trillo, Mauricio. 2020. *Latin America: The Allure and Power of an Idea*. Chicago, IL: University of Chicago Press. https://press.uchicago.edu/ucp/books/book/chicago/L/bo25581658.html.

Thompson-Hernández, Walter. 2015. "Afro-Mexicans Are Pushing for Legal Recognition in Mexico's National Constitution." *ReMezcla* (blog). September 11, 2015. https://remezcla.com/culture/afro-mexicans-legal-recognition-constitution-mexico/.

Universidad Nacional Autónoma de México, and Instituto de Investigaciones Históricas IIH-UNAM. n.d. "Noticonquista." Noticonquista. Accessed February 18, 2023. http://www.noticonquista.unam.mx/main.

Vaughn, Bobby, and Ben Vinson III. 2008. "Memín Penguin, Changing Racial Debates, and Transnational Blackness." *E-misférica 5.2: Race and Its Others*. https://hemi.nyu.edu/hemi/en/e-misferica-52/vaughnvinson.

Villarreal, Andrés. 2010. "Stratification by Skin Color in Contemporary Mexico." *American Sociological Review* 75 (5): 652–78. https://doi.org/10.1177/0003122410378232.

Viveros Vigoya, Mara. 2015. "Social Mobility, Whiteness, and Whitening in Colombia." *The Journal of Latin American and Caribbean Anthropology* 20 (3): 496–512. https://doi.org/10.1111/jlca.12176.

Viveros Vigoya, Mara, and Mónica G. Moreno Figueroa. 2022. "Anti-Racism, Intersectionality, and the Struggle for Dignity." In *Against Racism: Organizing for Social Change in Latin America*, edited by Peter Wade and Mónica Moreno Figueroa, 123–44. University of Pittsburgh Press.

Wade, Peter. 2010. *Race and Ethnicity in Latin America: How the East India Company Shaped the Modern Multinational*. 2nd edition. Pluto Press. https://doi.org/10.26530/oapen_625258.

Warren, Jonathan, and Christina A. Sue. 2011. "Comparative Racisms: What Anti-Racists Can Learn from Latin America." *Ethnicities* 11 (1): 32–58.

Woo-Mora, L. Guillermo. 2022. "Unveiling the Cosmic Race: Racial Inequalities in Latin America." SSRN Scholarly Paper 3870741. Rochester, NY: World Inequality Lab Paper. https://doi.org/10.2139/ssrn.3870741.

Yankelevich, Pablo. 2009. *Nación y extranjería: la exclusión racial en las políticas migratorias de Argentina, Brasil, Cuba y México*. Universidad Nacional Autónoma de México.

Yankelevich, Pablo (ed.). 2015. *Inmigracion y Racismo: Contribuciones a la Historia de los Extranjeros en Mexico*. Mexico, D.F.: El Colegio de Mexico.

Yankelevich, Pablo. 2020. *Los otros: Raza, normas y corrupción en la gestión de la extranjería en México 1900–1950*. El Colegio de Mexico.

Yeh, Rihan. 2015. "Deslices del 'Mestizo' en la Frontera Norte." In *Nación y Alteridad: Mestizos, Indígenas y Extranjeros en el Proceso de Formación Nacional*. Mexico City: UAM and Ediciones EyC.

Yeh, Rihan. 2017. *Passing: Two Publics in a Mexican Border City*. Chicago, IL: University of Chicago Press. https://press.uchicago.edu/ucp/books/book/chicago/P/bo27256524.html.

Zollá, Emiliano. 2022. "Racismo y mestizaje: apuntes para complejizar una discusión ineludible." *Revista Común* (blog). June. https://revistacomun.com/blog/racismo-y-mestizaje-apuntes-para-complejizar-una-discusion-ineludible/.

# RACE IS
# AN ILLUSION

## Jumko Ogata-Aguilar Translated by Ellen Jones

There is no such thing as race. There are no meaningful biological differences that allow us to claim the existence of categories known as "races." However, although they are arbitrary constructions, they do have tangible consequences for our bodies and determine how we move through the world—the kinds of violence we will or will not encounter. This is why the term *racialization* has emerged, based on an understanding of race as:

> an ontologically empty sociohistorical construct, the result of complex processes of identifying, dividing up, and differentiating human beings according to phenotypical, cultural, linguistic, regional, and ancestral criteria, among others. (Campos-Garcia 2012)

In other words, it's not that we *belong to* a race, but that our bodies are read and then quickly defined and categorized by those who look at us. Racialization as white or whitened is considered ideal or desirable, while racialization as a person of color is thought to be inferior.

Although race is an imaginary category that has no scientific basis, US historian Ibram X. Kendi holds that, within antiracism, it is important to identify ourselves racially in order to understand what privileges and dangers we will face according to the body we inhabit. That said, racialization is also a flexible means of categorization insofar as races are constructed and perceived differently in different spaces.

From the age of three months to nine years, I lived in Riverside, California, a small city an hour from Los Angeles, where one of the University of California campuses can be found. My mom and dad were doing their PhDs there and so the first years of my life played out according to a US understanding of race. Racism in the United States is segregationist; the nation was founded on genocide and the dispossession of Native American peoples, and on their later confinement to reservations. There was never any attempt to integrate these populations into the new American nation because their supposed inferiority was thought to be irreparable.

Later, after the abolition of slavery, the "Jim Crow" segregation laws were passed, preventing Afro-American people from voting, from accessing education, and even from occupying certain seats on public transport. Although the civil rights movement in the second half of the twentieth century abolished those laws, at a systemic level there is still a deeply segregationist logic that manifests as the violence still suffered by people of color in hospitals,[1] in schools,[2] and in the street.[3] Even people like Abraham Lincoln, considered a key forerunner of the US struggle for racial equality, claimed that:

> There is a physical difference between the white and the black races which I believe will forever forbid the two races living together on terms of social and political equality.[4]

The Statue of Liberty, one of the country's most important patriotic symbols, has a poem by Emma Lazarus inscribed at its base. Its most frequently cited lines read:

> Give me your tired, your poor,
> Your huddled masses yearning to breathe free,
> The wretched refuse of your teeming shore.
> Send these, the homeless, tempest-tost to me,
> I lift my lamp beside the golden door!

US discourse praises its migrant-origin population, but in practice it is clear that certain kinds of people are given preference over others.

In any case, in Highland Elementary School we were taught that racism was a thing of the past; that racism was what Martin Luther King Jr and Rosa Parks had marched for, and so there was nothing for us to worry about anymore. I remember feeling tremendous relief when this period of history was explained. What a terrifying thought! If we still lived in a racist society, things would not have gone well for me, I was sure, because I was not white. During my years in Riverside, I had always been very conscious of the supposed race of people around me. I would think: "He's white," "she's Asian," without really knowing why these categories were important or ought to be identified.

My third-grade classroom was dominated by us Latinos; the rest of my classmates were white, African American, or Asian. Our teacher, Guadalupe Hernández, was US American with Mexican heritage, and she made a huge effort to practice the little Spanish she knew with her Mexican students. I was never included in these conversations. I thought it must be because neither my first nor my last name was Hispanic, so she had no way of knowing I too was Mexican. In the playground all the Mexican girls played together and although I used to approach them and talk to them in Spanish, I never really felt like part of their group. I wasn't sure why, but I did notice that the girls didn't look like me. Some were white, some were darker skinned, but none of them had hair like mine.

According to my mum (I have no memory of this), I was always very clear about my racial identity while we lived there. "Mamá, I'm Black," I used to say.

A little before my ninth birthday we returned to Xalapa and I was enrolled in Enrique C. Rébsamen Primary School. There we were taught that our ancestors were Indigenous Americans and Spanish. They took us to Cempoala to see the "ruins" of great native civilizations and to the Xalapa Anthropology Museum to see the impressive Olmec heads. I do not remember being told anything about present day Indigenous people; there seemed to be a disconnect between what they showed us in the museums and any contemporary ethnic group.

Later, in secondary school, they made us study the eighteenth-century casta paintings in great detail; if I close my eyes, I can almost see the names we noted down in our books: *indio, español, mestizo, mulato, criollo*...The categories got more and more complicated—*lobo, saltapatrás* (*wolf, leap backwards*)—and, though I can hardly believe it, I used to compare those family portraits with my classmates. We were as different from each other as the people in the paintings: dark hair, blonde hair, straight, wavy, different colored skin, and equally diverse facial features. It was never said directly, but the message was very clear: we could no longer know for certain which category we belonged to, but the word "mestizo" was all we needed to identify ourselves as the result of this great mixing. The term *racism* never figured in these classes; so maybe it didn't exist. After all, they'd all had children together, hadn't they? And of course, what I had been taught at school in the United States reinforced that idea, that racism only existed in there, not here.

In Mexico the dynamics of racism are assimilationist. In other words, races are still said to exist, but, unlike a segregationist system, which understands racial differences to be irreparable, assimilationist racism believes that inferior races will gradually catch up with the more developed races. We must "better the race" at all costs. Compared with a segregationist system, it's much harder to identify violence and racism with the clarity afforded by the segregation of groups. How can you say there is racism in Mexico if mestizaje—that great foundational myth—is based on the mixing of two different races?

José Vasconcelos's *cosmic race* allows us to unravel the logic that both drives racial mixing and, at the same time, asserts the inferiority of certain races and the idea of mestizaje as a process of whitening. The racism of Vasconcelos's conception lies in part in its belief in races as biological categories and in part in its naturalization of white supremacy. This supremacy is never questioned but rather assumed to be the apex of development for a new, fifth race, a perfect race that would result from mixing the four already existing races. Racism in this context has a much more subtle dynamic than in the United States segregationist system, meaning that it can go unperceived.

In retrospect, many memories of my adolescence were changed and deformed as I gained full knowledge of the context and underlying logic of racism in Mexico. I remember friends who, on seeing themselves in photos, would lament how "prieta" they looked—how dark skinned. The white girls were always the popular girls at school, and nobody disputed that they were also the prettiest. I think about what it was like to receive comments about my "messy," "untamed" hair, and watching my straight-haired classmates proudly pull out their hairbrushes at break time, knowing that, in my case, brushing would only make my hair frizzier and more tangled. I felt the sadness of knowing I was ugly without understanding why.

When I turned nineteen, I moved to Mexico City to start my undergraduate degree at the School of Latin American Studies in the Faculty of Philosophy and Letters at the National Autonomous University of Mexico. Every class hit me harder than the last as I started to learn about African enslavement in Mexico during the colonial era. The topic fascinated me. I didn't know why, but I wanted to know more about Black people here. I learned that the state of Veracruz has one of the largest Afro-descendent populations in the country... and it was as though the scales had fallen from my eyes. The first time I went back to Xalapa, to Otatitlán and Tuxpan (where my parents are from) for the holidays, I not only saw Black people clearly, I also realized they were everywhere: in the streets, in the shops, and, especially, in my family. Sure, we had always affectionately called them "negro" or "negra"...but my mind had never made the connection between that adjective and Africanness. And now of course, it seemed so obvious. It was almost ridiculous to have realized so late.

It was also in Mexico City where the people with whom I interacted and established relationships made me realize I too was *other*; that I didn't fit the Mexican mold either. I had never stopped to think about my own racial identity because in the spaces where I grew up it wasn't something that made me substantially different from those around me. Now, in the City, the gazes categorizing me were drastically different and I had to face being racialized in a new way. Not only was I seen as *other*, I was now also frequently exoticized by those around me.

In Xalapa, my classmates had always led me to believe I was ugly. They never made fun of any particular feature, like they did with the other children...but I knew there was something about me I could not change. My experiences and the places where I have lived and spent time have shown me that "race" is not something we are born with. It is assigned to us by other people's gazes, through our skin, our hair, our names; it is the arbitrary combination of physical and cultural characteristics on which our individuality is built. The danger of believing race to be an important biological category lies in its ability to define our identity. Our identity, in itself, changes constantly according to who is looking at us, and every gaze brings with it a burden of expectations that turns us into a completely different person depending on where we are. That is why it is important to see racialization only as a category that allows us to understand our place in a hierarchy established by a racist system and to identify the forms of resistance most appropriate to our experience. That is all.

We are the only ones who can define our identity, and it is important to understand that race is not the only criteria available to us; for example, we might consider our connection to a place, the traditions we grew up with, the food that makes us feel at home, the music we dance to when we are happy, or the ancestors who told us stories about where we came from.

## Notes

1   Roni Caryn Rabin, "Huge Racial Disparities Found in Deaths Linked to Pregnancy," *New York Times*, May 7, 2019. Available at: nytimes.com/2019/05/07/health/pregnancy-deaths-.html.
2   Jodi S. Cohen, "A Teenager Didn't Do Her Online Schoolwork. So a Judge Sent Her to Juvenile Detention," ProPublica Illinois, July 14, 2020. Available at: propublica.org/article/a-teenager-didnt-do-her-online-schoolwork-so-a-judge-sent-her-to-juvenile-detention.
3   Ruben Vives, "Caught on Video: Man flips over Street vendor's cart in Hollywood, unleashing public anger," *Los Angeles Times*, July 25, 2017. Available at: latimes.com/local/lanow/la-me-hollywood-street-vendor-dispute-20170724-story.html.
4   George M. Johnson, *All Boys Aren't Blue*, New York, Farrar Straus Giroux, 2020, p. 57.

## Reference

Campos-Garcia, Alejandro. 2012. "Racialización, Racialismo y Racismo. Un Discernimiento Necesario." *Universidad de La Habana Journal 273*, June. https://www.academia.edu/6283861/Racializaci%C3%B3n_Racialismo_y_Racismo_Un_discernimiento_necesario.

# CHAPTER 1

# Key Aspects of Mexican Racism: "Blanquitud," Nationalism, and Mestizaje

## Eugenia Iturriaga Translated by Ellen Jones

Through the claim of "we are all mestizos," the existence of racism in Mexico has repeatedly been denied. People have sought to understand difference, including vast social and economic inequality, through class or ethnic discrimination, erasing racism from the social scene. For this reason, I think we have to ask: why has it been, and is still, so hard to talk about racism in Mexico, given that most Mexicans experience it daily? I believe the answer has to do with "blanqueamiento" or whitening, with nationalism, and with the discourse of mestizaje. Using the concept of "blanquitud"—the behaviors, identity, and ethos associated with "blancura" or epidermal whiteness—as a guiding thread, in this chapter I propose to show how the Mexican national project, which was begun at the end of the nineteenth century and has been justified discursively through a drive towards nationalism and mestizaje, has invisibilized racism in Mexico. I will try to explain how the national sentiment promoted by governing elites yearned for a homeland that would eventually become white. For this reason, the African-origin population was erased from national history and progressive whitening was held up as a means of achieving that objective.

This chapter is divided into four parts: in the first part I reflect on "blanquitud" as the great trap of Mexican mestizaje, because the ideology sustaining it seeks to naturalize a system of categorization in which whitening can be effective for individual but not collective upward social mobility. In the second part, I delve into the past and explain colonial era social classifications or "castas," as well as the nineteenth-century visions of "race," because I believe that only by understanding the past are we able to comprehend the present specificities of Mexican racism and its differences from other Latin American national projects. In the third part, I analyze how postrevolutionary governments consolidated the discourse of mestizaje and used Indigenista policies to attempt to deprive Indigenous communities of their varied identities by imposing on them a single language and culture. Lastly, I reflect on the importance the debate over skin color has acquired in recent years, and on the paradoxes of "blanquitud" in contemporary Mexico.

## Mexican Racism

Those of us who live in Mexico have all heard someone say: "they look like a decent person." It's no coincidence that the person in question is always fair-skinned. It is also common to hear how pretty a blonde child is, or that someone is "morenito, but handsome." And, of course, the phrase: "we must better the race." These and many other expressions uttered daily in Mexico contain a form of normalized, encrypted racism.[1]

I understand racism as the belief that certain human beings are better than others; as an idea that links physical appearance to culture, morals, and intellectual capacity. Racist thinking locates people's bodies in a specific place from which they are not permitted to leave; a place determined by appearance, because it is believed that physical features determine certain practices, behaviors, and ways of thinking. Racism implies hierarchization and this produces inequalities that are justified by passing them off as natural. This hierarchy allows us to accept that people in one group have privileges over people in another group. Racism is a social relationship of power and domination that manifests in repeated behaviors that are considered normal (Wieviorka 2009; Castellanos Guerrero 1998, 2000; D'Appolonia 1998; Gall 2016).

In Mexico, racism is not only directed towards Indigenous communities and Afro-descendent people; it also affects the majority group: moreno mestizos. For me it is important to think about mestizaje not only as the prevailing racial discourse within the nationalist discourse but also as a logic that structures and underpins Mexicans' everyday lives; as a logic that rewards physical whiteness and grants privileges to those who possess it. The discourse of mestizaje has given most Mexicans the chance to sporadically enter privileged spaces by marking their distance and difference from the Indigenous population. Mexicans have played the "game" of upward social mobility through mestizaje, which promised, through clever alchemy and a bit of luck, a whitening effect that would grant them a better social position. However, skin color is never enough; in order to belong to the Mexican elite, it is necessary to move in the same circles and networks as them, to share their spaces, tastes, and patterns of consumption (Iturriaga 2016). The Mexican elite tend to be nationalist and, thanks to the narrative of "we are all mestizos," they have managed to preserve and consolidate political power and economic and social control. The discourse of mestizaje—deployed in Mexico by the elite and by post-revolutionary governments—has managed to make the boundaries between different social groups blurry and ambiguous. This ambiguity has held off total discrimination, but at the same time it has allowed inequalities to persist and be reproduced. It constitutes, as Reygadas puts it, "a covert racism, largely buttressed by its own flexibility" (Reygadas 2008, 127).

In this country there has been little reflection on the process of whitening that has gone hand in hand, usually silently, with the ideology of mestizaje. At the end of the first decade of the twenty-first century, the Marxist philosopher Bolívar Echeverría reflected on this topic and developed the concepts of "blancura," "blanquitud," and "blanqueamiento." For Echeverría, "blancura" refers to the phenotypical features of "white" humans; to epidermal whiteness; to skin color. Meanwhile, "blanquitud" refers to *ethical* features associated with epidermal whiteness. Understood in this way, "blanquitud" ceases to be a color and becomes instead a group of power relations. Thus, not all those who have fair skin possess "blanquitud," and it is possible for people who do not have fair skin to achieve "blanquitud" through a process of "blanqueamiento" or whitening, which is to say, by following certain cultural practices and practices of consumption.

As Bolívar Echeverría proposes, "blanquitud" is "a pseudo-concrete identity trait intended to replace the absence of real concreteness that characterizes the identity imposed on human beings in modernity" (Echeverría 2010). The author explains that *homo capitalisticus*'s pseudo-concreteness includes the ethical aspects of the whiteness of the "white" man, a modern, capitalist human being. Thus, "blanquitud" is a way of behaving, a cultural identity, an ethos—the capitalist ethos that seeks the accumulation of capital and upward social mobility. The concept of "blanquitud" helps problematize privileged spaces, because it not only refers to a physical feature or to skin color.[2] "Blanquitud" also takes in social class and cultural and social capital. In Bourdieu's (1991) terms, it retains a direct relationship with *habitus*.

Unlike in the United States, in Mexico government policies do not talk about "races." However, as Stavenhagen (1994) has warned, a racist ideology can prosper even without talk of "race." Mexicans do not define themselves in terms of race, and yet processes of racialization are permanently present in its society. Following Campos (2012), I understand racialization as the social production of human groups (bodies, cultures, and ethnicities) in racial terms. Socially racialized groups are the result of practices, doctrines, and productions of knowledge. The processes of racialization "produce more or less lasting, more or less consensual typologies that homogenize groups considered to be similar" (Campos 2012, 187). In Mexico, Indigenous people have been strongly stigmatized and racialized as in need of modification. For this reason, it is not strange that most Mexicans do not want to appear Indigenous, or that the word "indio" ("Indian") can function as an insult (Navarrete 2017). The codes that reproduce and normalize racial hierarchies have been so powerful and effective that, for centuries, they have kept not only Indigenous and Afro-descendent people but also moreno mestizos in a subordinate position, thus legitimating the role of "white" or whitened people. This can be seen in everyday life in the aesthetic and moral guidelines that have been normalized and implanted in the culture (Moreno Figueroa 2013; Iturriaga 2016; Ceron-Anaya 2019). Popular refrains such as "aunque la mona vista de seda, mona se queda"—"a monkey may dress in silks but it'll still be a monkey"—is a good example of this.

In order to account for racism in Mexico, I propose we focus on processes of racialization, in discourse and in practice, because this will allow us to reveal the mechanisms through which racism operates in this country. Concentrating on racialization, as Moreno Figueroa (2016, 105) points out, "also implies rethinking mestizaje not just as a historical moment or even a historical, postrevolutionary ideology, but also as a lived experience, embedded in everyday and institutional life, that shapes and organizes relationships in Mexico."

Racial discrimination in Mexico has not operated under a system of exclusions protected by law, as was the case with segregation in the United States or apartheid in South Africa, because the Mexican State promoted policies and laws based on supposed equality and supported by the discourse of mestizaje. Mestizaje has not prevented there from being clear segmentation of society. There is no doubt that, over the years, both epidermal whiteness and "blanquitud" have been conditions *sine qua non* of a position at the top of the social pyramid. In Mexico it has been possible to obtain "blanquitud" through schooling, economic capital, "good taste," and the adoption of a bourgeois lifestyle. Historically, insertion into the church or the armed forces offered others the possibility of whitening. However, although whitening and upward social mobility have been possible, this does not mean ethnic or racial differences have disappeared, nor has the preference for epidermal whiteness either in public spaces or in family or intimate spaces. Although class divisions can be flexible, they only open the way for certain individuals, and their mobility does not constitute a collective betterment.

## Colonial Classifications and the Role of "Race" in the Construction of the Nation State

During the colonial era the population was classified according to their temperaments and qualities (López Beltrán 2004). New Spain distinguished between people of different qualities: Spanish, "Indians" ("indios"), "blacks" ("negros"), and "castas," as the different mixes were known. The different peoples of America, with their various languages and cultures, were grouped under the same name: Indians, thus homogenizing a very diverse population. The different mixes had different names depending on the region and the era.

It's important to make clear that there was no segregation in New Spain. Although New Spain was divided into the "república de indios" ("republic of the Indians") and the "república de españoles" ("republic of the Spanish"), this division did not last for long, because the Crown and Church did not maintain strict separation between the different populations. Indigenous communities, or the republic of Indians, had their lands recognized and Indian nobles maintained their hierarchies. The African and Afro-descendent population, which at first lived side by side with the Spanish, began to mix with them. It is important to point out that during the seventeenth and eighteenth centuries, the African-origin population was the second largest group in New Spain (Velázquez and Iturralde 2016, 36); in some regions where the Indigenous population had been decimated it was the largest group (Castañeda 2021). The different mixes or "castas" were growing, and mestizos, as well as other mixes such as "mulatos," and "pardos," were appearing all over New Spain. There were also differences among Spaniards: a Spaniard born on the Iberian Peninsula was of higher quality than a Spaniard born on American territory, because the diet and the climate with which they grew up were different. The Iberian-born Spanish occupied higher economic and social positions. In Mexico's censuses and parish electoral registers (contemporary tools for counting the population for the payment of a tribute), people were registered with the following qualities: español, indio, negro, mulato, and pardo. Not all of the more than forty castas found in eighteenth-century casta paintings from different parts of the Spanish empire appear in the official registers. These paintings were commissioned by the metropolitan elites to display the viceroyalty's social and cultural diversity to those visiting New Spain, or to those they met in Europe, and were not accurate reflections of the social structure of the period. However, thanks to the figures depicted in the casta paintings, the idea that New Spanish society was structured according to the types appearing in these images became popular. Although this was far from reality, the idea is still promoted today in basic education in Mexico.

The paintings present the possibility of progressive whitening (López Beltrán 2004), in which certain combinations of Indigenous people and Spaniards would, over time, become just Spanish.[3] At the same time, they show that mixing with the Black population makes whitening impossible, because, although a certain whiteness can temporarily be achieved, after several generations a "salta pa'trás" (a leap backwards, i.e., a Black person) will appear. This idea permeated society and remains current even today in stereotypes of and prejudices against morenos. Claudio Lomnitz (1995 274) points out that amid

> the ethnic manipulation that characterized the eighteenth century in Mexico, whiteness was the only position people were not trying to escape [. . . because] whiteness represented a kind of purity as the only position in which wealth, status, and power could be in balance.

When the struggle for independence was over, new Mexicans had to form a state and build a nation. "Race," as Tomás Pérez Vejo (2017) points out, plays a key role in imagining nations. In some nations, race becomes a mark of nationality—"a nation is a race" (Pérez Vejo 2017, 61)—while in others, race is a factor that favors or impedes the progress and civilization of nations as they move towards modernity. It was the second scenario that characterized Latin American nation-states, because they were formed from multiethnic populations. In Mexico, it wasn't until the 1940s that the nation was posited as a community of race, language, and culture. Previously, Pérez Vejo points out, "the leaders of independence were worried about the State, not the nation. Neither they nor their immediate successors proposed the need for an ethno-cultural definition of the nation" (Pérez Vejo 2017, 64). For this reason, in the early decades of independence, the "Indian problem" did not have a racial explanation. On February 24, 1821, Vicente Guerrero and Agustín de Iturbide signed the Plan of Iguala, which declared Mexico's Independence. The document begins thus:

> Americans! By whom I understand not only those born in America, but also the Europeans, Africans, and Asians who reside there: be so kind as to hear me. Great nations around the world were dominated by others; and only when they found the desire to become a nation themselves did they achieve their emancipation. (Chinchilla 2021, 29)

During the early decades of the nineteenth century the aim was to create a civic state; a state with its own sovereign territory, institutions, and constitutional rules. In order to build this civic state, it was necessary to turn subjects into citizens, to eliminate all colonial encumbrances, and to abolish all forms of slavery. Afterwards came the construction of the *ethnic state* and with it the construction of national identity. It was with the building of the ethnic state that the narrative of mestizaje began. Intellectuals such as José María Luis Mora (1794–1850), considered the father of Mexican liberalism, were the first to propose the need to dissolve the Indian population in the crucible of mestizaje. He proposed to "melt the Aztec race into the general masses," keeping the division of classes but allowing Indians to enjoy "the benefits of [modern, capitalist] society" (Mora 1950 [1836]).

The Plan of Iguala mentioned Africans and Asians as inhabitants of the territory, but the historical tale told by the ethnic state erased them completely because their presence did not fit into the idea of the longed-for nation. History was constructed as though they had never inhabited these lands, nor formed an important part of the new country. When they were freed, the state made them citizens with equal rights, but at the same time stopped mentioning their existence specifically. When stratified society legally disappeared, to be replaced by the notion of "citizenry" in independent Mexico, the Afro-descendent population also disappeared from official documentation (Velázquez and Iturralde 2016).

After Independence, both at national and regional level, the Mexican ruling classes all over the country struggled to hold onto their projects, whether liberal or conservative, which meant that the nineteenth century was characterized by constant confrontations and a permanent state of war. In the middle of the country, the liberal elite was convinced that the lack of progress was the result of the backwardness of the Indigenous population and that they therefore must be integrated as soon as possible. Francisco Pimentel (1832–1893) is a good example of this position. In his text, *Memoria sobre las causas que han originado la situación actual de la raza indígena de México y medios de remediarla* (Memoir about the causes of the current situation concerning the Indigenous race in Mexico and ways of solving it), published in 1864, explains why equality for Indians was necessary for nation-building:

> As long as the natives remain as they are today, Mexico cannot aspire to the rank of nation, in the proper sense of the word. A nation is a gathering of men who profess common beliefs, who are dominated by the same idea, and who are reaching for a single goal. (1864, 217)

Pimentel argued that, by bringing education and the Catholic faith to Indigenous people, by proclaiming equality among citizens and establishing a regime of private property, a new nation would begin to emerge. Among his four proposed solutions, Pimentel included the promotion of immigration from Europe:

> Fortunately, it is possible to modify a race rather than destroy it, and this is achieved through *transformation*. We will achieve the transformation of the Indians through European immigration [...] The mixed race would be a *transitional* race; after a short time everyone would become white [...] (1864: 234)

We want the names of races to disappear from our midst not only de jure but also de facto; we want the country to share the same customs and the same interests. We have already indicated the means: immigration. (1864, 240, my emphasis)

Thus, although the decline of the Indigenous "race" had a historical and cultural explanation in the mistreatment they received from the Spanish, the idea of progressive whitening was also held up as a possibility, a means of eliminating the different identities of the country's Indigenous populations entirely.

In the last quarter of the nineteenth century, the understanding of race underwent an important change. European positivism replaced the idea that the backwardness of Indians was due to colonial domination and imposed a "scientific" perspective that "conceptualized the backwardness of certain groups through modern raciological theories" (Urías 2000, 79). In this way, racist thinking at the end of the nineteenth century was essentially built on two claims. The first, the existence of "races" in the human species, and the second, the classification of those races according to a scale of values in which there is one superior race and others that are inferior. Thus, in addition to being represented as culturally backward beings, Indians were represented as having defects and deficiencies linked to their nature. It was no longer enough to change Indians' living conditions; mestizaje had to be promoted in order to better the race. Pablo Yankelevich (2015, 9) points out that immigration policy was rooted in large part "in the biological contribution the foreigner would make, the benefit they would bring to a race that could not be conceived of as anything but white."

## The Discursive Construction of the Mestizo

The poverty and marginalization most Mexicans experienced at the beginning of the twentieth century generated a new trend that explained the nation's problems as a consequence of economic failures. Andrés Molina Enríquez, in *Los grandes problemas nacionales* [The Nation's Great Problems] (1909), maintained that in order to be a real nation, Mexico needed many kinds of property, and that they should therefore eliminate latifundia[4] and the appropriation of small plots of land. These proposals influenced the Revolutionary ideologues of 1910, who saw in land distribution the possibility of lifting

Indigenous people and campesinos out of poverty and inserting them into capitalist progress.

The racial question occupied a preeminent position in Molina Enríquez's thinking. For him, the homeland could not exist without race, since racial unification generated community cohesion. Molina Enríquez understood a race as "a group of men who, because they have lived for a long time in similar conditions, have come to acquire certain uniformity of organization, marked by a certain uniformity of type" (2016, 65). For Molina, the mestizo would become a new race: the Mexican race. This race, derived from Indigenous people and Spanish people, would receive the best of both. "In our opinion, the greatest benefit we owe to the formation of the republic is that of having created civil equality that has favored the contact, mixing, and confusion of races, thus preparing the formation of a single race" (Molina Enríquez 2016, 69). Following Zermeño-Padilla's (1999, 19) reading of the construction of nation states, we can say that Molina Enríquez belongs to a generation of intellectuals nourished by the desire and hope of being part of progress and modernity, whose ultimate limit lay in a future not yet achieved. In order to achieve the longed-for progress, it was crucial that the people should not be irrational, ignorant, or in need of protection. Mestizaje was the discursive solution adopted by Mexico's intellectual class for a large part of the twentieth century.

Molina Enríquez, along with other intellectuals of the period, was convinced that over time mestizos would come to occupy all social spaces. The mestizo, the new Mexican, would synthesize the best characteristics of the two races: Indigenous people's ability to adapt to their environment and the intellectual and cultural superiority of the Spanish. That said, while mestizos were to be "better" human beings, they were not yet leading the nation, they did not occupy the highest positions, nor did they have the greatest social recognition, because they were not yet ready for such tasks—their time would come.

When the revolutionary process came to an end, governments encouraged a nationalism that located the mestizo as the official protagonist of history, making clear, according to official institutions, that there was only one way to be Mexican. Anthropologists took charge of resolving the "Indigenous problem" and their research was compliant with the demands of nationalist politics. Afro-descendent people still had no role in the story; the discourse of mestizaje did not take their presence into account, nor that Mexican mestizaje, throughout the nineteenth century and even as far back as the eighteenth century, had a large African-origin population. Governments imposed on the population an image of an integrated Mexico, a country sustained by a glorious Indigenous past and a prosperous present, based on evolution, scientific advancements, and the progress of the western world (Florescano 2001 and Pérez Montfort 2003).

The Indigenismo of the first half of the twentieth century was another chapter in the policy of modernizing society and invisibilizing racism in Mexico, because by promoting the supposed equality inherent in mestizaje, society's hierarchical relationships were kept hidden. Manuel Gamio published *Forjando Patria* (Forging a Homeland) in 1916, in which he built on Franz Boas's theses and rejected all forms of racism. For Gamio, the nation sustained a superior type of spiritual unity that had to be constructed through the application of scientific laws. Anthropology, with the help of other sciences, was a crucial instrument in the nation-building process, since the ultimate goal was the integration of Indian cultures into modernity (De la Peña 1996). Gamio, following Boas's thinking, argued:

> we do not know how the Indian thinks, we are ignorant of his true aspirations; we prejudge him with our criteria when we should be able to understand him on his own terms [. . .] This is not the task of the leader or the educator; it is exclusively the task of the anthropologist, and in particular of the ethnologist, whose apostolate requires not only enlightenment and self-denial, but above all approaches and points of view that are entirely devoid of prejudice. This applies to racial prejudices. (1982, 25)

While Gamio shared with his teacher, Boas, the idea of studying without prejudice, his interest was not wholly scientific, and as a revolutionary he thought that Mexican anthropologists ought to help change Indians' culture and insert them into the capitalist model. He was convinced Mexico needed linguistic unification and that it was down to anthropology to bring about both the linguistic and cultural homogenization that would allow for the formation of a true nation.

While Gamio was proposing cultural homogenization, postrevolutionary governments had set about redistributing land and opening schools, convinced that both processes would help transform and modernize the country. José Vasconcelos formally proposed the incorporation of Indians into national culture through education. As Secretary for Public Education, he drove the creation of "casas del pueblo"—community schools—and cultural missions. Moisés Sáenz (another great Mexican Indigenista) coincided with Vasconcelos in seeing the rural school as a tool for developing and integrating Indigenous people into national society. And yet his position was very different. While he thought Indians ought to be "made mestizo" and civilized through education, he maintained that this had to happen in their own languages. Preserving their languages would prevent them from rebelling against civilizing efforts (Pérez Monfort 2000, 44). Indians, one way or another, would have to learn Spanish because that was the only way for the Revolution to achieve its social justice objective. Sáenz thought Indigenous people had to be integrated into the regional economy, and for him, building roads to connect towns and communities was a priority, because this would not only facilitate the process of acculturation but also contribute to modernization and the country's economy. Despite being a pedagogue, Sáenz was in the habit of saying "when it comes to the indigenous problem, I'm more for roads than for schools" (Hewitt 1988, 34).

Luis Chávez Orozco, who headed up the Autonomous Department of Indigenous Affairs (1938–1940), agreed with Sáenz about the need to change the way education was imparted to Indigenous people. Spanish would no longer be imposed as the dominant language of everyday life but rather would be a second language to complement their traditional languages. However, unlike Sáenz, who sought to integrate Indigenous people, Chávez Orozco, like the great Mexican trade unionist Lombardo Toledano, defended Indigenous people's autonomy. They analyzed the structural elements of Indigenous people's poverty from a Marxist perspective and proposed that agrarian reform, in addition to returning land, should also provide credit and technology in order to improve their standard of living. Both attacked the integrationist tendencies of education policy and proclaimed the right of Indigenous groups to preserve their own customs and languages (Hewitt 1988, 35).

In sum, in the 1930s there were three main opinions on how to solve the "Indigenous problem": 1) Manuel Gamio supported the socioeconomic and cultural integration of Indigenous groups into national life; 2) Moisés Sáenz sought to strengthen a rural Mexican conscience through education, and 3) Luis Chávez Orozco and Vicente Lombardo Toledano defended the rapid development of the countryside while at the same time arguing for cultural pluralism (Hewitt 1988, 38). The Indigenista policy pursued by the postrevolutionary Mexican state—with Alfonso Caso at the head of the National Indigenista Institute—agreed with the first two stances: economic and cultural integration and a strengthening of Mexican consciousness through education. The Secretary of Public Education placed the notion of mestizaje at the heart of nationalist symbols (De la Peña 1996).

Until the mid-twentieth century, Indigenismo's main concern had been learning about Indigenous groups and concerning itself with their acculturation and integration into the nation. Julio De la Fuente, a close collaborator of Caso at the National Indigenista Institute, insisted that the country's education policy had neglected a fundamental issue: interethnic relations. For him, it wasn't right to talk of "the Indigenous problem"; those who did so believed Indians to be a source of *national shame* (1977, 41). For De la Fuente, Indians were characterized by their culture rather than their "race," and he claimed their difference was marked not by racial but by cultural features, of which language was the most important (1965, 51). Despite recognizing how contentious interethnic relations were, Julio De la Fuente could not visualize the racism inherent in them, and thought a correct command of Spanish and a change of clothing would put an end to the ethnic discrimination suffered by Indigenous peoples.

When the Second World War came to an end and people learned of the Nazi genocide of Jewish people, science made it clear that "races" did not exist and that all human beings, regardless of visible phenotypical differences, were equal. From the forties onwards, Mexican anthropologists and Indigenistas stopped using the concept of "race" and began to replace it with ethnicity. Over time, the Mexican State also stopped using "race," substituting it with ethnic groups. Indigenistas were convinced that by changing the culture and integrating Indigenous peoples into regional economies and establishing class relations, ethnic discrimination would come to an end.

In the fifties, Gonzalo Aguirre Beltrán (a doctor and anthropologist who dedicated his life to the study and integration of Indigenous peoples in Mexico) formulated a new theoretical and conceptual framework that guided the Mexican state's Indigenista discourse and action between 1950 and 1976. For him, the work of Indigenismo was to expand industrial, urban, rational, and modern Mexico. Aguirre Beltrán defined Indigenismo as "a policy formulated not by Indians, to solve their own problems, but rather by non-Indians, with regard to the heterogeneous ethnic groups who receive the general label of Indigenous" (1976, 24). Aguirre Beltrán thought that Indigenous people themselves could not propose an Indigenista policy because "the scope of their world was reduced to a narrow, homogenous, pre-classist community, in which they had only a very vague sense and notion of nationality" (1976a, 25).

The Indigenista practice driven by Aguirre Beltrán was based on a regional conceptualization in line with President Miguel Alemán's (1946–1952) development policy. It sought to extend the model of national development not just to small localities, but rather to broad regions, with the goal of opening a path to industrialization. In 1951, Aguirre Beltrán proposed the creation of the Indigenista Coordination Centers, units focused on research and on bringing about social change. These centers, which were dependent on the National Indigenista Institute, would facilitate the movement from casta-based social relations to class relations, which would allow for the upward social mobility of Indigenous people (Iturriaga 2015).

The Indigenistas were eager to bring the justice of the Revolution to Indian communities and to consolidate the Mexican nation; they refuted the idea that discrimination against Indians was racially motivated, understanding it as a form of social exclusion that would disappear as the process of acculturation and integration advanced. They were convinced that cultural change among Indigenous people, through different clothing, a good command of Spanish, and modern farming techniques, would integrate them into the modern nation, where they would find a place in the system of capitalist production and ascend the social ladder, thus lifting themselves out of poverty and marginalization. They would, in this way, become mestizos— real Mexicans.

Rodolfo Stavenhagen's *Las clases sociales en las sociedades agrarias* (Social Classes in Agrarian Societies), published in 1969, distinguishes between *social stratification* and *social classes*. While the former refers to social position and status, the latter is linked to the position an individual occupies in the social structure in relation to the means of production. Stavenhagen argues that, to understand social stratification in Latin American societies, we must take into account other factors, such as religion, ethnicity, casta, and race. For him, unlike for the Indigenistas, social mobility in the economic structure did not necessarily involve a rise in status. In this way, Stavenhagen incorporated the dimension of social classes and stratification into the study of ethnicity for the first time (1976, 41):

Classes are incompatible with one another, by which I mean they are mutually exclusive, but the same is not true of strata in various systems of stratification. This means an individual can have various statuses in society, and participate in various stratifications, but they can only belong to a single class.

Contrary to Aguirre Beltrán's approach, Stavenhagen explains that interethnic relations cannot be reduced to their class components since ethnicities can permeate social classes and still be discriminated against in terms of social stratification. This stance broke with the hegemonic explanation of inequality in Mexico and made it possible to look at ethnicity from a different angle. From several perspectives, new generations of anthropologists began to criticize integrationist Indigenismo, which in the preceding decades had become State policy, thus initiating a debate that began to cast serious doubt on its theoretical basis (Warman et al. 1970). After the 1970s, Indigenista policies began to change, becoming first participatory and then, soon after, self-managed, at least in name.

Within this framework, the anthropologist and civil servant Guillermo Bonfil proposed a public policy aimed at strengthening ethnic culture, as well as Indigenous peoples' right to self-determination, autonomy, and self-management (Anguiano 2003). In several of his publications, Bonfil (1989, 1995) developed a concept that was useful for understanding the process by which cultural domination gave rise to the loss of the original group's identity: deindianization. Bonfil noted that the process of deindianization differs from mestizaje. While mestizaje is a biological phenomenon, deindianization is a historical process through which populations that originally possessed a particular and distinctive identity based on their *own culture* saw themselves forced to give up that identity. According to Bonfil, the process of deindianization—which has been going on for more than five centuries—has caused large parts of the population to view the world from the conquistador's perspective. Bonfil made clear that Mexico is not a mestizo country, as the Indigenistas and the Mexican State had maintained, but rather a deindianized country.

As we have seen so far, to the extent that new generations of anthropologists—in the late 1960s and early 1970s—criticized the assimilationist policies of official Indigenismo, they opened the door to making visible what years later would be recognized as racist practices promoted by the Mexican state. In my opinion, the concept of deindianization formulated by Guillermo Bonfil is in dialogue with Bolívar Echeverría's ideas described at the beginning of this chapter. As I see it, deindianization is implied in the notion of whitening, since it not only brings about the loss of Indigenous identity but also causes people to internalize and live according to the values of *homo capitalisticus*, which is to say, to enter into a process of whitening. I think deindianization allows us to think about racism and the symbolic violence inflicted on the Indigenous population, and that whitening allows us to reflect on racism in Mexico beyond the Indigenous and Afro-Mexican populations and to extend it to Mexico's enormous, brown-skinned, mestizo majority.

**The Second Decade of the Twenty-First Century: Debates About Skin Color**
Throughout this chapter, I have tried to show how "blanquitud," nationalism, and mestizaje are interlinked keys to understanding why Mexican racism remained hidden for so long. Today the conditions have changed. "Blanquitud" is called into question by the large swathes of urban population with access to new technologies, nationalisms around the world are in crisis, and Mexican mestizaje has not fulfilled its promise of social equality.

When I began my studies on Mexican racism in 2007 there were few academics working in this area. Even many of my colleagues at the Autonomous University of Yucatán thought my choice strange, arguing that racism didn't exist either in Mexico or in the Yucatán and that my research would find nothing but classism. Fourteen years later, Mexican racism is discussed not only in academia but also in the media and has even been recognized by the President of the Republic as a national problem that needs tackling. What happened? Obviously, there is no single explanation.

The Zapatista movement, as Alicia Castellanos (2000) and Jorge Gómez Izquierdo (2002) argue, highlighted racism towards Indigenous peoples. Academia very slowly began to recognize racism and to reflect on the relationship between Indian communities and the nation state. Research continually pointed to the Mexican state, its institutions, and its policies, as responsible for the racism towards and discrimination against Indigenous peoples (Iturriaga 2016). In the 1990s, both academics and activists began to make Afro-Mexican people visible (and eventually managed to get them recognized in the Mexican constitution in August 2019). However, it wasn't until the twenty-first century that people began to recognize that Mexican racism also affected the majority population—the moreno mestizos—and the role of skin color in social relations began to be questioned.

In 2010 the PERLA (Project on Ethnicity and Race in Latin America) project used a color palette to measure racial discrimination in four Latin American countries (Brazil, Colombia, Mexico, and Peru). In 2017, an intergenerational social mobility survey by Mexico's National Institute of Statistics and Geography (INEGI) discovered, again through the use of a color palette, that people who self-describe as having darker skin tones have a lower level of education. In 2019, the sociologist Patricio Solís published *Por mi raza hablará la desigualdad* (Inequality will speak for my race) in which, returning to data from the social mobility survey, he shows the correlation between skin color and socioeconomic status. As these studies clearly show, skin color plays an important role in social relations in Mexico and forms part of Mexican racism. However, we mustn't lose sight of the fact that racism is not limited to skin color. Racism is a structural system that operates in different contexts and different ways, and so limiting it to skin color would be to reduce the phenomenon to just one of its variants.

Donald Trump's election success in 2016 and his repeated anti-Mexican rhetoric aroused huge discontent in several areas of Mexican society. The upper middle and upper classes defended themselves from these attacks by saying that the US president's accusations were unfair because "not all Mexicans are the same." This contradicts the Mexican discourse of mestizaje in which "all Mexicans are," indeed, "the same." In 2018, there was a Netflix series titled *Made in Mexico*, a reality show in which a group of young Mexicans tries to show the world that in Mexico there are "pretty people" with cosmopolitan tastes, who drink Aperol spritzes—the latest fashionable summer drink—and whose lifestyle resembles that of people who live in Beverly Hills. Around the same time, the Twitter account @losWhitexicans appeared, exposing a privileged sector of Mexican society, people who seem to live in a bubble and not understand the reality of the country in which they live. Many people reacted to tweets from this account by describing it as *inverse racism*. The film *Roma*, which premiered in 2018, and Yalitza Aparicio's subsequent Oscar nomination, generated multiple reactions from Mexican society. There were those who said that it didn't count as acting if you just played yourself, because anyone could do that—assuming they were a domestic worker—as well as those who defended Aparicio as a great actress. In this context, an explicit connection between skin color and social class began to emerge.

Donald Trump's openly racist comments about Mexico also prompted certain sectors of society to take a good look in the mirror and begin to question the racism operating within Mexican society itself. The mirror revealed different ways of being Mexican and the social status and privileged—or not so privileged—position from which each person gazes. In the debates we now see in the media, reference is made to "privilegio blanco" ("white privilege") and social distinctions are made between "los blancos" (white people), "los morenos" (brown people), and "los prietos" (dark-skinned people). After the Mexican Revolution, it was rare to find people with fair skin described as "blanco" or "blanca"; references to "güeros" and "güeras" were more common. It seems this essentialization is the result of categories imported from the United States, which is a topic that requires further reflection.[5]

The emerging public debate has highlighted the weight skin color has had and still has in social relations in Mexico. Actors like Tenoch Huerta, Maya Zapata, and Yalitza Aparicio have denounced the racism of which they have been victims because of their skin color, and, in May 2021, they joined the social media campaign with the hashtag #poderprieto (#dark-skinnedpower or perhaps even #Blackpower). Through social media platforms like Facebook, Twitter, Instagram, and YouTube channels, people who did not have access to mainstream media could now express their opinions and reach an audience beyond their immediate circle. Similarly, new technologies have made it possible for a wide public to consume content not produced by large television consortiums. Through social networking platforms, the opulence and profligacy of the upper classes have become visible, for instance in videos of graduation parties or trips around the world published on Instagram. At the same time, there has been a proliferation of videos, jokes, and memes about brown-skinned people considered to be middle or lower class, especially with regard to their physical appearance and lack of money or refinement.

Although the meaning of epidermal whiteness and "blanquitud" have changed over time, the desire for the former and the possibility of obtaining the latter through the alchemy of progressive whitening or by adopting the identity of *homo capitalisticus* remains. The nationalism that has been constructed since the end of the nineteenth century and which was strengthened after the Mexican Revolution was based on the figure of the mestizo, the product of a "union" between Spanish and Indigenous blood. This idea is still present in textbooks and is taught to children all over the country. What is never said is that the result of this mixing *does* matter, and that the result, for better or worse, has a significant impact on Mexican social relations.

Nationalist intellectuals of the nineteenth and early twentieth century hoped that European immigration would "better the race" and saw in the mestizo the realization of a future project. Through basic education, post-revolutionary nationalism impressed upon the population the idea that being Mexican meant being mestizo. That all Mexicans, no matter their appearance or social class, would be mestizos. The elites made themselves mestizos by becoming deeply nationalistic, by being "proud Mexicans." And why not, if the State privileged them and helped consolidate their position by implementing protectionist economic policies like the import substitution model in the mid-twentieth century?

Today it is clear that the promise of mestizaje has not been fulfilled and that whitening is not enough. Many moreno mestizos are raising their voices and demanding full citizenship, demanding not to be made to feel like second- or third-class Mexicans. They are denouncing the way the color of their skin has prevented them from occupying certain spaces or being accepted on equal terms rather than in frank asymmetry with lighter-skinned people. It is a battle that must be fought, but it is not the only one, because racism, as this chapter has sought to show, goes beyond skin color.

## Notes

1  See further examples in the chapter by Alejandra Leal in this book.
2  This is why I do not think it is enough to speak of a pigmentocracy, because it reduces a complex problem to just one factor.
3  At the edges of the paintings we can read: Spanish and Indian produce mestizo, Spanish and mestizo produce castiza, Spanish and castiza becomes Spanish.
4  Editors' note: Latifundia refers to vast extensions of land destined to agriculture owned by a single person.
5  There are some reflections on this topic in Alejandra Leal's chapter in this book.

## References

Aguirre Beltrán, Gonzalo. 1976. "Un postulado indigenista." In *Obra polémica*, 21–28. México: Instituto Nacional de Antropología e Historia/Secretaría de Educación Pública.

Aguirre Beltrán, Gonzalo. 1976a. "Estructura y funciones de los Centros Coordinadores." In *El indigenismo en acción: XXV aniversario del Centro*

*Coordinador Indigenista Tzeltal-Tzotzil, Chiapas*, coordinated by Gonzalo Aguirre Beltrán, Alfonso Villa Rojas and Agustín Romano Delgado, 27–40. Mexico: Instituto Nacional Indigenista.

Anguiano, Marina. 2003. *Las culturas indígenas vistas por sus autores*. Mexico: UPN/Miguel Ángel Porrúa.

Bonfil Batalla, Guillermo. 1989. *México Profundo: una civilización negada*. Mexico: Grijalbo/Consejo Nacional para la Cultura y las Artes.

Bonfil Batalla, Guillermo. 1995. "Descolonización y cultura propia." In *Obras escogidas de Guillermo Bonfil*, Vol. 4, edited by Lina Odena, 351–367. Mexico: Instituto Nacional Indigenista/Centro de Investigación y Estudios Superiores en Antropología Social/Instituto Nacional de Antropología e Historia.

Bourdieu, Pierre. 1991. *Sentido práctico*. Madrid: Taurus.

Campos, Alejandro. 2012. "Racialización, racialismo y racismo. Un discernimiento necesario." *Universidad de la Habana* 273 (January–June): 184–199.

Castañeda García, Rafael. 2021. *Esclavitud Africana en la fundación de la Nueva España*, Colección México 500. Mexico City: Universidad Nacional Autónoma de México.

Castellanos Guerrero, Alicia. 1998. "Nacion y racismos." In *Nación, racismo e identidad*, edited by Alicia Castellanos Guerrero and Juan Manuel Sandoval, 11–36. Mexico D.F.: Editorial Nuestro Tiempo.

Castellanos Guerrero, Alicia. 2000. "Antropología y racismo en México." *Desacatos* 4: 53–79.

D'Appolonia, Ariane Chabel. 1998. *Los racismos cotidianos*. Barcelona: Bellaterra.

Chinchilla, Perla. 2021. *Del Plan de Igual a los Tratados de Córdoba*. Mexico: Secretaría de Cultura.

Ceron-Anaya, Hugo. *Privilege at play: Class, race, and golf in México*. New York: Oxford University Press.

De la Fuente, Julio. 1965. *Relaciones interétnicas*. Mexico: Secretaría de Educación Pública /Instituto Nacional Indigenista.

De la Fuente, Julio. 1977. *Educación, antropología y desarrollo de la comunidad*. Mexico: Instituto Nacional Indigenista.

De la Peña, Guillermo. 1996. "Nacionales y extranjeros en la historia de la antropología mexicana." In *La historia de la antropología en México, fuentes y transmisión*, edited by Mechthild Rutsch, 41–81. Mexico: Universidad Iberoamericana/Plaza y Valdés/Instituto Nacional Indigenista.

Echeverría, Bolívar. 2010. *Modernidad y "blanquitud."* Mexico: Era.

Florescano, Enrique. 2001. *Etnia, estado y nación.* Mexico: Taurus.

Gall, Olivia. 2016. "Hilando fino entre las identidades, el racismo y la xenofobia en México y Brasil." *Desacatos* 51: 8–17.

Gamio, Manuel. 1982. *Forjando patria,* Mexico: Porrúa.

Gómez Izquierdo, José Jorge. 2002. "Estudios sobre el racismo en México. Enfoques preexistentes, antecedentes y estado de la investigación." *Cuadernos de Trabajo. Sociología y Ciencia Política,* no. 31 (working paper). Puebla: Instituto de Ciencias Sociales y Humanidades de la Benemérita Universidad Autónoma de Puebla.

Hewitt de Alcántara. Cynthia. 1988. *Imágenes del campo: La interpretación antropológica del México rural.* Mexico: El Colegio de México.

Iturriaga, Eugenia. 2015. "Discurso y práctica indigenista en Yucatán (1959–2003): el Centro Coordinador de Peto." *Temas Antropológicos* 37 (2, April—September): 43–73.

Iturriaga, Eugenia. 2016. *Las élites de la ciudad blanca: discursos racistas sobre la Otredad.* Mexico: Universidad Nacional Autónoma de México.

Lomnitz, Claudio. 1995. *Las salidas del laberinto.* Mexico: Joaquín Mortiz.

López Beltrán, Carlos. 2004. *El sesgo hereditario. Ámbitos históricos del concepto de herencia biológica.* Mexico: Universidad Nacional Autónoma de México.

Molina Enríquez, Andrés. 2016. *Los grandes problemas nacionales: 1909, y otros textos, 1911–1919.* Mexico: Era.

Mora, José María Luis. 1950 [1836]. *México y sus revoluciones.* Paris: Librería de Rosa.

Moreno Figueroa, Mónica. 2013. "Displaced looks: The lived experience of beauty and racism." *Feminist Theory* 14 (2): 137–151.

Moreno Figueroa, Mónica. 2016. "El archivo del estudio del racismo en México." *Desacatos* 51 (May–August): 92–107.

Navarrete, Federico. 2017. *Alfabeto del racismo mexicano.* Barcelona: Malpaso ediciones.

Pérez Montfort, Ricardo. 2000. *Avatares del nacionalismo cultural: cinco ensayos,* Mexico: CIESAS.

Pérez Montfort, Ricardo. 2003. *Estampas de nacionalismo popular mexicano.* Mexico: CIESAS.

Pérez Vejo, Tomás. 2017. "Raza y construcción nacional. México, 1810–1910." In *Raza y política en Hispanoamérica,* edited by Tomás Pérez Vejo and Pablo Yankelevich, Mexico: Bonilla Artiga editores/El Colegio de México.

Pimentel, Francisco. 1864. *Memoria de las causas que han originado la situación actual de la raza indígena de México y medios de remediarla*. Mexico: Imprenta de Escalante y Andrade.

Reygadas, Luis. 2008. *La apropiación. Destejiendo las redes de la desigualdad*. Barcelona: Anthropos.

Stavenhagen, Rodolfo. 1976. *Las clases sociales en las sociedades agrarias*. Mexico: Siglo XXI.

Stavenhagen, Rodolfo. 1994. "Racismo y xenofobia en tiempos de la globalización." *Estudios Sociológicos* 12 (34): 9–16.

Urías Horcasitas, Beatriz. 2000. *Indígena y criminal. Interpretaciones del derecho y la antropología en México, 1871–1921*. Mexico: Universidad Iberoamericana.

Velázquez, María Elisa and Gabriela Iturralde Nieto. 2016. *Afrodescendientes en México. Una historia de silencio y discriminación*. Mexico: Comisión Nacional de los Derechos Humanos/Consejo Nacional para Prevenir la Discriminación/Instituto Nacional de Antropología e Historia.

Warman, Arturo, Guillermo Bonfil Batalla, Margarita Nolasco Armas, Mercedes Olivera Bustamante and Enrique Valencia. 1970. *De eso que llaman antropología mexicana*. Mexico: Nuestro Tiempo.

Wieviorka, Michel. 2009. *El racismo. Una Introducción*. Barcelona: Gedisa.

Yankelevich, Pablo (coord.). 2015. *Inmigración y racismo. Contribuciones a la historia de los extranjeros en México*. Mexico: El Colegio de México.

Zermeño-Padilla, Guillermo. 1999. "Condición de subalternidad, condición postmoderna y saber histórico: ¿Hacia una nueva forma de escritura de la historia?" *Historia y grafía* 12: 11–47.

# WHAT IS DISGUST FOR? ANTI-BLACK RACISM IN MEXICO

Mónica G. Moreno Figueroa Translated by Ellen Jones

"One consequence of racism is that white people find Black people disgusting." So declared a participant in a workshop I held alongside the Colectivo para Eliminar el Racismo (Collective for the Elimination of Racism) some years ago. What is disgust for? What does the feeling of disgust allow us to do? What does it save us from? Answering these questions helps us understand anti-Black racism and its central role in how racism works in Mexico.

The recent furore over racism has been very welcome, especially during the pandemic. Social inequalities are being paraded unashamedly before our eyes, waiting to be seen and examined. Moreover, we seem to be paying much more attention to movements both internal and external: emotional turmoil and social upheavals. Our feelings are raw, close to the surface. "Look, a Black man! He's saying he can't breathe, why has that policeman got his knee on his neck?"

Perversely, we might think the attention being paid to racism in the United States has served as a good distraction from the pandemic in Mexico.

Or better still, we might say that this pandemic is such a turning point that we have had to pause, sit down and wait; that we've reached the point when we are ready to listen and to notice our own feelings of disgust, feelings that some of us have had about our own bodies and which many people involuntarily feel towards others, feelings expressed through a grimace, pursed lips, a wrinkled nose, or with surprise: "There are Black people in Mexico? Where?" Leaving suspicion aside, I've also noticed a genuine interest that manages, albeit timidly, to say: "And what about us, right here? What's it like for me?" I want to make the most of that attention.

In many of the conversations I've had about racism in recent months, I haven't got round to talking about Black people in Mexico. This isn't because we're avoiding the subject, but because I insist, when asked my opinion on the situation with George Floyd and the Black Lives Matter movement in the United States, on responding in a way that recognizes what is happening here, and the long process, begun by the Zapatista Nacional Liberation Army in 1994, in which a preoccupation with racism in Mexico began to emerge. It's also an opportunity to examine how the false national pride one gets from comparing oneself favorably to others is self-delusion ("We Mexicans aren't like that, ever! How could you think us capable of a thing like that?"). This distracts in two ways: it gets us comparing apples with pears, and then it silences us.

I also make a point of ensuring that I go about answering the question about Black people by first explaining what racism is, as a system of distribution of oppression and privilege, and then pause for a moment to focus on how the idea of "race" is just an idea and to question whether "races" even exist. Finally, it's important for me to make clear that the ideology of mestizaje is key to understanding how our racism works, which is to say, mestizaje is the Mexican racial project, one characterized by pretending to accept racial mixing while all the while undertaking violent processes of assimilation that are propped up by anti-Indigenous, anti-Asian, and anti-Black racism.

This preamble seems crucial to me if we are to see that what is happening in the United States, whose racial project is one of segregation and the rejection of mixing, is very different to what is happening in Mexico—although disgust is a shared logic in both spaces and projects. In both places, disgust for *blackness* serves to dehumanize and especially to set limits according to the dominant ideology: in the United States, these limits control and separate off Black people; in Mexico, they maintain Black people's unusual and contradictory status as both denied and entirely visible. The idea that in Mexico people have denied the existence of a Black population and, when challenged, refused to recognize the Black population as Mexican is partially correct. It's true that many people are surprised; that many people seem not to know there are Black people in this country, nor where they are. However, if there is one thing Mexicans do see, it's *blackness, darkness, brownness.*

Although whitening is one of the central logics of mestizaje, even in our analyses we fall into the trap of turning towards whiteness without realizing that this movement implies a distancing from blackness. Brownness in Mexico is organized according to this same logic: dark brown, then light brown, fair, and finally white. If we were to catalogue all the activities, attitudes and even social dynamics that are designed to distance us from blackness, we would fill several volumes. Who we love, who we feel attracted to, who we like and who we fear, who we trust and who is dangerous, who we want to sit in our living room and eat with us, who we help, who we demand things of, who is fascinating and exotic, who is admirable and lovable, who is repugnant and disgusting.

As well as being a political and racial project of assimilation and whitening, in contemporary Mexico mestizaje is a daily experience that structures social relations and distributes power and privileges in society. Historically, mestizaje has depended on a thorough anti-Black racism in order to rationalize the logic of whitening it presupposes. The strength, success, and effectiveness of mestizaje in Mexico have been such that, even in this moment of multicultural openness, the country reacts to and resists the emerging positioning of the Black population.

Mexico's racial history and mestizo logic help us to understand the desire of enslaved peoples to get away from the stereotype of inferiority and the experience of disadvantage that was or is represented by the Black person. Given this, it's not surprising that the seductive move towards whiteness and away from blackness is a deep-rooted, collective intention, developed over time, which characterizes the logic of mestizaje and feeds the fire of whiteness-oriented racial mixing.

We can therefore understand how anti-Black racism is responsible for ensuring that mestizaje, as the Mexican racial project, continues to run smoothly, thereby maintaining the stability of our national identity. What is more, in order for Mexican mestizaje and its racism to function, it is necessary both to maintain a permanent aversion to *blackness* as an idea and to keep the population racialized as Black at a persistent disadvantage. Which is to say that the idea of Mexicanness is based on the assumption that: 1) there are no Black Mexicans and 2) we must distance ourselves from what blackness represents. Hence, the apparent negation and exclusion of the Black population from the national imaginary is necessary to conserving national identity or the idea of Mexicanness. Disgust for blackness and Black people greases the wheels of Mexican racism. While it is hoped that Indigenous people will be integrated, Black people are used as a reference point for what to avoid.

Independent of what is observable about people's bodies—whether they look "Black" or "afro-descendent" or not, whether they have afro-textured hair, whether they have a wide-ish nose, or dark skin, or whether their cultural heritage is known as *Black*—mestizaje's racial project seems to depend on the dehumanization of the Black subject, the Black-ish subject, the Black-adjacent subject. The idea is to position them as the ultimate limit point, never to be approached, and to let the concept of "Black" become the filter that regulates our daily interactions. That ongoing aversion and persistent disadvantaging can be called *anti-Black racism*.

Racism requires certain guarantees, certain assumptions in order for it to function. In the case of mestizaje as a racial project propped up by the racialized and racist structuring of society, its guarantees are based on the assumption that racial mixing eliminates the emphasis on ideas about "race" and the body, while at the same time maintaining blackness as the limit case that regulates that very same mixing. Which is to say, mestizaje requires a degree of arbitration to ensure that the limit of blackness is very clear to everyone, to protect that border and make sure we don't cross it, thereby guaranteeing that the mixing continues along its trajectory towards whiteness. This arbitrator is anti-Black racism, mestizaje racism, which appears to want to save us from shame and disadvantage. For Black people, anti-Black racism is the fine thread of internalized oppression. For white-mestizos, "light" brown skinned people, or the fair-skinned, rural, working-class individuals known as "güeritos de rancho," anti-Black racism is there to remind us of the direction of the trajectory and its limits. That's what disgust is for: it regulates us, and, like an electric fence, its very presence keeps us at arm's length. Or if we decide to get too close, a sharp shock will do the trick.

# CHAPTER 2

# Notes on the History of Racial Capitalism and Slavery in Mexico

## Perla Valero Translated by Ellen Jones

This chapter sets out to offer some reflections on the concept of racial capitalism, a term coined by the Afro-American thinker and activist Cedric Robinson, but from the perspective of Mexican and Latin American historical experience. It is an open dialogue with Robinson's work, which returns to his hypotheses in order to illustrate connections with the phenomena of slavery, racialization, and the evolution of capitalism in Mexico.

### Latin American Racial Capitalism?

Social sciences in Latin America have been slow to develop a study of racism and its concrete expressions in our societies; it was only in the 1980s and 1990s that the discipline first began to be recognized within academia. The late development of its theoretical examination can be explained by the generalized presence of racial prejudices and ethnic discrimination, but also, more importantly, by the success of nationalist ideologies focused on defending racial and cultural mestizaje (París Pombo 2002, 289–310).

In Latin America and the Caribbean, mestizaje has been defined in many different ways: it is both "biological mixing" and cultural syncretism (Gruzinski 2000); a process of creolization, understood as cultural mixing (Muteba Rahier 2014); a process of "codephagy" (the cannibalism of signs) (Echeverría 2000); a modernizing State ideology (Basave Benítez 1992) that imposes the homogenization of socio-racial identity (Appelbaum, Macpherson, Rosemblatt (eds.) 2003); and an ethnocidal policy that has resulted in the whitening of the population (Gould 1998). But in Mexican culture, mestizaje is the essence of national identity.

Mexico is perhaps the most developed example of a state discourse based on mestizaje. There has been fierce criticism of the racism implicit in the nationalist ideology of mestizaje, which was constructed by the postrevolutionary State alongside the development of the capitalist economy, and which still dominates popular discourse in Mexican society. One notable critic is Mexican historian Federico Navarrete Linares, who defines the ideology of mestizaje as a racial and nationalist doctrine developed by intellectual elites and leaders during the nineteenth and twentieth centuries.

This racial ideology, which Navarrete Linares (2016) terms "mestizophilia," is based on the invisibilization of Indigenous, Afro-descendant, and other identities of non-European descent who are excluded from the national discourse. Either their identity is obscured by the figure of the mestizo or they are discriminated against for not being "Mexican," and through exploitation—or enslavement, as we shall go on to see—their labor underpins the profits of the great capitalist centers. However, the state discourse of mestizophilia also covers for white political identities that are hidden or obscured within the ambiguous category of mestizo.[1]

Navarrete himself distinguishes the discourse of mestizophilia from the process of "social mestizaje," understood as the sociocultural and identity transformation that many Indigenous communities and people experienced throughout the eighteenth, nineteenth, and twentieth centuries. This social mestizaje resulted in forms of "de-Indianization" and de-collectivization, which is to say the destruction of Indigenous peoples' forms of organization and cultural identities as a correlate of economic modernization (Bonfil Batalla 2019). After independence, the process of disentailing communal property—that is, the forced expropriation of land belonging to the Catholic Church, unused land, and communal land belonging to municipalities and Indigenous peoples so it could be put up for sale—accelerated. Essentially, this meant that land existing outside the capitalist market was incorporated into it as a result of State action. In the case of Indigenous peoples, the protection of their communal rights was revoked as part of the dismantling of the old corporative and class order that sought to convert them into individual property owners, citizens of the nation, and market participants. Dissolving Indigenous peoples' communal property meant dissolving the political community, its identity, and its culture. It meant the uprooting of community members, who became dispossessed migrant workers later socialized as mestizos, thus constituting a process of "de-Indianization."

The monopolization and unequal appropriation of communal lands, a very complex and nuanced process, contributed to the formation of new landowning elites and consolidated the old owners of large latifundia (Prien and Martínez de Codes 1999). There were cases of communal lands transformed into small properties; other communities organized their own land redistribution where it suited the interests of their dominant factions. In other cases, the communities themselves leased and sold individual property rights within their territory, although this responded not only to their peoples' political agency but also to the enormous pressure exerted by economic factors, such as the emergence of new agricultural markets that positioned the privatization of communal land as part of the process of capitalist development. And, of course, other communities resisted, especially in the south, where some managed to keep their land despite the disentailment laws (Kourí 2017).

The process of so-called disentailment can be understood as a form of original accumulation of capital: a disassociation between workers and their means of production. Essentially, this amounts to the separation of direct producers from communal property, which results in the appropriation and privatization of land, leading to the creation of large private estates and dispossessed "campesindios"[2] who must sell their labor to survive. Karl Marx theorized so-called original accumulation, defining it as a process that spans the entire history of capitalism and is reproduced over and over again on ever larger scales as part of the general law of capitalist accumulation (Marx, 2014). Marx finds historical expressions of original accumulation or the genesis of capitalist development in the spoliation of ecclesiastical property, the fraudulent transfer of unused land, the theft of communal property, and the transformation of corporative property into private property, as well as colonization and the slave trade. These processes, which Marx finds in Europe, undoubtedly also occurred in Latin America. Marx did not address the sociocultural impact of original accumulation; however, in the case of Mexico, it seems to have resulted in de-Indianization or social mestizaje. As Navarrete puts it: "collective mestizaje was a product of the forces of capitalist economic development" (Navarrete Linares 2004).

This correlation between mestizaje and capitalism in Mexico can also be observed in historical sources, such as in the discourse of the nineteenth century Porfiriato's intelligentsia, which formed part of the State ideology of mestizophilia. General Porfirio Díaz's[3] regime developed an idealized figure of the mestizo, much more identifiable by their moral qualities than by their physiognomy. The mestizo embodied the representation of "positive" and "civilized" modern societal values: a versatile, entrepreneurial, cheerful, daring subject, eager for economic advancement, representative of "a new, dynamic, entrepreneurial spirit at both rural and factory level" (Zermeño 2011, 297). In other words, they embodied the productivist subjectivity and liberal values demanded by capitalism, which, a century later, the Mexican-Ecuadorian philosopher Bolívar Echeverría would term "blanquitud"—"whiteness"— a concept that defines the ethos of capitalism: a particular way of being and being present in the world in accordance with modern values and subjectivity (Echeverría 2010).

This particular Porfirian discourse on mestizaje as a symptom of subjective, cultural, and economic modernization was developed in the context not only of Latin America's definitive integration into the global agro-export market at the end of the nineteenth century; but also of the deployment of policies intended to annihilate Indigenous peoples, who were enslaved and exploited as laborers on haciendas. One example is the Yaqui community in the northeast of Mexico, who were suppressed, enslaved, and forcibly displaced onto henequen-producing haciendas in the southwest of the country, in the Yucatán region (Padilla Ramos 2018).

The enslavement and extermination of Indigenous communities had been carried out all over Latin America and the Caribbean ever since the conquest, but it had a resurgence in the second half of the nineteenth century. This coincided with the consolidation of the capitalist economy which required lands to be "liberated" for the production of raw materials and for the laying of railway tracks, and masses of workers to sustain production. In his book *Indios, ejército y frontera* (Indians, the Army, and the Border) (Viñas 1982), the Argentine intellectual David Viñas analyzed this process, demonstrating that towards the last third of the nineteenth century Latin American states set in motion a process of frontier expansion in which they appropriated territories for cattle ranching and the planting of raw materials and food; a correlate of their position as dependent economies. This brought with it ethnocidal and genocidal practices wielded against Indigenous peoples, who were often subjected to various forms of forced and slave labor and discriminated against because of their origin, culture, language, and political traditions. Yet another expression of racial capitalism, which historically has gone hand in hand with racism and enslavement, as Cedric Robinson tried to demonstrate.

## The Robinson Hypothesis: Racial Capitalism and Permanent Slavery

In his work *Black Marxism: The Making of the Black Radical Tradition*, originally published in 1983 and only translated into Spanish in 2021 (Robinson 2000), the Afro-American thinker Cedric J. Robinson (1940–2016), professor at the University of California and activist for several radical Black organizations, proposed the concept of racial capitalism.

What today we call capitalism was defined by Karl Marx as a mode of production, distribution, and consumption founded on the appropriation and exploitation of other people's labor for monetary gain. It presupposes the existence of a market in which money and commodities circulate on a massive scale, including labor power—dispossessed workers forced to sell their labor—and the means of production—land, tools, and production technology (Marx 2014). These goods are bought by the capitalist and put to work in the productive space to generate new goods with surplus value that will result in profits. This happens under a regime of mainly—though not exclusively—free (that is, not slave labor) and wage labor. But, as Robinson notes, capitalism has overwhelmingly employed other forms of non-free and non-wage labor.

The uniqueness of Robinson's proposal lies in the idea that the systems of racial enslavement are inherent to capitalism and the basis of its evolution. For Robinson, it was not capitalism that re-signified slavery but rather slavery, especially in feudal Europe, that allowed the genesis of capitalism.[4] This meant that African enslavement and the trafficking of "pieces of the Indies," which would reach a climax in the eighteenth century, was not truly a capitalist invention but rather the natural continuation of the racial order of feudal Europe, only extended, expanded, and established on a planetary scale by modern capitalism.

Robinson's hypothesis challenged classic interpretations of slavery and the phenomenon of racism as elaborated by the so-called "Marxist tradition." Those readings had tended to interpret slavery as a pre-modern institution that disappeared after the expansion of free labor under capitalism. Slavery, then, was understood as a kind of remnant of feudalism that survived only in early capitalism, only to later fade away. But Robinson's work reveals that this was not the case; rather, slavery and its inherent racial order have had an essentially uninterrupted, if not unchanging, presence from Medieval Europe throughout the development of capitalism.

In his work, Robinson tries to demonstrate that the forms of slavery developed in Medieval Europe fell on so-called "barbarian" immigrant populations who were sold on the slave markets from the thirteenth to the early fifteenth century. These populations would be rapidly assimilated as an enslaved workforce in agriculture and domestic service. Robinson is careful to point out that these people, enslaved and sold by Mediterranean traders, were not white, but rather ethnically diverse: Tartars, Greeks, Armenians, Russians, Bulgarians, Turks, Circassians, Slavs, Cretans, Arabs, Africans, and Chinese people. This observation allows him to note that the processes of enslavement have tended to fall on non-white people—which is to say, those who lack what we might call a kind of "social whiteness"[5]—thus indicating a link between slavery and a racial order. Now, what Robinson observes about slavery in feudal Europe remained in place—although not without changes—with the development of capitalism on the American continent. During the colonial period, between the sixteenth and nineteenth centuries, native Indigenous and African groups enslaved by Europeans were exploited in mines, textile factories, and on plantations, industries that were the backbone of the colonial economy, as well as being sold as domestic slaves in Europe as well as America (Taladoire 2017 and Van Deusen 2015).

These enslaved populations in America, like those enslaved in medieval Europe, were, in reality, multiethnic. The native American and African populations were made up of culturally very diverse groups that were homogenized within the colonial categories of "indio" (Indian) and "negro" (Black). But among the enslaved populations there were also groups of southeast Asians originating in China, Japan, Malaysia, and the Philippines whose ethnic and identity diversity were, similarly, reduced to the category of "chinos" (Chinese). This means, as Robinson rightly notes, that the enslaved populations working in the industries that facilitated the development of the medieval European economy and later the global capitalist economy were overwhelmingly multiethnic and subjected to processes of racialization.

Racialization is the process of marking differences among groups of humans in relation to hierarchical discourses that seek to naturalize biological, cultural, and/or moral differences, established in colonial encounters and surviving in the legacy of modern nations (Appelbaum, Macpherson, and

Rosemblatt 2003). It means that people receive favorable or discriminatory treatment based on the racial category society attributes to them, a category constructed within a social framework based on ethnic, sex, gender, and class markers. As a result, Latin America and the Caribbean's impoverished, dispossessed, and racialized populations have historically been discriminated against, both for their position in the order of production and for their condition as colonized subjects and their identities and cultural traditions that do not meet those of the western-origin, modern, dominant culture.

In Cedric Robinson's work there are no clear definitions of the concepts "race" and "racialization." But he indicates that the discourse on race became, in large part, a way of rationalizing the domination, exploitation, and extermination of "non-Europeans," describing a process of racialization of non-white populations and, with it, the invention of blanquitud. This connects with US Afro-Caribbean philosopher Charles W. Mill's proposal that the processes of racialization imply the continuing validity of a kind of "racial contract" (Mills 1999). He defines this racial contract as a tacit agreement—occasionally made explicit—between dominant white European groups to proclaim, promote, and maintain the ideal of white supremacy in the face of the rest of the world. Underlying this racial contract is a colonial relationship.

As Robinson sees it, the enslavement of non-white populations, which involves a form of colonial domination, is a phenomenon with a very long history, reaching back to the thirteenth century. That said, it is not an unchanging phenomenon, because each era and place has its own particularities, changes, and continuities. Although the idea of "permanent slavery" might seem exaggerated, studies of contemporary slavery show the permanence of the phenomenon and its similarities with forms that preceded it.

Contemporary forms of slavery are linked to the colonial plantation and the exploitation of non-white populations. As the Afro-Caribbean historian Eric Williams claims, the needs of the plantation were the origin of the demand for slave labor on the American continent (Williams 2011). Cuban historian Manuel Moreno Fraginals (Moreno Fraginals. 2001) defined the plantation as an institution with exclusively productive ends, characterized by an antisocial, prison-like organization founded on the isolation of its members. Plantations tended to be located in uninhabited areas where homogenous work groups operated under the absolute command of individuals. This same structure was implemented in mines across the whole of the American continent, making them another form of plantation.

The plantation has gone hand in hand with forms of enslavement throughout history, right up to the present day. In a 1999 study of the role of slave labor in the neoliberal economy, the US sociologist Kevin Bales recorded 27 million enslaved people around the world. The overwhelming majority were exploited in agricultural latifundia in Asia, where the local population is not white European (Bales 2000). Data from 2018 recorded 40 million enslaved workers, a number that has continued to increase (WalkFree Foundation 2018).

**Permanent Slavery in the History of Mexico?**

The history of Latin America and the Caribbean has been marked by slavery. This includes the enslavement of Indigenous communities (Taladoire 2017), African communities brought over by force,[6] so-called "contracted white servants" (Williams 2011) (impoverished European migrants often brought against their will), and southeast Asian peoples enslaved under the false status of "settlers" and described using the pejorative term "coolies" (Young 2014, and Williams 2009). These victims of forced labor and human trafficking, which comprised various forms of enslavement, came to coexist simultaneously during the colonial period and throughout the nineteenth century, contributing to the development of a clearly racial capitalism.

The phenomenon of African enslavement has been widely studied, both in Mexico and in the rest of Latin America, compared to Indigenous enslavement, which has not received the same attention. It is often claimed that the latter disappeared during the colonial period and reappeared in sporadic form in independent Mexico, but in reality Indigenous slavery persisted all the way into the twentieth century in almost uninterrupted form, as Andrés Reséndez's recent study has shown (Reséndez 2019). His work echoes Robinson's ideas about permanent, long-lasting slavery being necessary to sustain the evolution of capitalism.

Although formally abolished by Charles V's New Laws of 1542,[7] Indigenous slavery survived in the New World in illegal and clandestine form, encouraged and tolerated by the colonial authorities because it was an instrument of the conquest that provided the Spanish encomenderos and hacienda owners with a workforce. The New Laws put limits on Indigenous slavery but did not eliminate it completely. While they offered Indigenous people protection and laid the foundations for a new legal culture allowing them to begin legal proceedings to denounce their status as slaves and be freed under the protection of the law, these legal proceedings (Van Deusen 2015) were much easier to carry out in the metropolis, in Spain, thousands of miles away from conquest and colonization. Meanwhile, in the kingdoms of the Indies, such as New Spain, the reality was very different, because Indigenous slavery was such a profitable business that the authorities looked the other way.

Indigenous slavery had to be banned once again through various edicts and decrees prohibiting the enslavement of Mapuche peoples in Chile and Peru (1662 and 1667) and freeing enslaved Indigenous peoples in Santo Domingo and Paraguay (1672), as well as in New Spain (1673). This abolitionist legislation culminated in a continent-wide royal decree in 1679, prohibiting the enslavement of native peoples, including in the Philippines (with the exception of Muslim slaves in Mindanao and "anthropophagic Indians").

As a result, the trade was diverted out of the hands of colonial authorities and into those of private intermediaries associated with certain Indigenous groups in the north, such as Comanches, Utes, and Apaches, who provided them with enslaved Indians of different ethnicities (Reséndez 2019). This involved subsuming the old practice of "capturing people"—which was common in pre-Columbian America and responded to ritual and warlike logic (Ibarra Rojas 2012)—to new market interests now controlled by capital and its representatives: settlers, traders, hacienda owners, and crown authorities, who supplied forced labor to mines, haciendas, textile factories, and for domestic service.

In the nineteenth century, after the wars of independence and especially after the Mexican–American War (1846–1848), Indigenous enslavement spread and became more established in the territories lost after the conflict, flourishing in California and New Mexico, where it experienced a "renaissance" (Reséndez 2019). An important market for enslaved Indigenous people was established there, at a time when African slavery was still legal in the United States. As Reséndez observes, this booming slave market soon also traded in Mexican peons, who were taken to haciendas to carry out forced labor. It would not be until 1924 that Indigenous slavery was abolished in the United States, when Native Americans were granted citizenship; however, in practice forced labor continued among these populations.

For Reséndez, peonage is very close to a form of slavery, as a regime in which the worker and their family, who were usually from dispossessed and displaced Indigenous populations, became the property of hacienda owners[8] despite the legal fiction of a work contract that made it look like free labor.

Yet it could easily be said, returning to Cedric Robinson's proposals, that this constituted yet another expression of racial capitalism in Mexico.

Here, the continuity between colonial Indigenous slavery and the work carried out by peons in haciendas during the Porfiriato is undeniable. The Yaquis, enslaved and sold by Porfirio Díaz's government, followed the age-old routes that other enslaved Indigenous people had walked before them, centuries before. These forms of slavery, with their various expressions, have been overwhelmingly imposed on colonized and racialized populations. For Reséndez, colonial-origin institutions such as the encomienda[9] and peonage constitute, in real terms, forms of Indigenous slave labor, although the law did not formally consider them as such (Reséndez 2019).

Today, well into the twenty-first century, the enslavement of racialized populations continues, especially of migrant and Indigenous peoples. Their labor is exploited through trafficking, in the sex trade, and in domestic work (a longstanding institution of colonial, racial, and patriarchal servitude, as Aura Cumes claims) (Cumes Simón 2014), but also in the agricultural work of day laborers who are exploited on modern plantations, institutions that require slave labor or forms of servitude that come very close to it, in order to meet the needs of large-scale industrial production (Williams 2009).

NGOs and journalists have denounced the existence of workers in "slavery-like conditions" in various parts of Latin America. In Brazil, workers in sugarcane fields are often victims of debt bondage. Between 1995 and 2006, eighteen thousand rural workers were rescued from conditions of semi-slavery, where three in every four were Black or mixed race (Castro et al. 2019). The same has been reported in Mexico, where agricultural workers in sugarcane fields are indebted to the stores located on the plantations after paying inflated prices for food and daily necessities which their salaries of seven dollars a day cannot cover (U.S. Department of State 2020).

For five hundred years, capitalism has been based on the forced labor of the dispossessed and colonized masses on which a racial order has been imposed, according to Aníbal Quijano (2013), who observed in this unfolding of the global modern and colonial system the expansion of a racial classification of the global population. This racial order justified the creation of a new structure of labor control, which was able to articulate slavery and other historical forms of work under the dominance of modern economic relations subject to a global market. For Quijano, the racial order that divides the population into "white" dominators and oppressed people "of color" through an intersection of race, class, and colonial subjection is a pattern inherent to capitalism. Put differently: capitalism is always racial. And that being so, capitalism in its neoliberal moment also expresses this racial order and a close relationship to slavery, as we will see in the following section.

## Neoliberal Slavery: Forced and Racialized Labor in Mexico

Neoliberalism has been conceptualized as capitalism's contemporary expression, characterized by economic policies based on an unfettered free market, the dismantling of social security, the privatization of public enterprise, and the "reining in" of public spending, thereby obliging states to take on debt and encouraging corruption (Harvey 2007). Under the euphemistic term "structural adjustments," neoliberalism was implemented first in the peripheries as the colonial face of a new system that spread unevenly around the world, undermining sovereignty, entrenching inequality, acts of dispossession, and economic dependency.

Initially, it erupted as a way of counteracting the 1973 economic crisis caused by overproduction during the postwar economic boom (1945–1975), the result of a repeating capitalist cycle: accumulation-boom-overproduction-bust. To alleviate this crisis, during neoliberalism the costs of social reproduction were lowered or subjected to the rules of private capital. This resulted in a fall in real wages, the flexibilization of labor, and the privatization of much of social security, resulting in a sharp swing towards precarity for the working class.

In addition to this, the State's retreat from the social functions it previously oversaw left a vacuum that was filled by NGOs and private capital, both legal and illegal. It is easy to see how this situation allowed for the flourishing of black-market businesses, especially human and drug trafficking; this is especially evident in the case of Mexico, where the 1994 North American Free Trade Agreement sentenced the Mexican countryside to death, as is evident, twenty-eight years later, in the thousands of vulnerable, rural, working communities who are at the mercy of narco-capital.

It was precisely during the neoliberal period that the extractivist export model, based on the extraction of natural resources that are privately appropriated and traded on the global market, gathered new energy, an energy it has maintained, extended, and deepened during the twenty-first century (Seoane 2012). In Latin America, extractive capital has been strengthened by agrobusiness—through sugarcane, soy, palm oil, avocado, and banana plantations, to name but a few examples—and by gold, silver, copper, lithium, iron, niobium, and coltan mining (Castro et al. 2020)—industries that often rely on labor that approaches "slavery-like conditions."

As well as the poverty, overcrowding, violence, and exploitation that neoliberalism has imposed on the working classes, there is also the slave labor regime. Referred to as "forced labor" by the international community, it has been conceptualized by the International Labor Organization (ILO) as work carried out involuntarily and under the threat of a penalty of some kind, thus constituting a violation of human rights and a restriction of personal freedom (ILO 2021). This definition coincides with Kevin Bales's definition of neoliberal slavery as involving people held against their will through violence or the threat of economic exploitation, who are de facto turned into private property (Bales 2000).

The ILO gives the figure of 1.3 million people working in forced labor conditions in Latin America, despite the fact it is an illegal practice and a serious crime under penal codes across the region (ILO 2021). Mexico is in first place for forced labor in Latin America, with 341,000 people experiencing modern slavery (WalkFree Foundation 2018). Across Latin America, most enslaved people work in the mining and agricultural industries or in maquiladoras, as well as in domestic service and sex work.

In Mexico, a large part of this forced labor is found in agriculture, concentrated in the states of Sinaloa, Sonora, Chihuahua, and Baja California Norte, where laborers work up to fifteen hours a day, according to a 2018 study by the U.S. Department of Labor (Moreno Hoyos 2020). The most frequent victims are campesinos who migrate either temporarily or permanently from southern states to centers of production, as well as Central American migrants heading towards the United States who are forced to work in export crops (Moreno Hoyos 2020). These displaced populations retrace the flows and routes of slave markets that have existed in Mexico ever since the sixteenth century, albeit now with their own contemporary particularities.

As was the case in the colonial period, Indigenous communities today continue to be particularly susceptible to coercive recruitment and debt bondage. According to a report carried out by the National Human Rights Commission, 45% of underage victims of human trafficking belong to Indigenous communities (García 2021). Andrés Reséndez notes that a significant number of Indigenous people enslaved during the colonial period were women and girls (Reséndez 2019) and that this remains the case. In sex trafficking in

Mexico—another expression of forced labor—85% of victims are female and most are both migrants (*Vértigo política* 2021) and Indigenous (Olivares Alonso 2021).

These women and girls from Indigenous communities are sold into marriage, or bought as domestic, maquiladora, or sex workers. While some transactions are made with the consent of their families, most are tricked into it (García 2021) and all constitute forms of enslavement, as was the case with "servants" (poor white people taken from Europe to the New World, with work contracts that were never fulfilled, often under false promises, and sometimes as the result of kidnapping) (Williams 2011) and "coolie" workers.

These forms of forced domestic and sexual labor share a longstanding patriarchal logic, maintaining control not only over the women's work but also over their lives. This makes them not exclusively economic structures but rather structures that also involve the body and form a matrix of colonial, racial, and gender oppression, as Aura Cumes notes with reference to domestic labor (Cumes 2014).

Forced child labor in agriculture is also a reality in Mexico (*Sin embargo* 2020). In this sector, agricultural workers—whether adults, pregnant women, or minors—are exposed to grueling, subhuman working conditions. This is how various investigations into the case of day laborers at Los Pinos: Productora Industrial del Noroeste, in San Quintín, Baja California, have described the conditions there. Many of the workers are Indigenous migrants from the states of Guerrero and Oaxaca. Their status as migrants and their condition as racialized subjects makes them more vulnerable, under a racist and exploitative regime, to this kind of practice, because State institutions and Mexican society invisibilize groups who look mestizo or Indigenous.

This invisibilization becomes fertile ground for violence and dehumanization, which are widely tolerated when the victims are dispossessed and racialized, to the extent that in Mexico "the rule seems to be that the murder of a white, privileged person will provoke much more outrage and will be much more visible than the death of a darker skinned, more marginalized person," as Federico Navarrete Linares (2016) argues, illustrating the presence of a necropolitics of inequality. Part of this violence is expressed in the near slavery-like working conditions experienced by agricultural workers in San Quintín.

As is documented in several reports, the workers themselves at San Quintín have denounced poverty wages—and sometimes nonexistent wages—inhumane living conditions, permanent surveillance, perpetual debt to the company store, a lack of work contracts, and the daily sexual harassment of female workers (Sirenio 2015). All this embodies the new relationship between modern slavery and racialized subjects already observed by Cedric Robinson. These conditions exist because of the extractive industries that have caused territories to be despoiled and widespread misery and poverty, conditions that are exacerbated by corruption and the rise of the black-market economy. In other words, it is the correlate of a context, imposed by neoliberalism, that has massively increased the number of potential enslaved people, who are now superabundant, as Kevin Bales (2000) has observed. This is one of the major differences from previous forms of enslavement: that the number of enslaved people has increased enormously.

The Cameroonian philosopher Achille Mbembe agrees on this count, pointing out that the systemic risks to which African slaves were exposed during early capitalism constitute, in the neoliberal era, a fate threatening all subaltern peoples. This is due to a kind of universalization of the "Black condition," which today is accompanied by new imperial practices that adopt elements of old slaver logic such as capture and depredation.

The correlate of this phenomenon is the globalization of colonial logics of occupation, wars of annihilation, zoning, the militarization of borders, the parceling out of territories and the creation of autonomous spaces that operate under the informal law of a host of fragmented authorities and armed private powers. These conditions hit a new class of men and women indebted under the neoliberal regime, making them the "new Black people."

In other words, as Mbembe sees it (Mbembe 2016), we are experiencing the transnationalization of the Black condition, which, although it was originally incubated in the Atlantic where it had its epicenter, has today become a new planetary condition, the existential norm: it is a becoming-Black of the world, in which racialization and oppression are recalibrated. And it is here that we find the greatest difference between the conditions imposed by capitalism in its neoliberal phase and previous historical moments: the generalized broadening and entrenching of brutal conditions, in which we are all at risk of becoming disposable, and which make the dispossessed, colonized, racialized masses of the colonial margins even more vulnerable.

## Final Comments

Capitalism's tendency to maintain the presence of slave labor, especially in industrial scale agricultural production, has been accompanied by a racial order in which the differentiation and exaggeration of ethnic, cultural, and social differences turns them into differences of race, which go hand in hand with discourses that biologize and hierarchize cultural diversity. And therein lies the key to racism and slavery as phenomena inherent to capitalism, which underpin its inexorably racial nature, as Cedric Robinson observed.

Although this chapter has briefly tackled the problem of the racialization and enslavement of Indigenous peoples in Mexico in relation to the development of capitalism, a discussion of the racialization of the non-Indigenous working class remains pending. This is because these processes of racialization have been present not only in Latin America, the Caribbean, and the colonized territories of the non-European world; they have also been applied to colonized communities inhabiting Europe and the Global North itself, where the colonial dynamics of center-periphery are reproduced within their own territories.

Robinson's work and his proposal regarding racial capitalism have allowed us to sketch out a dialogue with Mexican history in the Latin American context, a dialogue which could be deepened through a transnational reading of the processes of racialization and blanquitud in the shared history of the Americas.

## Notes

1  In Latin America the word 'mestizo' has different geographies, temporalities, and meanings. This is even reflected in vocabulary: *cholo, criollo, mulato, pardo, caboclo, caipira* and *gaucho*, to name just a handful of terms. In their meanings, class differences and particular processes of racialization intersect, showing the diversity of meaning 'mestizo' has. Something similar occurs with whiteness, which possesses its own geography, temporalities, and lexicon on the subcontinent, where white often refers to a position of privilege.

2  This is category coined by the Mexican thinker Armando Bartra (2008) that mixes the words peasent (campesino) and indian (indio).

3  Porfirio Díaz was President of Mexico from 1876 to 1911. His period in government, known as the "Porfiriato," was characterized by the development of public works and economic modernization, through the delivery of natural resources and strategic infrastructure to foreign capitals. It was also notable for the "Frenchification"

of culture and for the repression of workers' and indigenous movements. It was in reaction to Porfirio Díaz's policies that the Mexican Revolution broke out in 1910.

4   With regard to this concept Robinson is a little problematic. Research by medievalist historians have discarded the blanket application of the feudal model to Europe, instead understanding it as a very particular mode of production developed only in very concrete and delimited areas of continental Europe (Guerrau 2002). Meanwhile, other historians, such as Le Goff (2008), have criticized the concept of the "Middle Ages," instead employing the term "Christian era." See *Una larga Edad Media*. Barcelona: Paidós. However, this more nuanced conceptualization of medieval society does not modify the processes of enslavement and racialization that Robinson finds present in various parts of Europe between the eighteenth and twenty-first centuries.

5   Social whiteness can be understood as the ability to access to a set of public and private privileges that in a material and permanent way guarantee one's basic needs, ensure survival, and, in some cases, are protected by the law and restricted to certain social groups (Harris 1993).

6   Ten million enslaved Africans (mostly young men) disembarked in America between 1525 and 1866, overwhelmingly destined to work in plantations and mines (Morgan 2017).

7   Encomienda was a form of dividing up Indigenous people among the Spanish. Indigenous people had to carry out a service or personal work and, in exchange, the Spanish encomendero was obliged to give them religious instruction and to defend the land that the Indigenous people worked. In fact, this institution constituted a form of control and exploitation of Indigenous peoples, who were forced to work for their entire lives and then pass on their role to their descendants. The New Laws of 1542 prohibited new encomiendas and the practice of forcing Indigenous people to carry loads or to dive for pearls. It recognized them as free vassals who could not be enslaved under any circumstances except in "special cases."

8   Peonage was a labor regime resembling a kind of servitude, where peons or day laborers were paid in kind and forced to run up debts at company-owned stores as well as in other grocery stores (Stavenhagen 1998).

9   Although harshly attacked by Fray Bartolomé de las Casas and other defenders of Indigenous groups, the encomienda system remained active until the New Laws were passed in 1542. Even then, however, much of the legislation that comprised the New Laws were not, in fact, enforced (Morales Padrón 1979).

## References

Appelbaum, Nancy, Macpherson, Anne and Rosemblatt, Karin Alejandra (eds). 2003. *Race and Nation in Modern Latin America*. Chapel Hill: University of North Carolina Press.

Bales, Kevin. 2000. *La nueva esclavitud en la economía global*. Madrid: Siglo XXI Editores.

Bartra, Armando. 2008. "Campesindios: Aproximaciones a los campesinos de un continente colonizado.," *Boletín de Antropología Americana* 44 (January–December): 5–24.

Basave Benítez, Agustín. 1992. *México mestizo: Análisis del nacionalismo mexicano en torno a la mestizofilia de Andrés Molina Enríquez*. Mexico City: Fondo de Cultura Económica.

Bonfil Batalla, Guillermo. 2019 [1987]. *México profundo. Una civilización negada*. Mexico: Fondo de Cultura Económica.

Castro, Nazaret, Aurora Moreno, and Laura Villadiego. 2019. *Los monocultivos que conquistaron al mundo. Impactos socioambientales de la caña de azúcar, la soja y la palma aceitera*. Madrid: Foca.

Cumes Simón, Aura Estela. 2014. *La "india" como "sirvienta": Servidumbre doméstica, colonialismo y patriarcado en Guatemala*. Doctoral dissertation in social anthropology, CIESAS, Mexico City.

Echeverría, Bolívar. 2000. *La modernidad de lo barroco*. México City: Era.

Echeverría, Bolívar. 2010. *Modernidad y blanquitud*. Mexico City: Era.

García, Ana Karen. "Trabajo forzado, matrimonio, embarazo infantil y explotación sexual, el destino de muchas mujeres indígenas víctimas de trata." *El Economista*, June 13, 2021, https://www.eleconomista.com.mx/politica/Trabajo-forzado-matrimonio-embarazo-infantil-y-explotacion-sexual-el-destino-de-muchas-mujeres-indigenas-victimas-de-trata-20210613-0005.html.

Gould, Jeffrey L., *To Die in this Way: Nicaraguan Indians and the Myth of the Mestizaje, 1880–1960* (Durham: Duke University Press, 1998).

Gruzinski, Serge. *El pensamiento mestizo* (Barcelona: Paidós, 2000).

Guerrau, Alain, *El Futuro de un Pasado: La Edad Media en el Siglo XXI* (Barcelona: Crítica, 2002).

Harris, Cheryl I., "Whiteness as Property," *Harvard Law Review*, 106, 8 (June 1993): 1707–1791.

Harvey, David. *Breve historia del neoliberalismo* (Madrid: Akal, 2007).

Ibarra Rojas, Eugenia. *Pueblos que capturan: Esclavitud indígena al sur de América Central del siglo XVI al XIX* (San Juan: Editorial UCR, 2012).

ILO. "Qué es el trabajo forzoso, las formas modernas de esclavitud y la trata de seres humanos," https://www.ilo.org/global/topics/forced-labour/definition/lang--es/index.htm.

Kourí, Emilio. "Sobre la propiedad comunal de los pueblos, de la reforma a la revolución," *Historia mexicana*, 66, 4 (April/June 2017): 1923–60.

"La producción de carne, azúcar, café, tabaco...en México se ligan a trabajo forzoso infantil, dice EU," *Sin embargo*, November 20, 2020, https://www.sinembargo.mx/20-11-2020/3897214.

Le Goff, Jacques. *Una larga Edad Media* (Barcelona: Paidós, 2008).

Marx, Karl. (2014) *El capital. Crítica de la economía política*, Vol. 1. Mexico: Fondo de Cultura Económica.

Mbembe, Achille. *Crítica de la razón negra: Ensayo sobre el racismo contemporáneo* (Buenos Aires, Futuro Anterior, 2016).

Mills, Charles W., *The Racial Contract* (Ithaca & London: Cornell University Press, 1999).

Morales Padrón, Francisco. *Teoría y leyes de la conquista* (Madrid: Cultura hispánica, 1979).

Moreno Fraginals, Manuel. *El ingenio: Complejo Económico Social Cubano del Azúcar* (Barcelona: Crítica, 2001).

Moreno Hoyos, Hernán Arturo. "La escalofriante realidad del trabajo forzoso en el campo mexicano," *Expreso*, October 24, 2020, https://www.expreso.com.mx/seccion/expresion/e-comunidad/247063-la-escalofriante-realidad-del-trabajo-forzoso-en-el-campo-mexicano.html.

Morgan, Kenneth. 2017. *Cuatro siglos de esclavitud trasatlántica*. Barcelona: Crítica.

Navarrete Linares, Federico. 2004. *Las relaciones interétnicas en México*. Mexico: UNAM.

Navarrete Linares, Federico. *México racista. Una denuncia* (Mexico City: Grijalbo: 2016).

Olivares Alonso, Emir. "Ocupa México tercer lugar a escala global en trata de personas," *La Jornada*, May 25, 2021, https://www.jornada.com.mx/notas/2021/05/24/politica/ocupa-mexico-tercer-lugar-a-escala-global-en-trata-de-personas-ong/.

Padilla Ramos, Raquel. *Los partes fragmentados: narrativas de la guerra y la deportación Yaquis* (Mexico City: Secretaría de Cultura/INAH 2018).

París Pombo, María Dolores. "Estudios sobre el racismo en América Latina," *Política y Cultura* 17, Spring (2002): 289–310.

Phillips, William D., *La esclavitud desde la época romana hasta los inicios del comercio trasatlántico* (Madrid: Siglo XXI España, 1989).

Prien, Hans-Jürgen, and Ana Rosa Martínez de Codes (coords). 1999. *El proceso desvinculador y desamortizador de bienes eclesiásticos y comunales en la América española, siglos XVIII y XIX*. Amsterdam: Asociación de Historiadores Latinoamericanistas Europeos.

Quijano, Aníbal. "El trabajo," *Argumentos*, 26, 72, (May-August 2013): 145–63.

Rahier, Jean Muteba. *Blackness in the Andes: Ethnographic Vignettes of Cultural Politics in the Time of Multiculturalism* (Palgrave Macmillan, 2014).

Reséndez, Andrés. *La otra esclavitud. Historia oculta del esclavismo indígena* (Mexico City: Grano de Sal/IIH-UNAM, 2019).

Robinson, Andy. *Oro, petróleo y aguacates: Las nuevas venas abiertas de América Latina* (Barcelona: Arpa, 2020).

Robinson, Cedric J., *Black Marxism: The Making of the Black Radical Tradition*, (Chapel Hill & London: The University of North Carolina Press, 2000 [1983]).

Robinson, Cedric J., *Marxismo negro: La formación de la tradición negra radical* (Madrid: Traficantes de sueños, 2021).

"Segob debe informar sobre acciones para combatir esclavitud y trabajo forzoso," *Vértigo política*, April 19, 2021, https://www.vertigopolitico.com/nacional/politica/notas/segob-debe-informar-sobre-acciones-para-combatir-esclavitud-y-trabajo-forzoso, accessed September 2021.

Seoane, José. "Neoliberalismo y ofensiva extractivista Actualidad de la acumulación por despojo, desafíos de Nuestra América," *Theomai* 26, July–December (2012).

Sirenio, Kau. "San Quintín: esclavos del siglo XXI," *Pie de Página*, December 7, 2015, https://piedepagina.mx/san-quintin-esclavos-del-siglo-xxi/, accessed November 2021.

Stavenhagen, Rodolfo. *Derecho indígena y derechos humanos en América Latina México* (Mexico City: COLMEX/IIDH, 1998).

Taladoire, Éric. *De América a Europa. Cuando los indígenas descubrieron el Viejo Mundo (1493–1892)* (Mexico City: Fondo de Cultura Económica, 2017).

Urías Horcasitas, Beatriz. *Historias secretas del racismo en México (1920–1950)* (Mexico City: Tusquets, 2007).

U.S. Department of State. 2020 (June). *Trafficking in Persons Report*. 20th edition. Online report. www.state.gov/wp-content/uploads/2020/06/2020-TIP-Report-Complete-062420-FINAL.pdf.

Van Deusen, Nancy. *Global Indios: The Indigenous Struggle for Justice in Sixteenth-Century Spain* (Durham and London: Duke University Press, 2015).

Viñas, David. *Indios, ejército y frontera* (Mexico City: Siglo XXI, 1982).

WalkFree Foundation. 2018. *The Global Slavery Index*. Online report. https://cdn.walkfree.org/content/uploads/2023/04/13181704/Global-Slavery-Index-2018.pdf.

Williams, Eric. *Capitalismo y esclavitud* (Madrid: Traficantes de sueños, 2011 [1938]).

Williams, Eric. *De Colón a Castro: la historia del Caribe, 1492–1969* (Mexico City: Instituto de Investigaciones Dr. José María Luis Mora, 2009).

Young, Elliott. *Alien Nation: Chinese Migration in the Americas from the Coolie Era through World War II* (Chapel Hill: University of North Carolina Press, 2014).

Zermeño, Guillermo. 2011. "Del mestizo al mestizaje: Arqueología de un concepto." In *El peso de la sangre,* coordinated by Böttcher, Nikolaus, Bernd Hausberger and Max S. Hering Torres. Mexico City: COLMEX.

# CHAPTER 3

# Ethno-racial Inequality in Mexico: A Multidimensional Perspective

Patricio Solís and Braulio Güémez Translated by Ellen Jones

Mexico is a country with high levels of social inequality. Wealth is highly concentrated in the hands of a few, and almost half the population is affected by poverty. This inequality manifests not only in the unequal distribution of resources, but also in high inequality of opportunity. Studies have found that opportunities for upward social mobility in various environments, such as education, the labor market, and income, are to a large degree determined by background: both an individual's family's socioeconomic background and other social circumstances in which they grew up (Solís 2018; Serrano Espinosa and Torche 2010).

In addition, several studies have shown racist stereotypes and prejudices to be rife in Mexico, stigmatizing Indigenous people, Afro-descendant people and people with darker skin (Barabas 1979; Castellanos Guerrero 2005, 1994; López Santillán 2011) and giving symbolic and social advantages to characteristics associated with whiteness, such as having lighter skin, "European" physical features and foreign surnames (Moreno Figueroa 2010; Krozer and Urrutia Gómez 2021; Iturriaga 2011; Nutini 1997; Navarrete Linares 2016).

These racist prejudices and stereotypes are reflected not only in the discursive environment but also in systematic practices of discrimination in key environments such as family relationships, school, the labor market and the health system (Arceo-Gomez and CamposVazquez 2014; Solís et al. 2019). Taken together, these practices contribute to the reproduction of socioeconomic inequality and the unequal distribution of dignity and social respect (Lamont 2018).

Until a few years ago, studies of inequality of opportunity and intergenerational social mobility had not paid sufficient attention to structural racism expressed as a result of the relationship between the people's ethno-racial characteristics and socioeconomic inequality. This situation has changed over the last decade, since the publication of several studies that focus on this relationship (Solís, Avitia, and Güémez 2020; Villarreal 2010; Monroy-Gómez-Franco, Vélez-Grajales, and Yalonetzky 2022; Campos-Vazquez and Medina-Cortina 2019; Telles 2014). The main objective of this chapter is to deepen that analysis through an empirical analysis of data from the Project Survey on Ethno-Racial Discrimination in Mexico (PRODER), carried out in 2019.

This survey includes information about the interviewees' occupational, economic, and educative origins and outcomes, as well as a wide range of questions about their ethno-racial characteristics. The 2019 PRODER survey also includes new questions and methods of identifying how people classify themselves and are classified in terms of their ethno-racial characteristics, including, importantly, questions about how people describe themselves and are identified according to ethno-racial categories, as well as the use of digital optical colorimeters to obtain direct, unbiased measurements of people's skin tone. Based on the availability of these new data, our work tries, on the one hand, to further the discussion of how people perceive themselves and are perceived based on their ethno-racial features, and the multidimensional character of these perceptions (Roth, 2016); and on the other hand, to examine how far different ethno-racial characteristics are linked with socioeconomic origins and outcomes.

The chapter is organized as follows: after this introduction we discuss the theoretical and methodological background to the work. Then we lay out the methodological strategy and present the main results of the research. Finally, we discuss the results and present our conclusions.

**Previous Studies**

Studies of racism tend towards one of two theoretical perspectives (Golash-Boza, 2016).[1] The first puts emphasis on the content and logic of racist *ideology*; for example, through prejudices and stereotypes or discourses, as well as the creation of racialized identities (Wieviorka 2007; Taguieff 2001; Bonilla-Silva 2006; Lamont 2018; Barabas 1979; Cornell and Hartmann 1998). The other strand examines *structural* aspects of racism (Bonilla-Silva 1997; Feagin and Elias 2013; Reskin 2008; González Casanova 2006), such as how institutions contribute to the reproduction of ethno-racial inequality in different socioeconomic and political areas.

Our work belongs to the second strand and in particular to a "macro" focus on inequality of opportunity (Breen and Jonsson 2005), which examines the relationship between "adscriptive," or background characteristics, and the educational, occupational, and economic opportunities people access. Most studies in Mexico that tackle this question focus on analyzing the influence of social class or socioeconomic background on people's socioeconomic outcomes (Solís and Dalle 2019; Solís 2018; Delajara and Graña 2017; Serrano Espinosa and Torche 2010; Solís and Boado 2016; Solís 2007; Cortés and Escobar Latapí 2005). These studies all indicate a strong association, especially at the extremes of the distribution, between socioeconomic origins and outcomes, which has led to Mexico being characterized as a highly stratified society where there is widespread inequality and low social mobility.

While studies of Mexico have consistently acknowledged the importance of class background in inequality of opportunity, the role of ethno-racial factors, beyond recognizing that speakers of Indigenous languages live in poverty, has received less attention. This neglect of the ethno-racial as an organizing element in social stratification is partly due to the fact that throughout most of the twentieth century it was assumed that Mexico's inequality problem was explicable mainly by class or socioeconomic factors. This assumption is likely due to the influence of the ideology of mestizaje, especially the idea that because most Mexicans are "mestizo," ethno-racial divisions don't exist or are not relevant in explaining the country's inequality (Moreno Figueroa 2016; Knight 1990).

Despite the emphasis on aspects of class, in recent years a growing body of research has emerged that touches on elements associated with ethno-racial characteristics in analyses of inequality of opportunity (Solís and Güémez

2021; Monroy-Gómez-Franco, Vélez-Grajales, and Yalonetzky 2022; Monroy-Gómez-Franco and Vélez-Grajales 2020; Campos-Vazquez and Medina-Cortina 2019; Reeskens and Velasco Aguilar 2020; Trejo and Altamirano 2016; Solís, Güémez, and Lorenzo Holm 2019; Villarreal 2010; Villarreal and Bailey 2020). This work has led to a revision of the way ethno-racial stratification is researched, in two regards. The first is that ethno-racial inequality is now conceived as a problem which, while intimately connected to social class, is not entirely reducible to it. The second is that this work characterizes Mexican racism as a problem that needs addressing beyond the dichotomy of belonging or not belonging to an Indigenous community.

What does transcending this Indigenous/non-Indigenous dichotomy involve? We'd like to draw attention to three things: a) the acknowledgement that membership of an Indigenous community cannot be judged only on the basis of linguistic ability; b) the incorporation of other ethno-racial categories that reflect the diversity of the Mexican population; and c) the incorporation of other ethno-racial characteristics that go beyond categorization, among which racialized physical appearance is front and foremost. We will detail each of these in what follows.

This revised approach to the study of ethno-racial relations in Mexico and its relationship with social inequality involves recognizing that Indigenous belonging involves more than just language ability (Telles and Torche, 2018). For much of the twentieth century, the only official criterion used by State information collection agencies to identify Indigenous people was whether or not they spoke an Indigenous language (Loveman 2014). This was a considerable limitation on structural analyses of ethno-racial inequality (Ramírez 2002). As a result of pressure from Indigenous activists (Bengoa, 2000; Loveman, 2014), as well as the signing of international treaties such as Convention 169 of the International Labor Organization (ILO), which criticized the use of language as the only marker of Indigenous identity, this tendency was revoked in the 2000 Census, when a question about Indigenous self-designation was incorporated into the general questionnaire, in addition to the question about language.[2]

Although these changes have contributed to our understanding of Indigenous self-designation in Mexico, they do not help us identify the ethno-racial classification of the majority of the population, which neither ascribes to that category nor speaks an Indigenous language. This brings us to the second point of change: it is necessary to recognize that there are other ethno-racial designations beyond the Indigenous/non-Indigenous dichotomy, which can hide important variations in terms of social inequality.

State-collected information sources have gradually become more flexible and begun to incorporate other ethno-racial categories as a result of political pressure both at home and from abroad. Following international agreements and political activism by Afro-Mexican collectives, as of 2015 a series of official surveys and censuses, such as the 2015 Intercensal Survey, the National Discrimination Survey (ENADIS) and the 2020 Census, all carried out by the National Institute for Statistics and Geography (INEGI), incorporate questions about self-designation as Black or Afro-Mexican. The inclusion of the Afro-Mexican and Indigenous populations in official statistics is the result of political mobilization by collectives from these communities seeking both symbolic recognition and a way to channel public resources towards alleviating social disadvantage. People who identify themselves using the ethnoracial categories of "white" or "mestizo" have not sought recognition in the same way, in large part because of the ideology of mestizaje, which maintains that every Mexican is "mestizo" or a "mixture of everything," and that as such any distinction among them would be irrelevant (Moreno Figueroa 2012). Likewise, given those identified as "white" or "mestizo" tend to be in positions of greater social and political advantage, they have less incentive to seek out statistical representation. As such, only one official INEGI survey (the Module on Intergenerational Social Mobility from the National Housing Survey) has asked people whether they identify with the categories of "white" and "mestizo" as well as "Indigenous" and "Black." Incorporating multiple ethno-racial categories has made it possible to transcend the classic dichotomy (Indigenous/non-Indigenous) that led to the country's ethno-racial inequality in the first place, and which has allowed for a deeper understanding of the link between ethno-racial categories and social inequality, as well as of the socioeconomic privilege associated with "whiteness" and mestizaje ((Telles and Flores 2013; Moreno Figueroa 2010; Painter, Noy, and Holmes 2019; Krozer 2019; Krozer and Urrutia Gómez 2021; Solís, Güémez, and Lorenzo Holm 2019).

However, seeing as, with the exception of the category of "Indigenous," ethno-racial categories are not routinely used in Mexico by either individuals or institutions (for example, in job applications or school or university registration), it is possible that the options for self-designation appear artificial or distant to the survey's respondents. For this reason, it is important to pay close attention to the responses to questions about ethno-racial self-designation, an issue that we will return to when we present the descriptive results of the 2019 PRODER survey.

The third point of change is that to understand the association between ethno-racial characteristics and social inequality we must consider not only how people describe themselves in terms of ethno-racial categories, or whether they speak an Indigenous language, but also how other people identify them based on their racialized physical features. One of the most relevant, because it is identifiable at first glance, is skin color. The way people are identified and classified according to the color of their skin often influences discriminatory practices in different social spaces (Solís et al. 2019; Krozer 2019; Arceo-Gomez and Campos-Vazquez 2014; Telles 2014). What is more, in a society like Mexico's where ethno-racial categories, especially "mestizo" (Martínez Casas et al. 2014), have high "color elasticity" (Telles and Paschel, 2014), skin color is useful for detecting "intracategorical" inequalities, which is to say, among people who describe themselves or are described as belonging to the same ethno-racial category (Ryabov 2016; Chavez-Dueñas, Adames, and Organista 2014; Reeskens and Velasco Aguilar 2020).

However, as with ethno-racial self-designation, skin color can be measured in multiple ways, each leading to different results in analysis (Dixon and Telles, 2017). For example, some studies have found that the levels of discrimination interviewees report having personally experienced are higher among dark-skinned people when the interviewee's own perception of their skin color was used, rather than the interviewer's perception of it (Roth 2016, 1317). Monk (2015) argues that is because people's perception of their own skin color is influenced by how they have been treated by others (whether negatively or positively) throughout their lives—their "embodied social status," which cannot be perceived by the interviewer (Monk 2015, 412). In analyses of ethno-racial inequality, on the other hand, there is sometimes a "whitening" effect in perceptions of skin color (Freeman et al, 2011; Saperstein and Penner 2012; Schwartzman 2007; Freeman et al. 2011), in which people self-describe and are described by others as having lighter skin than they actually have because of their socioeconomic status.[3]

This whitening effect could lead to an overestimation of the effects of skin color, in which part of the relationship, observed in the surveys, between perception of skin color (both the interviewee's and the interviewer's) and socioeconomic status is explained by a tendency to assign people lighter skin tones, rather than by inequality of opportunity associated with skin color. One way of avoiding this bias is to use skin color measurements that do not rely on the subjective perceptions of either interviewer or interviewee. In the 2019 PRODER survey we used digital colorimeters to obtain these measurements, and based our estimates of the link between skin color and socioeconomic status on them knowing they were not affected by the biases inherent in interviewer and interviewee perceptions.

Although skin color is one of the most visible and studied racialized physical characteristics, there are others, such as hair color and type and eye color, which could also be associated with cognitive patterns of ethno-racial profiling (Brubaker 2009; Brubaker, Loveman, and Stamatov 2004) and through them with discriminatory practices and inequality of opportunity (Lamont, Beljean, and Clair 2014). It's possible, therefore, that these other racialized physical characteristics might, independently of skin color, be linked with socioeconomic status. We will analyze this possibility in some detail when we present the results of the 2019 PRODER survey.

In sum, we argue that in order to analyze the link between ethno-racial characteristics and inequality of opportunity in Mexico, it is necessary to adopt a multidimensional perspective on ethno-racial characteristics (Roth 2016; Gullickson 2016), which considers how different dimensions (language, self-determination, racialized physical features, etc.) are associated with opportunity, as well as the effects derived from possible interactions between them. A multidimensional approach begins with the constructivist assumption that the ethno-racial is socially constructed and multifaceted, and that there is therefore no univocal or biological criterion for ethno-racial classification, as would be assumed by an essentialist approach that takes the existence of groups with inherent, essential, or innate characteristics as a given (see Wimmer 2008; Brubaker 2004). Conceptualizing race and ethnicity from a constructivist perspective allows us to disaggregate ethno-racial characteristics into various constitutive elements that are socially and politically relevant (Roth 2016; Sen and Wasow 2016) and which affect people's opportunities in life.

Finally, to adequately take stock of the link between ethno-racial characteristics and inequality of opportunity, it is also important to distinguish between the effects of historically accumulated disadvantage and those linked to persistent, present-day racism and the discriminatory practices associated with it (Flores and Telles 2012; Solís, Güémez, and Lorenzo Holm 2019).

Indigenous and Afro-descendent communities have historically experienced social disadvantage associated with structural racism, which makes it more likely that people belonging to these communities will be born and raised in socioeconomically disadvantaged families. These inherited disadvantages, accumulated over generations, have a negative impact on people's opportunities in life, regardless of whether racism and discrimination persist in the present. As well as "historical accumulation of disadvantage," it is important to add disadvantage accumulated over the course of a lifetime as a result of persistent racism and discrimination. In our empirical analysis we present an exercise that tries to distinguish the effects of historical accumulation from those associated with persistent, present-day racism when it comes to inequality of socioeconomic opportunity.

## The 2019 PRODER Survey

In our analysis we use the Project on Ethno-Racial Discrimination in Mexico's survey, carried out towards the end of 2019 and targeting residents of private homes in Mexico, aged between 25 and 64. In addition to the national sample, oversampling was carried out in five regions: four metropolitan areas (Mexico City, Monterrey, Mérida, and Oaxaca) and the southern part of the Yucatán peninsula,[4] where a high proportion of Maya speakers reside. Appropriate weighting was designed to compensate for the regional oversampling and to allow for valid inferences to be made on a national level. The total sample includes approximately 7187 respondents.

The 2019 PRODER survey questionnaire was based on questionnaires from conventional surveys of intergenerational social mobility, so it includes very detailed information about interviewees' economic, educational, and occupational origins and outcomes. Several sections on people's ethno-racial characteristics and issues associated with racism and ethno-racial discrimination were also incorporated. Taken together, this detailed information about social mobility and ethno-racial characteristics allows us to deepen our analysis of inequality of opportunity associated with ethno-racial features.

### Ethno-racial Characteristics

With respect to ethno-racial characteristics, the survey developed several different approaches, considering the perceptions of both interviewers and the interviewees themselves. Table 3.1 presents the original questions used in the questionnaire.[5]

**Table 3.1.** Questions about ethno-racial classification in the PRODER questionnaire.

| Aspect of ethno-racial identity | Questions |
|---|---|
| Ethno-racial self-designation (open) | *In our country there are people with various different characteristics and backgrounds. What race do you consider yourself to be? and what ethnic group do you consider yourself to belong to?* |
| Ethno-racial self-designation (multiple choice) | *Do you consider yourself to be (INDIGENOUS, BLACK, WHITE, MESTIZO)?*<br>1. Yes 2. No<br>**READ ALL THE OPTIONS, EVEN IF YOU HAVE ALREADY RECEIVED A POSITIVE RESPONSE** |
| Skin color (interviewer's perception) | *With reference to the color scale (see Card 1), what is the interviewee's skin color?* |
| Other ethno-racial characteristics (interviewer's perception) | *What color hair does the interviewee have?*<br>1. Black 2. Brown, 3. Natural blonde, 4. Dyed blonde, 5. Bald, 6. Grey 7. Other<br>*What type of hair does the interviewee have?*<br>1. Very wavy/curly, 2. Wavy/curly, 3. Unruly straight, 4. Smooth straight 5. Bald<br>*What colour are the interviewee's eyes?*<br>1. Black 2. Brown 3. Green 4. Blue |

The 2019 PRODER survey included three questions about ethno-racial self-designation. The first two questions are open: In our country there are people with various different characteristics and backgrounds. What **race** do you consider yourself to be, and what **ethnic group** do you consider yourself to belong to? These questions allow us, on the one hand, to evaluate the extent to which race and ethnic group are recognized categories, and on the other hand how people self-identify in these two areas. So as not to bias the interviewees' responses, during their training we asked interviewers not to offer any definition of the terms race and ethnic group, but rather to register what the interviewee understood by them.

Following these two questions, the interviewees were asked to identify themselves ethno-racially using predetermined categories: 3.3a. Do you consider yourself to be 1) Indigenous 2) Black 3) White 4) Mestizo? One of the reasons for asking this question is to find out whether the boundaries between the multiple-choice categories are clearly delimited or sufficiently flexible that people identify with several of them at once. For this reason, we opted to allow interviewees to choose multiple options.

As we indicated earlier, as well as ethno-racial self-designation, we are interested in how people are perceived by others as a result of their physical features. One of the most visible of these is skin color. There are multiple instruments for obtaining approximate measurements of interviewee skin tone in a survey context, including color palettes, ordinal classifications ("light brown," "pale," etc.), images of people and optical colorimeters (Dixon and Telles 2017; Roth 2016). The PRODER questionnaire uses several of these measurements; however, here we use two, one obtained from a color palette and another captured using a colorimeter applied to the interviewee's wrist and the back of their hand.

Information about the interviewee's skin color was collected at the beginning of the interview and recorded by the interviewer. The instruction was as follows: 1.6) With reference to the color scale (see Card 1), what is the interviewee's skin color? The color palette, comprising 11 tones, with an emphasis on medium tones, is presented in Figure 3.1.

The colorimeter measurements were represented in a continuous, three-dimensional space; it was convenient for our purposes to represent them using the CIELAB color space, which has been recommended for a more precise classification of skin tone for scientific purposes (Weatherall and Coombs, 1992). The CIELAB space expresses color according to three values: $L^*$ for lightness, $a^*$ for color variations from green to red and $b^*$ for variations from

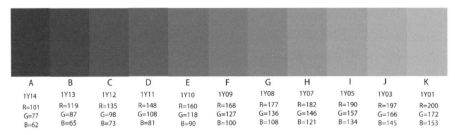

| A | B | C | D | E | F | G | H | I | J | K |
|---|---|---|---|---|---|---|---|---|---|---|
| 1Y14 | 1Y13 | 1Y12 | 1Y11 | 1Y10 | 1Y09 | 1Y08 | 1Y07 | 1Y05 | 1Y03 | 1Y01 |
| R=101 | R=119 | R=135 | R=148 | R=160 | R=168 | R=177 | R=182 | R=190 | R=197 | R=200 |
| G=77 | G=87 | G=98 | G=108 | G=118 | G=127 | G=136 | G=146 | G=157 | G=166 | G=172 |
| B=62 | B=65 | B=73 | B=81 | B=90 | B=100 | B=108 | B=121 | B=134 | B=145 | B=153 |

Figure 3.1. Proder Color Scale.

*Source*: Authors.

blue to yellow. An important advantage of the CIELAB space compared to other color space representations (such as RGB[6]) is that it isolates lightness or luminance (L*), the most relevant measurement for the purposes of our study, because this dimension defines levels of skin lightness or darkness. This allows us to focus on it while controlling for secondary variations in tone and skin color. In the case of the L* value obtained using the colorimeter, we used an average of the measurements obtained from the back of the hand and the wrist in order to reduce measuring errors (Dixon and Telles, 2017). While our analysis focuses on lightness, the other measurements taken by the colorimeter (a* and b*) are incorporated as control variables in the statistical regression analysis. To facilitate interpretation, the results associated with these variables are presented in their standardized versions.

In addition to skin color, in our analysis we also consider eye color and hair type and color, three racialized physical characteristics possibly linked with inequality of opportunity that have not previously been analyzed. These data were collected from the beginning of the PRODER interview, in the first section of the questionnaire designed to be completed by the interviewer. The questions were as follows:[7] What type of hair does the interviewee have? (Very wavy/very curly, wavy/curly, unruly straight, smooth straight, bald); What color hair does the interviewee have? (Black, brown, natural blonde, dyed blonde, bald, grey, other); and What color eyes does the interviewee have? (black, brown, green, blue).

Finally, regarding linguistic ability, we adopt a more conventional focus, offering two possible responses to questions about the interviewees and their parents' ability to speak an Indigenous language: 1) people who do not speak an Indigenous language and 2) people who speak or understand an Indigenous language.

### Socioeconomic Background and Current Status

One of our main objectives is to analyze the link between ethno-racial characteristics and inequality of socioeconomic opportunity. People's socioeconomic status can be evaluated by studying several factors. Research on intergenerational social mobility usually defines people's socioeconomic outcomes by looking at their occupation, income, or wealth (Neckerman and Torch, 2007). In this study we concentrate on economic factors. We determine people's socioeconomic outcomes using socioeconomic status (SES), an index of assets, goods, and services in the home. In the absence of direct information, this type of index is a good proxy for information about permanent income and level of household wealth (Alkire and Santos, 2011; Filmer and Pritchett, 2001). The SES index was constructed using a principal component polychoric factor analysis. We used the first three components derived from the application of this technique, which between them make up 59% of the variance. In order to obtain the final index, we weighted each of the components according to their contribution to the total variance (29%, 20% and 10% respectively).

Some of the questions we formulated are related to family socioeconomic background and geographical origins. We used the Social Background Index (SBI) to measure family socioeconomic background. This index takes into account the educational conditions and working status of the household's main earner and the socioeconomic status of the interviewee's family when they were 14 years old. In the case of educational environment, we use the main earner's years of schooling as a benchmark. Position in the occupational hierarchy was measured using the main earner's occupational status, using the International Socioeconomic Index of Occupational Status (ISEI) designed by Ganzeboom and Treiman (1996). Finally, for economic environment we built an index of assets and services based on the availability of goods and assets and characteristics of an individual's housing when they were 14 years old. We obtained an SBI measurement by using polychoric factor analysis based on the variables corresponding to each of the dimensions described above. Finally, we standardized the SBI by five-year birth cohorts, to control for the effects of increasing access to goods and services over time. In this way, the Index reflects the relative position of the family in the interviewee's birth cohort.

## Race, Ethnic Group, Ethno-racial Categories and Self-designation

We begin the description of our results with two questions: to what extent do people recognize "race" and "ethnic group" as criteria for classification and self-designation in Mexico? What terms do they use to describe themselves in these two respects? In Figure 3.2 we show the distribution of responses to the two open questions about ethno-racial self-designation. The results show that few people categorize themselves in terms of "race" and "ethnic group." Almost 35% do not recognize themselves as belonging to a "race" and just over 50% identify with an "ethnic group." In other words, many people do not know how to respond when they are asked to identify themselves using

In our country there are people with different characteristics and backgrounds*
What do you consider to be your...

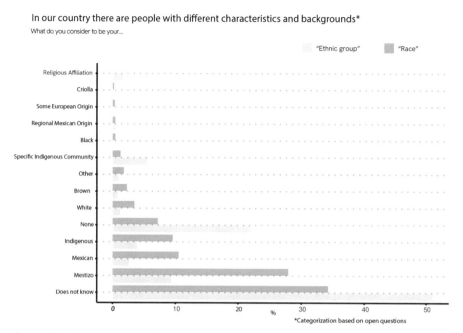

Figure 3.2.  In our country there are people with different characteristics and backgrounds.[a]

[a]Categorization based on open questions

these categories. At the same time, there is a high percentage of people who actively refuse to classify themselves in this way: 22% and 8% said they did not belong to any race or ethnic group, respectively.

For those who do self-designate, the most frequently mentioned term is "mestizo," with 28% of respondents reporting that that is their race, and 9.3% reporting that mestizo is their ethnic group. The next most frequently mentioned term is "Indigenous," both as a generic term and with reference to a specific Indigenous group, with 11% of mentions in race and 9.4% in ethnic group. Only 3.5% identified themselves as white and an even lower percentage (1.2%) as Black. It's worth noting the frequency with which nationality ("Mexican") was mentioned as an identifier of race.

These results coincide with the literature on ethnicity and race in Mexico, which indicates a weak formal use of "race" and "ethnicity" as a basis for ethno-racial classification (Wade, 2010). As Ceron-Anaya (2019) indicates, racialization occurs in informal cultural spheres, such as jokes, music, and popular sayings, but not in the form of fixed ethno-racial categories with clear boundaries. However, despite the low percentage of responses, we note that among those who did categorize themselves, the same terms are used to self-designate racially and ethnically, which suggests that there exists a degree of connection between the social construction of racial and ethnic categories. As was expected, too, the categories that *are* recognized are linked to the narrative of Mexico's mestizaje project: "Mexican," "Indigenous," and "mestizo" (Martínez Casas et al. 2014).

The panorama changes when people are asked directly whether they belong to specific categories. The responses to questions offering multiple identity categories are presented in Figure 3.3. We can observe that, by using specific categories, the percentage of people self-identifying grows considerably, with 81% of interviewees identifying with at least one category. A majority, 57.5%, consider themselves mestizo, which again reveals the importance of the ideology of mestizaje in the definition of ethno-racial identity in Mexico (Martínez Casas et al. 2014). This is followed by people who identify as Indigenous (27%), white (9.6%) and Black (3%); while 19% do not identify with any of the categories mentioned.[8] This tells us that, while people find it difficult to respond when they are asked broadly about their "race" or "ethnic group," a majority do recognize themselves in specific ethno-racial categories. Although people may not tend to use these categories in daily life, they do, however, have cognitive schemes (learned, in large part, at school or in official government discourse) (Martínez-Casas et al. 2014) that allow them to recognize themselves in them in the context of a survey.

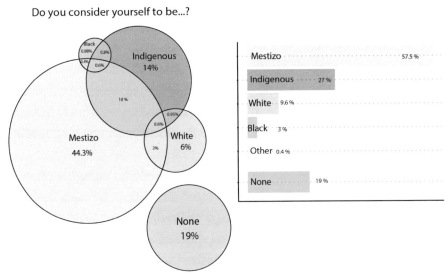

Figure 3.3. Ethno-racial self-designation in Mexico, 2019.

*Source*: Authors.

As we mentioned earlier, one of the new aspects of the PRODER survey is that it allowed people to identify with multiple categories. As is evident above, most people (nearly 65% of the total and 73% of those who identified with at least one category) identified themselves as belonging to a single category only. However, among the 15.2% who belonged to two or more categories it must be noted that most (10% of the total) declared themselves mestizo and Indigenous. This reveals the porosity between these two categories, which are at the heart of Mexico's official mestizaje narrative. On the other hand, the fact that more than a quarter of people define themselves as Indigenous and more than a third also describe themselves as "mestizo" could be indicative of a trend in claiming Indigenous cultural identity among people who in the past did not consider themselves Indigenous, thus weakening the boundaries between "mestizo" and "Indigenous" identity.[9]

Information about multiple designations is valuable for our analysis of ethno-racial identities but makes it very difficult to evaluate its relationship with inequality of socioeconomic opportunity. For this reason, in the statistical analysis that follows, we chose to use a simplified version of ethno-racial self-designation which only includes combinations that make up more than 1% of the sample. This leaves us with the following options: "mestizo," "Indigenous," "white," "mestizo and Indigenous," "mestizo and white," "Black (with any other category)" and "none." The individual categories group together cases where the person did not fall into any other category, with the exception of "Black," a category in which we included all combinations in order to obtain a sufficiently large sample.

## Skin Color, Colorimeter Measurements and Color Scales

The panorama emerging from the analysis of ethno-racial self-designation is of the predominance of three categories: mestizo, Indigenous and white, with high porosity in the category mestizo. What do we learn from an analysis of racialized physical features, and more specifically, skin color?

As we indicated earlier, a new aspect of the 2019 PRODER Survey is that it incorporates skin color measurements from optical colorimeters. Figure 3.4 shows the general distribution of values obtained in lightness (L*) and the color dimensions a* and b* for the average measures taken from the back of the hand and the wrist. As we can see, the main variations in skin tone detected by the colorimeter appear in the L* dimension, with a range between the 10th and 90th percentile, fluctuating between the values of 47 and 67,

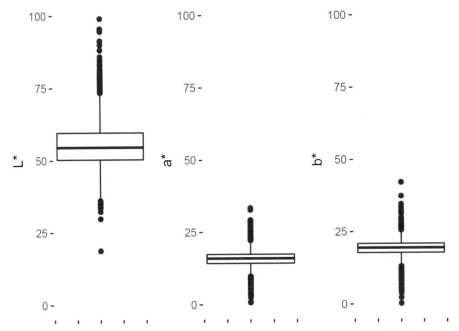

Figure 3.4. Distribution of lightness values (L) and color dimensions a* and b* for average readings from the back of the hand and the wrist.

*Notes*: a*= color variations from green to red; b*= color variations from blue to yellow.
*Source*: Authors.

with a median of 55. In contrast, variations in the a* and b* measurements are of lesser magnitude, from 12 to 19 with a median of 15 in the case of a*, and from 16 to 22 with a median of 19 in the case of b*. In other words, lightness is the most variable aspect of skin color among Mexicans. This characteristic is our main interest because of its association with pale skin, a central trait for social classification through racist cognitive schemes.

Recent research into skin color and social inequality in Mexico has used measurements taken using color scales, whether administered by the interviewer or by the interviewee. A key question is how these measurements compare to those taken using optical colorimeters. Figure 3.5 shows both the colorimeter measurements and those made by the interviewer using the color palette. In this case, unlike in Figure 3.3, we used the colorimeter measurements taken from the back of the hand only, as they are closer to the interviewer's visual perception of the interviewee.

As can clearly be observed, interviewers tend to assign lighter skin tones than those registered by the colorimeter. Thus, for example, the proportion

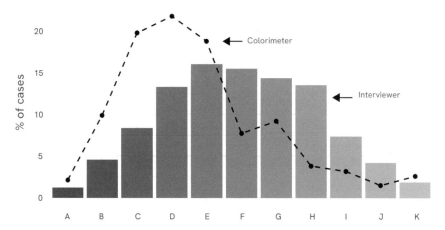

* The interviewer's perceptions appear as bars and the colorimeter readings appear as a dotted line.
The readings are assigned to the closest skin tone on the PRODER scale using the Delta method of measuring distance.

Figure 3.5.  Distribution by skin tone according to interviewer perception and colorimeter readings.[a]

[a]The interviewers' perceptions appear as bars and the colorimeter readings appear as a dotted line. The colorimeter readings are assigned to the closest skin tone on the PRODER scale. To determine the distances between colorimeter readings and PRODER colors, we used the Delta method.

of people with skin tone "H" according to the colorimeter is 4%; however, using the color palette, interviewers gave 13% of interviewees this same tone. Further analysis suggests that this skin lightening is directly related to interviewees' socioeconomic level, which could produce a biased assessment of the effect of skin color on SES.[10] In subsequent analyses we avoid this possible bias by exclusively using the measures taken by the colorimeter.

In Figure 3.6 we compare the distribution of L* with ethno-racial self-designation and linguistic ability. The different ethno-racial categories clearly correspond to a gradient of skin color where "Black," "Indigenous," and "mestizo/Indigenous" are at the darker end of the spectrum and "none," "mestizo/white" and "white" are distributed towards the right, indicating lighter skin. We note the same tendency in linguistic ability, where non speakers of Indigenous languages tend to have lighter skin than Indigenous language speakers or their children. However, while this gradient exists, the overlap between skin lightness, ethno-racial self-ascription and linguistic status is also striking. None of the categories, whether ethno-racial or linguistic, is entirely clear cut in terms of skin color. As Martínez-Casas et al. (2014) have pointed out, these categories show high elasticity of skin tone, which

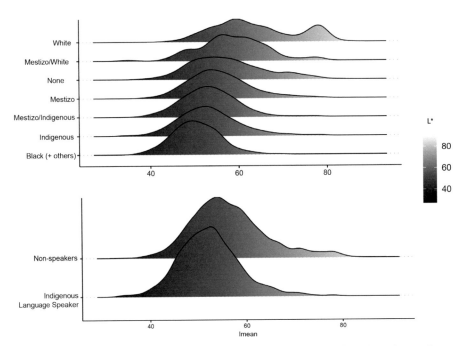

Figure 3.6. Distribution of skin tone according to ethnoracial self-designation and Indigenous language speaker status.

*Source*: Authors.

allows us to rule out a univocal association between ethno-racial and linguistic ascriptions and racialized physical traits.

## Ethno-racial Characteristics, Socioeconomic Background and Current Socioeconomic Status

Once we have considered certain important characteristics of ethno-racial self-designation and the distribution of skin color, we can move on to look at the link between ethno-racial characteristics and inequality of socioeconomic opportunity in Mexico.

As we indicated in the initial discussion, one thing that is important to bear in mind when analyzing these results is that the link is the result of two mechanisms: the historic accumulation of disadvantage and the persistence of racist and discriminatory practices today. In the case of the former, the implication is that people with ethno-racial characteristics linked to groups in a subordinate position (Indigenous and Afro-descendent people) are more likely to be born and grow up in families with low SES, because of the disadvantages their families accumulated throughout previous generations.

Regarding the 2019 PRODER survey data specifically, this should imply a lower SBI for these people.

In order to evaluate this issue, we present Figure 3.7, which shows the SBI distributions according to ethno-racial characteristics discussed so far in this chapter. When it comes to skin tone, we observe that greater skin lightness is linked to higher SES. Thus, for example, the 29.8% of those in the upper quintile for skin lightness come from families in the upper quintile for SES. In contrast, only 11.5% of those with the darkest skin tone have families with this same SES.

Regarding linguistic ability, we found starker contrasts. Practically half of Indigenous language speakers come from families in the lowest quintile for SES. This is more than three times the percentage of people who do not speak an Indigenous language in the same quintile for family SES (15.1%).

Finally, people who self-designate as belonging to multiple ethno-racial categories vary substantially when it comes to their family's SES. Among people who self-describe as "white," a greater proportion come from families with high SES: the proportion whose families come from the highest quintile is 33%. In contrast, those who self-describe as "Indigenous" or "Black" more often come from families with low SES, with 40% and 38% respectively in the lowest SBI quintile.

To what extent do these adverse origins translate into disadvantage in people's socioeconomic achievements? Is it possible to identify, in addition to the inequality of opportunity associated with family background, disadvantage attributable to the persistence of racist practices and ethno-racial discrimination in the present? To explore this question, we rely on an ordered logistical regression model (Powers and Xie 2008), in which the dependent variable is the socioeconomic quintile the interviewee is currently in (their socioeconomic outcome), and the independent variables are their ethno-racial self-designation, their ability to speak an Indigenous language, the color of their skin, their eye color, their hair type and color, and other sociodemographic characteristics that serve as statistical controls. We fit two models, one without controlling for SBI (M1), which reflects the total effects of ethno-racial characteristics, and another that includes SBI (M2), which allows us to evaluate the effects of ethno-racial characteristics once the effects of the historical accumulation of disadvantage are discounted.

We would like to highlight four aspects of these results. First, in M1—the unadjusted model, the three features examined (physical characteristics,

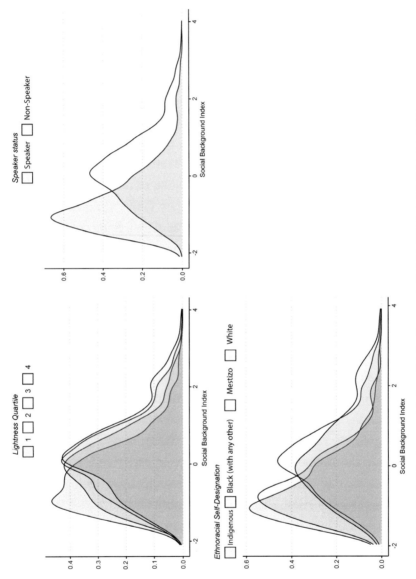

Figure 3.7. Social Background Index distribution according to ethnoracial characteristics.

*Source:* Authors.

linguistic ability and self-designation) all show a statistically significant relationship with socioeconomic outcome. Each feature therefore has an *independent* link with socioeconomic outcome, which reaffirms the importance of studying ethno-racial characterization from a multidimensional perspective.

Second, the intensity of the association varies for each category within each dimension. Thus, for example, for each standard deviation of skin lightness, the probability of moving into a higher SES quintile increases by 37%. We also observe a significant link with the hair color variable. Those with brown hair increase their chances of moving into a higher SES quintile by 22% compared to those with black hair. Among those with natural or dyed blonde hair, the probability more than doubles (2.21 and 1.77 respectively). People's eye color also appears to have a significant link with current SES: those with green eyes increase their chance of moving into a higher SES quintile by 55% compared to those with brown eyes. In contrast, the probability of people with black eyes moving up is reduced by 23% relative to people with brown eyes.

When it comes to linguistic ability, we see that people who do not speak an Indigenous language have an 85% higher chance of achieving a higher SES than their Indigenous language speaking counterparts. Finally, we found that self-designation as "mestizo" is associated with a 68% greater chance of achieving a higher SES than those who self-describe as "Indigenous." It is worth noting that this gap is greater in the case of those who self-describe as "mestizos and white" (odds ratio (OR) = 2.35), which highlights the importance of considering multiple self-designations in order to adequately understand ethno-racial inequality.

The third element to highlight is that, as shown in Table 3.2, the best fit of M2 (the adjusted model) and the significant coefficient for the SBI variable indicate that, as confirmed by other studies (Flores and Telles, 2012; Solís and Güémez, 2021), family SES is a variable strongly associated with socioeconomic outcome. For each unit increase in the standard deviation of the SBI, the probability of moving up in SES increases by 182%. On the other hand, it is important to mention that when SBI was included (in M2) the coefficients of the rest of the ethno-racial characteristics decreased, and in the case of self-designation ceased to be significant. This reaffirms that a substantial part of the link between ethno-racial characteristics and SES (M1) is explained by the unequal accumulation of disadvantage affecting family socioeconomic background.

**Table 3.2.** Results of ordered logistic models.

| | M1 | M2 |
|---|---|---|
| Skin lightness (Std.) | 1.37*** | 1.27*** |
| **Linguistic ability** | | |
| Speaker of an Indigenous language | (**Ref.**) | (**Ref.**) |
| Non-speaker of an Indigenous language | 1.85*** | 1.45** |
| **Ethno-racial self-designation** | | |
| Indigenous | (**Ref.**) | (**Ref.**) |
| Mestizo | 1.68*** | 1.17 |
| White | 1.48* | 1.08 |
| Mestizo and Indigenous | 1.54** | 1.04 |
| Mestizo and white | 2.35*** | 1.35 |
| Black (with any other category) | 0.95 | 0.75 |
| None | 1.15 | 0.84 |
| **Hair color** | | |
| Black | (**Ref.**) | (**Ref.**) |
| Brown | 1.22** | 1.02 |
| Natural blonde | 2.21** | 1.77* |
| Dyed blonde | 2.10*** | 1.69*** |
| Bald | 0.54 | 0.47 |
| Grey | 1.3 | 1.2 |
| Other | 1.65* | 1.42 |
| **Hair type** | | |
| Smooth straight | (**Ref.**) | (**Ref.**) |
| Very wavy | 1.13 | 1.2 |
| Wavy | 1.07 | 1.07 |
| Unruly straight | 0.83* | 0.85* |
| Bald | 2.60* | 3.63** |
| **Eye color** | | |
| Brown | (**Ref.**) | (**Ref.**) |
| Black | 0.77*** | 0.84* |
| Green | 1.55* | 1.11 |
| Blue | 1.43 | 1.31 |
| **Social Origin Index (Std.)** | | 2.82*** |
| **Pseudo R2** | 0.11 | 0.17 |
| **N** | 6991 | 6991 |

*Notes*: M1=model 1; M2=model 2. M1 is not adjusted for social background index (SBI). M2 is adjusted for SBI. The models include statistical controls by sex, age, marital status, region, and rural/urban area. *** p<.001; ** p<p.01; * p<.05

However, even after controlling for SBI, a statistical relationship remains between socioeconomic outcomes and Indigenous language speaker status, skin color, and hair and eye characteristics. Non-Indigenous language speakers have a 45% greater probability of bettering their SES compared to speakers of an Indigenous language. In turn, the probability of reaching higher SES increases by 27% for each unit increase in the standard deviation of skin tone lightness. For hair color, the probability of reaching a higher SES quintile for those with natural or dyed hair is 77% and 69% respectively, in contrast to those with black hair. Likewise, those who were identified as having "unruly straight" hair have a 15% lesser chance of reaching a higher SES quintile than those with "smooth straight" hair. Finally, having black eyes makes a person 16% less likely to reach a higher SES quintile than a person with brown eyes.

Taken together, these results suggest that while self-designation loses power as a factor associated with socioeconomic outcomes once the effects of the historical accumulation of disadvantage are neutralized, other characteristics that are more easily identifiable by third parties, such as Indigenous language ability and physical traits—skin color, hair type and color, and eye color—maintain their association with inequality of socioeconomic opportunity, probably—among other reasons—because these traits operate as triggers for discriminatory practices.

## Discussion and Conclusions

In this chapter we have analyzed the association between ethno-racial characteristics and inequality of economic opportunity in Mexico. We adopted a macro-social approach, which considers ethno-racial characteristics as an important axis of social stratification and the intergenerational reproduction of social inequalities.

In this final section we highlight four aspects of our analysis: the importance of taking a multidimensional approach to ethno-racial characteristics; the confluence of the historical accumulation of disadvantage and the persistence of racist and discriminatory practices in explaining the persistence of ethno-racial inequalities; confirmation of the substantive effects of skin color by using unbiased measurements taken with digital devices; and the importance of including not only skin color but also other racialized physical traits that act as "social markers" generating social inequality.

Our theoretical-methodological orientation is based on a constructivist approach that assumes ethnicity and race are social constructions whose meanings and consequences vary historically and have multiple dimensions. This approach is appropriate for analyzing a context, such as Mexico, where the use of ethno-racial categories is rare, as it conceptualizes ethno-racial classification from several points of view rather than just the perspective imposed by the observer. The result is a non-essentialist interpretation of ethno-racial categories that does away with the assumption that they are *necessarily* associated with clearly delimited groups.

Despite the weak formal and institutionalized use of ethno-racial categories in Mexico, we find that ethno-racial characteristics are strongly associated with socioeconomic origins and outcomes. We argue that this double link results from the confluence of two processes that contribute to the persistence of ethno-racial inequality: on the one hand, the effects of past racism, expressed as accumulated disadvantage in the families of Indigenous, Afro-descendent or dark-skinned people, and on the other hand, the effects of present racism associated with discriminatory practices.

Finally, our work includes two innovations relevant to the study of ethno-racial stratification. The first is that it incorporates a skin tone measurement taken with a digital colorimeter that is therefore unaffected by the perceptual biases that might classify people as lighter than they really are due to their SES. With this new measure, which overcomes the endogeneity problem associated with skin color and inequality, we confirm skin lightness as an important relevant factor in explaining inequality of economic opportunity in the present. The second innovation is the introduction of other racialized physical traits in addition to skin color that have a significant link with individuals' socio-economic outcomes. We believe that the incorporation of these variables and the approach we adopt contribute to expanding and refining analytical approaches to understanding ethno-racial stratification in Mexico.

## Notes

1  That said, in recent years there has been an interest in creating theoretical bridges between the two (Lamont, Beljean, and Clair 2014; Reskin 2008; Moon-kie 2015).

2  The question reads: "Is (name of interviewee) nahuatl, maya, zapoteco, mixteco, or a member of another Indigenous group?', to which 6% responded that they were. In 2010, INEGI changed the phrasing of the question to the following: "according to (name of interviewee)'s culture, does s/he consider her/himself Indigenous?" to which 15% responded positively. As Vázquez Sandrin and Quezada (2015) indicate,

this significant increase over the course of ten years could be because the reformulated question implied a restrictive less criterion ("culture") for Indigenous self-designation.

3  See Roth, Solís and Sue (forthcoming) for an analysis of the effects of "whitening" and "lightening" of skin with data from the 2019 PRODER survey.

4  The municipalities that were oversampled were: Hopelchén, Calakmul, José María Morelos, Cantamayec, Chacsinkín, Chankom, Chikindzonot, Maní, Mayapán, Ozkutzcab, Tahdziú, Teabo, Tekom, Tixcacalcupul, Tixmehuac and Yaxcabá.

5  The survey questionnaire includes other questions related to this topic that we do not analyze in this research. To see the questionnaire and additional details about the PRODER survey, visit discriminacion.colmex.mx.

6  RGB stands for Red, Green, Blue and it is a widely used model for representing colors based on the addition of the three primary light colors, red, green, and blue.

7  We recognize that one limitation of these questions is that they might not capture other racialized physical characteristics associated with people of Asian descent. This should be taken into account in future studies.

8  This distribution is comparable, with a few slight changes, to the distribution obtained in recent studies using a similar methodology for ethno-racial self-designation, such as PERLA (Telles, 2014) or the Intergenerational Mobility Module in Mexico (Monroy-Gómez-Franco, Vélez-Grajales, and Yalonetzky 2022; Campos-Vazquez and Medina-Cortina 2019).

9  Regarding the increase in claims to Indigenous identity, it is worth pointing out that the percentage of people who self-identify as Indigenous went from a little over 15% in the 2010 Census (Martínez Casas et al, 2014) to 19% in the 2020 Census (the Census's own calculations). The disparity between these percentages and the 27% shown in the 2019 PRODER Survey might be due to sampling variation, different phrasing of questions, and the fact that the Census data is obtained in an indirect way by relying on a key informant in each household, whereas in PRODER it was done through individual interviews.

10  For an analysis of the lightening of skin and its relationship to socioeconomic status in the 2019 PRODER survey, see Solís, Ruth, Sue (forthcoming). For an analysis that directly compares the link between different measurements of skin color and socioeconomic status, see (Solís, Güémez, and Campos-Vazquez, n.d.).

## References

Alkire, Sabina, and María Emma Santos. 2011. "Acute Multidimensional Poverty: A New Index for Developing Countries." *Proceedings of the German Development Economics Conference*, Berlin 2011, No. 3, ZBW - Deutsche Zentralbibliothek für Wirtschaftswissenschaften, Leibniz-Informationszentrum Wirtschaft, Kiel und Hamburg.

Arceo-Gomez, Eva O., and Raymundo M. Campos-Vazquez. 2014. "Race and Marriage in the Labor Market: A Discrimination Correspondence Study in a Developing." *The American Economic Review* 104 (5): 376–80.

Barabas, Alicia M. 1979. "Colonialismo y Racismo En Yucatán: Una Aproximación Histórica y Contemporánea." *Revista Mexicana de Ciencias Politicas y Sociales* 97: 105–39.

Bengoa, José. 2000. *La emergencia indígena en América Latina*. Mexico: Fondo de Cultura Económica.

Bonilla-Silva, Eduardo. 1997. "Rethinking Racism: Toward a Structural Interpretation." *American Sociological Review* 62 (3): 465. https://doi.org/10.2307/2657316.

Bonilla-Silva, Eduardo. 2006. *Racism without racists. Color-blind racism and the persistence of racial inequality in the United States*. 2nd ed. Lanham: Rowman & Littlefield Publishers.

Breen, Richard, and Jan O. Jonsson. 2005. "Inequality of Opportunity in Comparative Perspective: Recent Research on Educational Attainment and Social Mobility." *Annual Review of Sociology* 31 (1): 223–43. https://doi.org/10.1146/annurev.soc.31.041304.122232.

Brubaker, Rogers. 2004. *Ethnicity without groups*. Cambridge: Harvard University Press.

Brubaker, Rogers. 2009. "Ethnicity, Race, and Nationalism." *Annual Review of Sociology* 35: 21–42. https://doi.org/10.1146/annurev-soc-070308-115916.

Brubaker, Rogers, Mara Loveman, and Peter Stamatov. 2004. "Ethnicity as Cognition." *Theory and Society* 33 (1): 31–64. https://doi.org/10.1023/B:RYSO.0000021405.18890.63.

Campos-Vazquez, Raymundo M, and Eduardo M. Medina-Cortina. 2019. "Skin Color and Social Mobility: Evidence from Mexico." *Demography* 56 (1): 321–43. https://doi.org/10.1007/s13524-018-0734-z.

Castellanos Guerrero, Alicia. 1994. "Asimilación y Diferenciación de Los Indios." *Estudios Sociológicos* 12 (34): 101–19.

Castellanos Guerrero, Alicia. 2005. "Exclusión étnica en ciudades del centro y sureste." In *Urbi Indiano, la larga marcha a la ciudad diversa*, coordinated by Pablo Yanes, Virginia Molina and Óscar González. Mexico: Dirección General de Equidad y Desarrollo Social, Gobierno del Distrito Federal.

Ceron-Anaya, Hugo. 2019. "An Ostensibly Raceless Nation." In *Privilege at play: Class, race, gender, and golf in Mexico*. Oxford University Press.

Chavez-Dueñas, Nayeli Y., Hector Y. Adames, and Kurt C. Organista. 2014. "Skin-Color Prejudice and Within-Group Racial Discrimination: Historical and Current Impact on Latino/a Populations." *Hispanic Journal of Behavioral Sciences* 36 (1): 3–26. https://doi.org/10.1177/0739986313511306.

Cornell, Stephen, and Douglas Hartmann. 1998. "A Constructionist Approach." In *Ethnicity and race. Making identities in a changing world*. Thousand Oaks: Pine Forge Press.

Cortés, Fernando, and Agustín Escobar Latapí. 2005. "Movilidad Social Intergeneracional." *Revista de La CEPAL* 85.

Delajara, Marcelo, and Dositeo Graña. 2017. "Intergenerational Social Mobility in Mexico and its Regions." *Working document 6/2017*. Mexico: Centro de Estudios Espinosa Yglesias.

Dixon, Angela R., and Edward Telles. 2017. "Skin Color and Colorism: Global Research, Concepts, and Measurement." *Annual Review of Sociology* 43: 405–24. https://doi.org/10.1146/annurev-soc-060116-053315.

Feagin, Joe, and Sean Elias. 2013. "Rethinking Racial Formation Theory: A Systemic Racism Critique." *Ethnic and Racial Studies* 36 (6): 931–60. https://doi.org/10.1080/01419870.2012.669839.

Filmer, Deon, and Lant Pritchett. 2001. "Estimating Wealth Effects without Expenditure Data or Tears: An Application to Educational Enrollments in States of India." *Demography* 38 (1): 115–132.

Flores, René, and Edward Telles. 2012. "Social Stratification in Mexico: Disentangling Color, Ethnicity, and Class." *American Sociological Review* 77 (3): 486–94. https://doi.org/10.1177/0003122412444720.

Freeman, Jonathan B., Andrew M. Penner, Aliya Saperstein, Matthias Scheutz, and Nalini Ambady. 2011. "Looking the Part: Social Status Cues Shape Race Perception." *PLoS ONE* 6 (9). https://doi.org/10.1371/journal.pone.0025107.

Ganzeboom, Harry B. G., and Donald J. Treiman. 1996. "Internationally Comparable Measures of Occupational Status for the 1988 International Standard Classification of Occupations." *Social Science Research* 25 (3): 201–239. https://doi.org/10.1006/ssre.1996.0010.

Golash-Boza, Tanya. 2016. "A Critical and Comprehensive Sociological Theory of Race and Racism." *Sociology of Race and Ethnicity* 2 (2): 129–141. https://doi.org/10.1177/2332649216632242.

González Casanova, Pablo. 2006. "El Colonialismo Interno." In *Sociología de La Explotación*. Buenos Aires: Consejo Latinoamericano de Ciencias Sociales.

Gullickson, Aaron. 2016. "Essential Measures: Ancestry, Race, and Social Difference." *American Behavioral Scientist* 60 (4): 498–518. https://doi.org/ 10.1177/0002764215613398.

Iturriaga, Eugenia. 2011. "Las Élites de La Ciudad Blanca. Racismo, Prácticas y Discriminación Étnica En Mérida, Yucatán." Doctoral thesis. Universidad Nacional Autónoma de México.

Knight, Alan. 1990. "Racism, Revolution, and Indigenismo: Mexico, 1910–1940." In *The Idea of Race in Latin America, 1870–1940*, edited by Thomas Skidmore, Aline Helg, and Alan Knight. Austin: University of Texas Press.

Krozer, Alice. 2019. "Élites y Racismo: El Privilegio de Ser Blanco (En México), o Cómo Un Rico Reconoce a Otro Rico." *Nexos*, March 2019.

Krozer, Alice, and Andrea Urrutia Gómez. 2021. "Not in the Eyes of the Beholder: Racialisation, Whiteness and Beauty Standards in Mexico." Working paper 5. México: El Colegio de México.

Lamont, Michèle. 2018. "Addressing Recognition Gaps: Destigmatization and the Reduction of Inequality." *American Sociological Review* 83 (3): 419–44. https://doi.org/10.1177/0003122418773775.

Lamont, Michèle, Stefan Beljean, and Matthew Clair. 2014. "What Is Missing? Cultural Processes and Causal Pathways to Inequality." *Socio-Economic Review* 12: 573–608.

López Santillán, Ricardo. 2011. *Etnicidad y Clase Media. Los Profesionistas Mayas Residentes En Mérida*. Mérida: Universidad Nacional Autónoma de México/Instituto de Cultura de Yucatán.

Loveman, Mara. 2014. *National colors. Racial Classification and the State in Latin America*. New York: Oxford University Press.

Martínez-Casas, Regina, Emiko Saldívar, René Flores and Christina A. Sue. 2014. "The Different Faces of Mestizaje: Ethnicity and Race in Mexico." In *Pigmentocracies. ethnicity, race, and color in Latin America* by Edward Telles. Chapel Hill: The University of North Carolina Press.

Monk, Ellis P. 2015. "The Cost of Color: Skin Color, Discrimination, and Health Among African-Americans." *American Journal of Sociology* 121 (2): 396–444. https://doi.org/10.1086/682162.

Monroy-Gómez-Franco, Luis A., and Roberto Vélez-Grajales. 2020. "Skin Tone Differences in Social Mobility in Mexico: Are We Forgetting Regional Variance?" *Journal of Economics, Race, and Policy* 4 (4): 257–74.

Monroy-Gómez-Franco, Luis A., Roberto Vélez-Grajales, and Gastón Yalonetzky. 2018. "Layers of Inequality: Social Mobility, Inequality of Opportunity and Skin Colour in Mexico." *Working Paper No. 03/2018.* Mexico: Centro de Estudios Espinosa Yglesias.

Moon-kie, Jung. 2015. "Introduction: Reconsidering Racism and Theory." In *Beneath the surface of white supremacy.* Stanford: Stanford University Press.

Moreno Figueroa, Mónica G. 2010. "Distributed Intensities: Whiteness, Mestizaje and the Logics of Mexican Racism." *Ethnicities* 10 (3): 387–401. https://doi.org/10.1177/1468796810372305.

Moreno Figueroa, Mónica G. 2012. "'Yo nunca he tenido la necesidad de nombrarme': Reconociendo el Racismo y el Mestizaje en México." In *Racismos y otras formas de intolerancia. De Norte a Sur en América Latina,* coordinated by Alicia Castellanos Guerrero and Gisela Landázuri Benítez (15–48). Mexico D.F.: Universidad Autónoma Metropolitana y Juan Pablos Editor.

Moreno Figueroa, Mónica G. 2016. "El Archivo Del Estudio Del Racismo En México." *Desacatos* 51 (May–August: 92–107.

Navarrete Linares, Federico. 2016. *México Racista: Una Denuncia.* Mexico City: Penguin Random House.

Neckerman, Kathryn M., and Florencia Torche. 2007. "Inequality: Causes and Consequences." *Annual Review of Sociology* 33 (1): 335–357. https://doi.org/10.1146/annurev.soc.33.040406.13175.

Nutini, Hugo G. 1997. "Class and Ethnicity in Mexico: Somatic and Racial Considerations." *Ethnology* 36 (3): 227–38.

Painter, Matthew A., Shiri Noy, and Malcolm D. Holmes. 2019. "Skin Tone and Asset Inequality in Latin America." *Journal of Ethnic and Migration Studies* 46 (18): 1–28. https://doi.org/10.1080/1369183X.2019.1592881.

Powers, Daniel, and Yu Xie. 2008. *Statistical methods for categorical data analysis* (2nd cd.). Emerald.

Ramírez, Alejandro. (2002). México. In *Indigenous peoples, poverty and human development in Latin America,* edited by Gillette Hall and Harry Anthony Patrinos (150–198). Palgrave Macmillan.

Reeskens, Tim, and Rodrigo Velasco Aguilar. 2020. "Being White Is a Full Time Job? Explaining Skin Tone Gradients in Income in Mexico." *Journal of Ethnic and Migration Studies* 47 (1): 1–23. https://doi.org/10.1080/1369183X.2020.1775071.

Reskin, Barbara F. 2008. "Including Mechanisms in Our Models of Ascriptive Inequality." In *Handbook of employment discrimination research. rights and realities*, edited by Laura Beth Nielsen and Robert L. Nelson, 75–97. New York: Springer.

Roth, Wendy D. 2016. "The Multiple Dimensions of Race." *Ethnic and Racial Studies* 39 (8): 1310–38. https://doi.org/10.1080/01419870.2016.1140793.

Ryabov, Igor. 2016. "Educational Outcomes of Asian and Hispanic Americans: The Significance of Skin Color." *Research in Social Stratification and Mobility* 44: 1–9. https://doi.org/10.1016/j.rssm.2015.11.001.

Saperstein, Aliya, and Andrew M. Penner. 2012. "Racial Fluidity and Inequality in the United States." *American Journal of Sociology* 118 (3): 676–727.

Schwartzman, Luisa Farah. 2007. "Does Money Whiten? Intergenerational Changes in Racial Classification in Brazil." *American Sociological Review* 72 (6): 940–63.

Sen, Maya, and Omar Wasow. 2016. "Race as a Bundle of Sticks: Designs that Estimate Effects of Seemingly Immutable Characteristics." *Annual Review of Political Science* 19: 499–522. https://doi.org/10.1146/annurev-polisci-032015-010015.

Serrano Espinosa, Julio, and Florencia Torche (eds). 2010. *Movilidad Social En México. Población, Desarrollo y Crecimiento*. Mexico City: Centro de Estudios Espinosa Yglesias.

Solís, Patricio. 2007. *Inequidad y Movilidad Social En Monterrey*. Mexico City: El Colegio de México.

Solís, Patricio. 2018. "Barreras Estructurales a La Movilidad Social Intergeneracional En México. Un Enfoque Multidimensional." *Serie Estudios y Perspectivas* 176. https://doi.org/10.15713/ins.mmj.3.

Solís, Patricio, Marcela Avitia, and Braulio Güémez. 2020 (July). "Tono de Piel y Desigualdad Socioeconómica En México." COLMEX. https://discriminacion.colmex.mx/wp-content/uploads/2020/07/info1.pdf Mexico: El Colegio de México.

Solís, Patricio, and Marcelo Boado. 2016. *Y Sin Embargo Se Mueve...* Mexico City: Centro de Estudios Espinosa Yglesias.

Solís, Patricio, and Pablo Dalle. 2019. "La Pesada Mochila Del Origen de Clase. Escolaridad y Movilidad Intergeneracional de Clase En Argentina, Chile y México." *Revista Internacional de Sociología* 77 (1): 1–17.

Solís, Patricio, and Braulio Güémez. 2021. "Características Étnico-Raciales y Desigualdad de Oportunidades Económicas En México." *Estudios Demográficos y Urbanos* 36 (106): 255–89.

Solís, Patricio, Braulio Güémez, and Raymundo M. Campos-Vazquez (forthcoming). "Skin Tone and Inequality of Economic Outcomes in Mexico: A Comparative Analysis Using Optical Colorimeters and Color Palettes." *Sociology of Race and Ethnicity*.

Solís, Patricio, Braulio Güémez, and Virginia Lorenzo Holm. 2019. *Por Mi Raza Hablará La Desigualdad. Efectos de Las Características Étnico-Raciales En La Desigualdad de Oportunidades En México.* Mexico City: Oxfam México.

Solís, Patricio, Alice Krozer, Carlos Arroyo Batista, and Braulio Güémez. 2019. "Discriminación Étnico-Racial En México: Una Taxonomía de Las Prácticas." In *La Métrica de Lo Intangible: Del Concepto a La Medición de La Discriminación*, coordinated by Jesús Rodríguez Zepeda and Teresa González Luna Corvera (55–94). Mexico City: Consejo Nacional para Prevenir la Discriminación.

Taguieff, Pierre André. 2001. "El Racismo." *Debate Feminista* 12 (24): 3–14.

Telles, Edward. 2014. *Pigmentocracies. Ethnicity, race, and color in Latin America.* Chapel Hill: The University of North Carolina Press.

Telles, Edward, and René Flores. 2013. "Not Just Color: Whiteness, Nation, and Status in Latin America." *HAHR - Hispanic American Historical Review* 93 (3): 411–50. https://doi.org/10.1215/00182168-2210858.

Telles, Edward and Florencia Torche. 2018. "Varieties of Indigeneity in the Americas." *Social Forces* 97 (4): 1543–1570. https://doi.org/10.1093/sf/soy091.

Trejo, Guillermo, and Melina Altamirano. 2016. "The Mexican Color Hierarchy. How Race and Skin Tone Still Define Life Chances 200 Years after Independence." In *The double bind: The politics of racial and class inequalities in the Americas*, edited by Juliet Hooker and Alvin B. Tillery Jr. (1–14). Washington, D.C: American Political Science Association.

Vázquez Sandrin, Germán, and María Félix Quezada. 2015. "Los indígenas autoadscritos de México en el censo 2010: ¿revitalización étnica o sobreestimación censal?" *Papeles de Población* 21(86), 171–218.

Villarreal, Andrés. 2010. "Stratification by Skin Color in Contemporary Mexico." *American Sociological Review* 75 (5): 652–78. https://doi.org/10.1177/0003122410378232.

Villarreal, Andrés, and Stanley R. Bailey. 2020. "The Endogeneity of Race: Black Racial Identification and Men's Earnings in Mexico." *Social Forces* 98 (4): 1744–72. https://doi.org/10.1093/sf/soz096.

Weatherall, Ian, and Bernard D. Coombs. 1992. "Skin Color Measurements in Terms of CIELAB Color." *The Journal of Investigative Dermatology* 4 (99): 468–473.

Wieviorka, Michel. 2007. "La mutación del racismo." *Perspectivas Teóricas: Revista Mexicana de Ciencias Políticas y Sociales* 49 (200): 13–23.

Wimmer, Andreas. 2008. "Elementary Strategies of Ethnic Boundary Making." *Ethnic and Racial Studies* 31 (6): 1025–55. https://doi.org/10.1080/01419870801905612.

# CHAPTER 4

# The Double Standard of Success: Narratives of Inequality, Social Mobility, and "Meritocratic Mestizaje"

Máximo Ernesto Jaramillo-Molina Translation
by Ellen Jones

## Introduction

It is increasingly common to find social movements, civil society organizations, and other actors who seek to identify and visibilize the injustice of inequality and the fallacy of the meritocratic narrative, as well as the historical presence of racism in Mexico. Despite this, society is still structured according to a stratification that is hugely unequal: the majority of wealth remains in the hands of the few, while everyone else has almost nothing.

In 2019, Credit Suisse (2020) estimated that the poorest 50% in Mexico owned 4% of the country's wealth, while the richest 10% had accumulated 65%, which means that Mexico has a Gini coefficient—a standard measure of inequality—of 0.77 (a coefficient of 0 means that all the wealth is distributed equally among the population, whereas a coefficient of 1 means that all the wealth is concentrated in a single person). Worse still, several institutions estimate an exacerbated increase in inequality (economic and otherwise) in the context of the economic crisis related to the pandemic in 2020 and 2021 (CIEP et al. 2021). Moreover, this inequality is not only economic, but also intersects with other social categories beyond class, such as gender, ethno-racial characteristics, and age (Solís et al. 2019).

In the light of this, there are questions that need to be asked about the exacerbated and sustained increase in inequality over recent decades, as well as the observable increase in the frequency with which meritocratic, racial, and stigmatizing narratives are made public: what relation (if any) is there between classist and racial narratives in Mexico? What effect do ethno-racial characteristics have on the various narratives of inequality? Do they have any effect on the perception of "success" or "failure," or in general on social mobility?

This article attempts to explore in depth how society perceives, reproduces, and legitimizes narratives of inequality. In short, it analyzes narratives about meritocracy, mestizaje, poverty, inequality, and social mobility, with the aim of creating hypotheses, finding some answers, and posing questions about how these narratives are legitimized. In this way, it seeks to make connections with categories of stigmatization, which tend to have a differential value (or double standard) when it comes to how we perceive and value the achievements and responsibilities (or culpabilities) of different social groups. The objective is to provide evidence so that future studies can continue to explore the topic of the legitimacy of inequality by observing the intersection between different narratives, with the term "meritocratic mestizaje" offered as one possible term for that intersection.

The second section details the sources of information used. The third section focuses on the perception of social mobility and possible associated variables. The fourth section involves a detailed analysis of interviewees' social mobility alongside their skin color. The fifth section uses qualitative analysis tools to deepen our understanding of the narratives that have already been discussed. Finally, the chapter closes with some conclusions.

## Sources of Information and Methods

In order to find connections between narratives of meritocracy, inequality, poverty, wealth, and social mobility, all of which play important roles in the broad process of reproducing inequality, this article combines information gathered in interviews for quantitative analysis, with qualitative information acquired using digital ethnography techniques.

In principle, data from the Social Mobility Survey (EMOVI) from the year 2017 are used (Centro de Estudios Espinosa Yglesias [CEEY] 2019). But given the limitations of a survey in terms of the amount of information that needs gathering for analysis and the level of depth required by the object of study, in this article the data is complemented by qualitative information: a corpus built using web scrapping tools. In short, a set of information was gathered from different social networks. More than a thousand tweets associated with the hashtags #CosasRarasDeLosPobres (#StrangePoorPeopleThings) and #PrietosEnAprietos (#PrietosInAPredicament) were downloaded and then analyzed according to the number of times they were shared and their relationship to the narratives mentioned above. In addition, I also analyzed social media posts (specifically Facebook) posted by the Mexican government and the comments left by users on these posts: most posts advertised social policy programs, and one asked about the perceived causes of poverty.

## The Illusion of Betterment

Social mobility can be defined as "the changes people experience in their economic condition" (CEEY 2019). When this mobility is vertical, that is when someone passes from one socioeconomic stratum to a higher or lower one, they are experiencing upward or downward social mobility. It is also important to distinguish absolute social mobility from relative social mobility: the first refers to an absolute change in the standard of living between different generations, while the latter refers to a person's change in position in the social hierarchy relative to the rest of society in comparison with their parents. Both are forms of objective social mobility.

Studies of subjective or perceived social mobility[1] have very different, and especially important results. In general, at a global level, people are more likely to *think* that they have had upward social mobility compared to their parents (Evans & Kelley, 2004) than to have actually experienced it.

What studies of social mobility in Mexico find depends in large part on their methodology, and especially on the type of question used for analysis. For example, Torche (2010) finds, using data from 2006, that 51% of people in Mexico perceive themselves to have experienced upward social mobility. However, information from Centro de Estudios Espinosa Yglesias (CEEY 2013) using data from 2011, found that people in Mexico perceive greater immobility (or at least limited social mobility) than they actually experience. And finally, Yaschine (2015) finds that 19% of the population consider themselves to have experienced upward social mobility, 70% do not think their situation has changed, and 11% think they have had downward social mobility.

One of the most interesting and important dimensions of analysis of these data is the difference or "social mobility bias," which is to say, the difference between subjective and objective perceptions of social mobility. Why would someone who had experienced upward social mobility not perceive that to be the case? What explains why someone who, in objective terms, has experienced downward mobility believe themselves to be better off? These discrepancies become important given the size of the population group that presents them. For example, Duru-Bellat and Kieffer (2008) found that nearly half of the population has these subjective and objective social mobility biases: 30% of the population overestimates their social mobility and 20% underestimates it.

As well as those authors, Heath, de Graaf, and Li (2010), Torche (2010), and Yaschine (2015) sketch out possible reasons for these biases: 1) confusion between absolute and relative objective social mobility on the part of the interviewees; 2) the assessment being made based on the people around them (rather than on society or the country as a whole); 3) different dimensions being evaluated (rather than just wealth, income, or work, on which analyses of objective social mobility are usually based), and 4) the father's occupation being assessed in terms of its current relative stratification.

EMOVI's data on subjective or perceived social mobility are shown in the Table 4.1. In sum, Table 4.1 shows that 41.5% of the Mexican population perceive themselves to have experienced upward social mobility with respect to the home they now live in, while 37.1% perceive themselves to be in the same social stratum (totals can be obtained by adding the percentages in the main diagonal in the table) and the remaining 21% perceive themselves to have experienced downward social mobility.

First, Table 4.1 shows a perception bias when it comes to social mobility, similar to that found in previous studies. In fact, according to these results there is a greater percentage of the country's population that perceives themselves to have had social mobility (42%) compared to those who have objectively experienced it (34%). In other words, this result indicates that people's perceptions of social mobility are more optimistic than reality.

**Table 4.1.** Quintiles of perceived childhood and current living conditions, 2017.

|  |  | Current living conditions | | | | | |
|---|---|---|---|---|---|---|---|
|  |  | I | II | III | IV | V | Total |
| Childhood living conditions | I | 7.1 | 13.5 | 6.5 | 0.6 | 0.1 | 27.9 |
|  | II | 3.4 | 9.7 | 11.5 | 3.0 | 0.1 | 27.7 |
|  | III | 1.0 | 6.1 | 14.2 | 5.4 | 0.2 | 27.0 |
|  | IV | 0.3 | 2.5 | 5.6 | 5.5 | 0.4 | 14.3 |
|  | V | 0.1 | 0.3 | 0.9 | 1.3 | 0.6 | 3.2 |
|  | Total | 11.9 | 32.1 | 38.7 | 15.9 | 1.5 | 100.0 |

*Source*: Author's own, using data from CEEY (2019)

How is the perception of upward social mobility closely linked to objective experience? Of the population that perceives themselves to have had upward social mobility, only 4 out of 10 objectively presented it, with 6 out of 10 remaining in the same income quintile or having moved to a lower one (the results can be observed in Table 4.2). Put a different way, for most people who believe themselves to have experienced upward social mobility, this is nothing more than an illusion in objective terms.

## Does "Success" Depend on Skin Color?

Beyond the relationship between subjective and objective social mobility and the biases that accompany them, it is essential to try to understand the reason behind the subjects' perceptions of their "successes" in life. For example, perception of upward social mobility might be related to other contextual variables or associated factors, beyond simply objective or experienced social mobility. For example, the interests, aspirations, and relative social mobility of people around you, the demands of social norms, as well as mobility observed in the press and on social media, can all help shape our perceptions of social mobility.

Among these associated factors, ethno-racial characteristics may determine the formation of subjectivity about upward or downward social mobility or, relatedly, perception of one's own successes or failures. For example, Sánchez et al.'s (2011) study of Afro-American people in the United States found that 1) it is clear that there are fewer opportunities for this ethno-racial minority, which means they therefore achieve lower results (for example,

**Table 4.2.** Objective and subjective social mobility, 2017.

| Subjective social mobility | Objective social mobility | | |
|---|---|---|---|
| | Not upwardly mobile | Upwardly mobile | Total |
| *Not upwardly mobile* | 42% | 17% | 59% |
| *Upwardly mobile* | 24% | 17% | 41% |
| Total | **66%** | **34%** | **100%** |

| Subjective social mobility | Objective social mobility | | |
|---|---|---|---|
| | Not upwardly mobile | Upwardly mobile | Total |
| *Not upwardly mobile* | 71% | 29% | **100%** |
| *Upwardly mobile* | 58% | 42% | **100%** |
| Total | **66%** | **34%** | **100%** |

*Source*: Author's own, using data from CEEY (2019).

they earn lower salaries); 2) for this reason, everyone else tends to have lower expectations of Afro-American people's performance, and 3) their skin color and ethno-racial characteristics always weigh heavily on them, and will be the first thing other people observe about them, before their social class (whether lower, middle, or upper), and regardless of any upward social mobility they may have experienced. In the same way, when Oh and Kim (2016) studied students from two different ethno-racial contexts (Asian and Mexican) living in the United States, they found that their families and other people close to them shaped students' expectations and the criteria for them to be perceived as having "achieved success" in very different ways.

In sum, there is a robust body of literature showing the close relationship between ethno-racial belonging and the formation of expectations, the perception of "success" (especially in very academic contexts), and those who have achieved it (Enriquez, 2011; Fuligni, Tseng, & Lamb, 1999; Jiménez and Horowitz 2013; Kao & Tienda, 1998; Qian & Blair, 1999; Solorzano, 1992).

Relatedly, a couple of important hypotheses have emerged from work with low-income Afro-American and white people in the United States with regard to their aspirations: the first mentions that their aspirations in life are shaped more by the position they occupy within their ethno-racial group than by the position of said group in relation to society in general, while the alternative hypothesis suggests the contrary, in which the position of the ethno-racial group with respect to society in general is more important than the position of the individual within the ethno-racial group (Lorenz 1972).

In Mexico, there are no studies that directly link ethno-racial characteristics and/or belonging with subjective social mobility. On the one hand, there is research that shows subjective factors that are linked to subjective social mobility, such as the formation of expectations about life or subjective wellbeing, but especially Indigenous identity or belonging to an Indigenous community. For example, Segura Salazar et al. (2016) analyze Indigenous university students' expectations about the workplace and about success in life, focusing on students from the Autonomous University of Chapingo, while other studies indirectly analyze those expectations in relation to strategies Indigenous students must adopt due to their experience of discrimination in certain spaces (Arellano 2008). Another study shows that subjective wellbeing, specifically satisfaction with life, is experienced less often by people who speak an Indigenous language, once the effects of social class or level of education have been controlled for (Jaramillo-Molina 2016).

But in all these cited studies, the ethno-racial dimension is only approximated through Indigenous community belonging, which in turn is usually approximated through ability to speak an Indigenous language or through self-identification (Carrasco & Alcazar 2009). In fact, the distinction made by Hopenhayn and Bello (2001) when studying ethno-racial discrimination and xenophobia in Latin America is that "race" tends to be associated with "biological distinctions attributed to genotypes and phenotypes," among which they highlight skin color, while ethnicity is associated with "cultural factors." The authors also highlight that these two dimensions of discrimination—race and ethnicity—tend to be difficult to separate, which is why this chapter prefers the concept of the "ethno-racial."

It has been only a few years since the concept of the ethno-racial began to be studied widely, beyond whether or not someone belonged to an Indigenous community. Practically speaking, the key variable that has often allowed for recent studies of the "ethno-racial" has been skin color (Aguilar Pariente 2011; Arceo-Gomez & Campos Vázquez 2014; Campos Vázquez & Medina-Cortina 2019; Flores & Telles 2012; Monroy-Gómez-Franco et al. 2022; Solís et al. 2020; Torres et al. 2019; Villarreal 2010). In fact, discrimination based on skin color in Mexico is almost as prevalent (23% in men, 15% in women) as discrimination based on social class (25% in men, 21% in women) (INEGI 2020).

Perhaps the most relevant study was carried out by Campos Vázquez & Medina Cortina (2017). Using an experimental design, they found that stereotypes associated with skin color in Mexico affect young people's expectations, aspirations, and even performance (in this specific case, young people in middle school in Mexico City). Will these effects on expectations and aspirations reflect a probable effect on how people with different skin colors in Mexico evaluate their own social mobility?

Given all the above, it is clear skin color can be extremely interesting when analyzing the subjectivity of social mobility. Although no research has been conducted in Mexico that delves specifically into the relationship between, on the one hand, the appropriation of narratives of success and subjective social mobility, and, on the other hand, this proxy variable for the ethno-racial, the body of research already indicated generates certain hypotheses about its relationship with our perception of social mobility. For example, a first hypothesis is simply that there is a significant link between skin color and subjective social mobility, with an additional effect on other socioeconomic and demographic variables that may also be related. A second hypothesis, regarding the direction of the effect, is that darker skin tones associated with discrimination and related inequalities lead people to underestimate change to their own socioeconomic conditions and social mobility. An alternative hypothesis would be that, faced with the disadvantages recognized as being associated with having darker skin, their achievements are overvalued, and therefore subjective social mobility outstrips objective social mobility.

The EMOVI data help provide answers here. The descriptive statistical analysis shows that people with lighter skin tones are less likely to perceive themselves as having experienced social mobility, although the difference is not especially great (see Figure 1). While 27% of people with lighter skin tones (from I to K on the PERLA scale) perceive themselves as having experienced upward social mobility, 42% of people with darker skin tones (from A to H on the PERLA scale) report having experienced social mobility. This rises to 42% for everyone else (from A to H on the PERLA scale). In addition, it is once again people with the lightest skin tones who most often think they have experienced downward social mobility or simply no mobility at all (although here the percentage is almost the same as for people with the darkest skin tones, from A to E).

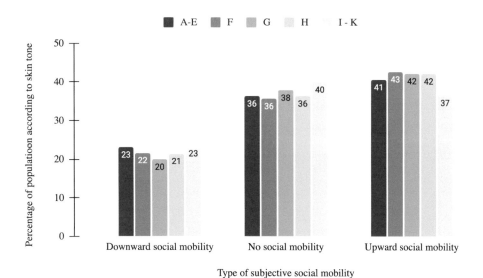

Figure 4.1. Subjective social mobility, according to skin tone (PERLA scale).

*Source*: Author's own with data from CEEY (2019).

This would indicate that people with darker skin more often perceive themselves to have had upward social mobility than people with lighter skin. But such results do not take into account the objective prevalence of social mobility in accordance with the skin color of the interviewee. Put a different way, they do not consider how many of those people who *perceive* themselves as having had social mobility truly had it in objective terms. To control for this skin color variable, and also to account for the effect of other variables that could intervene in perceptions of whether or not someone is socially mobile, the following binominal logistic model was considered.

This binomial logistic model was created to estimate the chances of the interviewee perceiving themselves as having experienced upward social mobility with respect to the independent variables shown in Table 4.3. With respect to the control variables, the results show that the chances of someone perceiving themselves as having experienced (subjective) upward social mobility increase by 65% if the person actually experienced that social mobility in objective terms. On the other hand, currently living in poverty and being over 45 years old also increases those chances, with statistical significance. On the contrary, having felt discriminated against due to a lack of money is associated with a lower probability of reporting subjective upward mobility.

For its part, the effects of skin color on one's perception of social mobility are interesting because it shows that, once all the previously mentioned variables are controlled for, the coefficient for lighter skin tones (I to K) turns out to be significant, and reduces the chances of perceiving oneself as having had upward social mobility by 18% (taking skin tone G as a reference category, the median category of the skin tones used). In turn, the coefficient for darker skin tones (A to E) is also significant, where changes in perceptions of social mobility are reduced by 18% compared to the reference category. The effect seems to be equally great for both categories at the extremes of the skin tone spectrum.

These results show that skin color is significantly associated with subjective social mobility, even after taking into account variables, including objective social mobility, which explain it to a large extent. These results confirm the first of the hypotheses mentioned above: skin color is significantly linked to subjective social mobility, and has an additional effect on other socioeconomic variables and demographics that may also be related.

The results of the statistical model do not reject the second hypothesis (to remind readers: "a darker skin color, associated with discrimination

**Table 4.3.** Odds ratio (OR) of the binominal logistic regression model to estimate the probability of perceiving upward social mobility.

| Variable | Model 1 | | | Model 2 | | |
|---|---|---|---|---|---|---|
| | Odds ratio | Lim. Sup. | Lim Inf. | Odds ratio | Lim. Sup. | Lim Inf. |
| **Skin tone (ref. G)** | | | | | | |
| A–E | 0.819 | 0.719 | 0.933 | 0.812 | 0.713 | 0.925 |
| F | 0.995 | 0.904 | 1.096 | 0.988 | 0.897 | 1.088 |
| H | 1.020 | 0.943 | 1.104 | 1.053 | 0.973 | 1.139 |
| I–K | 0.818 | 0.731 | 0.915 | 0.886 | 0.791 | 0.992 |
| Objective upward social mobility | 1.650 | 1.543 | 1.765 | 1.490 | 1.390 | 1.598 |
| Poverty (quintiles I and II) | 1.417 | 1.319 | 1.523 | 2.263 | 1.998 | 2.563 |
| Financial discrimination | 0.895 | 0.818 | 0.980 | 0.913 | 0.834 | 0.999 |
| Age (ref. under 30) | | | | | | |
| Between 30 and 44 | 1.088 | 0.989 | 1.197 | 1.003 | 0.910 | 1.106 |
| 45 and over | 1.199 | 1.088 | 1.322 | 1.076 | 0.973 | 1.190 |
| Sex/Woman (ref. man) | 1.053 | 0.986 | 1.123 | 1.025 | 0.960 | 1.095 |
| Region | | | | | | |
| North-West | 0.945 | 0.842 | 1.061 | 0.920 | 0.819 | 1.033 |
| Center-North | 1.094 | 0.984 | 1.216 | 1.092 | 0.982 | 1.214 |
| Center | 0.938 | 0.854 | 1.031 | 0.963 | 0.876 | 1.059 |
| South | 0.960 | 0.865 | 1.064 | 0.913 | 0.822 | 1.014 |
| Wealth of childhood home (ref. quintile I) | | | | | | |
| Quintile II | | | | 1.024 | 0.929 | 1.128 |
| Quintile III | | | | 1.986 | 1.774 | 2.225 |
| Quintile IV | | | | 1.573 | 1.409 | 1.757 |
| Quintile V | | | | 1.000 | | |
| Constant | 0.580 | 0.459 | 0.734 | 0.420 | 0.330 | 0.537 |

| | | | | | | |
|---|---|---|---|---|---|---|
| | Number of obs = | | 16,441 | Number of obs = | | 16,210 |
| | LR chi2(16) = | | 569.5 | LR chi2(16) = | | 700.39 |
| | Prob > chi2 = | | 0 | Prob > chi2 = | | 0 |
| | Pseudo R2 = | | 0.0253 | Pseudo R2 = | | 0.0315 |

*Source*: Author's own with data from CEEY (2019).

and related inequalities, leads people to underestimate their own change in socioeconomic circumstances and social mobility"). They show that people with the darkest skin tones tend to underestimate their achievements and do not perceive their own upward mobility, even when it is objectively present. But the results are yet more complex, because the same effect is observed in people with the lightest skin tones: they too underestimate their own upward social mobility compared to their actual experiences.

It is a little complicated to know how to interpret this last result. What it shows is that regardless of the social mobility people have actually experienced, and regardless of sociodemographic and discrimination variables, people with the darkest and lightest skin tones are less likely to perceive their own upward social mobility. We can investigate the mechanisms at play by proposing various hypotheses. In the case of those with the darkest skin tones, we can hypothesize that underestimating personal achievements (and having a lesser propensity to perceive upward social mobility) is linked to inequality, discrimination, stigma, and stereotyping that weigh on people according to their ethnic and racial characteristics. We can even make a link with the results of Campos-Vázquez and Medina-Cortina's (2017) study, which shows how skin tone affects expectations, aspirations, and even performance. Is the perception of success or of upward social mobility less reported by people with darker skin tones, who are also those who experience most discrimination? Despite their objective mobility, do these people not claim a success narrative because of the discrimination they continue to experience? Or, coinciding with Sánchez et al. (2011), are people with the darkest skin always judged, on first impression, based on their ethno-racial characteristics, before their current social status is perceived, and might this in turn affect their perception of their own social mobility? In colloquial terms, if you were born "moreno," is it true that you'll always be moreno, even if you climb up the social scale?

On the other hand, regarding people with the lightest skin, we can pose questions and create hypotheses that are equally complex to interpret. Can we explain the fact that people with lighter skin are less likely to perceive their own social mobility (despite that perception not corresponding with objective experience) in part because of a greater demand for achievements (such as upward social mobility, wealth, or higher academic degree) that are markers of success for this group of people? Or are they less likely to perceive their own social mobility because of higher expectations or aspirations, given the advantages they started off with in life, at least in stereotypical terms (because actually the effects of that start in life are controlled for in the logistical model)? Another hypothesis might be that, given that in large part this social group begins from a more advantaged position than those in other social strata, perhaps there is no more space available above in the pyramid of social stratification in which upward social mobility could be perceived. Similarly, the distance between the richest stratum at the top of the pyramid and everyone else is growing wider, which makes social mobility more difficult to achieve in this context.

In this way, and in summary, the main result of the statistical model is that skin color has an important, particular effect over and above sociodemographic factors, childhood wealth/poverty, objective social mobility, and perceived discrimination. Skin color matters. While the results are not conclusive when it comes to exactly how skin color affects the perception of upward social mobility, there is evidence that there are different standards of evaluation when it comes to people's success, that these standards vary along with ethno-racial characteristics, and that people with the darkest and lightest skin tones seem to have a self-perception that seems more biased than people in the middle range of skin tones.

## The Double Standard of Deserving Success

The previous analysis showed a significant relationship between ethno-racial characteristics and the perception of social mobility, and proposed some hypotheses regarding the different understandings of "success" among different social groups. The current section provides some more concrete ideas about the possible relationship between ethno-racial characteristics and certain narratives of achievement, success, or meritocracy itself. To further deepen the understanding of the relationship between these aspects of distributive justice, the results of the qualitative analysis on the subject are shown below.

In order to deal with narratives of success, let's analyze the other side of the coin: narratives about "failure"; that is, narratives about the causes of poverty. The stigmatization of poverty is caused by a series of assessments that use different yardsticks (or standards) to judge people in such a situation (i.e., socially identified as poor) with respect to the rest of the population, imposing different demands on them and legitimizing them in different ways in terms of the degree to which they are deserving. Moreover, this classist assessment often has a clear racist correlate, so that ethno-racial characteristics cannot be left out of the analysis.

In Mexico, in 2019 (a year after president López Obrador began his term in office there were changes in the discourse around redistributive policies discursive, changes that unleashed or increased the visibility of *stigmatizing* or *meritocratic*, *classist*, and *racist narratives* that questioned the legitimacy and deservingness of beneficiaries.

Among the most important changes in the social policies of the current presidential administration is the strong criticism of previous social programs, based on the suspicion of corruption and inefficient use of intermediaries in the rollout process, which led to a restructuring of social programs. The most important program during the 1997–2018 period was the PROSPERA program that sought to break the intergenerational transmission of poverty through investment in "human capital" for the youngest members of those households, which was roundly criticized for years but also made some important achievements. It came to represent up to 25% of income for the poorest households (Boltvinik and Jaramillo-Molina 2019; Valencia and Jaramillo-Molina 2019). This program was criticized and replaced by a program of grants (called Becas Benito Juárez) that replicated most of PROSPERA's problems, but which had a considerably smaller budget. On the other hand, the Pension for Older Adults program (for over 65s) takes up over half of the total budget dedicated to social programs for 2022, and does not prioritize people suffering from poverty, but rather seeks to be universal.

While in objective terms the social programs implemented during this new term in office do not have bigger budgets or a greater effect on the reduction of poverty (although it has been proven that they are less effective at reducing inequality), they are more often debated on social media and in the press and have caused particular controversy for their perceived risk of creating clientelism. This frequent public discussion might be behind the greater stigmatization of beneficiaries of these social programs.

As previously mentioned, there are numerous historical studies that point to the stigmatization of beneficiaries of redistributive policies, especially those aimed at people affected by poverty. "The undeserving poor" (Katz 1989) is a socially constructed category that stigmatizes the beneficiaries of social programs, especially those aimed at people living in poverty, since it blames them for their situation and classifies them as lazy, dependent on the state, and not legitimate recipients of "social assistance" through taxpayers' money. In this way, meritocratic perceptions of the causes of poverty, so important and generalized in Mexico, start to materialize, undermining any sense that those living in poverty have a legitimate claim to or are deserving of redistribution.

This stigmatizing representation of poverty is extremely frequent in the opinion columns of newspapers and other media outlets in Mexico. For example, Barba and Valencia (2019) show that the narratives about poor people in national newspapers are stigmatizing and that they depict the poor as a danger to public security and to society. Maria Amparo Casar (2019), a famous opinion writer, characterized social programs as "clientelist"—thus portraying beneficiaries of such programs as "clients"—because "nothing is asked of them in return." Such examples abound.

Stigmatizing narratives about the working classes are common in Mexico. According to the National Discrimination Survey (INEGI, 2017), at least two out of every five people agree that "poor people make little effort to pull themselves out of their poverty." Moreover, 65% of the population agrees that the programs aiming to fight poverty make people dependent on the government, and 57% believe that they incentivize them to not work, according to my own calculations based on the National Poverty Survey data (Cordera 2015).

Combined with this, the stigmatization of poverty in Mexico has historically had a racial element. The narrative of mestizaje has for centuries spread scorn on the working classes and often on people with darker skin, qualifying them as backward, immoral, chaotic, and threatening (Leal 2016). There is therefore a historical aspect to the racialization of the urban poor to be discussed (Knight 1990), one that has been denied by the ideology of mestizaje (Leal 2016). Based on the above, a hypothesis proposed in this chapter is that the working classes, who are "dangerous" to society (Barba and Valencia 2019), and the beneficiaries of social programs, who are "dependent" on the state (Casar 2019; Riva Palacio 2019), tend to also be racialized under these stigmatizing narratives.

Let's try to go a couple of steps further: why is this type of stigmatizing narrative about people who are identified or perceived as poor or with dark skin and who are beneficiaries of social programs in Mexico so popular? A second hypothesis put forward in this section is that the social construction of someone who deserves to benefit from social programs (also a reflection of whether they deserve to achieve "success") is based principally on a series of myths about the beneficiaries of these programs, especially about people who are socially identified as poor and/or with ethno-racial features that point to an Indigenous origin—myths that are taken as truths despite being completely removed from reality. These myths tend to relate people living in poverty, people with dark skin, and single mothers, among other stereotyped figures, with individualist and meritocratic narratives that hold them responsible for their own situation.

In this section I will use a corpus compiled from social media analysis to provide evidence of stigmatizing narratives of poverty and redistribution. Table 4.4 shows some comments in response to a publication in which the question "What do you think the causes of poverty are?" was asked.

The meritocratic narrative and the ideology of mestizaje coincide in their depiction of the "failure" of the lower classes and racialized people, who are blamed for the vulnerable conditions in which they live, which are seen as the simple result of their actions, culture, customs, and way of life. In this sense, some of these opinions shared on social media reproduce narratives in which specific behaviors of those identified as poor are questioned. These behaviors, it is important to mention, would not be questioned or reproached for any reason in people who are not socially classified as poor, or in people who have light skin (without racialized features). One source of various comments on this topic was the social media trend that took off in 2019 (although it has had sporadic new life since then) with the hashtag "#CosasRarasDeLosPobres" (#StrangePoorPeopleThings), which allows people to share criticisms of behavior characterized as "illogical" or "naco"[2] by people identified as poor according to familiar stereotypes.

These viral tweets confirm ideas already presented above, such as fecundity ("To have a bunch of kids and not be able to afford them. #StrangePoorPeopleThings" or "StrangePoorPeopleThings to have kids and then complain you can't afford to feed them"), or the idea of dependence on the state ("Believing you deserve to be maintained by those of us who actually work").

Like these tweets, there are also others who question the aspiration to success when it is linked to skin color. The popular trending hashtag "#PrietosEnAprietos" (#PrietosInTightSpots) gave rise to tweets such as: "Calling lack of talent victimization. When will they understand that success is achieved through effort and true talent, not self-pity. #PrietosEnAprietos" in reference to a tweet by Yalitza Aparicio with the hashtag #PoderPrieto

**Table 4.4.** Comments on the perceived "causes of poverty."

| ID | Comments |
|---|---|
| 1 | Ignorance. Both on the part of those managing the economy and on the part of the layabouts waiting for everything to be handed to them on a plate. |
| 2 | The first cause is to feel poor and the second is to feel incapable of no longer being poor. |
| 3 | Mentality. |
| 4 | All the prejudices you're fed since birth like, for example, that money is bad, that if you are born poor you die poor, because of mediocre comments that you believe. |
| 5 | Laziness |
| 6 | Overpopulation, lack of desire to be productive. Living under the expectation that someone else will do it. |

*Source*: Author's own

(#PrietoPower) (Faure 2021) which sought precisely to vindicate the situation of people in Mexico who have historically been oppressed because of their skin color.

In another example, an account titled "PrietosMX" shared a photo of a young man on the metro wearing a suit, with the ironic caption: "Lowly skin color is no impediment to SUCCESS. Interested? Go on, mate, ask me how." It's clear that this reference to success is entirely formed through the stigmatization of people based on their ethnic characteristics and skin color, rather than just because they live in poverty. Why should it be surprising that a person with dark skin is "successful"? As I have mentioned, meritocracy and mestizaje form a double narrative in which poor people (and people with Indigenous ethno-racial characteristics or dark skin tones) are blamed for "being poor," but it is also assumed that these people cannot be successful, so others are "surprised" if they do indeed "achieve."

As the above cited phrases make clear, there is widespread stigma within individualist and meritocratic narratives and the narrative of mestizaje, of people living in poverty, people with racialized features, and people who are beneficiaries of social programs. But these stigmas are not extended to other social actors who receive transfers from the government, directly or indirectly. When have you seen, for example, people who are entitled to government subsidies or IMSS (the country's main social security organization) or ISSSTE (social security for state employees) recipients being stigmatized? When have those who benefit from electricity, water, or gas subsidies, or from taxes such as "la tenencia" and "el predial" (the country's main property taxes) been questioned in this way? Why is it only poor people benefitting from these redistribution efforts who are stigmatized?

There is obviously a double standard in the evaluation of merit and justice around the distribution and redistribution of funds that individuals and social groups receive from the state and in general from society. But it is not only redistribution: this double standard means people's success and the "value of their effort" are judged in different ways.

I will outline at least two hypotheses to try to understand the cause of the existence and reproduction of this double standard. The first is proposed by Mettler (2011) and mentions that many citizens are critical of direct transfers but are more likely to promote and accept what are called "submerged policies"—indirect transfers that are less visible, such as fiscal incentives and subsidies. The role of these submerged policies is not clear to citizens, who often do not understand their function fully, much less their impact on the reproduction of inequality, which is why there are few who oppose them or stigmatize their beneficiaries.

The second hypothesis (Jaramillo-Molina 2019) is an explanation of the stigma contained in these narratives, due to a belief that the beneficiaries of those social programs lack legitimacy and merit, summed up in tweets and other social media: "they do not legitimately deserve society's help." As I mentioned before, this narrative ensures that "a poor person is to blame for their own situation. They need to be taught to fish. Unless something is done, they'll end up dependent on the government." This narrative tends to be extended to racialized people, through the narrative of mestizaje. The obvious consequence is that these people are not considered deserving of any social program.

But within that narrative there are several exceptions. It is possible for poor people to become deserving if there is a hint of "effort," "initiative," or "merit" involved. The evidence is clear, both in the results of related studies (Jaramillo-Molina 2019; Oorschot 2000, 200; Reeskens & van der Meer 2019) and in comments on social media. Thus, proof of "effort" becomes the bargaining chip to diminish stigma against beneficiaries of social programs: good qualifications, "entrepreneurism," ingenuity, etc. At the end of the day, according to the dominant view, poverty caused by structural factors is not legitimate enough to deserve justice. This double standard reinforces the idea that it is illegitimate to provide redistribution to the poor, but simultaneously justifies giving to "deserving," non-poor, non-racialized people.

## Conclusions: Meritocratic Mestizaje

This article provides evidence of the existence of a double standard in the dominant discourses and narratives that operate in Mexico around the perception of success and failure, of "effort" and "conformism," of deserving and undeserving. Such narratives establish a double standard about what it takes to be considered successful at the same time as perpetuating stigmas based on a biased understanding of "failure," to the detriment of the working and racialized classes. In this way, we can identify a kind of double linked narrative that we can call the narrative of "meritocratic mestizaje," a term that ought to be used more widely in order to highlight the close correlation between the two narratives and their mutual dependence on one another.

To get closer to the evidence on this matter, the results of the analysis clearly show that skin color, as a proxy for the interviewees' ethno-racial characteristics, plays an extremely important role in the judgement of success, approximated from the subjective representation of social mobility.

Moreover, the effect of skin color on the assessment of upward social mobility goes over and above the variables of childhood wealth, experienced (objective) social mobility, and other sociodemographic variables that were integrated into this analysis. Despite this, there remain some open questions about the different ways skin color affects the perception of mobility, especially when the results show that not only people with darker skin tones, but also those with the lightest skin are less likely to perceive upward social mobility. In any case, the evidence clearly shows that the perception of social mobility in Mexico is racialized.

On the other hand, analysis of the corpus compiled through the observation of narratives related to classism and racism on social media, including the narratives of meritocracy and of mestizaje, clearly shows how people living in poverty with racialized features are held responsible for their own situation. By referring to habits or customs that are supposedly "incomprehensible" or "detrimental to themselves," the double narrative of "meritocratic mestizaje" explains, justifies, and legitimizes the precarity of the working classes in this country.

Pointing to a supposed generational and historical inheritance of a certain 'backward," "vulgar," and "inefficient" culture that weighs on poor and racialized people, "meritocratic mestizaje" is an example of how classist and racist discourses are intimately linked in societies such as Mexico, although the existence of both stigmatizing and exclusionary processes is often denied.

## Notes

1 In terms of analysis of subjectivities, this study begins with a theoretical framework drawn from the sociology of valuation and evaluation (SVE), which allows us to analyze the narratives of deservingness and of distributive justice from the point of view of the subject, pointing out that valuative and evaluative practices are permeated by a series of conditions and factors that give rise to such a valuation, by stabilizing and institutionalizing it (Lamont 2012, 7).

2 Translator's note: See Hugo Ceron-Anaya's chapter in this volume for a full discussion of the historical and current usage of the insult "naco," which he defines as "a person who is unrefined or lacking formal education, who belongs to the working classes; they can also be an Indigenous person."

## References

Aguilar Pariente, R. (2011). *The tones of democratic challenges: Skin color and race in Mexico*. http://repositorio-digital.cide.edu/handle/11651/1350.

Arceo-Gomez, E. O., & Campos Vázquez, R. M. (2014). Race and Marriage in the Labor Market: A Discrimination Correspondence Study in a Developing Country. *American Economic Review*, 104(5), 376–380. https://doi.org/10.1257/aer.104.5.376

Arellano, M. E. C. (2008). Ser indígena en la educación superior ¿desventajas reales o asignadas? *Revista de la Educación Superior*, 37 (148), 31–55.

Barba, C., & Valencia, E. (2019). La construcción social de la pobreza y la desvalorización de los pobres en México en quince años del diario *El Universal*. *Espiral: Estudios sobre Estado y Sociedad*, 26(76), 183–232.

Boltvinik, J., Damián, A., & Jaramillo-Molina, M. E. (2019). Crónica de un fracaso anunciado. Ha llegado la hora de remplazar el Progresa-Oportunidades-Prospera (POP). In *El Progresa-Oportunidades-Prospera, a veinte años de su creación*, coordinated by Gonzalo Hernández Licona, Thania Paola de la Garza Navarrete, Janet Zamudio Chávez, Iliana Yaschine Arroyo. Consejo Nacional de Evaluación de la Política de Desarrollo Social.

Campos Vázquez, R. M., & Medina Cortina, E. M. (2017). Identidad social y estereotipos por color de piel. Aspiraciones y desempeño en jóvenes mexicanos. *El Trimestre Económico*, 85(337), 53. https://doi.org/10.20430/ete.v85i337.659.

Campos Vázquez, R. M., & Medina Cortina, E. M. (2019). Skin Color and Social Mobility: Evidence from Mexico. *Demography*, 56(1), 321–343. https://doi.org/10.1007/s13524-018-0734-z.

Carrasco, V. T., & Alcazar, C. T. (2009). Los pueblos indigenas y los censos en Mexico y America Latina: La cultura en la definicion de su identidad. In *Derechos de los mexicanos: Introducción al derecho demográfico*, edited by Luz María Valdés. Universidad Nacional Autónoma de México. https://archivos.juridicas.unam.mx/www/bjv/libros/6/2638/18.pdf.

Casar, M. A. (2019, March 1). El Gran Benefactor. *Nexos*. https://www.nexos.com.mx/?p=41305.

Centro de Estudios Espinosa Yglesias (CEEY). (2013). *Informe Movilidad Social en México 2013. Imagina tu futuro*. https://ceey.org.mx/wp-content/uploads/2018/06/Informe-de-Movilidad-Social-en-M%C3%A9xico.-Imagina-tu-futuro.pdf.

Centro de Estudios Espinosa Yglesias (CEEY). (2019). *Encuesta ESRU de movilidad social en México 2017 (ESRU-EMOVI 2017)*. https://ceey.org.mx/contenido/que-hacemos/emovi/.

CIEP, FUNDAR, Centro de análisis e investigación, & Oxfam México. (2021). *La vacuna contra la desigualdad*. https://lavacunacontraladesigualdad.org/wp-content/uploads/2021/05/VACUNAVSDESIGUALDAD.pdf.

Cordera, R. (2015). *Percepciones, pobreza, desigualdad: Encuesta Nacional de Pobreza* (1st edition). Universidad Nacional Autónoma de México.

Credit Suisse. (2020). *Global wealth report 2019*. Credit Suisse. https://www.credit-suisse.com/about-us/en/reports-research/global-wealth-report.html.

Duru-Bellat, M., & Kieffer, A. (2008). Objective/subjective: The two facets of social mobility. *Sociologie du Travail*, 50, e1–e18. https://doi.org/10.1016/j.soctra.2008.07.001.

Enriquez, L. E. (2011). "Because we feel the pressure and we also feel the support": Examining the educational success of undocumented immigrant Latina/o students. *Harvard Educational Review*, 81(3), 476–499. https://doi.org/10.17763/haer.81.3.w7k703q050143762.

Evans, M. D. R., & Kelley, J. (2004). Subjective Social Location: Data From 21 Nations. *International Journal of Public Opinion Research*, 16(1), 3–38.

Faure, Vanesa. 2021. A falta de talento, el victimismo. Cuándo entenderán que el éxito se consigue con esfuerzo y verdadero talento, no con autocompasión. #PrietosEnAprietos 🫠🍒 [Tweet]. @Vanesa_Faure, May 26. https://twitter.com/Vanesa_Faure/status/1397759408927608833.

Flores, R., & Telles, E. (2012). Social Stratification in Mexico: Disentangling Color, Ethnicity, and Class. *American Sociological Review*, 77(3), 486–494. https://doi.org/10.1177/0003122412444720.

Fuligni, A., Tseng, V., & Lam, M. (1999). Attitudes toward Family Obligations among American Adolescents with Asian, Latin American, and European Backgrounds. *Child Development*, 70, 1030–1044. https://doi.org/10.1111/1467-8624.00075.

Heath, A., Graaf, N. D. de, & Li, Y. (2010). How Fair is the Route to the Top? Perceptions of Social Mobility. In A. Park, J. Curtice, E. Clery, & C. Bryson, *British Social Attitudes: The 27th Report: Exploring Labour's Legacy* (29–50). SAGE Publications Ltd. https://doi.org/10.4135/9781446268254.n2.

Hopenhayn, M., & Bello, A. (2001). *Discriminación étnico-racial y xenofobia en América Latina y el Caribe*. Santiago de Chile: Naciones Unidas, CEPAL, Div. de Desarrollo Social.

INEGI. (2017). *Encuesta Nacional sobre Discriminación (ENADIS) 2017*. https://www.inegi.org.mx/programas/enadis/2017/.

INEGI. (2020). *Estadísticas a Propósito del Día Internacional de la Eliminación de la Discriminación Racial (21 de Marzo)* (Press release 133/20). INEGI. https://www.inegi.org.mx/contenidos/saladeprensa/aproposito/2020/DISCRIMINAC_NAL.pdf.

Jaramillo-Molina, M. E. (2016). Mediciones de bienestar subjetivo y objetivo: ¿complemento o sustituto? *Acta Sociológica*, 70, 49–71. http://dx.doi.org/10.1016/j.acso.2017.01.003.

Jaramillo-Molina, M. E. (2019). *Yo (no) merezco abundancia: Percepciones y legitimidad de política social, pobreza y desigualdad en la Ciudad de México*. Doctoral dissertation, El Colegio de México. www.researchgate.net/ publication/334495442_Yo_no_merezco_abundancia_Percepciones_y_ legitimidad_de_politica_social_pobreza_y_desigualdad_en_la_Ciudad_de _Mexico'.

Jiménez, T. R., & Horowitz, A. L. (2013). When White Is Just Alright: How Immigrants Redefine Achievement and Reconfigure the Ethnoracial Hierarchy. *American Sociological Review*, 78(5), 849–871. https://doi.org/ 10.1177/0003122413497012.

Kao, G., & Tienda, M. (1998). Educational Aspirations of Minority Youth. *American Journal of Education*, 106(3), 349–384. https://doi.org/10.1086/ 444188.

Katz, M. B. (1989). *The undeserving poor: From the war on poverty to the war on welfare*. Pantheon Books.

Knight, A. (1990). Racism, Revolution, and Indigenismo: Mexico, 1910–1940. In *The Idea of Race in Latin America 1870–1940*, edited by Richard Graham, 71–113. University of Texas Press. https://hemi.nyu.edu/course-nyu/nat ion/materials/text/knight.html.

Lamont, M. (2012). Toward a Comparative Sociology of Valuation and Evaluation. *Annual Review of Sociology*, 38, 201–211.

Leal, A. (2016). La ciudadanía neoliberal y la racialización de los secto- res populares en la renovación urbana de la ciudad de México. *Revista Colombiana de Antropología*, 52(1), 223–244. https://doi.org/10.22380/ 2539472X9.

Lorenz, G. (1972). Aspirations of Low-Income Blacks and Whites: A Case of Reference Group Processes. *American Journal of Sociology*, 78(2), 371–398.

Mettler, S. (2011). *The Submerged State: How Invisible Government Policies Undermine American Democracy*. University of Chicago Press. https://press. uchicago.edu/ucp/books/book/chicago/S/bo12244559.html.

Monroy-Gómez-Franco, L.A., R. Vélez-Grajales, and G. Yalonetzky. 2022. "Layers of Inequality: Social Mobility, Inequality of Opportunity and Skin Colour in Mexico." Working Paper 03/2018. Mexico: Centro de Estudios Espinosa Yglesias.

Oh, C. J., & Kim, N. Y. (2016). "Success Is Relative": Comparative Social Class and Ethnic Effects in an Academic Paradox. *Sociological Perspectives*, 59(2), 270–295.

Oorschot, W. van. (2000). Who should get what, and why? On deservingness criteria and the conditionality of solidarity among the public. *Policy & Politics*, 28(1), 33–48. https://doi.org/10.1332/0305573002500811.

Qian, Z., & Blair, S. L. (1999). Racial/Ethnic Differences in Educational Aspirations of High School Seniors. *Sociological Perspectives*, 42(4), 605–625. https://doi.org/10.2307/1389576.

Reeskens, T., & van der Meer, T. (2019). The inevitable deservingness gap: A study into the insurmountable immigrant penalty in perceived welfare deservingness. *Journal of European Social Policy*, 29(2), 166–181. https://doi.org/10.1177/0958928718768335.

Riva Palacio, R. (2019, April 30). La 4T: El Efecto Cobra. *El Financiero*. https://www.elfinanciero.com.mx/opinion/raymundo-riva-palacio/la-4t-el-efecto-cobra/.

Sánchez, F. J., Liu, W. M., Leathers, L., Goins, J., & Vilain, E. (2011). The subjective experience of social class and upward mobility among African American men in graduate school. *Psychology of Men & Masculinity*, 12(4), 368–382. https://doi.org/10.1037/a0024057.

Segura Salazar, C. M., Chávez Arellano, M. E., Segura Salazar, C. M., & Chávez Arellano, M. E. (2016). "Cumplir un sueño": Percepciones y expectativas sobre los estudios profesionales entre estudiantes indígenas en la Universidad Autónoma Chapingo. *Revista mexicana de investigación educativa*, 21(71), 1021–1045.

Solís, P., Avitia, M., & Güémez, B. (2020). *Tono de piel y desigualdad socioeconómica en México. Reporte de la Encuesta Proder # 1*. El Colegio de México. https://discriminacion.colmex.mx/wp-content/uploads/2020/07/info1.pdf.

Solís, P., Güémez, B., & Lorenzo Holm, V. (2019). *Por mi raza hablará la desigualdad* (p. 98). Oxfam México. https://www.oxfammexico.org/sites/default/files/Por%20mi%20raza%20hablara%20la%20desigualdad_0.pdf.

Solorzano, D. (1992). Chicano Mobility Aspirations: A Theoretical and Empirical Note. *Latino Studies Journal*, 3, 48–66.

Torche, F. (2010). Cambio y persistencia en la movilidad intergeneracional en México. In *Movilidad social en México. Población, desarrollo y crecimiento*, edited by J. Serrano and F. Torche (71–134). Centro de Estudios Espinosa Yglesias.

Torres, F., Salgado, M., Mackenna, B., & Núñez, J. (2019). Who Differentiates by Skin Color? Status Attributions and Skin Pigmentation in Chile. *Frontiers in Psychology*, 10. https://doi.org/10.3389/fpsyg.2019.01516.

Valencia, E., & Jaramillo-Molina, M. E. (2019). *El Programa Progresa-Oportunidades-Prospera en el régimen de bienestar dual mexicano.* CONEVAL.

Villarreal, A. (2010). Stratification by Skin Color in Contemporary Mexico. *American Sociological Review, 75*(5), 652–678. https://doi.org/10.1177/0003122410378232.

Yaschine, I. (2015). Percepciones de la movilidad intergeneracional en México. In *Percepciones, pobreza, desigualdad. Encuesta nacional de pobreza.* Universidad Nacional Autónoma de México. http://www.humanindex.unam.mx/humanindex/consultas/detalle_capitulos.php?id=23238&rfc=WUFBSTcxMDYyMw==&idi=1.

# MIRRORS FOR GOLD: THE PARADOXES OF INCLUSION

Yásnaya Elena A. Gil Translated by Ellen Jones

It's not that mirrors didn't exist in these lands before the European invasion. They did, and they were beautiful, as only obsidian mirrors tied to the sacred world can be. In many representations of the Mexican divinity Texcatlipoca, he bears an obsidian mirror on his chest. The relationships we establish with these strange objects, which try to reflect the world by showing us a representation of it, are mediated by cultural interpretations.

As I child, I was constantly told to avoid seeing my own face in the mirror after nightfall, so as not to risk wisp-like beings or threatening figures smiling in the glass behind me. In other cultures, mirrors are needed for divination, because their surfaces can reveal the future. Different traditions teach that breaking a mirror will bring years of bad luck, or that they can open doors to other worlds and dimensions. Mirrors appear to have symbolic relevance in many cultures and traditions, which makes sense if we think just how strange it is that they can create visual doubles of our faces, bodies, and the objects that inhabit the world.

Despite the value we assign to these objects, according to popular Mexican nationalist culture, the Spanish cheated the native American population when they exchanged mirrors for gold at the start of the wars we refer to today as the conquest. It probably doesn't help that those mirrors are often referred to in the diminutive: espejitos or espejuelos were given in exchange for gold. I won't go into the complexities of the trade in objects established by emissaries of Moctezuma and Hernán Cortés; undoubtedly these exchanges meant something different to each party, with exceedingly complex implications. In any case, it certainly wasn't as simple as the Spanish handing over mirrors in exchange for the deceived, naïve, native peoples' gold. But we can't deny that the Spanish troops prized gold almost to the point of obsession, making it the driving force behind most of their actions.

Beyond recognizing the complex events and circumstances influencing this historical moment, I'd like to pay attention to the shades of meaning the phrase "mirrors for gold" has acquired over time. The words are often used to warn people not to succumb to abuse and lies: don't let yourself be tricked by mirrors into giving away your gold. In a country where indigenous communities are still being exploited, it is, lamentably, a common, thriving practice for lies or half-truths to be told, for instance about the nature of a government megaproject and its implications for indigenous peoples and communities. The expression that warns us, however, not to exchange "mirrors for gold" takes as given that there is only one correct value system: the one dictating that gold—rather than mirrors—is valuable. Accepting this warning in some sense also implies accepting that value can only be established according to a single value system—that gold is the valuable item in a trade that strengthens the system belonging to those who seek to exploit us. How can we warn people about exploitation and deceit without strengthening the idea that what we consider valuable can only be dictated by our oppressors?

Now that the discussion about racism has reached Mexico's elites, who have long ignored the antiracist struggles of indigenous and Afro-descendent communities, it is essential that we confront the paradox implied by recognizing just one value system: the one imposed by oppressive entities. In fact, the idea that we have only begun to talk about racism in Mexico in the wake of recent antiracist protests in the United States implies that the discussion is only relevant when it reaches those elite members of society who pay careful attention to our northern neighbors despite systematically ignoring the voices of community members racialized as inferior who have been talking about this for years. Even discussions of racism are more relevant when they involve people who are categorized as superior according to the value system created by their own racist structure.

One thing emerging from the discussions about racism in Mexico that have taken place recently in privileged digital spaces has been the implicit suggestion that the only thing necessary for racism to be dismantled is for the value systems created by oppressive entities to recognize the bodies of racialized people as valuable. For example, fashion magazines whose pages have not historically included dark-skinned bodies (which are linked with the categories of indigenous and Afro-descendant) now recognize them by including them on their covers; the system, however, not only remains the same but is actually reinforced through these acts of recognition. The value systems dictating what is desirable, beautiful, or valuable are also racialized; oppression cannot be dismantled unless we consider the numerous other value systems that have been attacked and invisibilized. It strikes me as fundamental to the antiracial struggle for those of us in oppressed sectors of society to be able to create and strengthen our own value systems with criteria that do more than just replicate the parameters of value created by supposedly superior sectors of society.

There is no use in a soft drink company suddenly including racialized bodies (which are read as indigenous, dark, or Afro-descendant) in their adverts if that same company keeps robbing indigenous communities of their access to water, thus supporting a racist system that permits it because it has created a hierarchy in which indigenous is inferior. Nor can we fall into the trap of thinking that including individuals who are racialized as inferior on the boards of directors of companies (which reproduce capitalist oppressions) implies the destruction of a racist system. Social class is also racialized: structurally, poverty has been assigned a skin color, and the fact that some people can escape the class to which the system confines them does not imply the destruction of the structures that racialize class. What this tells us is that it is not possible to fight racism without fighting capitalism. To do so would leave intact a structure that could further validate itself by including a diverse range of individuals from whom it would profit economically.

Attempts to combat racism by strengthening the very value systems racism created generates a peculiar situation: the inclusion of specific individuals in order to create a sense of recognition that allows us to avoid destroying the value system. This situation gives rise, for example, to the phenomenon of celebrating "the first indigenous person" to win a prestigious prize in the oppressive value system; the first indigenous person to appear on such-and-such a cover, the first indigenous person to star in a telenovela, the first indigenous person to be elected president of a national political party, the first indigenous person to be reflected in the mirror held up by the oppressor. This doesn't mean people racialized as inferior who are recognized by hegemonic value systems lack merit, or that they haven't had to negotiate endless obstacles in order to see themselves reflected in those mirrors; it doesn't mean they don't deserve acknowledgement or that those acknowledgements are never worth celebrating. The problem is the existence of a single hegemonic mirror dictating what is worth reflecting. It would be different if we could see ourselves reflected in multiple mirrors that return and thus acknowledge our image in all its diversity.

Is it important for hegemonic value systems to account for the diversity of the world? Yes, it is, but it's even more important that our own mirrors, which by nature are many and diverse, are strengthened. As the Zapotec cinematographer Luna Marán puts it, in a text describing the creation of her own audiovisual mirror in the Sierra Norte in Oaxaca, there is a political urgency to the creation of our own value systems. Luckily, this is happening and has always happened in the resistance.

At an important indigenous women's convention, one official gave a lecture during which she said, among other things, that while she was of course pleased indigenous women were participating in the political life of our self-governing community structures, it was time for us to participate in "real politics," party politics. According to this stance, the only political system with real value is the one created by oppressors, while our own system is seen to be inferior, worth less. Racism cannot be destroyed by thinking in this way, only transformed under the guise of inclusion, while the hierarchy reproducing and strengthening it is maintained.

Of course, we need to fight to prevent hegemonic value systems from continuing to oppress. But at the same time, we must not forget to build and strengthen our own systems; this seems to me an even more important task. More than just demanding to see ourselves reflected in a mirror created, maintained, and held in an iron first by our oppressors, let's demand to see ourselves and the world reflected in our own obsidian mirrors, carved and polished by our own hands. In a future that is no longer hierarchical, the world and our faces will be reflected in many different mirrors corresponding to multiple, equally important and necessary systems—a world in which the oppressor no longer endlessly repeats that gold is the only thing of value.

# CHAPTER 5

# "Whiteness" and the Afterlives of Mestizaje in Neoliberal Mexico

## Alejandra Leal

### Prietos, Morenos, Blancos[1]

On May 25, 2021, a number of public figures, most notably female and male actors, took to Twitter to denounce discrimination based on their skin color in the film and television industries, taking the hashtag #PoderPrieto (#PrietoPower). The idea behind this social media campaign was to celebrate their skin color in a system that devalues and discriminates against them, relegating them to stereotypical roles of violent gangsters, poor workers and house cleaners. Within hours, a wide variety of people with a wide variety of skin tones and phenotypes had posted their pictures on Twitter replicating the hashtag. There were academics, activists, performance artists, visual artists, influencers, students, and countless Twitter users celebrating their #PoderPrieto. In the following days, numerous newspapers and news sites picked up the story, which they labeled a "campaign against racism." Some critics within social media called the hashtag "reverse racism" and were quickly rebuffed and reminded that there is no such thing. Others wondered if categories such as prieto or moreno designated fixed racialized markers and were criticized for speaking from their privileged blanco positions. Indeed, many posts repeated the claim that Mexican blancos are a privileged minority that has long oppressed prietos and is unwilling to accept that Mexico is a profoundly racist country. A prominent actor and one of the most vocal figures behind the hashtag explained in a video posted on social media that their motivation for using prieto in a positive light was to appropriate "the saber that wounded us in order to dismantle the system that still oppresses us."

It would be a mistake to approach this social media campaign as representative of an expansive grassroots movement against racism in Mexico. Its influence extends to academic, cultural and (particular kinds of) activist circles participating in social and other digital media. However, it does reflect a shift in the languages available to conceptualize and talk about racism in Mexico's public sphere. As part of this recent shift, prieto and blanco have come to appear as fixed racial categories designating clearly identifiable groups of people, as if they were part of biology-based racial frameworks that assign particular and unchanging traits and colors to particular races. As this chapter will explain, this appears to be at odds with other understandings of Mexico's racial imaginaries as not grounded in supposedly biological features but instead in more elusive ideas of culture and modernity, and as deeply intertwined with class. Indeed, there is a dissonance between the apparent fixedness of the notions prieto and blanco as mobilized in the #PoderPrieto campaign and the wide variety of skin colors and class markers represented in the countless pictures attached to the #PoderPrieto hashtag. Many of those faces could in fact equally be positioned within the fluid category of güero, which indexes both relatively fair skin and a privileged class position.

In this chapter, I critically analyze the proliferation of such racial languages in contemporary Mexico. More than taking them as an indication that racism is finally being discussed publicly, I explore why these seemingly fixed understandings of race and skin color have become a meaningful way to think and talk about racism in recent years, especially among Mexico City's middle class and educated sectors, in both academia and the public sphere. As early as the 1970s some scholars were already writing about racism in Mexico, but the topic only started to gain centrality in the late 1990s. Earlier studies focused their attention on racism against the country's indigenous population (Castellanos Guerrero 2000), but they gradually expanded to other racialized minorities such as Mexican blacks and afromestizos (Hoffmann 2006), as well as to racism within and amongst the *mestizo* majority (Ceron-Anaya 2019; Moreno Figueroa and Saldívar Tanaka 2016; Iturriaga 2020; Moreno Figueroa 2010; Saldaña Tejeda 2013). These works have contributed to positioning the topics of race and racism not only in academic circles but also in Mexico's public sphere. Indeed, the last decade has witnessed a veritable explosion of a wide variety of forums for discussing them, from academic seminars to governmental institutions, from public events to websites and social media campaigns like #PoderPrieto.

Writings about race and racism in Mexico often argue that while mestizaje—the racial ideology that functioned to legitimize national identity during most of the twentieth century—made race invisible, disavowing explicit racial categories in public life, notions of racialized difference permeated, and continue to permeate, everyday private and public interactions. As Ceron-Anaya put it, studies have attempted to understand the *obscured visibility* of race in popular discourse and everyday life despite its *invisibility* in institutional settings (Ceron-Anaya 2019,95). Moreover, most studies and public discussions approach *mestizaje* as a racial/racist ideology that continues to delineate racialized distinctions and racial discrimination in twenty-first century Mexico. There is less attention, however, to how Mexico's racial imaginaries have changed in the wake of the post-revolutionary regime's lost hegemony since the mid-1980s and the gradual move towards a neoliberal hegemony. Inasmuch as studies discuss transformations or ruptures within mestizaje, they do so in relation to the advent of multicultural discourses, projects and constitutional changes since the last decade of the twentieth century, but give less consideration to the broader changes that have taken place within national imaginaries in the context of neoliberalization (Martínez-Casas, Saldívar, and Sue 2014).

This is due, at least in part, to the preeminence of the conceptual history of *mestizaje* over its political and social histories or, in other words, to an absence of works that reflect on how the ideology of mestizaje was embedded within the larger post-revolutionary state project, and on the past and present effects of such embeddedness. Conceptualizing mestizaje as both a racial ideology *and* a state project, I interrogate whether we can continue to assert that *mestizaje* alone informs racial discrimination in contemporary Mexico. Exploring the ambivalences at the heart of the post-revolutionary *mestizo* national subject, I argue that in a profoundly changed ideological, political, social and economic landscape mestizaje has lost its unifying force. The new languages that have emerged for thinking and talking about race and racism in this context have reified skin color as a defining category, effectively erasing class from public discussions about racial discrimination. This, I suggest, has excluded from such discussions the historically racialized urban masses, who were once at the center of nationalist discourses and state projects, as if they could not be part of (re)claiming a #PoderPrieto in neoliberal Mexico.

## The Ambivalent Temporalities of the Mestizo[2]

*Mestizo* existed as a category since early colonial times to refer to mixed persons (and more concretely to the offspring of Spanish and native Indian parents), but it was late nineteenth century intellectuals and post-revolutionary ideologues who placed it at the very center of Mexican nationalism. While prevalent racial theories at the end of the nineteenth and the beginning of the twentieth century condemned miscegenation for its degenerative tendencies, nineteenth century writers and post-revolutionary nationalists placed racial mixing as the basis for Mexico's national unity and its integration into civilization and modernity (Tenorio Trillo 2009). They posited the mestizo as the embodiment of a racially and culturally unified and forward-looking nation, one that, they hoped, would be capable of playing as equal in the international field (Lomnitz 2001).

Recent writings about mestizaje and racism remind us that these ideologues never considered the mestizo's two constituent elements as equal. On the contrary, the superior European element would elevate the inferior Indian. Yet more than merely "inferior," the Indian who entered the national equation was a highly ambivalent figure. He/she was inscribed at the very heart of the mestizo national subject and, at the same time, racialized as backward and inferior. He/she was both a redeemable, civilizable figure, to be incorporated into the nation by a paternalistic state, and a quintessential other against which the contours of a modern and civilized national collective were drawn (Bartra 1992). Likewise, more than merely "superior," the mestizos's European element was also ambivalent. Proponents of mestizaje saw him/her not only as the source of the mestizo's elevating racial element, but also as a threat in the form of colonialism and (American) expansionism. In other words, much like the Indian, the European had ambivalent connotations as simultaneously desired and dreaded.[3] He/she was a source of civilization and, at the same time, a danger to Mexico's independence.

There are two points regarding these ambivalences that are crucial for my argument in this chapter. First, they express particular understandings of race, which combined nineteenth and twentieth century racist views and colonial imaginaries alike. Indeed, the introduction of race as a scientific concept in late nineteenth century Mexico interwove with earlier colonial imaginaries. In those imaginaries, "race" was associated with descent and not with unchanging biological attributes, thus it could not easily be read out of the body (Lewis 2003). It more often referred to the moral quality of persons and their (in)ability to be civilized. Therefore, unlike race as it came to be understood in the Anglo colonies, in Mexico's mestizaje, as elsewhere in Latin America, it did not refer to ostensibly unambiguous biological differences, but mainly to cultural traits and dispositions, language and moral quality, all of which could be transformed (Poole 1997). To be sure, skin color did play a role as a marker of difference in post-revolutionary Mexico, but as Hugo Ceron-Anaya has argued, "in the mestizo framework, phenotype is not a conclusive marker of racial belonging" (Ceron-Anaya 2019, 96). Or as Marisol de la Cadena claimed in discussing Latin American racial ideologies more broadly:

> [A person's] assigned racial "color" does not necessarily correspond to [his or her] skin [color]. It also depends on the quality of the individual. (…) In Latin American categories phenotype comes in and out. (…) It is obvious that the logic is not the same for all "colors." They have a history and the association between color and quality depends on this history. (de la Cadena 2009, 24)

Second, the ambivalences of both the Indian and the European expressed the anxieties of nineteenth century intellectuals and twentieth century post-Revolutionary ideologues about their own temporal and spatial place in Western modernity (and what they perceived as the civilized world), with which they had an agonizing relationship. The point to be made, then, is that discourses of mestizaje attempted to tame *both* ambivalences by positing that modern Mexico would be neither European nor Indian but mestizo. Yet the ambivalences remained.

Consider, for example, the figure of the Indian in depictions of the post-revolutionary mestizo Mexican, where it appears not in reference to concrete, sociological subjects, but rather as a spectral presence threatening mestizo aspirations to modernity. Samuel Ramos' book *Profile of Man and Culture in Mexico*—the foremost text, published in 1934, in a wide body of literature concerned with defining the national character—is a prime example of how the specter of the Indian haunts the mestizo.[4] Ramos' general argument is that the Mexican has a "feeling of inferiority," which is generated by the gap between his desire to be part of universal (European) culture, and a national reality of backwardness. These are two forces in continuous tension as well as two conflicting temporalities: the historical time of universal civilization and the permanence and immutability of the Indian:

> It must be supposed that the Indian has had an influence on the soul of the other Mexican groups (the mestizos and whites living in the city); of course, because he has mixed his blood with them. (...) The Indian is like those substances called "catalytic," which provoke chemical reactions just by their presence. No Mexican thing can be subtracted from this influence, because the indigenous substance (masa indígena) is a thick element that covers everything in the country. (Ramos 1934, 78)

The Indian, then, is a passive but ubiquitous presence: a series of primitive traits indelibly inscribed at the very heart of the mestizo national subject. Indeed, Ramos calls it "a ghost within the Mexican" (Ramos 1934, 65). The inescapability of the Indian is more forcefully expressed in the figure of the pelado, the stereotypically uncouth and violent lower class man of Mexico City, who has lost his rural anchors but is not quite at home in urban modernity, which for Ramos stands as the exemplary Mexican (Ramos 1934, 71–72).[5] Ramos' representation of the pelado as a racialized urban other, an unmoored Indian, resonated with a history of racialization of class in Mexico and, more specifically, a racialization of the poor in the urban context (expressed in such iconic figures as the lépero in the nineteenth century). Yet the point is that in Ramos's text the pelado appeared as a racialized category of distinction, deeply intertwined with class, to situate oneself and others visa-vis the specter of the Indian. While for Ramos, surely, this specter was more clearly present in poor mestizos, his "bourgeois Mexican" could never be entirely sure of his position as a modern subject. The Indian within could appear at any moment, for example, during bouts of anger. In other words, Ramos' text divulged longstanding elite and middle-class anxieties about a slippage between the Indian in the other and the Indian in the self. Therefore, far from being an unambiguous category that entailed a straightforward process of whitening or Europeanization, as often posited in recent arguments about mestizaje and racism, the post-revolutionary mestizo was a constitutively split subject, continually oscillating between the two conflicting yet ambivalent temporalities of the Indian and the European.

## Beyond Mestizaje

As I argued in the previous section, in some post-revolutionary nationalist writings, the mestizo/pelado represented the not-yet-civilized urban masses. However, it is important to consider that he was also a central part of el pueblo that triumphantly emerged from the Revolution and, as such, he was the subject of a modernizing state under whose protection and guidance he would eventually domesticate his Indian atavisms and become a full-grown modern subject (Lomnitz 2001, 54). In other words, the mestizo/pelado was at the same time a racialized other *and* a paradigmatic element of the national collective. Let us remember that the post-revolutionary state erected itself as the representative of the revolutionary (mestizo) pueblo—that is, the popular masses who had revolted against oppression—and based its legitimacy on its capacity to mediate between multiple group interests and class-based demands. It governed through what Aaron Ansell and Ken Mitchell (2011) call "corporate clientelism," dividing society into three corporate "sectors" (peasant, worker, and the popular sector) with the state as the ultimate patron. Indeed, as Mauricio Tenorio Trillo has argued, mestizaje was central to post-revolutionary Mexico's particular form of the 20th century welfare state. That is to say, beyond its intellectual history, the social history of mestizaje is the history of state corporatism, of popular education, public health, land rights and (partial and conditioned) social security (Tenorio Trillo 2009, 61).

As the post-revolutionary regime cohered and evolved after the 1920s, the racial content—and the racial anxieties—that had suffused debates about the mestizo national subject in the late 19th and early 20th centuries gradually lost centrality. The Indian became the privileged domain of anthropology, while the mestizo became an unmarked, unmentioned, taken for granted category, synonymous with the Mexican. Such disavowal of the racial referents of mestizaje, combined with the post-revolutionary state's capacity to integrate different class interests into its corporate structures and its social programs, made a national "we" viable in the post-revolutionary era. In nationalist discourses mestizaje entailed not only the incorporation of the Indian into the mestizo national subject, but also of the criollo (European) Mexican (who could not legitimately posit himself as superior), as well as the disparagement of public displays of excessive luxury and wealth. In Mauricio Tenorio's words, mestizaje was a "cult to the average," or the halfway (Tenorio Trillo 2009, 51). All of this provided legitimacy to the idea that "we are all mestizo,"

despite entrenched class inequalities and pervasive racialized discrimination. In other words, profound and persistent injustices notwithstanding,
post-revolutionary nationalism held the promise that inequalities would,
if not disappear, at least be reduced and that *we*, Mexicans, would finally
arrive at the future. It is clear that the state never fully realized its promises of incorporation and that the poor remained the majority of the urban
and rural populations despite a period of economic growth and expansion of
the middle classes between the 1940s and the 1970s. However, the crucial
point is that in this political and ideological context, the poor underwent
a significant process of both discursive and material inclusion through the
state's corporate structures; they were not only racialized others, but crucial
members of the nation.[6]

Like many other countries, Mexico began a process of neoliberalization
in the years that followed the debt crisis of 1982. Alongside a move from a
protectionist to a free market economy, which included a process of dereg-
ulation and privatization of state industries, of austerity and job precarity,
important changes began to take place in the national imaginary. The 1982
crisis furthered the crisis of legitimacy of the post-revolutionary regime and
its "corporate clientelism." In this context, the Revolution ceased to function as a source of legitimacy for the state and its policies, and was gradually
re-signified—in an expanding liberal public sphere—as inseparable from the
state's authoritarianism and corruption (Rousseau 2010). The *pueblo* too was
resignified in this new context: from being the legitimate national collective
and the subject of the social rights promised by the Revolution, it gradually
came to be represented as a residue from the past, a collection of passive
and dependent individuals created by the post-revolutionary regime. This
is because neoliberalization also entailed the resurgence and resignification
of liberal vocabularies about citizenship and democracy, the state and civil
society, as well as a recasting of poverty as an individual problem—related to
lack of effort, or to moral deficiency—and decoupled from inequality. As I will
explain in more detail below, the liberal narrative of the country's democratization celebrated the country's gradual move from clientelism and corporatism to a mature civil society and citizenship; it celebrated the replacement of
the old dependant *pueblo* by an expanding middle class.

Contrary to these triumphalist narratives, as Esquivel has demonstrated,
while income inequality has decreased since the 1990s, overall inequality has
grown: we face "two contradictory events: income per capita has increased

but poverty has stagnated in the country. This is because growth is concentrated in the highest strata of the distribution" (Esquivel Hernández 2015, 7). According to Esquivel, the top 1% concentrates 21% of all national income, while the top 10% concentrates 64.4 % of all national wealth. Moreover, the mega rich in Mexico increased by 32% between 2007 and 2012, while in the rest of the world they decreased by 0.3% in the same period (Esquivel Hernández 2015, 7). At the same time, Esquivel underlines the extreme growth in the income and wealth of the superrich, a handful of families who benefited from the privatization of state industries that began in the late 1980s and early 1990s (Esquivel Hernández 2015, 20). Alongside such astronomical concentration of wealth, social mobility has been foreclosed for the majority of the population. The country has experienced an explosive growth of unemployment, precarious employment and the proliferation of so called informality, especially in urban contexts, as well as a spectacular increase of insecurity and violence.

It is clear, then, that Mexico's (old and new) elites were the main beneficiaries of the breakdown of the post-revolutionary regime. In addition to growing inequality, the expansion of the super-rich brought about new and extravagant displays of wealth and luxury. In other words, the extremely wealthy elites increased not only in size and capital, but also in their penchant for publicly flaunting their status, money and power. This is not to say that post-revolutionary elites were not prone to boasting, but as Ricardo Raphael has argued in a book about this phenomenon, "they would have been unmercifully judged by a political regime that, on its façade, claimed to be revolutionary and a guarantor of social justice" (Raphael 2014, 26). Both state and society, in other words, imposed some restraints so that the elites "tried to keep the exhibition of their enormous buying capacity, their eccentricities and their excesses behind the palace walls" (Raphael 2014, 26–27). This is no longer the case.

Considering this significantly altered ideological, political, social, and economic landscape, the question that arises is whether we can assume—as many do—that the racial ideology of mestizaje continues to function today as it did before. In other words, does mestizaje as an ideology and a set of discourses, practices, and policies that served to unify the national collective during post-revolutionary nationalism continue to function in its aftermath? Does the mestizo continue to be the ideal national subject? Not much has been written about these questions in the literature about racism in Mexico, but there have been some attempts to grapple with them. Consider, for example, Rafael Lemus' reflection on the fate of the mestizo within neoliberal ideologies in a recent book about Mexican neoliberalism. He argues that already by the early 1990s, it was clear that the post-revolutionary nationalist discourse did not reflect the new political rationality of the regime:

> Even more cumbersome for neoliberal administrations was the national subject, the Mexican, which revolutionary nationalism had created and placed at the center of its narrative. That Mexican (. . .) is not, by far, the entrepreneurial subject that neoliberalism already by then required. On the contrary, the singularity of that national-revolutionary subject, its identitarian difference, is precisely being and not being modern. (Lemus 2021, 65)

On a similar note, Lomnitz argued that in the 1980s certain fissures within Mexican nationalism were already evident. Specifically, he identified an increasing disconnect between nationalism and modernity. Nationalism, he wrote, had moved "from being a tool for achieving modernity to being a marker of *dismodernity* and a form of protest against the (. . .) reorganization of capitalist production" (Lomnitz 2001, 111). In other words, Lomnitz argued that while the emerging leftist opposition parties had started to appropriate post-revolutionary nationalism as a discourse against neoliberalization, liberal ideologues and neoliberal politicians saw it as a hindrance to overcome, a burden from the past. Take as an example an article by Jorge Castañeda and Hector Aguilar Camín published in the magazine *Nexos* in 2009 titled "A Future for Mexico," later released as a book. Following the genre of the manifesto, the text is an exhortation for the country to finally look towards the future by overcoming the legacies of the Revolution:

> Mexico is imprisoned by its history. Inherited ideas, sentiments and interests prevent it from swiftly moving towards the place that its citizens yearn. The history accumulated in the head and sentiments of the nation— in its laws, in its habits and fantasies—obstruct the path to the future (...) (Castañeda and Aguilar Camín 2009)

The text does not mention mestizaje or the mestizo explicitly, but it seems safe to assume that both are part of the burdens and "fantasies" of the

Revolution. Another article published in *Nexos*, which also became a book, titled "Clasemedieros" and authored by Luis de la Calle and Luis Rubio, further illuminates the fate of the pueblo mestizo in neoliberal discourses (de la Calle and Rubio 2010). The text's central argument is that Mexico is no longer poor but has become a majority middle-class country. The authors define this middle class as aspirational, hardworking, invested in education, autonomous, and—crucially—the opposite of the corporatist subjects of the *ancien regime*. While the latter exploit their assigned privileges, the former are known for their "quotidian assumption of risks," and their orientation towards the future. Therefore, the authors claim, "in the current moment democracy fits naturally with the qualities of the middle class."

To sum up, I have argued that the post-revolutionary mestizo was a highly ambivalent figure, not a straightforward category of identification or a clear process of whitening. Mestizo was synonymous with Mexican—that is, not Indian—but nonetheless, the mestizo was haunted by the latter's specter. Moreover, in some nationalist writings, mestizo referred to the poor urban masses (those supposedly more clearly traversed by the specter of the Indian) who had lost their rural moorings but were not yet fully civilized, modern subjects. At the same time, the mestizo was the subject and the object of a protectionist and modernizing state, which promised to transform him through corporatist protections and rights. However, as I have also argued, political and intellectual elites started to abandon the premises and promises of the Revolution from the 1980s, with the unraveling of the post-revolutionary regime. In the aftermath of this regime, mestizaje ceased to be a hegemonic narrative. Instead of being the ideal national subject, the pueblo mestizo was resignified as retrograde and dependent, an obstacle to be overcome. As an inherently ambivalent figure in need of state tutelage and protection, the mestizo appeared as the opposite of the upstanding, middle-class individual that neoliberal ideologues envisioned as the ideal subject of the new era. As I will explain in more detail in the following section, being a crucial element of the disgraced pueblo mestizo, the urban poor did not find a legitimate place in this reimagined national collective; they remained, as racialized others, at its margins.[7]

## "Whiteness" and the Afterlives of Mestizaje

It is in light of the changes in national imaginaries, wealth distribution, and inequality I have briefly outlined above that I now return to the #PoderPrieto

(#PrietoPower) hashtag with which I opened this chapter. I noted that the category of prieto, as mobilized in this social media campaign, appears to have a certain fixedness, as if it referred to a more or less identifiable color that, moreover, is clearly different from blanco; the latter is a site of racialized privilege ("privilegio blanco"), the former of racialized oppression. This particular campaign originated among actors, aimed at the film and advertising industries, where a somewhat rigid, and evidently racist, chromatic, and phenotypic scale predominates. However, as I said, the campaign took a life of its own and moved well beyond specific grievances against these industries to denounce racism in Mexican society as a whole. As such, it echoed other recent instances where race and racism have become contentious topics in social and other digital media.

As in the #PoderPrieto campaign, these other instances, too, mobilize skin color as a central element of racialization. Echoing some academic discourses, these renditions of racism condemn mestizaje as a racist ideology that privileges "whiteness" while continuing to deny that racism exists (Navarrete 2016). But as I argued previously, post-revolutionary ideologues were ambivalent towards mestizaje. While they strived to distance themselves from the specter of the Indian—that is, the racialized negative traits that traversed this category of identification—they did not identify themselves as white. How, then, did the ambivalent terrain of mestizaje become so neatly divided into clearly identifiable groups? And how did these differences get so clearly mapped onto skin color? How, moreover, did "whiteness" become a meaningful category of (non) identification?

Scholars of racism in Mexico started to use "whiteness" (in English) as an analytic category in the last decade. Moreno Figueroa, for example, conceptualizes whiteness as a site of privilege, "a core structuring motif" that has been obscured by mestizaje (Moreno Figueroa 2010, 388). She argues that whitening embodies "the process of homogenization represented by mestizaje," and analyzes how different people perceive and experience what she calls "mestizaje logics" in their everyday lives (Moreno Figueroa 2010, 390). At the same time, scholars writing in Spanish have drawn on Bolivar Echeverría's notions of "blancura" and "blanquitud" (both of which could be translated as whiteness) to differentiate between, as Forssell Méndez explains, a "racial identity defined as the phenotypic expression of a Western body" and "the habitus of (western) modernity" (Forssell Méndez 2019). While these works conceptualize whiteness as a position of privilege within

Mexico's racial hierarchy, and not as a chromatic or phenotypic feature, they nonetheless gesture towards discussions happening in places dominated by biology-based racial ideologies such as the United States, where skin color and phenotype are central to processes of racialization.

At the same time, quantitative sociologists, demographers and economists have introduced skin color as a variable in studies about racial discrimination and inequality in Mexico. The book *Pigmentocracies* was the first to introduce skin color, and the category of blanco, as a variable for understanding ethnicity and race (Telles 2014). Using a pantone with hues ranging from white to dark brown, researchers asked interviewees to position themselves within it (researchers also positioned interviewees within the pantone). Later, in 2016, the National Institute of Statistics and Geography (INEGI) used this pantone in a national survey about "intergenerational mobility" within Mexican households, which was later analyzed by different scholars alongside other categories of identification, such as self-adscription to different ethno-racial categories (white, mestizo, indigenous, afro-Mexican) or use of indigenous languages. Correlating these categories with educational attainment, occupation, and income, among others, some of these studies have concluded that those who position themselves in the darker hues of the pantone occupy the worst positions in Mexican society (Solís and Güémez 2021). However, they have also shown that skin color is rather slippery, that blanco is not a very significant category of identification and that racialized discrimination is particularly acute against people who identify themselves as indigenous and afro-Mexican.

Fragments of these scholarly arguments—especially the notion of skin color as determinant of opportunities and life trajectories—have circulated in a multiplicity of sites and registers, from websites dedicated to racism to digital panels and television programs where experts and activists discuss racism, from newspaper columns and opinion pieces to videos, infographics, and books written for the wider public. Without the nuances of some of the aforementioned scholarly works, and overlapping with idioms taken from struggles against racism in the United States, such as "white privilege" (privilegio blanco) or "black [here prieto] power," these settings mobilize color as a reified category that, alone, seems to explain racial discrimination in Mexico. Consider, for example, an infographic that circulated widely in social media based on a scholarly report that analyzed the INEGI survey that I mentioned above (Solís, Güémez, and Lorenzo Holm 2019), which asked people to self-identify their skin color within a color palette. Titled "The Privilege of Being Whitexican" (Forssell Méndez 2020),[8] (see Figure 1) this infographic is divided into three columns, each explaining an aspect of "white privilege." The first, illustrated with three circles—one pinkish, one light brown and one dark brown—claims that "1 out of 3 people with white skin belong to the richest 25% in Mexico." The second column, using the same circles, asserts that 35% of women and 17% of men with "dark skin tones are at risk of not having a primary education." The third column displays two female silhouettes, one pinkish, the other dark brown, and asserts that for "white women it is easier to get a prestigious and well remunerated job." All the analytic complexities of the report have been lost, there is no explanation of what these colors refer to, or of how the report reached these conclusions. Echoing arguments from the United States, the message is that white skin in Mexico equals privilege. And yet, while the infographic purports to illustrate how skin color is a central variable explaining inequality, the reification of color actually erases class from public discussions about racial discrimination.

Class, is conspicuously absent in #PoderPrieto and other similar campaigns, where prieto appears not only as an independent category, but also as single-handedly explaining discrimination and oppression. Therefore, as I mentioned before, the hashtag proposes to re-appropriate and resignify prieto in a positive light. The social media account (Instagram and Twitter) @poderprieto, created following the #PoderPrieto campaign, attempts to do just that. Alongside announcements of events related to racism, links to news on the topic, and highlights of a variety of indigenous and afro-Mexican movements and struggles, it publishes highly aestheticized and glamorized pictures with the hashtag #PrietosChingones (#BadassPrietos). Some are portraits of hip artists, intellectuals, athletes, and other prominent public figures accompanied by texts that detail their accomplishments: an actor that starred in recent blockbuster movies, a trans human rights activist who created a shelter for transwomen, an Olympic medalist. Others are pictures of indigenous women donning traditional clothing, also accompanied by texts explaining why they are awesome: a young Zapotec rapper, a Raramuri runner, an indigenous rights activist. Conspicuously absent are pictures of ordinary indigenous persons, as well as pictures, mentions, or even references to the historically racialized urban poor—the majority of whom are dark-skinned—that crowd the streets and public spaces of Mexican cities. It is as if poor urban Mexicans—the old pueblo mestizo of the Revolution—cannot partake of the resignification of prieto—as if they cannot claim the position of #PrietosChingones.

Reflecting on contemporary racial politics in the United States, Dawson and Ming Francis remind us that "racial orders change over time as the political economy and the institutional context of race change" (Dawson and Francis 2016). They argue that a neoliberal racial order has emerged in the United States, where "racial divisions have become magnified in economic policies and civil society," while the state claims to have become post-racial (Dawson and Francis 2016). All contextual differences notwithstanding, these insights invite us to analyze how processes of neoliberalization have transformed the racial logics of mestizaje in Mexico. What I want to suggest, then, and in contrast with many scholars, is that it is precisely the undoing of mestizaje as both dominant ideology and state project—not its permanence—over the past few decades that has created the conditions for both the emergence of novel forms of racialized distinction and discrimination, and for the proliferation of new ways of thinking and talking about race and racism in Mexico's public sphere. In other words, more than mestizaje, what informs these forms and languages is what we can conceptualize as its afterlives. This term refers to the persistence of the racial imaginaries and anxieties at the heart of mestizaje—what I have called the specter of the Indian—without the post-revolutionary state's promises of integration, social justice, and redistribution, which gave meaningful content to the idea that "we" are all mestizo.

It is in this context that certain elites unabashedly flaunt their wealth and privilege in an expanding public sphere, especially in social media platforms such as TikTok, Instagram or Twitter, where they post videos of extravagant parties, expensive shoe collections or luxurious trips abroad. They even proudly—though often also ironically—identify themselves as white(xican). It is also in this same context that middle- and upper-class Mexicans can position themselves as victims of racialized oppression together—and seemingly at the same level—with indigenous and afro-Mexican populations, effectively erasing class differences and the severe historical and contemporary marginalization of those populations. And it is in this same context that other historically racialized groups, like the urban poor, are excluded from discussions about racism. While the latter continue to be racialized as backward—as wearing, as it were, the specter of the Indian on their sleeves—they are portrayed as dependent and residual subjects.

In the same article I mentioned previously (Lomnitz 1996, 58), Lomnitz noted another change or fissure in the national imaginary, namely, "a growing horror toward the masses," which he in part attributed to the "tremendous growth of urban unemployment and crime" in the aftermath of the 1980s crisis. In my own work I have explored how the explosion of so-called informal street activities since the 1980s in major cities, and most notably in Mexico City, has prompted widespread condemnation in the liberal public sphere and beyond. I have examined different processes of urban renewal in central areas of Mexico City—from the revitalization of the historical center, to the renovation of a mayor bus hub, to the installation of parking meters—that have entailed the (often forcible) removal of street workers in the name of rescuing public space for "all."

A wide variety of actors participating in these projects, including urban planners, experts, private investors, neighborhood activists, and journalists, have represented the urban poor who take to the streets to work—from street vendors to informal parking attendants—as obstacles to be removed; as belonging to powerful and corrupt mafias; as residues from the clientelist structures of the post-revolutionary regime; and as dirty, violent, and even criminal figures. In such representations, dirtiness (street workers are often called "pigs," "filthy," "disgusting") appears as constitutive of who *they* are, as something akin to their essence. Moreover, these representations render street workers as lacking capacity to change, to become civilized; they render them as incommensurable others and thus as not being part of any legitimate (urban, national) "we." The point is not that these racialized representations of the urban poor—the pelados of old—are new, but rather that whereas the post-revolutionary national project sought to elevate them through their integration into the corporate structures of the regime, neoliberal discourses and policies render them as uncontainable, dangerous, and residual. This happens in at least two ways: they are excluded from neoliberal economic policies and they are perceived as the opposite of the upstanding, middle-class individuals of neoliberal imaginations.

## Conclusion

The social, economic, political, and cultural changes brought about by more than four decades of neoliberalization have necessarily transformed Mexico's national imaginary. While a new hegemonic national narrative has not emerged, it is misleading to explain contemporary idioms of distinction, including racializing languages, as the result of a seemingly unchanged mestizaje, understood both as ideology and as state project. In contrast with such an explanation, in this chapter I have suggested that the reification of skin color in contemporary public discussions of racism and racial discrimination—evident in the #PoderPrieto campaign—can be understood as an effect of mestizaje's undoing, not of its permanence, in the context of neoliberalization. An effect of such reification has been the erasure of class distinctions and differences from those discussions, when in fact processes of racialization in Mexico have been historically articulated with class.

This class–race link is evident in the subtle yet pervasive idioms of racialized difference that traversed and continue to traverse quotidian interactions.[9] More than referring to "race" mainly as a set of immutable biological traits or to "color" as a clearly recognizable physical, chromatic feature, these idioms are indexes of one's status as a modern subject. They point to a series of racialized, moral, and aesthetic attributes associated with modernity, from intelligence to responsibility or beauty, as well as to one's class position. By contrast, the reification of color positions discussions of racism closer to biology-based racial frameworks that assign particular and unchanging traits and colors to particular races. Here the question of (linguistic, analytical, ideological) translation is crucial: prieto does not easily translate as "brown" and güero is not equivalent to white. What gets lost in translation, then, is precisely how the specter of the Indian that haunted the mestizo national subject referred to much more than color, indexing one's capacity to become a civilized, modern subject. It is precisely the mestizo as pelado—as not only a racialized other but a legitimate member of the national collective—that has been erased from contemporary discussions of race.

## Notes

1   I use these terms in Spanish to highlight the problem of translation or, in other words, the non-correspondence of terms that index class and racialized difference in Mexico with English terms that refer to racialized physical attributes. Prieto and moreno usually refer to dark phenotypes (the former can in some contexts be used as an offensive term, that is to say, to disparage someone for being too dark). Blanco is the color white.

2   The arguments in this and the next sections appear in a more extensive form in the (Leal 2016).

3   Ana María Alonso has argued that the racialized identities of Mexican elites—and of Latin American elites more generally—cannot be reduced to "European" or "white,"

as they have in turn been racialized as "non-European" in Europe and the United States (Alonso 2004).

4 Ramos was one of a number of (male) writers, philosophers and public intellectuals who, throughout the twentieth century, wrote essays that sought to define the essence of "the Mexican."

5 For a more in-depth analysis of the pelado see: (Bartra 1992).

6 A caveat is in order here. What I am lumping together under the term "post-revolutionary regime" was, to be sure, a heterogeneous, malleable, ever changing and adapting set of ideologies, discourses, practices, institutions, policies, individuals and groups spanning several decades of the 20th Century. But despite this heterogeneity, and its different permutations, Mexico's post-revolutionary state was part of the larger historical context of the twentieth century social state, where the latter's legitimacy depended on its capacity (or promise) to guarantee the wellbeing of all citizens through the collectivization of risk, social solidarity and redistribution.

7 The seemingly hegemonic neoliberal narrative of Mexico's democratization—together with its displacement of el pueblo as the legitimate national collective—was dramatically disrupted when the center-left Andrés Manuel López Obrador won the country's presidency by a landslide in 2018.

8 This term, which combines "white" and "Mexican," started circulating in social media in the early 2000s. Lacking a clear meaning, it has become a popular, and somewhat satirical, slang to disparage privileged (white) Mexicans who enjoy flaunting their power and status in discriminatory ways. For a critical discussion of the term see: (Forssell Méndez 2020).

9 Examples include popular sayings like "no se me quita lo indio" (I cannot get rid of the Indian within) that are used when one exhibits ignorance, rudeness or backwardness. There is also the category of "naco" (a recent variation of pelado), a pejorative term used in reference to the urban lower classes or those who, despite being affluent, exhibit vulgarity and ignorance. There are aesthetic categories that divide "beautiful" and "ugly" people, such as "he is handsome, blond and blue-eyed" or "she's morena but pretty;" and the elusive category güero, a common form of address in public space, which, depending on context, can refer to a blond person, or to someone with perceived fair skin, and is often associated with relative affluence.

## References

Alonso, Ana María. 2004. "Conforming Disconformity." *Cultural Anthropology* 19 (4): 459–90. https://doi.org/10.1525/can.2004.19.4.459.

Ansell, Aaron, and Ken Mitchell. 2011. "Models of Clientelism and Policy Change: The Case of Conditional Cash Transfer Programmes in Mexico and Brazil." *Bulletin of Latin American Research* 30 (3): 298–312.

Bartra, Roger. 1992. *The Cage of Melancholy: Identity and Metamorphosis in the Mexican Character*. New Brunswick, N.J.: Rutgers University Press.

Cadena, Marisol de la. 2009. "Introducción." In *Formaciones de indianidad: articulaciones raciales, mestizaje y nación en América Latina*, 7–34. Envión. https://books.google.com/books?id=igI7AQAAIAAJ.

Calle, Luis de la, and Luis Rubio. 2010. "Clasemedieros." *Nexos*, May 1, 2010. https://www.nexos.com.mx/?p=13742.

Castañeda, Jorge, and Héctor Aguilar Camín. 2009. "Un futuro para México." *Nexos*, November 1, 2009. https://www.nexos.com.mx/?p=13374.

Castellanos Guerrero, Alicia. 2000. "Antropología y racismo en México." *Desacatos* 4: 53–79. https://doi.org/10.29340/4.1234.

Ceron-Anaya, Hugo. 2019. *Privilege at Play*. Global and Comparative Ethnography. Oxford, New York: Oxford University Press.

Dawson, Michael C., and Megan Ming Francis. 2016. "Black Politics and the Neoliberal Racial Order." *Public Culture* 28 (1 (78)): 23–62. https://doi.org/10.1215/08992363-3325004.

Esquivel Hernández, Gerardo. 2015. "Desigualdad Extrema En México. Concentración Del Poder Económico y Político." *OXFAM México*. https://dds.cepal.org/redesoc/publicacion?id=4045.

Forssell Méndez, Alfonso. 2019. "Entre blancos y güeros. Desigualdad y privilegio en el discurso popular." *Nexos*, November 24, 2019. https://cultura.nexos.com.mx/entre-blancos-y-gueros-desigualdad-y-privilegio-en-el-discurso-popular/.

Forssell Méndez, Alfonso. 2020. "Whitexican: hacia una definición crítica." *Nexos*, July 2020. https://cultura.nexos.com.mx/whitexican-hacia-una-definicion-critica/.

Hoffmann, Odile. 2006. "Negros y afromestizos en México: viejas y nuevas lecturas de un mundo olvidado." *Revista mexicana de sociología* 68 (1): 103–35.

Iturriaga, Eugenia. 2020. "Desencriptar el racismo mexicano: mestizaje y blanquitud." *Desacatos*. 64 (December): 148–63. https://doi.org/10.29340/64.2339.

Leal, Alejandra. 2016. "'You Cannot Be Here': The Urban Poor and the Specter of the Indian in Neoliberal Mexico City." *The Journal of Latin American and Caribbean Anthropology* 21 (3): 539–59. https://doi.org/10.1111/JLCA.12196.

Lemus, Rafael. 2021. *Breve historia de nuestro neoliberalismo: Poder y cultura en México*. Penguin Random House Grupo Editorial México.

Lewis, Laura A. 2003. *Hall of Mirrors: Power, Witchcraft, and Caste in Colonial Mexico*. https://doi.org/10.1215/9780822385158.

Lomnitz, Claudio. 1996. "Fissures in Contemporary Mexican Nationalism." *Public Culture* 9 (1): 55–68. https://doi.org/10.1215/08992363-9-1-55.

Lomnitz, Claudio. 2001. *Deep Mexico, Silent Mexico: An Anthropology of Nationalism*. U of Minnesota Press.

Martínez-Casas, Regina, Emilio Saldívar, and Christina A. Sue. 2014. "The Different Faces of Mestizaje: Ethnicity and Race in Mexico." In *Pigmentocracies: Ethnicity, Race, and Color in Latin America*, edited by Edward Telles, 36–80. University of North Carolina Press.

Moreno Figueroa, Mónica G. 2010. "Distributed Intensities: Whiteness, Mestizaje and the Logics of Mexican Racism." *Ethnicities* 10 (3): 387–401. https://doi.org/10.1177/1468796810372305.

Moreno Figueroa, Mónica G., and Emiko Saldívar Tanaka. 2016. "'We Are Not Racists, We Are Mexicans.'" *Critical Sociology* 42 (4–5): 515–33. https://doi.org/10.1177/0896920515591296.

Navarrete, Federico. 2016. *México racista: Una denuncia*. Mexico: Grijalbo.

Poole, Deborah. 1997. *Vision, Race, and Modernity: A Visual Economy of the Andean Image World. Vision, Race, and Modernity*. Princeton University Press. https://doi.org/10.1515/9780691234649.

Ramos, Samuel. 1934. *El perfil del hombre y la cultura en México*. Mexico: Imprenta Mundial.

Raphael, Ricardo. 2014. *Mirreynato: la otra desigualdad*. 1st edition. 1 online resource (247 pages) vols. Mexico, D.F.: Temas 'de hoy. https://www.overdrive.com/search?q=F4FC8C73-C7F0-405B-A9E9-80351BFDF9C2.

Rousseau, Isabelle. 2010. "Las Nuevas Élites y Su Proyecto Modernizador." In *Del Nacionalismo al Neoliberalismo, 1940–1994*, edited by Elisa Servín, 242–94. https://www.digitaliapublishing.com/a/64189/del-nacionalismo-al-neoliberalismo--1940-1994.

Saldaña Tejeda, Abril. 2013. "Racismo, proximidad y mestizaje: el caso de las mujeres en el servicio doméstico en México." *Trayectorias* 15 (37): 73–89.

Solís, Patricio, and Braulio Güémez. 2021. "Características Étnico-Raciales y Desigualdad de Oportunidades Económicas En México." *Estudios Demográficos y Urbanos* 36 (106): 255–89.

Solís, Patricio, Braulio Güémez, and Virginia Lorenzo Holm. 2019. *Por Mi Raza Hablará La Desigualdad. Efectos de Las Características Étnico-Raciales En La Desigualdad de Oportunidades En México*. Mexico City: Oxfam México.

Telles, Edward. 2014. *Pigmentocracies. Ethnicity, Race, and Color in Latin America*. Chapel Hill: The University of North Carolina Press.

Tenorio Trillo, Mauricio. 2009. "DEL MESTIZAJE A UN SIGLO DE ANDRÉS MOLINA ENRÍQUEZ." In *En Busca de Molina Enríquez*, edited by Emilio Kourí, 1st ed., 156:33–64. Cien Años de Los Grandes Problemas Nacionales. El Colegio de Mexico. https://doi.org/10.2307/j.ctvhn0b22.4.

# CHAPTER 6

# Mestizaje in Mexico and the Specter of Capital

Alfonso Forssell Méndez Translation by Ellen Jones

Haven't they taken your land? Your parents' land and their grandparents' land? Aren't you victims too? —José Revueltas, *El luto humano* (Human Mourning)

## Introduction

Mestizaje has often been seen as the basis of a *nationalist* identity built and reproduced by the actors and cultural institutions of the Mexican state at the level of discourse, symbols, and representations, with the aim of homogenizing the population and hiding endemic racism behind a mask of inclusion. Within the framework of "racial capitalism," which has emerged in recent years in projects in the global North which highlight the production of difference alongside the production of capital (Ralph and Singhal 2019), no one has yet examined a racial project such as Mexican mestizaje—which does not seek to differentiate but rather to homogenize the population—in the light of capitalist logics. Faced with this gap in our knowledge—and with the urgent need to more effectively understand and combat Mexico's particular kind of racism—this chapter seeks to broaden and refine the interpretation of mestizaje from the perspective of the elements that make up the backbone of historical materialism: land ownership, modes of production, and class relations. Using these as a starting point, this article will seek to understand mestizaje as a specific form of capitalist social relations in Mexico rather than merely as a consciousness deliberately established by the Mexican nation-state. This will make it possible to trace its material origins and to find the figure of the modern mestizo in the working class by calling attention to the "peculiarity" of the conditions of their birth and their praxis. Once these premises have been established, the chapter will explore how, through the national bourgeoisie[1] and its state party's intervention in the political economy, mestizaje formed a postrevolutionary democratic ideology that sought to legitimize and naturalize the laws of capitalist production; to integrate ethnically diverse populations into a system based on wage labor; to corporatize the fledgling mestizo's class independence; and to disguise the bourgeoisie's status as a class by universalizing its interests, identifying them with those of Mexican society at large. In parallel, the chapter will discuss the limitations of critiques of mestizaje by the main schools of antiracist thought, in order to apprehend the logics of racism in relation to class in Mexico. This chapter shows a materialist view on mestizaje to be a necessary appendix if we are to understand Mexican racial capitalism from an emancipatory perspective that transcends affiliation to specific identity groups.

## The Limits of Traditional Critique of Racism and Mestizaje

Until very recently, the topic of racism was an anthropological rarity in Mexico, drowned out by the influence of the post-racial identity of mestizaje (Moreno Figueroa 2010) and only belatedly brought onto the national scene in 1994 with the Zapatistas' uprising, whose demands for autonomy and justice exposed the cracks in the country's feigned national unity. As the critical anthropologist Bonfil Batalla (1989) shows, racism seemed to be a problem that specifically concerned and affected indigenous populations, especially their relationship with a *nationalist* state devoted to internal colonialism. Among the Mexican nation's majority, a racially coherent and homogenous population, the main recognizable form of discrimination was based on social position. Officially, mestizaje is understood as the racial and cultural mixing between Spanish and indigenous people that produced an in-between race: the Mexican race. In academia, on the other hand, mestizaje tends to be formulated as a project intimately connected with the creation of the nation-state, whose foundation was the Europeanizing nationalism taught by criollos and their learned acolytes (Araujo 2015; Acevedo Rodrigo 2015) who understood "mestizo culture" in opposition to "indigenous culture" (Ruz 1997). According to this version, the ideology emerged during the

Porfiriato (1876–1911) from the minds of intellectuals such as Pimentel and Riva Palacio, who were looking for a solution to the "indigenous problem." It wouldn't be until 1909 that Andrés Molina Enríquez would formulate the discourse of mestizaje as a key national issue in *Los grandes problemas nacionales* (2016). Its later consolidation and institutionalization as an assimilationist project would be led by postrevolutionary ideologues such as Manuel Gamio—the so-called father of Mexican anthropology—and José Vasconcelos, who would give it narrative consecration in his magnum opus *La raza cósmica* and assure its pedagogical reproduction through the recently founded Ministry of Public Education. These trends would converge in the state's indigenist cultural policies of the mid-twentieth century. Seen thus, the so-called project of mestizaje is inexorably linked to the popular spirit of the state party born from the Revolution, and is, in essence, the single framework within which the history of Mexican racism has been analyzed. Recently, in part because of the "decolonial turn" (Castro-Gómez and Grosfoguel 2007) and Latin America's growing academic and cultural integration with the United States (Wacquant and Bourdieu 1999), in Mexico the epistemic dams preventing the discussion of racism as a phenomenon of national dimensions have been pulled down.

For this reason, one of the main axes of antiracist criticism—whose broad discursive arc brings together decolonial and anticolonial arguments, and even liberal identity politics—has been articulated in a kind of counter-pedagogy of mestizaje that seeks to expose it as a racial ideology and a nationalist project. In fact, by pulling it apart it becomes clear that Mexico's entire social hierarchy is organized according to a continuum of pigmentations that contradicts the supposed homogeneity on which it is based. Seen in this light, it also becomes clear that the closer you get to the top of the social pyramid, the lighter that pigmentation tends to get. Such a patent feature of Mexican society, which has been established in an unusual—although symptomatic—way through recent empirical studies of racism such as the one carried out by Oxfam (Solís et al. 2019), has evolved into a critical reading of mestizaje that considers the processes of whitening—not just in relation to the white body but also as an organizing principle of modern subjectivity (Echeverría 2010)—as an inherent aspect of its dynamics (Moreno Figueroa 2010). According to its critics, the official version of mestizaje, imagined as a cultural encounter on equal terms, is based on Euro-American civilizing processes (Bonfil Batalla 1989).

However, it is possible to argue that the traditional critique of mestizaje falls into racial reductionism. By this I mean that it succumbs to the circularity that affects major antiracist discourses more broadly: in order to escape its equalizing framework, it recreates a logic of difference from what is outside it, based on a notion of stable identity that does not account for the social and political contradictions within. In this sense, just as the myth of mestizaje does at a national level, antiracist critique of mestizaje takes for granted affinities and coherence at a group level on the basis of a trait that remains essentially the same throughout the class structure: race (understood in sociological terms).[2] Race brandished as political identity, Stuart Hall suggests (2007), goes from being a marker of socially constructed difference to a sameness that lacks internal differentiation. In this sense, race-centered critique atomizes mestizaje and strips it of its "universality" in order to offer only partial relief: to assume other displaced and decentralized positions constructed within the racial paradigm. As an antiracist tactic, it pulls apart a hegemonic ideology that racially disguises the ruling classes in order to make space for other identity-based forms of situating oneself and resisting. But as a strategy seeking transformation it soon finds its limitations, because it cannot transcend the binary structure of "mestizaje versus everyone else." It remains established, therefore, within its scheme, without troubling or interrupting its class matrix. In this way it yields to strategic essentialism, as Spivak termed it, which implies not the overcoming of but rather a yielding to what is understood as a mestizo social body. Strategic antiracism therefore falls into an apparently unresolvable contradiction in which categories emerging from colonialism and slavery are accepted and embraced in order to make political demands that simultaneously recodify and reify those categories. This kind of operation limits the urgency of overcoming them and building the "new man" that Franz Fanon (2019), in dialogue with revolutionary Marxism in the context of anticolonial struggles in the Global South, envisioned in his greatest work: to destroy racial alienation so a truly universal society can emerge. Authors such as Judith Butler (1999) and Asad Haider (2018) refer to this trap as the "consolations of identity": attachment to identities recognized by the liberal state that reduce political agency to a matter of group affiliation. Such affiliation to identity, they warn, is maintained within a relationship of subordination that dismantles possible solidarities. This form of closing off therefore constitutes both the fundamental principle and the internal limit of theoretical and political projects centered on race (Mezzadra 2008; Hall 1980).

In this way it is possible to see how reductionist forms of understanding mestizaje and its relationship to racism lead to a dead end. Such understandings start from the assumption that race as a category can explain all social and historical phenomena, and that therefore all oppression and injustice can be causally reduced to race. The partial image they cultivate however, can be completed if racism and mestizaje are examined within the framework of "racial capitalism." In this sense, historical materialism, being a method of socioeconomic analysis that seeks to understand historical changes to class structure in order to produce social transformation, allows us to situate mestizaje within the framework of racial capitalism not only to penetrate its logic but also to acquire the tools to potentially overcome it. It is thus possible to shed light on dynamics that remain obscure when mestizaje is understood mainly as a national identity resulting from a racist ideological project of the Mexican state. As we will see in the next section, materialism presents a broader picture of the question of the nation and the role it plays in the "mestizofication" of racialized classes.

## The Material Foundations of National Consciousness

While it is true that Mexican Independence in 1821 put an end to the Spanish colonial domination of most of the territories of New Spain, we can also see how this event would open the door to free market imperialism driven by the great capitalist powers of the time (Marini 1973). The advance of the global market under European rule, which reached its zenith in the second half of the nineteenth century, would bring with it a new set of imperatives in the old American colonies whose weak governments were not able to determine their own destinies (Córdova 1973; Chibber 2021; Hobsbawm 2019). Despite its political independence and the ongoing internal wars and reforms, Mexico maintained the demographic and administrative backbone forged during the Viceroyalty, meaning that land issues and semi-feudal bonds of servitude were not fundamentally altered (Silva Herzog 1959). The most important obstacle to the process of capitalist development in Mexico, therefore, continued to be latifundia ownership[3] by large landowners, whose position had been strengthened by the abolition of Spanish colonialism (Collado 1987). In these conditions, the stagnation of land ownership left over from the colonial period would increasingly be subjected to the pressures of import and export trade taking place within the realm of US influence (Cosío Villegas 1976). As a consequence, the nascent dynamics of a capitalist system within

Mexico would produce a new kind of economic colonization and a new type of oppressor class dependent on western monopolies. This would be based not only on the desire for the kind of wealth typical of feudal leaders, or on the larceny of Novo-Hispanic colonialism, but rather on an outward expansion of the same imperatives of competitive production that drove the internal market of northwestern European countries, and which in Mexico would be endorsed by US enterprise (Meiksins Wood 2002, 152).

In the middle of the nineteenth century, the liberals, led by Benito Juárez who sought to establish a democratic republic free of the influence of the church, saw in the global expansion of the market economy the opportunity to disentail through Reform Laws any land holdings that were not covered by the concept of private property, such as those belonging to the clergy and to indigenous communities (Collado 1987). This would lead Mexico to become a country of practically landless communities, surrounded by haciendas that ran on the labor of a growing number of poor and dispossessed peons and agricultural laborers (Kourí 2015). When the obstacles to Mexico's full development as part of the global economy were removed, the federalist liberals—representatives of progressive, bourgeois, and urban interests in territory that was essentially rural and indigenous—were poised to form an independent state and a unified nation. In opposition to the conservatives' centralist, monarchist ideology, they proposed a process of national unification that would later converge with the political structure of the state. Liberal nationalism would thus become the foundation of a program aimed at shaping these political structures in accordance with changing economic and territorial conditions. In this sense, the boundaries of the nation-state would be defined through the demands of capital expanding to form territorially defined markets with legal frameworks guaranteeing the rights to property and investment and legally regulating the kinds of contract required by "free labor." Porfirio Díaz's rise to power in 1876 would represent the intensification, along absolutist rather than liberal lines now, of the nation-building project based on integration and development. Indeed, the regime would be justified by its ideologues by the *overwhelming* need to create stable conditions that would attract foreign capital, on which the national policy of modernization depended (Córdova 1973).

Since then, and especially after the Mexican Revolution (1910–1917), an integrationist policy represented the main method of underpinning the construction of a capitalist national project based on a market economy and a population educated in accordance with the needs of the emerging social division of labor (Castillo Ramírez 2014). This period of integration would lay the foundations for the state's educational and cultural institutions that would begin the task—functioning according to the productive dynamics of the market—of imposing national uniformity through the teaching of the "national language" and the values of modern society. Against this background, the working classes—laborers, servants, and campesinos—would enter or emerge during the final stages of the nationalist movement to embody, with all its inherent contradictions, the idealized "national subject." The first and most threatening group, able to institute an identity that threatened bourgeois nationalism, would be the new proletariat, which, as we will see, would for this reason become the focus of the corporative-democratic program. Importantly, Hobsbawm (1998, 159) observes that in this period of imperial expansion (1875–1914), not only in Mexico but throughout the westernized world, "the nation" would become the counterweight to everything that demanded loyalty to something other than the state: religion, an ethnic group not identified with the state, and particularly *class*.

In this context, we can appreciate how the nationalist elites promoted modernization and state formation through the pressures of governing within a global capitalist economy. Under the demands of global capitalism, peripheral nations (old and new colonies) had to form local political structures articulated through a nationalist ideological paradigm—mestizophilia in Mexico's case (Lomnitz 2009)—in order to channel an ethnically diverse population towards the productive dynamics of the "free" market. Throughout the nineteenth century, but mainly in the twentieth, these indigenous and rural populations, lacking common lands, would feed the ranks of the emerging working classes who, forced by circumstance to renounce their cultural determinations in order to increase their material security, would group around a national identity. Although the Mexican state, through its discourse, saw the opportunity to reinterpret itself as a nation of equals, the new social division of labor was built on existing racial divisions, largely preserving colonial-era social hierarchies among "indios," "mezclados," and "criollos" (Granados 2016). Nationalist mestizaje, in this way, would play a crucial role not only in shaping and disciplining the emerging working classes, but also in maintaining and justifying the social organization into castes that had been forged during the Novo-Hispanic period. Seen in this light, the emergence of modern mestizaje in Mexico represents a period of transformation, in origin and meaning, that was internally determined by class. This is not to imply that the Mexican State, consolidated years after the Revolution, did not implement a conscious regime of cultural (Palou 2016) and indigenist policies (Acevedo Rodrigo 2015) that would consolidate the divide between the "indigenous person" and the "mestizo." Rather, it involves complicating the inherited understanding of mestizaje as a project belonging to intellectuals and politicians who rose above the imperatives of the global economy to deliberately construct the destiny of the nation and of its historical subject, the mestizo. It is thus possible to recognize both the role of collective praxis and the ruling classes' intervention in the face of advancing global capitalism, the social order it cemented, and the beliefs that would legitimate it.

This perspective opens the door to identifying the material origins of modern mestizaje in the land issues that emerged from Mexico's independence.

## The Material Origins of Mestizaje

If in the previous section I explained how the economic dynamics governing the relationship between nation-state formation in Mexico and global capitalism gave way to a nationalist ideology such as mestizaje, in this section we will see in more detail how issues to do with land are fundamental to understanding the material conditions in which mestizaje appears. As I mentioned, global north scholars writing in the tradition of "racial capitalism" tend to be inspired by Cedric Robinson's text, *Black Marxism: The Making of the Black Radical Tradition* (2021). In Mexico, there is a similarly canonical work which, since its publication in 1909, despite being hampered by that era's positivism, has been an important reference in discussions about the relationship between the national mestizo subject, agrarian reform, and the role of the state: *Los grandes problemas nacionales* (The Nation's Great Problems) by Andrés Molina Enríquez. Importantly, his work has been celebrated for its decisive criticism of latifundia which led to his contribution to the ideals of the Mexican Revolution, later enshrined in Article 27 of the 1917 Constitution (Kourí 2009). This article gave shape to what is considered the great social reform of the twentieth century: the ejido[4]. The Revolution's ejido emerged from the idea of reconstituting communal forms and practices of land tenancy and social organization considered characteristic of the indigenous peoples of Mexico, whose origins, in this view, could be traced back to colonial Indian communities and through them to the collectivist practices of the pre-Hispanic indigenous world (Kourí 2015). The sense of social justice that motivated the parceling out of land and reconstitution of communal property was forged in the centuries of dispossession suffered by indigenous and rural populations, originally during the three centuries of Spanish colonialism but mainly in independent Mexico, through the civil expropriation that took place under La Reforma (1855–1863) and through the privatization that took place during the Porfiriato (1876–1911).[5] Seen in this way, the popular rebellions of the Mexican Revolution—with the Zapatistas in the south and the Villistas in the north—were the inevitable outcome of the violent usurpation of land that became particularly severe after Independence in 1821. If we consider that during the nineteenth century, *freed* from the unproductive yoke of the Spanish tribute system, Mexico began to be annexed to the global economy under the liberalizing pressure of the great capitalist nations, we can begin to understand why the communal agrarian structure was an obstacle to instituting the type of private property and relations of production demanded by the market economy. The dissolution of communal lands, in turn, established a sense of alienation from their territory and community that would lead ethnically diverse populations to migrate to new urban and factory centers. These spaces would become the laboratory of Mexican nationalism, where people would seek to inspire a functional consciousness in the emerging dynamics of production, consumption, and the export of commodities. This is why Molina begins with the difficulties of nineteenth century agrarian reform when he visualizes the formation of the subject of twentieth century "mexicanidad": the mestizo (Lomnitz 2009). In this sense, we can understand problems to do with land as a key chapter of the history of the development of the modern mestizo under the type of racial capitalism that was to take place in Mexico. This is why it is important to recover a systemic, interconnected view of conflicts over land ownership, the state, the national subject, and racialized classes in Mexico. A materialist perspective allows us, in this sense, to establish the material basis of mestizaje in the specific phase of capitalist development known as "primitive accumulation." In some of his best-known passages, Marx illustrates the long history of plunder and expropriation that would establish new relations of production, with violence as the basis of national processes of accumulation. It is thanks to the "complete separation of the laborers from all property in the means by which they can realize their labor" (Marx 1976, 874) that the systematic need to develop productive forces under globally unprecedented economic imperatives will be born (Meiksins Wood 2002).

This approach explains why the birth of the mestizo national subject in turn represents the birth of a fundamental actor in capitalist relations: the proletariat, or the working class. If we understand the proletariat as the class without the means of production—such as land—who struggle to make a living through their capacity to work for a wage, then we can understand why historically it has been necessary to have, first, the violent expropriation of territory and, later, the forced or *voluntary* integration of the peoples that inhabited it into the capitalist nation-state project. As such, not only during the three hundred years of colonization but also in the two hundred years that Mexico has been an independent state, there has been an ongoing offensive against indigenous and campesino communities and peoples that seeks their subjugation, dispossession, and assimilation. Finally, the history of original accumulation in Mexico is the history of the growing deprivation of working-class populations that would lead to the loss of ways of life and, with it, the formation of a class with no means of subsistence other than to "freely" sell their ability to work in the labor markets: the mestizo class. This perspective helps clarify why the main "ethnocidal" transformations in Mexico did not occur during the colonial period but rather between the nineteenth and twentieth centuries (Navarrete 2021): in 1821, the year in which Independence was achieved, around 70% of the population spoke an indigenous language compared to 6.5% today (INEGI 2020).

However, the processes of mestizofication are not a question of the past but rather are ongoing. Throughout the nation, agrarian communities regularly defend their territory against extractive projects, and indigenous communities continue to resist, opposing their proletarianization through demands for their right to self-governance. The armed uprising of the Zapatista Nacional Liberation Army in Chiapas in 1994 represents a key recent episode in these processes of resistance that go back 500 years. At the heart of the Zapatistas' calls for autonomy is the fight for their land, because they understand the violent dispossession of territory as inherent to the capitalist relations of production, which require not only the continuous annexation of territories in order to maintain their imperatives of expansion and accumulation, but also a wage laborer population engendered by dispossession and alienation. Such are the material bases on which the homogenizing processes of proletarianization historically thrived, and continue to thrive today. That is why, in Mexico, conflicts over territory and self-determination represent ongoing resistance to the "complete separation of the laborers from all property in the means by which they can realize their labor." In this case, this means land, through which they find not only the possibility of subsistence but also their rootedness in a collective, their political and cultural place in the world, and their metabolic relationship with nature. As Fanon put it, "For a colonized people the most essential value, because the most concrete, is first and foremost the land: the land which will bring them bread and, above all, dignity."

Given the expansive and conflictive nature of capital (Bonefeld 2011; De Angelis 2001), the separation of workers from their land not only represents a violent point of departure for capitalist relations in Mexico, but also a current mode of coercive mestizofication. The systematic reproduction of those processes, as we can see, requires a centralized administrative apparatus that claims original ownership of the national territory that makes up the nation-state. In turn, capital depends on local and national forms of extra-economic support—procured by the state—to maintain local conditions that favor accumulation (Meiksins Wood 2002). This is the historically constituted material foundation of the mutual attachment between the state and capital. This is why, in Mexico, there must be a continuous engagement in coercive acts of land expropriation and policies that discriminate against speakers of indigenous languages in order to sustain and recreate the basis of accumulation itself: the mestizo working population. It is therefore possible to say that, as long as mestizofication continues to be the cultural logic of proletarianization, the narrative of original accumulation will retain its power in Mexico.

But what happens to those who have already been made mestizo; to the great de-indigenized and proletarianized majorities? Do the conflicts come to an end when a person ceases to *be* indigenous? As we shall see, the same logics continue to operate in populations that have been assimilated into the nation-state and turned into a class of wage earners stripped of their ethnic-territorial claims. In this way we can build an image of the mestizo as embodying an emerging counterforce within capitalist accumulation itself—in other words, the working class—which it must try to manage or assimilate, an interpretation already suggested in the distinguished work of José Revueltas.

## A Headless Mestizaje

With *Ensayo sobre un proletariado sin cabeza* (Essay About a Headless Proletariat) published in 1962, José Revueltas gave us one of the most lucid analytical studies of materialist thinking on the emergence and development of the modern state and capitalist relations in Mexico, based on its historical specificities. While this thesis does not allude directly to mestizaje—he would later dedicate literary works such as *El luto humano* (Human Mourning) to that topic—he lays the foundations for thinking about why racial homogenization by itself does not produce a unified class, something academia in the global north would come to understand through the tradition of racial capitalism following the early work of W. E. B. Du Bois.[6] Undoubtedly, when Revueltas alludes to the "peculiar characteristics" with which the working class was born in Mexico, it is hard not to see those characteristics, in the light of mestizaje, as a life process that has been intrinsically connected to the reproduction of capitalism.

One of the central concerns of Revueltas's work—the alienation and emancipation of the national being—is intimately connected here to the modern Mexican state that emerged from the 1910 Revolution. Indeed, he displaces the figure of the mestizo as the embodiment of the national subject—later to become a commonplace par excellence in Mexican intellectual history—because his analysis takes a materialist approach: classes assume leading roles in the development and organization of capitalist Mexico. But Revueltas openly formulated—half a century after Molina Enríquez's text—the material bases of modern Mexican history from which it is possible to study the emergence of the mestizo class and its eventual corporatization: his research on national integration and the working class's loss of independence—a summary of mestizaje—begins with the unsustainable contradictions between an agricultural system still organized on semi-feudal grounds and the thriving relations of capitalist property and production. Along these lines, we can see clearly how, in the context of an emerging class structure formed by the relationship between capital and wage labor, agrarian dispossession would push groups of mainly servants and campesinos towards the cities and industry. These populations, because of their alienation from their ethnic group and territory, would find in wage labor—possibly associated with the national conscience as a form of labor discipline—their main direction.[7]

In this context, the justification for mestizaje as an ideology can be found in Marx's argument about the ideological legitimization of the "natural laws of capitalist production" as though they were the "ordinary run of things." This premise shapes Revueltas's reading of the 1910 Revolution:[8] a democratic movement that allowed the national bourgeoisie to rise to power and found their state party on the idea of the Revolution as a "Revolution of the entire population"; the "Revolution made government." This mediation would allow the national bourgeoisie to deny its status "as a class," as though it "were already the totality of the movement and had been diluted within it"

(Revueltas 1962, 81). In such a way, hidden behind a "neutral state" built as the sum of all classes, the bourgeoisie puts its own stamp on "the process of ideological development, which, then, is nothing but its own myth." In the building of its own genealogy, we can unearth the roots of the ideology of mestizaje as an abstract category of universal citizenship behind which it hides intrinsic class and race relations. The discourse of mestizaje, then, ends up rounding off the claim of the bourgeois democratic state as an agrarian, nationalist, and workers' movement that is "essentially Mexican" (Revueltas 1962, 130), which, echoing Marx and Engels's argument, allows for the universalization of its own interests by identifying them with those of society at large. Equally crucial to the processes of original accumulation, it inherits the indigenist mantel by promoting its mission of liberating indigenous peoples from the base circumstances in which they live. Although the terms employed continue to echo euphemistic discussions of the nineteenth-century "indigenous problem"—"integration," "redemption," "progress" (Acevedo Rodrigo 2015)—in reality it seeks their redefinition through capital in order to transform the labor force into commodities (Palou 2016, 93).

In this period when the new system is being established, the fledgling bourgeoisie, witnessing a proletarian revolution on European soil, realizes that the still unconsolidated working masses constitute an antagonistic class capable of threatening their own position and resisting the ongoing processes of proletarianization, so their intervention becomes one of the central policies of the democratic bourgeois program: to be born mestizo, they must lose their ideological independence and thus all associations with class. It is clear that in the postrevolutionary period, the working classes were able to become active participants on the political stage, forcing public institutions to represent their social demands. However, between 1929 and 1938 they were attracted to a model of conciliation between social groups and classes, built during the Maximato[9] and cemented under Cardenismo, under the leadership of semi-official trade union organizations (Córdova 1973). In this way, the working masses became a critical source of support for national development policies, making them participants in a program of social reforms based on the promise of social mobility and workers' rights (Soto Reyes Garmendia 2016). Given this, understanding mestizaje as the imposition of a state project onto the working masses loses sight of the democratic freedoms achieved through social struggle, mass strikes, and popular rebellions that allowed them to burst into the heart of national politics in the first half of the twentieth century. The irony of their success, however, is rooted in the fact that the working classes would remain more fully integrated into the bourgeois order because they were positioned in class organizations associated with the state as corporative formations. This prevented the working classes from building their own organization of political power that would speak in the name of their entire social class. By making their ideological independence contingent, the fledgling mestizo class, as Tenorio Trillo (2009) suggests, would have no other option but to turn to the homeland.[10] The mestizo then becomes the national subject, not because they are a generic member of the Mexican state, but because they will come to represent the whole group of antagonistic relations between labor and capital—charged with all their contradictions and their racial specificities and specificities of gender and origin—arbitrated by the state.

In this way it is possible to trace how the ideology of mestizaje, mediated through the Revolution by union corporatism,[11] partly a field regulating the conflict between classes, will favor the weakening antagonistic capacity of the labor force while assuring commitment, through the granting of civil rights, to the workers. In this way the corporative pact is based on the necessary collaboration between classes to contribute to the national interest and the strengthening of a state committed, at least in name, to the country's majority population (Zamora 1995, 44–45). Any revolutionary movement that could propose the abolition of class itself would be replaced by a democratic nationalist policy that subordinates the "organized masses" under its command (Revueltas 1962, 167) and, therefore, penetrates "to the deepest layers of the population" to prevent "class competition."

Similarly, this arrangement will make it possible to ensure that the ethnic-political characteristics of dispossessed populations can be remodeled in order to adapt to the needs of modern production techniques. In order to establish its authority over the worker, capital will need to erase any trace of each worker's particular normative universe that might conflict with the extraction of the socially necessary work effort (Chibber 2013). In this context, the corporatist spirit of mestizaje will play a role in ensuring a disciplined work force that, by virtue of its morality and cultural adscriptions, adapts to the rhythms of production dictated by the capitalist division of labor. With the establishment of a trade unionist and democratic regime, the state and the capitalist class will come to consolidate a social order in which they can exert their political dominance to strengthen their control over the center of work. This will be the process by which the disciplinary logic of capital, as part of the drive to reach levels of efficiency demanded by market competition, will tend to homogenize workers' identity.

Union corporatism is for this reason the bearer of the ideology of revolutionary nationalism (Zamora 1995), the result of which is the formation of a social bloc able to extend its cultural, moral, and ideological influence over broad sectors of the population (Rendón Corona 2001). The need to maintain the stability of the corporatized bases will demand the appearance of apparent unity and unanimity—supplied by mestizophilia—which becomes a nationalist cult with rituals, idolized symbols, and ideological grandiloquence (Rendón Corona 2001, 18). In this way, the corporate regime of mestizaje, while it contributes to the *racial* homogenization of the working class, undermines the conditions for closer ties of solidarity with those in similar conditions. It is on the basis of this nationalist-corporatist pact, built on the structural inequalities of the capitalist economy, that mestizaje abandons its promise to reflect "universal interest" or to fully represent an inclusive project.

Seen in this way, it is no longer worth interpreting mestizaje strictly as a deliberate, premeditated project by agents of the Mexican state. Instead, it can be revealed as part of the disciplinary logic of the market that obliges both the dispossessed and landowners to act in accordance with its social norms of reproduction. This gives rise to an appreciation of mestizaje as a process structurally linked to the dominant forms of labor organization: an impersonal compulsion that transforms itself to meet new conditions. A dialectic approach[12] therefore avoids fixing it in a conscious ideological framework that moves unchanging through the vicissitudes of history. Mestizaje, seen thus, is brought up to date as a normative demand accompanying the movement of capital as it adjusts the national will to the requirements of the economic development of production. This is confirmed in the period of capitalist restructuring known as "neoliberalism," which took the form of a broad offensive against the working class—shaped under the Revolutionary Institutional Party's (PRI's) corporatist welfare model—that sought to reestablish adequate conditions for the accumulation of capital after the global crisis of the Fordist-industrial paradigm (Giori 2013). In parallel, these strategies were deepened during the government of Carlos Salinas de Gortari (1988–1994) with the counter reform that attacked the heart of the Mexican Revolution—Article 27 of the Constitution—which initiated the parceling out of land. This policy favored the privatization of the ejido in order to establish a property market that would facilitate a new concentration of land in the hands of large producers. As a result, the shift in the balance of power from labor to capital would delegitimize the ideological efficacy of the discourse of social mobility on which the mestizophilic postrevolutionary narrative was based (Palou 2016). It is therefore no accident that, in the face of the joint attack on campesinos and the working class, this period marks the rise of multiculturalist indigenist policies that sought to recast the discourse of mestizaje to embrace a fetishization of difference compatible with contemporary capitalist development. Thus, in 1992, constitutionally speaking Mexico went from being a "single and indivisible nation" to a "pluricultural nation," while strengthening economic conditions in favor of capital, dismantling the working classes' social base, and ramping up the expropriation of communal lands.

In sum, this allows us to appreciate how "mestizofication" is the already corporatized proletarianization, fruit of the wide arc of capitalist evolution in Mexico that can be seen in the ongoing expropriation of land, postrevolutionary corporatist unionism, and state indigenism.

## Towards a Horizon of Visibility

In this article I have proposed an understanding of mestizaje in Mexico as a category determined by class relations within the framework of racial capitalism. In this way I have sought to fill a gap in a tradition that has focused on projects that examine the production of *difference* alongside the production of capital. The materialist reading of mestizaje, in this sense, has allowed us to formulate tentative answers as to why a racial project that promotes *homogenization*, rather than differentiation, can also be made to serve capital.

There has been a focus on the material bases of mestizaje as part of the "life process" of capitalism in Mexico. We have seen why the continual interaction between the expropriation of communally owned land and the disciplinary logic of the market are key if we are to understand these historical processes that are still current today. So, faced with the traditional image of mestizaje as a *conscious state program*, the present materialist interpretation has made mestizofication part of the social processes internal to the logic of proletarianization in Mexico.

This perspective allows us to discern the analogy between the appearance of the mestizo and the working class in the difficult, dynamic trajectories of social and economic transformation. Contrary to the understanding of the mestizo as a product instrumental to the service of the state—a mere spectator to history—this proposal claims their active and creative role in history, one that has important political implications for transformation through social praxis. Part of the importance of a materialist approach, as I have mentioned, is precisely to open up and expose the active strength of the subaltern majority in the movement of history. This vision implies a common course for indigenous and mestizo peoples as *bearers* of social relationships rather than just mere *subjects*. It is thus possible to see a route towards the political transformation of the mestizo class in the light of their praxis: while it has been held captive by capital, its prospects for freedom lie outside itself, where mestizo loses meaning as a formula for nationalist identification. This argument calls into question the assumption that ethnic or racial autonomy exists outside the logic of capital's reproduction, an assumption that ends up fueling the false binary between the mestizo and everybody else: two faces, as we have seen, of the same cycle of dispossession, proletarianization, and accumulation that affects society as a whole.

It is productive, therefore, to remain outside this apparent antagonism. Historical and present-day indigenous populations repeatedly resist their own proletarianization. At the same time, they intensify the search for a common emancipatory ground as totalizing as the capitalist mode of production. Thus, by considering original accumulation as a recurrent strategy to combat the continuous character of those struggles, we can see a unified destiny for the working class and indigenous nations around the world. Faced with the irreversible historical fact of colonialism and imperialism, this interpretation shows that, far from representing opposing positions, mestizos as a class can find in indigenous peoples' resistance an example of a broader process in which both their origin and their historical trajectory are intertwined. In this way, from being an apparently subsidiary issue, indigenous peoples' autonomous rule with respect to the state suggests the possibility of the working majority rising above the imperatives of capitalism. Renewing the critique of mestizaje from the standpoint of historical materialism incorporates a mark of solidarity that allows us to conceive of paths of emancipation for the great, formidable majorities. These paths can dispel the specter of capital and lead us to reconnect with the lost class.

## Notes

1   The bourgeoisie is identified in the capitalist mode of production as the class that owns the means and structures of production, which establishes unequal relations with other classes, especially with the proletariat. The proletariat is the working class that does not own the means of production and must sell its labor power in exchange for a wage. The extraction of surplus value from their labor allows the accumulation and reinvestment of capital by the bourgeoisie.

2  In other words, that races do not exist in a biological sense, but rather are just a social and historical construction.

3  Latifundia were large rural properties where campesinos worked for landowners and local leaders under a regime based on tributes and slave labor.

4  System of distribution and communal possession of land that was institutionalized after the Mexican Revolution and that consists of granting land to a group of people for their exploitation.

5  The percentage of people around the country who lost their communal property reached a disturbing 95% in the three decades of Díaz's dictatorship (Katz 1974, 1).

6  In the global north, in contrast, the historical introduction of race is understood as an instrument of class division.

7  An understanding that is congruent with what Hobsbawm would observe as a phenomenon that began to unfold at a global level between 1875 and 1914.

8  More recently, Soto Reyes Garmendia (2016) takes a similar approach.

9  The Maximato was a political period that began in 1924 with the government of Plutarco Elias Calles and lasted until 1934, with Lázaro Cárdenas's reformist government.

10 In the broadest sense, Hobsbawm (1998, 180) warns how the international appearance of the labor movement and democracy would incite the bourgeoisie to deny publicly not only their existence as a class but also that of all classes.

11 The state strategy of co-opting union leadership and circumscribing its independent political capacity is known as "union corporatism." In this way, the labor aristocracy is established as a social bloc belonging to the state as a source of legitimacy capable of extending its influence over broad sectors of society.

12 As Marx claims in the 1871 epilogue to Capital, "dialectic . . . regards every historically developed social form as in fluid movement, and therefore takes into account its transient nature."

## References

Acevedo Rodrigo, A. 2015. "Incorporar al indio. Raza y retraso en el libro de la Casa del Estudiante Indígena." In D. Gleizer and P. López Caballero (eds), *Nación y alteridad. Mestizos, indígenas y extranjeros en el proceso de formación nacional* (pp. 165–196). Mexico: UAM Cuajimalpa.

Araujo, A. 2015. "Mestizos, indios y extranjeros: lo propio y lo ajeno en la definición antropológica de la nación. Manuel Gamio y Guillermo Bonfil Batalla." In D. Gleizer and P. López Caballero (eds), *Nación y alteridad. Mestizos, indígenas y extranjeros en el proceso de formación nacional* (pp. 197–242). Mexico: UAM Cuajimalpa.

Bonefeld, W. 2011. "Primitive Accumulation and Capitalist Accumulation: Notes on Social Constitution and Expropriation." *Science and Society* 75 (3): 379–399.

Bonfil Batalla, G. 1989. *México profundo: Una civilización negada.* Mexico: Conaculta/Grijalbo.

Butler, J. 1999. *Gender trouble: Feminism and the subversion of identity.* New York: Routledge.

Castillo Ramírez, G. 2014. "Integración, mestizaje y nacionalismo en el México revolucionario. Forjando Patria de Manuel Gamio: la diversidad subordinada al afán de unidad." *Revista Mexicana de Ciencias Políticas y Sociales,* 59 (221, May–August): 1–23. Universidad Nacional Autónoma de México: CDMX.

Castro-Gómez, S. and Grosfoguel, R. 2007. "Giro decolonial, teoría crítica y pensamiento heterárquico." In S. Castro-Gómez, R. Grosfoguel (eds), *El giro decolonial: reflexiones para una diversidad epistémica más allá del capitalismo global* (pp. 9–23). Bogotá: Siglo del Hombre Editores.

Chibber, V. 2021 (2013). *La teoría poscolonial y el espectro del capital.* Madrid: Ediciones Akal.

Collado, M. C. 1987. *La burguesía mexicana. El emporio Braniff y su participación política 1865–1920.* Mexico: Siglo Veintiuno Editores.

Córdova, A. 1973. *La ideología de la revolución mexicana. La formación del nuevo régimen.* Mexico: Ediciones Era.

Cosío Villegas, D. 1976. *Historia general de México,* vols 3 and 4. Mexico: El Colegio de México.

De Angelis, M. 2001. "Marx and primitive accumulation: The continuous character of capital's 'enclosures'." *The Commoner.* Issue 2: September. https://thecommoner.org/wp-content/uploads/2019/10/Marx-and-primitive-accumulation-deAngelis.pdf.

Echeverría, B. 2010. *Modernidad y blanquitud.* Mexico: Ediciones Era.

Fanon, F. 2019. *Los condenados de la tierra.* Mexico: Fondo de Cultura Económico.

Giorgi, A. 2013. "Punishment and political economy." In J. Simon and R. Sparks (eds) *The SAGE handbook of punishment and society* (pp. 40–59). SAGE Publications Ltd. https://www.doi.org/10.4135/9781446247624.n3

Granados, L. F. 2016. *En el espejo haitiano. Los indios del Bajío y el colapso del orden colonial América Latina.* Mexico: Ediciones Era.

Haider, A. 2018. *Mistaken identity. Race and class in the age of Trump.* New York: Verso.

Hall, S. 1980. "Race, articulation, and societies structured in dominance." In D. Morley (ed.), *Essential essays* (pp. 172–221). Durham: Duke University Press.

Hall, S. 2007. "Introducción: ¿quién necesita 'identidad'?" In S. Hall and P. Du Guy, (eds), *Cuestiones de identidad cultural* (2nd ed.), translated by Horacio Pons (pp. 13–39). Buenos Aires: Amorrortu.

Hobsbawm, E. 1998. *La era del imperio, 1875–1914.* Barcelona: Crítica (Grijalbo Mondadori).

Hobsbawm, E. 2019. *La era del capital, 1848–1875.* Barcelona: Ediciones Culturales Paidós.

Instituto Nacional de Estadística y Geografía (INEGI). 2020. *Censo de población y vivienda 2020.* Mexico: INEGI.

Kourí, E. 2009. "Introducción. Vida e impacto de un libro." In E. Kourí (ed.), *En busca de Molina Enríquez: cien años de los grandes problemas nacionales.* 1st ed. Vol. 156 (pp. 9–32). El Colegio de México. https://doi.org/10.2307/j.ctvhn0b22.3.

Kourí, E. 2015. "La invención del ejido." *Nexos.* January 1. www.nexos.com.mx/?p=23778.

Lomnitz, C. 2009. "Once tesis acerca de Andrés Molina Enríquez." In E. Kourí (ed.), *En busca de Molina Enríquez: cien años de los grandes problemas nacionales.* 1st edition, Vol. 156 (pp.65–78). El Colegio de México. https://doi.org/10.2307/j.ctvhn0b22.5.

Marini, R. M. 1973. *Dialéctica de la dependencia.* Mexico: Ediciones Era.

Marx, K., 1976. *Capital.* Vol. 1. Harmondsworth: Penguin.

Meiksins Wood, E. 2002. *The origins of capitalism. A longer view.* London: Verso.

Mezzadra, S., 2008. *La condizione postcoloniale: Storia e politica nel presente globale.* Verona: ombre corte.

Molina Enríquez, A. 2016. *Los grandes problemas nacionales.* Secretaría de Cultura, Instituto Nacional de Estudios Históricos de las Revoluciones de Mexico.

Moreno FigueroaMónica G. 2010. "Mestizaje, cotidianeidad y las prácticas contemporáneas del racismo en México." In *Mestizaje, diferencia y nación: Lo "negro" en América Central y el Carib*e [online]. Mexico: Centro. de estudios mexicanos y centroamericanos. http://books.openedition.org/cemca/164.

Navarrete, F. 2021. *Cómo los historiadores mexicanos "vencieron" a los indios*. Noticonquista, UNAM.

Palou, P. A. 2016. *Mestizo failure(s). Race, film and literature in twentieth century Mexico*. Boston: Art Life Lab, LCC.

Ralph, M., Singhal, M. 2019. "Racial capitalism." *Theory and Society* 48: 851–881. https://doi.org/10.1007/s11186-019-09367-z.

Rendón Corona, A. 2001. "El corporativismo sindical y sus transformaciones." *Nueva Antropología* 18 (59): 11–30.

Revueltas, J. 1962. *Ensayo sobre un proletariado sin cabeza*. Mexico: Ediciones Era.

Robinson, C. 2019. *Marxismo negro. La formación de la tradición radical negra*. Madrid: Traficantes de Sueños.

Ruz, M. H. 1997. "Etnicidad, territorio y trabajo en las fincas decimonónicas de Comitán, Chiapas." In R. Leticia (ed.), *La reindianización de América, siglo XIX*. Mexico: Siglo Veintiuno Editores.

Silva Herzog, J. 1959. *El agrarismo mexicano y la reforma agraria: exposición crítica*. Mexico: Fondo de Cultura Económica.

Solís, P., Güémez, B. and Lorenzo Holm, V. 2019. *Por mi raza hablará la desigualdad*. Oxfam México. https://www.oxfammexico.org/sites/default/files/Por%20mi%20raza%20hablara%20la%20desigualdad_0.pdf.

Soto Reyes Garmendia, E. 2016. "La revolución pasiva: motor del Estado Mexicano (1920–1940)." *Polis* 12 (2): 13–37. http://www.scielo.org.mx/scielo.php?script=sci_arttext&pid=S1870233320160002000013&lng=es&nrm=iso.

Tenorio Trillo, M., 2009. "Del mestizaje a un siglo de Andrés Molina Enríquez." In E. Kourí (ed.), *En busca de Molina Enríquez: cien años de los grandes problemas nacionales*. 1st ed., Vol. 156 (pp. 9–32). El Colegio de México. https://doi.org/10.2307/j.ctvhn0b22.4.

Wacquant, L. and Bourdieu, P. 1999. *Una invitación a la sociología reflexiva*. Argentina: Siglo Veintiuno Editores.

Zamora, G. 1995. Corporativismo sindical: ¿Institución sin futuro? *Política y Cultura* 5: 43–53. Universidad Autónoma Metropolitana Unidad Xochimilco.

# THE BLACK AFRO-MEXICAN MOVEMENT: A SPACE FOR WOMEN IN THE TWENTY-FIRST CENTURY

Itza Amanda Varela Huerta Translated by Ellen Jones

At the end of the 1990s, social movements in the southeast of Mexico were a major social and political-ideological force. Perhaps the strongest of these movements—and the one that received the most community, press, and political coverage—was the uprising of the Zapatista National Liberation Army (EZLN) in Chiapas in 1994.

In the 1990s and early twenty-first century, the EZLN opened up the national debate about difference, otherness, ethnicity, and national identity from the point of view of the Mexican southeast. The EZLN openly asked every level of the Mexican state what was understood by "Indigenous" or "Indian" ("indio"). By raising this question everywhere possible, Zapatismo called into question the racism embedded in the Mexican nation, a nation that publicly adored Indigenous people but whose projects meant that levels of poverty in their communities were higher than the national average, and whose racist discourse of mestizaje has excluded them from the national project of progress and change.

In studies of Zapatismo's media reach and social impact, most voices are linked with urban spaces, leftist organizations that preceded the armed Indigenous movement, or the National Indigenous Congress. There are few studies, however, that focus on spaces where the Zapatista voice created an important echo, or on regions like the Costa Chica, where questions about "Indianness" involved the creation of subjectivities such as black Afro-Mexican. But the beginnings of what we can recognize today as antiracist movements can be found in the echoes of neo-Zapatista politics, in which skin color was one of the ways that the identification of ethnic otherness marked Mexico's internal politics.

In this very brief interlude, I will concentrate on the organization of female black Afro-Mexican leaders in the Costa Chica region of Oaxaca, aiming to show the social process through which their identity was constructed.

## Costa Chica

The Costa Chica region straddles two southeastern Mexican states, stretching from Acapulco in Guerrero to Huatulco in Oaxaca. This subregion of the Mexican Pacific is home to various indigenous and Afro-descendent groups, as well as mestizo and white-mestizo people. It is one of the regions where the most field work has been carried out in relation to the black or Afro-Mexican population.

There are several cities in the area where we can observe a concentration of economic, political, and cultural activity: the first, Cuajinicuilapa, is in Guerrero, while the other two, Pinotepa Nacional and Jamiltepec, are in Oaxaca. Puerto Escondido is another a city with considerable economic activity, as it is a tourist center that attracts both Mexicans and foreigners to its surfing beach. Between these cities live black communities, communities that have come to question whether there are different kinds of mestizo Mexican identity, the apparently homogeneous Mexican identity created through the mixing of indigenous and Spanish people. This mestizo identity, as I have mentioned, has been called into question by indigenous Maya peoples of the southeast since the 1990s.

In 1995, the town of Charco Redondo, Oaxaca, hosted the first Black Communities Conference. This was possible thanks to various collectives, associations, and individuals who had been asking about their place on the Mexican identity map. These people were not indigenous according the state's specific understanding of the term, which linked indigenous identity with languages other than Spanish; their physical and social markers did not allow them to identify as part of the mestizo citizenry; and they clearly did not belong to the coastal region's small, tightknit pockets of whiteness either. These people were marked by physical differences such as features broadly associated with the African continent, as well as by ways of organizing economic, cultural, and religious life that were shared with the indigenous communities in the region.

As many educators in social sciences and humanities disciplines received training, the black population's important presence began to give rise to a discourse on difference, in a national context in which the EZLN had already questioned the idea that the whole country was mestizo. People began to seek ways to distinguish mestizo identity from cultural practices that could be identified as black Afro-Mexican.

Thus, the Black Communities Conference was born, to be repeated annually from 1995 to the present day. This political space was provided every year in municipalities in the Costa Chica region of Guerrero and Oaxaca—this being the epicenter of what is now a national mobilization—until 2017, when the conference took place in Mata Clara, Veracruz.[1]

The Black Communities Conference and other political gatherings in the region are important because they bring organizations and individuals together, and because they are where many of the black Afro-Mexican movement's ideas have emerged and gained strength.

In the second half of 2019, black Afro-Mexicans were recognized in the Mexican constitution, a government measure that changed the direction of civil society organizations' demands, because constitutional recognition had been one of their main requests of the federal government. In addition, in 2020, they were included for the first time in the Population and Housing

Census, another specific demand. This is how we know that in Mexico there are 1,381,853 people who self-describe as black, Afro-descendent, Afro-Mexican, or using another ethnonym used by the community. This constitutes 1.2 % of the country's total population, according to information provided by the National Institute of Statistics and Geography (INEGI).

In the early days of the black Afro-Mexican movement, the most important identity marker was skin color, along with others such as hair type and facial features. These markers have continued to be important over time, but other markers of political and cultural identity have also emerged, such as the tradition of the Danza de los Diablos (Dance of the Devils), means of self-description that go beyond just skin color, and a sense of belonging through place of origin and residence. This allowed the movement to distance itself from essentialisms, while also allowing other people who did not identify as black Afro-Mexican to recognize a familiar past in which they could seek features of Afro-descent through tradition, geographical origin, or phenotype.

## Women in the Movement

Through the organization of different groups on the Costa Chica, the question of black Afro-Mexican identity has been developing since the end of the 1990s. Before the mobilization began, historians recognized African descent as having existed during the colonial era, but not in the present-day population.

At the beginning of the twenty-first century, black Afro-Mexican women took up their place in this political mobilization. The Black Communities Conference, along with other political activities, was the ideal place for these women's voices to grow louder and bring the experiences of women and children from the community into public discourse.

In the Costa Chica of Guerrero and Oaxaca, being identified as black outside of your own hometown involves being marked by a series of stereotypes about your political and cultural identity, a series of obstacles sustained by discourses that have been developed and reformulated since the colonial era and which continue to leave black Afro-Mexican people unable to fully exercise their collective and individual rights.

The importance of women's community organization is not contained in the specific region I have discussed here, but is also part of the political discourses, narratives, and mobilizations deployed since the end of the 1970s in this country, which have had a slower impact in non-urban spaces. Specifically, because feminism in Mexico had rarely taken into account the contemporary existence of black Afro-Mexican people—no social movement or government institution had—it was much more difficult to enumerate the specific problems facing black Afro-Mexican women in the Costa Chica.

Based on field work carried out between 2008 and 2021, I have observed specific changes to the discourses around black Afro-Mexicans: they have gone from occupying a completely marginal discursive space, to occupying regional, state, and—since 2010—national spaces. By opening dialogues with other national and international organizations, questions about women's spaces also began to gain in importance, prompting the question: what are the particular demands of organized black Afro-Mexican women at this time?

The response is always partial, but it tends to be related to the different forms of violence they experience: obstetric violence, sexual violence, domestic violence, everyday racism, forms of exclusion from educational spaces, and the hyper-sexualization of their image at a national level. In addition, activists like Rosa María Castro denounce the lack of space for black Afro-Mexicans in feminist activist groups; Juliana Acevedo, another activist who self-identifies as a black woman, claims domestic violence is an epidemic in the region; and Elena Salinas speaks of the racism she experienced as a girl in primary school in Pinotepa Nacional, and how it affected how she understands and names herself as an Afro-Mexican woman.

Difference is key; difference has mobilized feminist discourses. Some women call themselves feminists and are interested in recognition for black Afro-Mexican people and communities but also in fully understanding the problems facing black Afro-Mexican women, who continue to experience the logic of racism and therefore exclusion in various aspects of their lives. Some problems frequently mentioned by women include a lack of schools and health centers with family planning facilities; a lack of work opportunities that allow them to lead a dignified life, both in economic terms and in terms of racism; the hyper-sexualization of their bodies at every stage of life; and ideas that link them with permanent sexual availability and which portray them as submissive women without the capacity to occupy social spaces in politics or science, for example.[2]

Black Afro-Mexican women have made many advances, perhaps one of the most important being to name themselves as such; to attend feminist schools set up by NGOs and build a specific kind of feminism and political struggle linked to their community spaces, that is, a kind of policymaking that does not conflict with networks of family or community care.

In the specific case of the black Afro-Mexican mobilization and its inter-section with feminist discourses, there is still the problem of who feminism is actually referring to when it discusses women as a homogeneous group. Activist women in the Costa Chica region have been critical of this kind of feminism, because in the political, social, and cultural context in which they operate, it is important to take community living into account once again. In other words, certain notions about women's freedom are brought into ques-tion when considered from the perspective of a different way of life in which individual autonomy exists in relation to a collective existence. On the other hand, these women have not been included as distinct collectivities either in national history or in public policy, as mestizo and indigenous women have. For this reason, black Afro-Mexican women continue reinventing new mean-ings for feminism as a political practice and as an epistemic understanding.

On the other hand, the possibility of naming themselves as feminist or activist women also made it possible to think about, imagine, and see young people and the LGBTI+ community. Although there are few spaces available to them, and although they require specific types of care such as access to health and sex education, these invisibilized populations are gaining more and more strength within black Afro-Mexican organizations.

It is important to understand that antiracist policies will not come from governments, or from NGOs, but rather from people organizing themselves in the same ways they have historically done in order to defend their terri-tories and fight for their own political frameworks and for versions of his-tory that reclaim their voices and experiences. This is currently happening with the Mobile Professorship of Afro-Mexican Women and the Mexico City Network of Afro-descendent Women, in which the central discussion is about the regional differences within black Afro-Mexican women's collectives, and about specifying ways of entering into dialogue with national history, public policy, and political representation, etc.

Various civil society organizations, along with the National Women's Institute, are interested in learning about the political processes that allow black Afro-Mexicans to speak out. We must make sure, then, that the dynam-ics reproducing this group's invisibility are not replicated by institutions, by discourses of ethnic opportunism, or by the dynamics of political and aca-demic representation. We must also be able to understand how black Afro-Mexican women in the Costa Chica have organized themselves so they can participate in the movement, sustaining it outwardly without putting their gendered work aside.

In recent years, black Afro-Mexican organizations have multiplied all over the country: from Mexico City, where migrants from the Costa Chica, Haiti, and other Afro-Latino regions live, to Coahuila, in the north of the country, where the Mascoga, who identify as an Afro community, live on the northern border. In the United States, groups of Mexicans assert their black Afro-Mexican identity by reviving festivities, gathering with community members for important holidays, and thinking about what it means to be Afro-descendant outside of Mexico.

In academic spaces, though, we still have a duty to think through ways of involving the black Afro-Mexican community, both as a student body, and as colleagues producing scientific and disciplinary knowledge. This, specifically, is what is at stake in an antiracist academy.

## Notes

1  Since 2017, the Conference has sought to widen the discussion about Black Afro-Mexican identity to states such as Veracruz, Coahuila, and Mexico City. While in these areas there are organizations working to achieve constitutional and historical recognition for this population, at a national level there is a slow but steady recognition of the current presence of Black Afro-Mexicans.
2  For more information on this topic, see Varela Huerta (2021).

## Reference

Varela Huerta, Itza Amanda. 2021. "Mujeres y movimiento negro afromexicano a través de la historia de vida." *Revista Estudios Feministas* 29 (1). https://doi.org/10.1590/1806-9584-2021v29n165072.

# CHAPTER 7

# The Racialization of Class as a Manifestation of Racial Capitalism

Hugo Ceron-Anaya Translated by Ellen Jones

## Introduction

Mexico has high levels of social inequality, a problem that has been studied mainly from an economic perspective (Bosch and Manacorda 2010; Esquivel and Cruces 2011; Lustig 2010; Winters and Chiodi 2011; Gilbert 2007; Boltvinik and Archer Mann 2016). Without denying the importance of this work, these studies have neglected to examine the role perceptions of epidermal schemas play in the reproduction of social inequalities.[1] This line of analysis has been discarded on the assumption that Mexico is principally a mestizo nation in which notions of race do not exist, and, as a result, where racism does not influence the organization of social inequalities (Wade 2005; 2010). According to this view, Mexican mestizaje has viewed itself as a flexible, inclusive, and tolerant model. Enrique Krauze, one of Mexico's best-known public intellectuals, summarized this argument in an opinion piece titled "Latin America's Talent for Tolerance," published in the *New York Times* on July 10, 2014. The author points out that Mexico's (and Latin America's) main problem resides in its class structures and dynamics, not in its racial practices, which, despite everything, show a high level of inclusivity. "Mexico's main problem is its gaping class divide—classism, more than racism," the author argues (Krauze 2014).

By way of example, Krauze claims that the term "mestizo" lacks currency in everyday speech, since nobody in contemporary Mexico defines themselves as mestizo. This fact demonstrates, he argues, that notions of race are irrelevant in this country (see Solís and Guemez in this book). Thus, Krauze continues, despite the existence of a certain level of animosity towards Indigenous people, Mexicans (like Latin Americans) operate according to a tolerant model in which the idea of race is not important in the daily life of its subjects (implicit in this argument is that anti-racism is similarly irrelevant). Despite the hegemony of this argument, recent studies have begun to question the idea that racialized perceptions have no influence on the perpetuation of inequality in Mexico (Moreno Figueroa 2010, 2013, 2017; Moreno Figueroa and Saldívar Tanaka 2016; H. Nutini and Isaac 2010; H. G. Nutini 1997; Sue 2013; Villarreal 2010; Wade et al. 2014; Iturriaga 2018; Vaughn 2005; Navarrete 2016, 2017). It should be noted that these studies do not seek to argue that Mexico operates under the same racial logic as the United States—a logic based on the supposed biological existence of races (Omi and Winant 2014). Rather, these studies seek to rethink how the relationship between mestizaje and social inequality in Mexico has been understood.

This chapter seeks to contribute to this discussion by emphasizing the close connection between class structures, dynamics of racialization, and perceptions of whiteness. For example, in Mexico there is a popular belief that "money whitens," which is to say that the greater a subject's accumulation of economic power, the whiter their epidermal schema is perceived to be. This idea would appear to be present in the popular saying "trabajar como negro para vivir como blanco" (work like a black man to live like a white man) in which racialization changes according to class position. The apparent subordination of racialized dynamics to class structure would appear to confirm the stale argument that Mexican mestizaje is a flexible model in which racialized categories become meaningless as soon as they are conditioned by class relations (Rosas 2014; González Casanova 1965; Krauze 2014). Some researchers have expressed doubts about the verifiability of the thesis that "money whitens," pointing out that the idea of whiteness lacks substance in Mexico and Latin America more broadly (Telles and Paschel 2014). However, this inconsistency is owing to the class dynamics and structures influencing racialized ideas—and perceptions of whiteness—that change depending not only on the national context, but also on the class position of individuals of the same nationality. This generates a model that lacks stability and varies across specific contexts and situations, hence the difficulty of capturing such dynamics in statistical models.

My ethnographic work among the upper and upper-middle classes in Mexico City confirms the existence of the notion that "money whitens," although not in the way it has commonly been understood (Ceron-Anaya 2019). My study found that money can change perceptions of epidermal schemas with greater efficiency among members of the middle and working classes; in contrast, money's ability to change racialized perceptions and perceptions of whiteness is reduced among the upper and upper-middle classes. This phenomenon is based on two principles. First, the fact that money's symbolic value changes according to its abundance or scarcity (Bourdieu 1986); and second, the strong correlation between the upper classes and the schema associated with whiteness, and between the middle and working classes—particularly the latter—and the opposite schema (H. Nutini 2008; H. G. Nutini 1997).

This article is divided into three sections. The first deals with the way mestizaje apparently eradicated the idea of race in Mexico, demonstrating that, although the notion isn't present in institutional spaces, outside those spaces Mexicans articulate a clearly racialized hierarchy. The second section turns to everyday language, especially insults, to show how that racialized hierarchy is inextricably linked with notions of class. The third section analyses how racialized dynamics and class relations produce a model in which the accumulation of capital can change perceptions of a person's whiteness. However, this process doesn't operate in a universal way; rather it is conditioned by class origins. These arguments propose a new understanding of the relationship between class, racialization, and whiteness in Mexico (and to some degree, in Latin America).

## The (Non)Existence of Racial Categories

Throughout the twentieth century, the notion of mestizaje came to have a central role in the definition of Mexico and Mexican-ness (see Iturriaga in this book; Krozer in this book; Sue 2013). In the middle of the twentieth century, the prominent sociologist Pablo González Casanova summarized what mestizaje represented in his book *La democracia en México* (González Casanova 1965), maintaining that "a man of Indigenous race with national culture doesn't feel the slightest discrimination because of his race: he might feel it based on his economic status, his occupation, or his politics. Nothing else"

(González Casanova 1965, 103). Mexico's problem, according to this interpretation, is a problem of class but not of racial inequality, since the concept of race lacks meaning for Mexicans. This argument continues to be the dominant paradigm in contemporary Mexico. The apparent lack of understanding of race might lead us to suppose that, at least in theory, racism doesn't exist either (Gargallo 2005; Monroy-Gómez-Franco 2017). However, in everyday life there exists a whole universe of practices and perceptions that use epidermal schema to classify subjects into different racialized groups.

Racialization creates groups of subjects that, while not racial in the strict sense of the word—because there is no purported scientific basis for the grouping (Fausto-Sterling 2008)—do maintain a kind of racial logic by assigning unique and supposedly inherent characteristics to all subjects and elements associated with the group in question (Gotkowitz 2011; Goldberg 2002). Processes of racialization essentialize all individuals who appear to share similar epidermal schemas, assigning them common characteristics (for example, an abundance or lack of work ethic, moral values, or intelligence). By using the term racialization, I seek to transcend the debate about what race *is* and move towards an analysis of what this concept *produces* in practical and everyday terms (Mora 2017, 14).

In Mexico and much of Latin America, the processes of racialization operate hand in hand with economic structures and dynamics; a relationship that is also present in the United States although in a different way. An individual's class position, and the experiences and deep-seated ideas that come with it, are constantly articulated alongside racialized ideas. The combination of these two dynamics creates a set of everyday words, phrases, and narratives that make ambiguous reference both to class and to racialized elements simultaneously. The relationship between class dynamics and racialized practices can be visualized on two intersecting axes. One axis establishes a hierarchy according to a socioeconomic logic—that is, according to the amount of capital a person possesses—while the other axis shows a scale with "white" and "not white" at opposite poles, in which the former is assigned a series of positive connotations and the latter a series of negative ones (this is not to suggest that the notion of race exists as a biological reality; I will return to this point later on). That said, it is important to note that the link between racialization and class does not operate according to a universal logic that cuts across all socioeconomic strata.

Before demonstrating how the dynamics of racialization and class vary across the socioeconomic pyramid, I will show how these ideas are widely reproduced through the everyday use of language. This usage escapes the mechanisms of institutional regulation because it is impossible to police and sanction what is expressed in the street. Everyday language is the "common sense" according to which the social world is understood (Ceron-Anaya 2019).

## The Racialization of Class and Everyday Insults

Insults, like humor, are a strategic window onto the way large social groups share perceptions of reality. Insults are terms resulting from an accumulation of negative emotions towards something or someone. The emotional character of an insult situates it at the opposite pole to the rational; an insult is an impulsive act that does not follow the logic used to analyze a complex problem. Insults emanate from beliefs about what one should not be within a given society. The social character of an insult makes it a linguistic weapon that requires both the insulted and the insulting to share the same cultural perceptions; if not, the insult is ineffective (this is why insults, like humor, are not easy to translate). In present day Mexico, the term *naco* has a special place among insults. "From the '70s onwards, the moniker naco has been enthroned as one of the most hurtful descriptors in Mexican Spanish, in large part thanks to its ambiguity. It is used in a way that discriminates on the basis of race, class, and aesthetics simultaneously" (Serna 1996, 747). The word naco gained currency in the mid-twentieth century. In his *Diccionario de mejicanismos*, originally published in 1959, Francisco J. Santamaría defines the word naco as "1. In Tlaxcala, an indian with white underwear. 2. In Guerrero, indigenous people native to that state, and by extension, a clumsy, ignorant, illiterate person" (Santamaría 1978). While clumsy and ignorant can be understood as generic insults, the term "illiterate" implies a lack of formal education, which, both in the 1970s and today, is a clear indicator of class. Essentially, a lack of formal education—illiteracy—is a characteristic of the working classes. In addition, the definitions use the words "indio" (Indian) and "indigena" (Indigenous) respectively to explain its meaning. These two terms are closely connected to an epidermal schema diametrically opposed to the schema linked to whiteness or Europeanness. For this reason, around the middle of the twentieth century, to be naco—according to the above dictionary definition—was simultaneously to be a lower-class subject and to possess an epidermal schema perceived as non-white.

In 2018, the *Diccionario del Español de México* offered three definitions of the same insult: "1. An Indian or Indigenous person in Mexico. 2. An ignorant or clumsy person, lacking education. 3. In poor taste, unrefined" (Colmex 2018). Today, the insult maintains the same logic as Santamaría's descriptions in the previous century. A naco is a person who is unrefined or lacking formal education, who belongs to the working classes; they can also be an Indigenous person. Zentella points out that the word naco was originally a contraction of "Totonaco," a term that, as well as naming a specific Indigenous community, came to be used more widely to refer to any Indigenous person (Zentella 2007, 30). Thus, naco refers to an epidermal schema linked to Indigenous corporeality, which is characterized by brown skin, black eyes, and straight black hair.

In whichever of its origins and definitions, anything "naco" is linked with indigeneity, as though one were an extension of the other and vice versa. However, as I have already mentioned, racialized logic in Mexico does not follow Anglo-American patterns. For this reason, in Mexico any individual can be accused of being naco if the individual lacks "class," even those associated with a white epidermal schema. In practical terms, to be accused of being "naco" is a symbolic attack on a person's racialized and class-based reputation. The insult seeks to cast doubt on the individual's mestizo character by showing how their manners, behavior, tastes, and understanding are not like those of other mestizos, but rather those of Indigenous people (non-white people). The word naco seeks to unmask and identify those who try to pass for mestizo or white without "actually" being so (I will come back to this point).

It is no coincidence that the term emerged in the '60s and '70s (Monsivais 1976), a period in which Mexico experienced considerable social mobility. The invention and popularization of the insult responded to the middle and upper classes' need to classify those who sought to pass for a higher class than they really were, and the racialized nature of the insult was a way of emphasizing that person's lower-class condition (Serna 1996; Shorris 2012). It is worth noting that during the 1980s, as part of a widespread, popular urban movement, the rock band Botellita de Jerez coined the phrase "todo lo naco es chido" (literally, everything naco is cool),[2] which acquired wide circulation. Following the same logic as the civil rights movement in the United States and its exaltation of blackness ("Black is beautiful"), the Mexican phrase sought to re-appropriate the expletive and turn it back into a source of pride. While the term naco maintains a racialized and class-based ambiguity, as I have pointed out, at base it refers to an epidermal schema linked to non-whiteness. As a result, we might translate "todo lo naco es chido" into English as "Brown is beautiful."

Another common insult that shows how the logic of the racialization of class operates daily in Mexico is the offensive phrase "güero de rancho," a term that puts together the categories of white (güero) and countryside (rancho). This insult discredits a person's whiteness by linking their epidermal schema with the rural world, and, by extension, with the working classes. A "güero de rancho" is a person whose schema is linked with whiteness (white skin and light-colored eyes), but whose tastes, manners, and body language denote a rural origin. It's important to note that this expression's delegitimization of the white epidermal schema is essentially based on the lower-class positionality of the person being insulted. The lack of "proper" manners, of "class" in their interactions with others, and the absence of "sophistication" in their world view, among other characteristics, situate this individual, whose epidermal schema is linked to whiteness, closer to the social positions reserved for nacos.

These two insults show how the racialization of class operates on two simultaneous axes. In the first, racialized notions create a scale in which white is principally associated with a series of positive notions and non-whiteness is principally associated with a series of positive notions and non-whiteness is primarily associated with the condition of lacking, such as a lack of formal education, manners, sophistication, and social distinction. In the second, legitimacy is articulated according to a logic of class in which a subject's position changes according to the kinds of capital they possess. The combination of these two axes is what determines an individual's range of possibilities and actions. The next section shows how the link between racialization and class structures is part of a broader social order that responds to a logic of racialized capitalism, understood as an economic system in which racialized dynamics and racism are both consequences of the system and one of the axes perpetuating it.

## The Racialization of Class

This section returns to the idea that "money whitens" in order to demonstrate that this perception doesn't function according to a universal logic that straddles class divisions. For this reason, I will begin by explaining why "money whitens" most efficiently at the middle and lower end of the socio-economic scale.

"The category 'middle class' has no unique and consistent meaning. As with poverty, the complexity of its conceptual and methodological connotations make it one of a number of terms across several disciplines whose definition lacks consensus in the literature" (Teruel et al. 2018, 447).[3] That said, in order to offer an estimate of the size and characteristics of the social classes in Mexico I will use the model developed by the Asociación Mexicana de Agencias de Inteligencia de Mercado y Opinion (Mexican Association of Market Research and Public Opinion Agencies, AMAI). This model divides the Mexican population into eight groups according to factors including income, living conditions, level of education, type of work, car ownership, and food budget, among others (AMAI 2018). The three groups that occupy the lowest rungs ("the working classes")[4] are characterized by precarious housing, a low level of education, a high percentage of income spent on food, and lack of internet access. These segments represent 55.5% of the population.[5] The following three groups ("the middle classes") spend nearly 30% of their income on food, have a higher level of education, usually own a car, live in sturdier housing and usually have access to the internet. These three groups represent 38.5% of the population.

Despite their higher income, the middle classes in Mexico are characterized by considerable economic fragility (Teruel et al. 2018, Atkinson and Brandolini 2014). A natural disaster, a severe health condition, or some other considerable misfortune can easily drag the middle classes down towards to the working classes. This means economic capital is a scarce commodity both among the working and the middle classes, and particularly in the former. As a result, the symbolic value of buying power intensifies, which isn't to say that the exchange value of money changes—the same number of objects can be bought in a shop regardless of the buyer's class—but rather that, because economic capital is an extremely scarce resource, its possession generates a greater symbolic good for its owner in the eyes of their peers. While this is the case in any market society, in the context of Mexican racial capitalism this process has two simultaneous effects.

On the one hand, the accumulation of financial capital can eventually be converted into other kinds of capital, thus increasing the subjects' potential agency (Bourdieu 1986). On the other hand, this class distinction intersects with a racialized hierarchy that situates whiteness and non-whiteness at opposite poles, assigning a series of positive elements to the first and negative elements to the second. The mass media never tire of reproducing this logic, for example, by using models whose phenotype almost exclusively conforms to what is understood by whiteness in Anglo-America to personify consumer power, and actors with these same characteristics to fill star roles and represent complex characters. The opposite is equally true, in that they almost exclusively use people with a non-white epidermal schema to embody lack of capital, moral deficit, limited intelligence, and a poor work ethic, and to represent one dimensional characters (Agis, González, and Aceves 2016; Iturriaga 2018; Winders, Jones III, and Higgins 2005; Bravo Regidor and Campa Butrón 2017). When class difference intersects with a racialized hierarchy, the result is the racialization of class, in which greater purchasing power modifies the way a person's epidermal schema is perceived, on the assumption that the possession of capital brings people symbolically closer to the white universe.

It is easier to change racialized perceptions among the working and middle classes because the latter comprise a kind of intermediary racialized zone, situated somewhere between the working classes, where dark skin tones and Indigenous- or African-origin features are statistically common, and the upper classes, where the epidermal schema associated with the west has overwhelming statistical presence (H. Nutini 1997, 2008; Iturriaga 2018; Solís, Güémez, and Lorenzo Holm 2019). Because of their relative diversity, middle-class spaces retain a level of racialized acceptance, allowing those lower-class individuals who have accumulated capital to be included to a certain degree, despite possessing epidermal schemas or social behaviors not linked with whiteness.

The transition from lower class to middle class status brings with it greater buying power and therefore a different symbolic link to the white schema. The acquisition of more expensive objects and services—private schools, access to social clubs, luxury cars, or homes in residential neighborhoods—produces an individual whitening effect in the eyes of people with the same social status or in the eyes of the working classes.[6]

### Money Whitens (But Not Always)
According to the AMAI's model, the upper and upper-middle classes are characterized by access to large, well-constructed houses, to all public services, and more than two cars. They also invest the most in and have the highest

level of education. Together these two groups represent 6% of the total population (AMAI 2018). The whitening power of economic capital doesn't operate as efficiently in these economic strata, for the same two reasons previously explained, though in reverse. On the one hand, economic capital is no longer a scarce commodity, but rather abounds in these groups. Again, it is not the value of money that changes, but rather the symbolic power of financial capital. For example, in the upper classes a luxury car is no longer a scarce commodity (as it is in the middle and especially the working classes) but rather an ordinary everyday object. This does not mean the vehicle loses its exchange value on the automobile market. What it loses is part of its symbolic value. The possession of luxury goods is no longer a source of prestige among peers, but rather the minimum prerequisite to be considered a member of those classes. Among all that abundance, money becomes a habitual good, and as a result, its capacity to generate symbolic forms of whitening is diminished.

Amid all that material abundance, other more costly forms of capital take precedence. There are kinds of capital that require constant exposure over long periods of time—as the result of privilege—if they are to be internalized in an "authentic" way. This is the case with embodied cultural capital such as the ability to speak another western language in addition to Spanish. For example, speaking a language with the accent and diction of a native speaker requires extensive exposure via formal education, tutors, and travel, as well as the consumption of various cultural artefacts over long periods of time. Only thus will a person be able to speak "well." It is for this reason that the upper classes prefer schools where the language teachers are native speakers—schools that tend to be extremely expensive in economic terms. Attendance at this type of school for just a year or two is not long enough for this kind of capital to be efficiently internalized. It is necessary to have extensive (and therefore expensive) exposure to these kinds of privileged spaces if one is to authentically acquire this kind of embodied cultural capital. It is worth pointing out that Indigenous languages are never seen as a source of prestige in any social class, despite their complexity or the difficulty involved in mastering them. Within the racialized hierarchy, these languages are associated with the same negative connotations as the epidermal schema of their speakers. In practical terms, these perceptions racialize languages not linked with the west by assuming they lack sophistication, elegance, or complexity. This process also takes place in certain parts of the United States in relation to Spanish, a language associated there with poor immigrants who "suffer" from low intelligence, poor work ethic, and scant moral values, and who have a non-white epidermal schema (Davis and Leo Moore 2014).

The second reason why the thesis that money whitens doesn't bear out as consistently among the upper classes is their strong correlation with a white epidermal schema. This means that the moderate racialized flexibility found among the middle classes gradually gives way to almost biological notions (thus is the idea of race understood in the Anglo-American world) that determine social belonging to the upper classes. For example, in his ethnographic work on the Mexican aristocracy, Nutini reports that deviations from the white epidermal schema in members of this group (light brown skin or a wider than average nose) are given negative emphasis, as though such features were a form of dishonor (H. Nutini 2008). Iturriaga's work on nightclubs and bars for young upper-middle- and upper-class adults in the southern Mexican city of Mérida shows a similar pattern to Nutini's work: epidermal schema is a fundamental factor determining who has access to those spaces (Iturriaga 2011).

**Caddies**

I would like to use some ethnographic material from my research to deepen my explanation of the link between class and racialization. In particular, I want to discuss caddies—workers who help out on golf courses and carry golf players' clubs—to further substantiate the thesis expounded in the previous paragraphs. Caddies tend to begin their careers at an early age, usually towards the end of their adolescence (although some, especially older caddies, began work alongside family members as children). This long exposure to golf allows them to get to know the game in depth. For example, a caddie aged around thirty-five who began working in the profession when he was about seventeen said jokingly to me: "I've walked around this course so many times I could do it with my eyes closed."

When I asked these workers how they learned the game, which is only played in exclusive private clubs as there are no public golf courses in Mexico City, almost all my interviewees responded with some variant of the following: "I learned by watching members play." The vast majority of caddies had a clear understanding of the game and some were extraordinary players (golf clubs were traditionally closed on Mondays for facility maintenance, and on that day the caddies had access to the course to play themselves). Despite the deep understanding of the game many of these players showed, almost every club member put forward a series of arguments as to why a caddie cannot be considered a real golfer.

The members' justifications for differentiating between themselves and the caddies were many, but they can be summed up in phrases like: caddies "don't understand the strategy of the game," "they're uneducated," "they don't know how to hit the ball, nobody has ever taught them," "unfortunately they have poor diets, just look at what they eat," "they have no work ethic," "no matter how much you help them, sooner or later they end up drinking [alcohol]," "it's the caddies who bring drugs into the clubs," or "not even putting together all the best caddies could you make a player who could compete in the world leagues." In short, the caddies lack the understanding, wisdom, nutrition, morality, determination, and character to succeed in this exclusive sport, and for that reason they cannot be considered golfers. These arguments are articulated in a context in which most club members have near-white epidermal schemas, whereas the overwhelming majority of caddies have schemas at the opposite end of the spectrum.

The exclusion of the caddies appears to be classist, given the emphasis on issues like their lack of education. However, that narrative is constantly racialized by the presentation of their limitations as innate characteristics shared homogeneously by the whole group (which also shares a similar epidermal schema), such as complaints about their lack of work ethic, propensity for alcoholism, or poor nutrition. This last complaint retains a surprising parallelism with the long-standing racialization of working-class food, which assumes that these groups are held back in material terms by their consumption of Indigenous-origin foods such as, among other things, corn and beans (Aguilar-Rodríguez 2011; Pilcher 1998). Arguments like these seem to indicate that the difference between caddies and golfers resides in a set of inherent, almost biological differences between the two groups.

During my field work I met several caddies with an extraordinary level of skill in the game, a skill that ought to have set them on a solid trajectory towards professional golf. However, the caddies reported that this was not an option for them because they lacked financial support from the clubs where they worked and from the Mexican Golf Federation. When I questioned the members of those clubs, some of whom were also on the board of the Federation, about the lack of support for these outstanding caddies, most interviewees blamed both the institutions, for not doing enough to support the caddies, and the caddies themselves, who had too many failings to be able to succeed in the sport. However, on one occasion an interviewee, speaking off the record,[7] explained the problem to be a result of the racialization of class:

> Before, you asked me why the clubs or the Federation don't help the caddies [to become professional players]. Off the record, I'll tell you what I think. I think the majority of golfers don't support the caddies, despite there being some very good players among them, because the caddies look like their domestic help. The caddies look like their servants and chauffeurs.[8]

This was the only interviewee who openly expressed a racialized explanation, involving phenotypes such as skin color, in which social class (employment in the service sector) and physical appearance (the similarity between chauffeurs, servants, and caddies) intersect to explain the caddies' marginalization. For this member, the lack of institutional support is based on the epidermal similarity between the caddies and other workers whose roles lack prestige in a similar way. In this case, social class and racialized hierarchy intersect, creating a single dynamic. While many participants used arguments with an ambiguous racialized charge (such as the mention of food) to express similar ideas, this was the only interviewee who explicitly used a racialized argument to explain the lack of financial support. It's worth noting that this interviewee went to university in the United States and lived there for several years before returning to Mexico. It's possible that this experience explains his questioning of the idea that racialized categories don't exist in Mexico.

**Undesirable Members**

As part of my field work, I met someone who had recently accumulated a considerable fortune and bought membership at a prestigious golf club. He was, however, socially rejected by many of the other members. Two members, who were not personal friends, explained why this player was socially excluded. One of them, after giving examples of the new member's lack of manners—such as his excessive desire to win,[9] which came to generate conflict—finished by saying, "look, I think he's a good guy, but at the end of the day he's a naco." The other player who broached the topic of the new member who was looked down on mentioned a confrontation in which the rejected member irately protested his defeat in a tournament. The interviewee who related this incident concluded by saying, "to cut a long story short, the frijolito [little bean] kept arguing, he didn't want to lose."

It is notable in both cases that the interviewees indicated a lack of appropriate manners as the motive for the man's exclusion and concluded their comments with the racialized terms "naco" and "frijolito" (in Mexico, black and brown varieties of beans are the most common). In the eyes of the upper and upper-middle classes that make up membership of this club, the new member's extensive economic capital did not immediately generate symbolic forms of whiteness. Meanwhile, the way he expressed his emotions more closely resembled the way anger is expressed among the working classes—with a higher degree of physical violence—than the hostile yet civil manner that characterizes confrontations among members of the upper classes. This is another example of how more costly forms of internalized cultural capital, like knowing the proper way to express one's emotions, are key to generating a whiter perceived epidermal schema among wealthy individuals.

**Driving Ranges**

During my research, I visited four different driving ranges on multiple occasions. These are small independent businesses that have no connection with the golf clubs. People visit them to learn the basics of the sport, which involves hitting the ball (an action that is much harder than it looks). The standard driving range includes no more than ten hitting stations situated at the opposite side of a large net, set up to prevent the ball from flying toward the street. A green square carpet with a flexible plastic golf tee (a small stand used to support the ball) affixed to one corner designated the hitting spots. Clients stood on these carpets to practice swinging a golf club and hitting balls off the tee. The ball travels no more than 75 meters before hitting the net. In contrast, each hole on a course in a golf club covers a distance of around 450 meters on average. The driving ranges' clientele is not made up of club members, but by members of the middle classes looking to get into golf, a sport which became fashionable in Mexico with Mexican player Lorena Ochoa's success in the US league (the most important in the world) between 2007 and 2010. She attracted unusually extensive media coverage for the sport, which more or less continues today.

It requires only a modest investment to start swinging at a driving range, because you don't have to pay for membership and can rent both clubs and balls at low cost in the venue itself. For 150 pesos a session (USD 7.50) the middle classes can feel like they are becoming golfers (along with all the class and racialized implications of that title). On the multiple occasions I visited these driving ranges I saw people who introduced themselves as professional golf teachers offering their services to clients. On talking to them, I learned that they were caddies who used their days off to teach golf here. These caddie-instructors invariably dressed in golfer outfits—hat, t-shirt, glove, an expensive brand of golf shoe, and khaki cotton trousers—keeping their own bag of golfclubs to hand so they could demonstrate technique and talk about the equipment. Here, the caddies were respected and treated as legitimate golfers. On several occasions I witnessed clients talking to caddies excitedly or organizing their first lessons. In these settings, caddies were not "butchers disguised as golfers," as a member of one of the city's most distinguished clubs described them in an interview.

As part of my field work, I spoke to the owner of one of these driving ranges, who on hearing that I was doing a study of golf decided to talk at length to me, wanting to hear what I thought about his business's failure to thrive. The interviewee complained bitterly that despite investing in decorations and paint, despite hiring waiters—dressed in the universal service uniform of white shirt and black trousers—to attend to the clientele, despite buying advertising space in specialist magazines and having personally spent several days outside a golf course handing out discount vouchers inviting people to visit his business, not a single golf club golfer had come. The owner observed that his business was only attended by "low grade office workers, [...] I want to attract executives." At that stage of the project, I didn't yet have sufficient information about how the members of clubs saw driving ranges, so I limited myself to recommending websites and some other magazines where he might advertise.

As I went on interviewing club members, I asked what they thought of the driving ranges. One of the interviewees answered my question by suggesting that their existence was very sad, because people looking to get into golf there would never succeed in becoming real golfers. For this member, the world of golf and the world of driving ranges were radically different places. To emphasize his argument, he used a play on words, referring to driving ranges (called "tiros de práctica" in Spanish) as "tiraderos," a word that could refer either to a place where things are launched or thrown (as a golf ball is thrown when hit by a club), or to a place where things are thrown *away* (as in a garbage dump). The interviewee summed up his disdain for driving ranges by saying "in the tiraderos, you hit the ball here and it comes down right there [pointing to a distance about ten or fifteen meters away]. I think it's pointless to go to places like that, they're not going to get you anywhere." Later in the interview, this participant returned to the impossibility of becoming an authentic golf player in a driving range, mentioning that the basic instruction given at the "tiraderos" was given by caddies, who in his opinion lacked even the most basic understanding of the sport. I heard this argument in several variations from other members of the clubs. The driving ranges were antithetical to the world of golf.

In the driving ranges, on the other hand, possessing golf-related objects and demonstrating a wide knowledge of the sport generated an aura of distinction and legitimacy that seemed to extend beyond traditional notions of class. One thing that was noticeable in those places was a desire to demonstrate greater buying power than other members of the middle class. For example, these driving ranges sell golf shoes and gloves which are unnecessary seeing as it's hard to practice there for more than an hour, unlike an average game of golf which lasts approximately four hours, but which nevertheless have an important value insofar as they allow beginners to get symbolically "closer" to the world of golf. The diversity of epidermal schemas among clients, owners, and caddie-instructors allowed a certain level of racialized flexibility, in which the possession of objects and knowledge linked to a sporting practice reserved exclusively for the privileged classes seemed to bring subjects closer to those groups and, symbolically, to the universe of white privilege in Mexico.

## Conclusion: Racial Capitalism

As I mentioned in the introduction, this chapter does not mean to suggest that the notion of race exists as a biological reality, nor to propose that Mexico has a racial logic like that of the United States. My work seeks to contribute to critical reflection on how the relationship between social inequalities and mestizaje has been understood. Working to debunk the benign, tolerant, and inclusive version of mestizaje propped up by the national discourse, I have shown that mestizaje is molded by racialized ideas that have whiteness center stage. Racialized perceptions are not openly expressed in institutional spaces, such as State-regulated sites and interactions, but can be found in everyday practices, in day-to-day life. This chapter has shown how social hierarchies in Mexico reproduce innumerable ideas expressing a racialized hierarchy in which whiteness is located at one pole and non-whiteness at the other. The final part of this chapter draws on the idea that "money whitens" to propose the concept of the racialization of class.

It's important to emphasize that arguing for the racialization of class has profound implications for our understanding of inequalities in Mexico. If, as I argue, the dynamics of class and racialization cannot be separated because they operate as a duality, then inequalities are not only the fruit of purely economic structures, they also respond to a racial logic. This means that, seen through the lens of racialized capitalism, social problems such as poverty, lack of opportunities, unemployment, limited state support, and social exclusion, among others, respond to class dynamics as well as racialized (and racist) logics. This explains why poverty is so closely linked to dark skin color whereas wealth is associated with "whiteness" (both its material realities and perceptions of it). The racialization of class is one way that racial capitalism manifests and is reproduced in Mexico.

## Notes

1 Frantz Fanon coined the term epidermal schema to explain how skin and eye color, hair texture, the shape of the nose and lips, as well as body fat are commonly used to organize subjects into groups that apparently have long-term biological and social characteristics in common (Fanon 2008, 84).
2 Chido is a colloquial term that denotes positive, virtuous, and useful characteristics.
3 For example, see the debate between Gerardo Esquivel and Roger Bartra about the meaning of the middle class in Mexico (Revista Digital Horizontal 2015).
4 I use the plural, "classes" to demonstrate the diversity within each of Mexico's social classes.
5 It is important to note that 20% of this group live in extreme poverty (CONEVAL 2014), which could situate them in a position similar to what Marx defined as the "lumpenproletariat."
6 In some parts of the country the difference between the epidermal schema of the working and upper classes does not differ much, for example in the northeast of the country. This generates forms of racialized anxiety which are expressed in a social need on the part of the lower-middle classes to possess objects commonly associated with the upper classes, such as luxury cars (even if the state of these vehicles is less than optimal). These objects are attempts to emphasize class difference in regions where epidermal schemas among the working and middle classes are very similar.
7 For a methodological and ethical discussion of the study of elites, see "Appendix: An Un/Ethical Approach" (Ceron-Anaya 2019).
8 The golfer used the third person to express this idea.
9 At the amateur level, popular sports are characterized by a desire to win at all costs, whereas elite sports are identified by the desire to maintain an emotional distance from the game (Ceron-Anaya 2010).

## References

Agis, Karla, Mireya González, and Javier Aceves. 2016. "Así Es Como Las Revistas Mexicanas Reflejan La Discriminación Racial En México," *Buzzfeed*. December 14, 2016. https://www.buzzfeed.com/mx/karlaagis/asi-es-como-se-refleja-la-discriminacion-racial-de-mexico-en.

Aguilar-Rodríguez, Sandra. 2011. "Nutrition and Modernity: Milk Consumption in 1940s and 1950s Mexico." *Radical History Review* 110: 36–58. https://doi.org/10.1215/01636545-2010-025.

AMAI (Asociación Mexicana de Agencias de Investigación de Mercado y Opinión Pública) (2018). "Nivel socioeconómico AMAI 2018." www. amai.org/nse/wp-content/uploads/2018/04/Nota-Metodolo%CC%81g ico- NSE-2018-v3.pdf.

Atkinson, Anthony and Brandolini, Andrea. 2014. "On the Identification of the Middle Class." In *Income inequality: economic disparities and the middle class in affluent countries*, edited by Janet C. Gornick and Marcus Jäntti (77–100). Stanford: Stanford University Press.

Boltvinik, Julio, and Susan Archer Mann. 2016. *Peasant poverty and persistence in the twenty-first century: Theories, debates, realities and policies*. Zed Books Ltd.

Bosch, Mariano, and Marco Manacorda. 2010. "Minimum Wages and Earnings Inequality in Urban Mexico." *American Economic Journal: Applied Economics* 2 (4): 128–49. https://doi.org/10.1257/app.2.4.128.

Bourdieu, Pierre. 1986. "Forms of Capital." In *Handbook of theory of research for the sociology of education*, translated by Richard Nice. Westport, CT: Greenwood Press.

Bravo Regidor, Carlos, and Homero Campa Butrón. 2017. "Afromexicanos: La discriminación visible," *Proceso*. March 26, 2017. https://www.proceso. com.mx/reportajes/2017/4/1/afromexicanos-la-discriminacion-visible-181 471.html.

Ceron-Anaya, Hugo. 2010. "An Approach to the History of Golf: Business, Symbolic Capital, and Technologies of the Self." *Journal of Sport and Social Issues* 34 (3): 339–58. https://doi.org/10.1177/0193723510377317.

Ceron-Anaya, Hugo. 2019. *Privilege at play. Global and comparative ethnography*. Oxford, New York: Oxford University Press.

Colmex, Colegio de México. 2018. "DEM | Diccionario Del Español de México." 2018. https://dem.colmex.mx/.

CONEVAL. 2014. "Pobreza En México 2014." https://www.coneval.org.mx/ Medicion/MP/Paginas/Pobreza_2014.aspx.

Davis, Tiffany Y., and Wendy Leo Moore. 2014. "Spanish Not Spoken Here: Accounting for the Racialization of the Spanish Language in the Experiences of Mexican Migrants in the United States." *Ethnicities* 14 (5): 676–97. https://doi.org/10.1177/1468796814523740.

Esquivel, Gerardo, and Guillermo Cruces. 2011. "The Dynamics of Income Inequality in Mexico since NAFTA [with Comment]." *Economía* 12 (1): 155–88.

Fanon, Frantz. 2008. *Black Skin, White Masks*. New York: Grove Press.

Fausto-Sterling, Anne. 2008. "The Bare Bones of Race." *Social Studies of Science* 38 (5): 657–94. https://doi.org/10.1177/0306312708091925.

Gargallo, Francesca. 2005. "México: El Racismo Que No Se Nombra." *La Jornada*, November 19, 2005. https://www.jornada.com.mx/2005/11/19/mas-gargallo.html.

Gilbert, Dennis L. 2007. *Mexico's middle class in the neoliberal era*. Tucson: University of Arizona Press. http://catdir.loc.gov/catdir/toc/ecip0 618/2006026215.html.

Goldberg, David Theo. 2002. *The racial state*. Malden MA: Wiley.

González Casanova, Pablo. 1965. *La democracia en México*. Mexico City: Ediciones Era.

Gotkowitz, Laura, ed. 2011. *Histories of race and racism: The Andes and Mesoamerica from colonial times to the present*. Durham, NC: Duke University Press.

Iturriaga, Eugenia. 2011. "Antropología en los antros: racismo y discriminación juvenil en Mérida." In *Niños y jóvenes en Yucatán: miradas antropológicas a problemas múltiples*, edited by Luis Vargués Pasos. Mérida, Yucatán, Mexico: Ediciones de la Universidad Autónoma de Yucatán.

Iturriaga, Eugenia. 2018. *Las Élites de La Ciudad Banca: Discursos Racistas Sobre La Otredad*. Mexico: UNAM. https://www.academia.edu/43394 061/Las_%C3%A9lites_de_la_ciudad_banca_discursos_racistas_sobre_ la_otredad.

Krauze, Enrique. 2014. "Opinion | Latin America's Talent for Tolerance." *The New York Times*, July 10. https://www.nytimes.com/2014/07/11/opinion/enrique-krauze-latin-americas-talent-for-tolerance.html.

Lustig, Nora Claudia. 2010. *Coping with austerity: Poverty and inequality in Latin America*. Brookings Institution Press.

Monroy-Gómez-Franco, Luis Ángel. 2017. "¿Importa el color de piel en México?" *Nexos*, June 20. https://economia.nexos.com.mx/importa-el-color-de-piel-en-mexico/.

Monsivais, Carlos. 1976. "No Es Que Esté Feo, Sino Que Estoy Mal Envuelto Je-Je (Notas Sobre La Estética de La Naquiza)." *Siempre!* January 20.

Mora, Mariana. 2017. *Kuxlejal politics*. Austin: University of Texas Press.

Moreno Figueroa, Mónica G. 2010. "Distributed Intensities: Whiteness, Mestizaje and the Logics of Mexican Racism." *Ethnicities* 10 (3): 387–401. https://doi.org/10.1177/1468796810372305.

Moreno Figueroa, Mónica G. 2013. "Displaced Looks: The Lived Experience of Beauty and Racism." *Feminist Theory* 14 (2): 137–51. https://doi.org/10.1177/1464700113483241.

Moreno Figueroa, Mónica G. 2017. "Institutional Racism, Indigenous Women and the Racialization of Health and Justice in Mexico." Lehigh University, February 15.

Moreno Figueroa, Mónica G., and Emiko Saldívar Tanaka. 2016. "'We Are Not Racists, We Are Mexicans.'" *Critical Sociology* 42 (4–5): 515–33. https://doi.org/10.1177/0896920515591296.

Navarrete, Federico. 2016. *México racista: Una denuncia.* Mexico: Grijalbo.

Navarrete, Federico. 2017. *Alfabeto Del Racismo Mexicano.* MALPASO. https://hchlibrary.org/Hoopla/14479106.

Nutini, Hugo. 1997. "Class and Ethnicity in Mexico: Somatic and Racial Considerations." *Ethnology* 36 (3): 227–38. https://doi.org/10.2307/3773987.

Nutini, Hugo. 2008. *The Mexican aristocracy: An expressive ethnography, 1910–2000.* University of Texas Press. https://utpress.utexas.edu/books/nutmex.

Nutini, Hugo, and Barry Isaac. 2010. *Social stratification in Central Mexico, 1500–2000.* University of Texas Press. https://utpress.utexas.edu/books/nutcen.

Omi, Michael, and Howard Winant. 2014. *Racial formation in the United States.* 3rd ed. New York: Routledge. https://doi.org/10.4324/9780203076804.

Pilcher, Jeffrey M. 1998. *Que vivan los tamales! Food and the making of Mexican identity.* UNM Press.

*Revista Digital Horizontal.* 2015. "La Verdad Sobre La Clase Media En México. Respuesta a Roger Bartra." http://horizontal.mx/la-verdad-sobre-la-clase-media-en-mexico-respuesta-a-roger-bartra/.

Rosas, Alejandro. 2014. "¿Classistas or Racistas?" *Milenio*, December 10, 2014.

Santamaría, Francisco J. 1978. *Diccionario de mejicanismos.* Mexico City: Porrúa.

Serna, Enrique. 1996. "El naco en el país de las castas." In *Las Caricaturas me hacen llorar*, 747–54. Editorial Terracota.

Solís, Patricio, Braulio Güémez, and Virginia Lorenzo Holm. 2019. *Por Mi Raza Hablará La Desigualdad. Efectos de Las Características Étnico-Raciales En La Desigualdad de Oportunidades En México.* Mexico City: Oxfam México.

Sue, Christina A. 2013. *Land of the cosmic race: Race mixture, racism, and blackness in Mexico.* Illustrated edition. Oxford, New York: Oxford University Press.

Telles, Edward, and Tianna Paschel. 2014. "Who Is Black, White, or Mixed Race? How Skin Color, Status, and Nation Shape Racial Classification in Latin America." *American Journal of Sociology* 120 (3): 864–907. https://doi.org/10.1086/679252.

Teruel, Graciela y Reyes, Miguel (2017). *México: país de pobres y no de clases medias*. Puebla: Universidad Iberoamericana-Fundación Konrad Adenauer.

Vaughn, Bobby. 2005. "Afro-Mexico: Blacks, Indígenas, Politics, and the Greater Diaspora." In *Neither enemies nor friends: Latinos, blacks, afro-latinos*, edited by Anani Dzidzienyo and Suzanne Oboler, 117–36. New York: Palgrave Macmillan US. https://doi.org/10.1057/9781403982636_6.

Villarreal, Andrés. 2010. "Stratification by Skin Color in Contemporary Mexico." *American Sociological Review* 75 (5): 652–78. https://doi.org/10.1177/0003122410378232.

Wade, Peter. 2005. "Rethinking 'Mestizaje.'" *Journal of Latin American Studies* 37 (2): 239–57.

Wade, Peter. 2010. "The Presence and Absence of Race." *Patterns of Prejudice* 44 (1): 43–60. https://doi.org/10.1080/00313220903507628.

Wade, Peter, Carlos López Beltrán, Eduardo Restrepo, and Ricardo Ventura Santos, eds. 2014. *Mestizo genomics: Race mixture, nation, and science in Latin America*. Mexico City: Fondo de Cultura Económica. https://doi.org/10.1215/9780822376729.

Winders, Jamie, John Paul Jones III, and Michael James Higgins. 2005. "MakingGüeras: Selling White Identities on Late-Night Mexican Television." *Gender, Place & Culture* 12 (1): 71–93. https://doi.org/10.1080/09663690500082984.

Winters, Paul Conal, and Vera Chiodi. 2011. "Human Capital Investment and Long-Term Poverty Reduction in Rural Mexico." *Journal of International Development* 23 (4): 515–38. https://doi.org/10.1002/jid.1664.

Zentella, Ana Celia. 2007. "'Dime Con Quién Hablas, y Te Diré Quién Eres': Linguistic (In)Security and Latina/o Unity." In *A Companion to Latina/o Studies*, edited by Juan Flores and Renato Rosaldo, 25–38. https://mymission.lamission.edu/userdata/casarera/docs/ebooksclub.org__A_Companion_to_Latina_o_Studies__Blackwell_Companions_in_Cultural_Studies_.pdf.

# CHAPTER 8

# Racialization and Privilege among Mexican Elites

Alice Krozer

## Introduction

Human beings rely on their senses and detailed training throughout their lives to locate, on average correctly, fellow humans' social status relative to their own. In the blink of an eye, we all make judgements about each other. In Mexico, to identify a person's level of wealth or poverty at a glance, there exists an effective shortcut: their skin color. In a context where over 60% of the country's white people belong to its richest quintile, while people with dark skin tones are 3.5 times more likely to end up in the poorest 20% of the population compared with their lighter skinned peers (Solís, Güémez, and Campos-Vázquez 2023), and almost six times less likely to reach higher education (Solís, Güémez, and Lorenzo Holm 2019), skin tones serve as a reliable heuristic (a mental shortcut to make sense of a complex world) to identify somebody's position on the social hierarchy.

But skin color goes beyond a question of pigmentation. We tend to inadvertently associate a wide variety of personal characteristics when referring to the attribute of "skin tone," including hair type, facial features, and body shape, but also bearing and dress. While for analytical purposes it can be useful to isolate one of those features and try to estimate its impact on social outcomes, in this chapter I wish to show how these cannot be meaningfully separated, either in people's heads or in their day-to-day interactions, as they are perceived simultaneously and mutually reinforce each other. Moreover, even where they would be theoretically separable from class positions, in practice they constitute an integral whole that mediates people's social experience of self and other.

To better understand the role skin tone plays as a social marker, and how it interacts with other racialized traits, it is revealing to examine the perceptions of social hierarchy with regards to these features among elites. Their strategies of distinction and reproduction encompassing "class and culture, corpus and color" (Castellanos Guerrero 2018) constitute more than just barriers to entry to the higher strata of society. They provide the key criteria for a social stratification based on the construction of "profiles" that fit specific racialized and classed categories, recognized both within and beyond elite circles. The legitimizing references that the symbolic preferences of the elites take on for large parts of the population convert these strategies into the fundaments of an underlying (and not, therefore, benign or innocent) racism, perpetuated via the passing on of these very preferences.

My main aim in this chapter is to analyze the perceptions elites hold with regard to appearance and social hierarchy. I look into the strategies of reproduction of class and cultural privilege, in ideological and corporeal terms, including the aesthetic ideals and exclusionary mechanisms of in-group creation related to aspirational "whiteness." Based on in-depth interviews with members of the elites, as well as empirical evidence on racism stemming from focus groups and semi-structured interviews, this chapter attempts to contribute to the discussion on the intersection of racism and capitalism in the global South, examining the relationship of wealth and racialization in a high inequality context.

To this end, in the following section I will describe the data I base my analysis on. In the section titled Racialization and Whiteness in Mexico I proceed to contextualize the social environment my participants navigate within the existing literature and theoretical insights on the subject. The next section, Elite Perceptions of Social Status Contingent on Class and "Race," lays out the empirical evidence with regards to elite perceptions, followed by the conclusion.

## Data and descriptive analysis

Certain particularities apply when researching elites of all types compared to data collection among other informants. As its members do not appear in official statistics or household surveys, it is necessary to collect primary data in direct interaction with them in order to learn more about their specific perceptions.

This chapter thus relies on empirical data collected in over 60 in-depth interviews with members of the Mexican elite conducted between October 2015 and July 2019, predominantly in Mexico City, but also in Monterrey, Oaxaca City, and Merida. Combining definitions offered by Reis and Moore (2005) and Khan (2015), I understand "elites" as loose groups that comprise individuals within the top 1% of the country's income distribution who also hold positions of potential influence, that is, those with vastly disproportionate access to, or control over, both economic resources *and* at least one other source of capital (political, social, cultural, symbolic). I thus selected participants from within the highest social and occupational classes: officials in public sector decision-making roles, including ministers and deputies; private sector managers or directors; and opinion-shaping academics, intellectual leaders, or media professionals. Compared to the population as a whole, members of this group are extraordinarily well educated. All of them have a first university degree; over half hold a Masters and/or MBA degree; about a third have, or are in the process of acquiring, a doctoral degree. At the national level, only 0.1% of Mexicans between 25 and 64 years old hold a PhD, the lowest level within the Organization for Economic Co-operation and Development (OECD 2019). Participants have attended the most prestigious, overwhelmingly private, national institutions (Instituto Tecnológico Autónomo de México; Tecnológico de Monterrey, but also Universidad Nacional Autónoma de México which is not private), and international universities (Oxbridge and US Ivy League).

At the time, individuals with a monthly per capita income of just over MXN 100.000 could be considered to belong to the top 1% of the Mexican income distribution.[1] According to this threshold, just over half of the interviewees fall within the 99th percentile of the income distribution. The remainder belongs to the top 0.1% and above (with incomes of up to MXN 2 million monthly).[2] At least half of the participants also have levels of wealth that place them within the top percentiles of the wealth distribution.

Certain difficulties arise in accessing this "hidden" population, as has been well-documented by other researchers studying elites, in Mexico and beyond (Inglis 2018; Ceron-Anaya 2019; Sherman 2017; Gaztambide-Fernández 2015). My particular positionality as a female researcher affiliated to an elite (foreign) university was of relevance in the context of this research, particularly with regard to the complex interaction of personal social and economic characteristics among the Mexican upper classes. Decisive for access were not only my credentials, knowledge of the local context (including language and cultural references), and personal acquaintance with some of the contact persons, but also a phenotypical appearance readable as northern European, arguably producing preemptive trust (and recognition), as well as my non-threatening status as a young, foreign, and female researcher.

Another challenge particular to elite research, the inversion of the power relation between researcher and interviewee, has a bearing on sampling choices. As many of them are trained in communicating with journalists and my interest was to reach beyond pre-prepared press statements, I identified potential interviewees via snowball sampling, since peers are best able to access hidden populations like the elite (to avoid "community bias," I started out interviewing people who did not know each other). Moreover, thanks to these personal referrals, I am perceived as a trustworthy peer in most situations. This increases the reliability of participants' declarations and provides internal validation. Where possible, I cross-checked information extended by interviewees with publicly available sources.

I did not aim to collect a representative sample of what statistically constitutes "the elite." Instead, my sample represents a variety of personal characteristics, including different political ideologies, religious beliefs, sexual orientations, ethnicity and migrational history, family status, and socioeconomic backgrounds.

Although I made deliberate sampling efforts to diversify the sample, women and ethnic minorities remain underrepresented. This is, however, also a defining feature of those at the top of most wealth distributions, of which 87% are male at the global level (Wealth-X 2016), a similar percentage as in my sample. Age within the sample ranges from 28 to 77 years; the average age of 45.6 years is well above the national average of 28. Interviews were conducted in Spanish, recorded and transcribed verbatim; direct quotes are indicated by double quotation marks. To maintain anonymity of informants upon citing them, I assigned a number to each interview.

Considering the public personae of some of the participants, personal characteristics are not disclosed where they could lead to recognition of the individual.

Interviews were analyzed around categories of ethnic/racial identity, perceptions of whiteness, "racialized" characteristics and the legitimation of wealth.[3]

## Racialization and Whiteness in Mexico

Before turning to the analysis of participants' accounts, I will first lay out some considerations about the concept of mestizaje and how it relates to racism in contemporary Mexico, which point to the impossibility of conclusively separating specific racialized traits from others and thus isolate the impact of any one particular trait. Speaking about racism, it is important to first emphasize that there is no scientific justification for the existence of "human races" as a biological reality, or as self-sustained, distinguishable groups that can be classified according to genetic characteristics.[4] Rather, "race" is a historical and social construction based on the false belief that genetic or biological differences exist that not only express themselves in certain (real or imagined) physical traits but these also translate into "natural" hierarchies among different groups and individuals with different traits, irrespective of their group affiliation (Iturriaga 2018). It is in this process of "racialization" that (generic) physical traits acquire relevance as criteria for discrimination and social exclusion, turning them into determinants of social inequalities (Solís et al. 2019). More directly, racialization is the process of linking specific external physical attributes with human qualities (Webster 1993; Segato 2010; Wade 2014; Gall 2016), and a key heuristic people use to make social classifications. The racialized physical trait of skin tone has been shown to be of particular importance as a predictor of social outcomes in the Mexican context (Chavez-Dueñas, Adames, and Organista 2014; Dixon and Telles 2017; Ortiz-Hernández et al. 2011; Monroy-Gómez-Franco and Vélez-Grajales 2020).

It is hardly surprising to any person attending to debates on "race," inequality or human social relations more broadly that the sorting of skin tones on the one hand and favorable/desirable characteristics on the other does not occur randomly, but follows particular patterns. Yet, explaining the micro mechanisms of how this matching comes about is not entirely straightforward in a context such as Mexico's which is multilayered, diverse, and rife with subtle cultural cues which are presupposed and naturalized by all members of an interaction and incorporated in mutual understanding (Hall and Hall 1959; Rubin et al. 1992). What further complicates matters is the relationship *between* different racialized characteristics, which tend to "package" several personal traits to form specific ethnoracial "profiles." For instance, the rich colloquial terms "whitexican" and "naco" explicitly entangle ethnoracial and socioeconomic characteristics, whitexican referring to wealthy, upper-middle class Mexicans, and naco to brown, (culturally) lower class persons (see also Ceron-Anaya's chapter in this volume). These deliberately vague terms succeed in matching physical and socioeconomic attributes because their connotations are understood by everybody within the reach of the Mexican cultural sphere. Often, skin tone is used, to varying degrees of accuracy, as a shortcut for these profiles, as I will explore further as follows.

In contemporary Mexico, whiteness constitutes an aspirational ideal (Navarrete 2017). In the collective imaginary of a country that has experienced a process of racialization since colonial times, being "white" carries a non-neutral meaning. Under colonial rule, somatic traits enabled classification into castes; unsurprisingly resemblance to the colonists implied higher social status. Neither the state doctrine of "mestizaje" or miscegenation, assumed as an anti-colonial nation-building project in the early 20th Century (Lomnitz-Adler 1993; Tenorio Trillo 2009) and promising eventual social, cultural, and ethnoracial equality on the basis of past intermarriage,[5] nor the generous passing of time and continuous mixing of peoples thereafter could eradicate a stubborn notion of "whiter" as superior. In such a context, the premise of mestizaje carries within it the possibility of change both at the individual and at the collective level. It thus illuminates two main functions of "whiteness" in contemporary Mexico: 1) demarcating and defending a location of personal power and status for those who "own" it; and 2) encapsulating a vehicle of potential social ascension for a "bronze race" striving to "whiten" itself towards an idealized European complexion.

As mestizaje upholds an illusion of racial social mobility within a highly stratified system, the intuition that "'light' is seen as 'right'" (Winders 2005, 72) permeates all levels of society.

This is remarkable considering almost 80% of the country's inhabitants self-identify as non-white. When asked to identify their ethnoracial identity, only about 3% of contemporary Mexicans spontaneously self-identify as white (this number increases to less than 10% if the question prompts individuals to identify with one category within a set of predefined options, including "white") (Solís, Güémez and Avitia 2020).[6]

In itself, this distribution does not say much about the relationship between appearance and wealth—until it is made explicit that the different ethnoracial characteristics are not randomly distributed across the population with regard to other characteristics, including socioeconomic status. Beyond the historical disadvantages of racialized individuals and groups, social inequalities in Mexico are linked to ongoing ethnoracial discrimination (Trejo and Altamirano 2016) both in the labor market (Arceo and Campos Vázquez 2014) and many other public and private spheres, including importantly social interaction with friends, family, and colleagues (Solís et al. 2019). On average, those with lighter skin color boast higher wages and higher levels of education compared to individuals with darker skin tones, skewing the distribution of opportunities (Monroy-Gómez-Franco, Vélez, and Yalonetzky 2018). They tend to have better employment opportunities (Arceo and Campos Vázquez 2014; Solís et al. 2019) and they are vastly overrepresented among positions of power in the public (Campos-Vázquez and Rivas-Herrera 2021) and private (Gómez Bruera 2020) sectors.

This privileged position whiteness holds on the class spectrum idealizes its bearers and leads to equating wealth with whiteness. Moreover, the constant media representation of whiteness as beautiful conjures its desirability (Navarrete 2017), aligning aesthetic appreciation smoothly with racialized models as part of a collective aspiration towards "white" body appearances within an ethnically mixed society (Krozer and Gómez 2023). At the same time, the successful and desirable are portrayed as consistently whiter than the majority of the population (Winders 2005; Iturriaga 2018). In combination, this intuitive superposition leads to an associative conflation of wealth and beauty epitomized in whiteness, which helps to internalize and normalize its reproduction over time.

Consequently, racialized profiles hold fixed socioeconomic positions in Mexico, with those perceived as whiter systematically occupying the upper rungs as an increasing number of studies highlights. But how does the interaction between the ethnoracial dimension and socioeconomic inequality come about in practice?

Racism, like other social stratification systems, is governed by relationships of power and privilege that establish its legitimacy to distribute resources under the pretext that systematic human differences warrant such distribution (for instance, specific skin tones, cultures, or genders restrict their bearers to particular positions on the social hierarchy). It expresses itself as a series of diverse structural and systematic exploitation practices and injustices that are triggered by particular racialized physical characteristics that elevate and subordinate, respectively, some individuals over others. For instance, the constant referral to and repetition of popular racial tropes like the one about babies being "pretty despite being brown" (*morenitos pero bonitos*) anchors racist discourses in the collective subconscious from an early age and transforms strategies to "improve the race" (*mejorar la raza*) into a collective social endeavor and individual aspiration. Enacting whiteness thus requires substantial investments of energy from both the racialized and racializing subjects in any social interaction (Castellanos Guerrero 2018).

Despite its ubiquity, whiteness remains an elusive and contentious category, in which the micro-interactions between class, "race" and gender are complex and not fully understood (Cerón-Anaya 2019). Rather than a challenge to its exclusionary power, this stretchable ambiguity plays an important role in the patterns of privilege accumulation across different environments. For instance, Cerón-Anaya (2019) shows that in the lower and middle classes a richer person can be perceived as whiter by exhibiting certain kinds of social status. Due to its "whiter" composition, the elite, however, is less likely to overlook non-conforming phenotypical features among aspirants to their circles (see also Leal 2016). Thus, although racialized notions and class-related assumptions form an amalgam in the "racialization of class" which negates its racism by focusing on socioeconomic differences only, its expressions at different levels within society differ markedly. Moreover, ethnic and racial components are virtually impossible to disentangle in Mexico, as questions of "essence" and "blood" creep into discussions about Indigenous customs and dress upon the slightest challenge (see also Solís et al. 2019).[7]

What we do know is that ethnoracial discrimination includes both individual and collective behavior that reproduces asymmetric social relations in a diverse range of social spaces (Solís et al. 2019). Despite its frequency, few studies in Mexico have analyzed them systematically (Solís et al. 2019; Oehmichen 2007; Moreno Figueroa 2016; Barabas 1979). Most of these studies focus on disenfranchised groups. However, perception of advantaged groups is equally marked by stereotypes and prejudice, which serve to locate power and point towards a hypothetical pathway to approach it. In a context of extreme inequality of resources and opportunities alike, as in the case of Mexico, exploring prevailing views on racism held by the economically privileged can shed some light on the vast and generally underestimated dimensions of the problem.

## Elite Perceptions of Social Status Contingent on Class and "Race"

Discriminated and discriminating behaviors exist in all socioeconomic segments, often even within the same person. Scrutinizing how specific racial stereotypes and expectations inform class identities through mundane practices of discrimination at the top can thus help understand how these concepts are socially constructed and validated. Therefore, in the following I will discuss the perceptions members of the Mexican elites hold, firstly with regard to the interaction between social classes, and secondly on how these relate to particular racialized profiles. I argue that while the segregation of physical and social spaces begets the lack of interaction with the Other, guarding these borders is also in the interests of privilege so as to safeguard its persistence, and is thus actively reinforced.

Both the tremendous success of mestizaje as a social narrative and its simultaneous failure in terms of achieving actual levelling have to be understood based on the inherent contradiction of the concept: it provides in one package a promise of equality, another of social mobility, and also (inconveniently) intrinsic obstacles to the fulfilment of either. These obstacles are difficult to overcome because of "how we have constructed society in Mexico; everything works so this does not happen" (#19). From the perspective of privilege, there are two powerful limitations. On the one hand, the spatial compartmentalization of society itself inhibits the (non-contractual) interaction between different groups. There is limited space where the rich and poor worlds touch: the use of space in Mexico City is highly segregated by socioeconomic level (Oxfam 2020). For education, gastronomy, leisure, and cultural activities, as well as living and public spaces, there is virtually no location shared between individuals from the highest and lowest deciles. Considering the exclusive private spaces frequented by the elites there is arguably even less opportunity for casual interaction—unless it is in these private spaces, which usually implies a contractual relationship, as non-eligible poorer people do not by themselves have access to these spaces "unless they are 'invited' (for some purpose) by an elite member, be that to their club or their home" (#21).

On the other hand, overcoming the obstacles would go against the self-interest of maintaining these privileges. Common sense thus dictates a preference for limited interaction across (socioeconomic) groups, as laid out by the following participant:

> In Mexico, [classes] are completely separated. It's not just a question of money. It's a cultural, racial and social issue. Yes, I mean I am not like that, but the majority of people in the high social strata don't like to interact with people they consider indigenous or Indio. Look, I think this happens in any society—people's relationships get constructed over shared activities, which are related to economic income: if I like to play golf, just to say something, well, I'll interact with people that can play golf. Another way of relating, I think, is to be able to talk, to have topics of shared interest. This might not be money as such, but it implies a vision, a shared way of understanding life. So, I think that when I say 'culture', the topics of interest between the two [wealthy and poor people] are different. And I think you tend to associate with people that have similar interests and activities. Somebody from a completely different world [...] wouldn't be compatible socially or family-wise. (#1)

This incompatibility is both real and imagined. It concerns different interests in terms of recreational activities like sports, as well as limits to shared public space in a society with fragmented health, educational, and even cultural and gastronomical service provision along lines of socioeconomic differences, and the social and family expectations of individuals marrying someone "alike" bear testament to this. However, it also implies a different mental space in terms of awareness of the Other´s presence on those occasions where their physical space does overlap. As Inglis (2019) cautions, relationships between elites and poor exist, and indeed are the necessary consequence of existing inequality. Thus there *is* interaction. However, this interaction happens in a confined space with predefined rules, akin to contractual labor/service relations between two highly unequal individuals, for example, domestic labor that only allows limited space for maneuver (with very few exceptions) in what constitutes socially acceptable behavior. Likewise, the differences in interests mentioned by the participant above are often mediated by pecuniary ability and standard of living (Veblen 1899), as the allegedly random yet frequently arising example of the expensive hobby of golf (or the "experience" of traveling to particular international holiday destinations) indicates.

Participants themselves seem unsure how to disentangle the individual from the social aspects of relationship forging; they disagree about the degree to which they select their personal relationships, including friends and partners, based on shared interests and given individual preferences, as opposed to simply meeting people due to socially predetermined conditions. They agree, however, that restrictions in the form of socially valued or dismissed behavior perpetuate this situation. Questioned about why interaction is limited, participant #46 responds "because we are *clasistas*. Relationships with people from lower socioeconomic levels are frowned upon." What holds for friendships does not extend to service relations. Here, perceived generosity characterizes the self-portrait of the wealthy employer, who holds that, as opposed to the norm, "of course I pay my maid more than the required minimum wage" (#30).[8]

Ceron-Anaya (2019), who reports on social relations between caddies and golfers in Mexico, shares similar observations of predefined patterns of behavior for any interaction, like learned (and shared) rules of the game in the case of golf (and most services). They display a studied performance from both sides: the elites acknowledge the poor conditions of their service providers, pay (genuine) lip service to improving the situation, but have no interest in changing the fundamental underlying conditions. The service providers have studied their dance of servility and deference (Inglis 2019) and/or alternative strategies of relying on direct, highly individualized support by their "benefactors." However, they do not usually challenge or even question the underlying "nature" of some individuals playing in a completely separate league.

Asked about how he can know an unknown person's wealth, a participant explains that "for starters, you can judge from the color. Someone with light skin and colored eyes is rich" (#46). He goes on to point out that this is "because the country is racist. Since their arrival, the Spaniards controlled all realms of power. Thus comes about the aspiration to whiten oneself" (#46). The rhetorical diversion of agency to an administrative body ("the country") 'being' racist allows the individual to slip from responsibility for any discriminatory behavior all the while cultivating a controlled outrage in denouncing an unfair situation. Instead of displaying active resistance towards, or acknowledging complicity in this unfairness, however, the strategy of coping with the ongoing influence conceded to faraway histori-cal events becomes a shrugging normalization of their uncomfortably con-venient consequences. Similar sentiments are shared by most participants:

> You will always think that somebody with Caucasian features belongs to the upper echelons economically speaking. That's normal in Mexico. I think that, on a sociological level, this has been the case since colonial times. (#4)[9]

The association between socioeconomic status and racialized traits seems so obvious and natural to my participants that they scarcely consider it worth elaborating on when it is mentioned. This is remarkable considering that, until recently, racial (self)identification was not collected in official statistics, nor a topic of much public discourse. Notwithstanding, there are clear, col-lectively held profiles of poor and rich people according to my participants, and they almost always feature racialized traits. Previous research confirms that there indeed seems to exist an agreed-upon social hierarchy of pheno-types irrespective of respondents' social standing (see for instance Solís et al. 2019).

The ranking attached to these profiles coincides with the overlap of money and racialized personal characteristics other authors have confirmed (Nutini 1997; Iturriaga 2018; Solís et al. 2019). Thus, the empirical experience of racialized poverty and wealth permeates society at all levels, and leads to palpable perceptional and behavioral consequences. In terms of perceptions, contrary to its self-image, Mexico isn't a colorblind society; it is far more likely for a rich person to be white (of my participants, only two self-identified as "brown," compared to over 80% of the population identifying as non-white on the national level (Solís, Güémez and Avitia 2020).

As to related behaviors, one strategy to legitimize the 'natural' pairing of certain bodies and wallets is precisely its (historical) normalization: handing down responsibility for stereotypes that racialize poverty, and by extension wealth, to events occurring five centuries ago. Without minimizing the impor-tance of the institution of "*la colonia*" in the establishment of these practices, it constitutes a comfortable exit strategy when talking about reasons for their unabashed existence today compared to confronting ongoing discrimination.

Although participants declare that, as a society, "we have not acknowl-edged just how racist we are and we still prejudge and discriminate" (#19), they don't necessarily see the whiteness of privilege as a potent mechanism of exclusion. In an unusual exception, a participant candidly acknowledges the difference in tolerance towards certain behaviors: upon insulting another man, that person laughed, whereas "if it had been a brown dude they would have said 'that *naco*, what nerve to come here and even think of saying something like that'" (#46). The subtlety of these "prejudices and discriminations" here shows in the observation that the aversion would be directed towards persons *perceived to be* Indigenous or poor, that is, there exist clear criteria for judging who belongs to which group and who doesn't.

Mechanisms of exclusion further extend to cultural aspects, identified as "paradigms and filters" that "one holds as an adult" to comply with certain conventions that need to be adhered to in order to be part of certain socio-economic strata (#19). For instance, one cannot invite poor friends to a restaurant without confronting the fear of being "judged by my friends, all the other clients in the restaurant, its staff . . ."—only because they *will* know as the friend *is visibly different*: "the different socioeconomic groups, they speak differently, they look different" (#19).

Appearance and speech are recurrent themes. Often, they are sufficient as indicators to establish a person's position on the social hierarchy, participants assert. However, there are also more indirect characteristics. In classic Bourdieusian manner, fluency in cultural references "typical of our stratum" (that is, "upper-class contexts"), such as "reading Shakespeare" (#15), help to construct easily identifiable access barriers to elite membership. A director wraps them into preoccupation about how the Other would feel in a context in which he didn't "fit in":

> I used to have a teacher [from a poor neighborhood] that I liked a lot. But I could have never invited him to a party with my friends because he wouldn't have felt comfortable. He was a bit shy; different strata operate by different behavioral codes. (#1)

In combination, these "codes" increase the distance between those who are "appropriate" in the way they talk, dress, and look and those who are not. Taken together, these criteria are used to create catalogues of social classification for *insiders* and *outsiders* that are "obvious" and "easy to recognize"—and effectively recognized by the respective groups (#20). The ease of recognition of individual codes and complete profiles, fomented through ubiquitous repetition until their eventual normalization, has the practical purpose of facilitating the reproduction of existing privileges by way of endogamy. As highlighted by the participants, key criteria include visible and audible differences (how a person looks or speaks) alongside cues like social capital (who they are surrounded by or associated with), cultural capital (education) and behavioral and even moral traits like apparent confidence or arrogance (see also Krozer and Gómez 2023). For instance, a participant explains how his appearance ("my color") raised expectations ("excitement") from his future in-laws when they first met him, because in the mating market "you have to prove that you have money. If you are white [*güerito*] it is kind of assumed already that you come from a wealthy family" (#46).

The resulting cultural patterns and social segregations are further consolidated through habits of assortative mating, which "whiten" an elite that chooses to reproduce among its peers: "families marry into the same levels of education, culture and money—the *couple's* [English in the original] and the parents'. That's how they reaffirm these levels, this stratification" (#31).

Participants feel that this "special" treatment goes both ways. Take these very different stories of two participants explaining the everyday consequences and restrictions of their appearance. On one hand, responding to the question about whether he uses public transport, a public sector director answers:

> I would like to, but no; because of my face it's not so easy, it doesn't help me much. The other day I asked the security guard at my new office where I could buy a soft drink or something, and she said: 'No, you'd better not get out'. Just here! And me: 'That bad?' And she said: 'Rather not'. Yep. It's a complicated zone, a tough area, and if they see a guy like this they think he surely must be a multimillionaire! Blondie ['güerito'], you know. I mean my hair is white now, but I am obviously a blondie. (#9)

Stating that his face inhibits him from moving freely in public spheres—presumed straightforwardly as dangerous for somebody with his features—he points out how his phenotypically white appearance would automatically trigger association with upper-class status, and hence expose him to risks. As the participant's exchange with the security guard shows, both the unspecified Other ("them") that he would face on public transport or on his way to the corner shop (taken to belong to different social strata) and the guard herself would similarly read these codes, namely that irrespective of a perceived or real safety threat to the participant, it is commonsense not to mingle with "them."

On the other hand, one of the few participants that do not comply with the stereotypical features speaks of a different sort of restriction. His personal story confirms ethnoracial preconceptions, but he also points out that, in his experience, social position "trumps" deeply internalized racist prejudice—as long as it is "obvious" enough:

> "I am very brown [*negrito*]. This is what I experienced: in my youth, there were environments or issues where there was certain segregation. This has decreased. I'm not sure whether this is because it actually disappeared, or rather because your position became more influential. I mean, it's not the same to snub a brownie ['morenito'] like me that comes walking along, or the one arriving at a high-end restaurant in a fancy car accompanied by four bodyguards, right? As a teenager, if we went to a club for example, all my friends that look like you [blond] just went in, and to me they said: 'no, this one doesn't pass.' And today wherever I go it's the opposite, they even say 'you, come!', right? Mexico has changed in this regard, I think classism is *much* stronger and more predominant today than racism." (#20)

This sentiment is confirmed by another participant (#99) from a very well-off family who, considering himself "brown," claims to have been denied entry to nightclubs due to his slightly darker skin tone compared to his friends, despite his wealth. He elaborates that, when he gave the club owner a call and made him come to the door to check on the situation, he would be admitted without problem. Rather than implying the predominance of one or the other discriminatory treatment (race or class), this shows how both categories can 'deceive' the gatekeepers where they are not displayed in the 'standard', expected combination, and lead to confusion among those addressed. They nonetheless remain clearly identifiable for the individual being discriminated against: as they tell their stories—just like others who recount observing similar events not concerning themselves directly—they never doubted that the treatment received related to their racialized features, even when the official response (the bouncer's) related to "the wrong shoes" (#99) (for "random" codes created by doormen, see also Mears 2020). This shows the constant translation work going on in both directions, as well as a degree of inter-changeability of categories as a pretext for exclusion.

It also points to the fact that privilege needs careful guarding. Indeed, none of these accounts challenged the existence of dissimilar treatment and exclusion per se, only their own position in them, particularly if these were perceived as placing them on the wrong side of dealings. Where diversity is not appreciated as a value in itself, and only tolerated within limited margins that do not threaten the established order, strict protocols are needed to rein-force the boundaries. Thus, even though in the example above the participant is grudgingly let into the club upon flashing his credentials (the owner con-nection), these ceremonies repeat every time a similar situation unfolds: they are no accident, but proclaimed rules (and doormen, for instance, are par-ticularly and explicitly trained in these performances). They are part of a rit-ual anticipated and expected, if not appreciated, by most everybody involved.

While some might feel that a classist discourse looks less bigoted than a racist one, this argument does not seem to be of concern for many people comfortable in their management of either of those discourses. Nonetheless, the renewed verve in the public discourse about racism in Mexico is start-ing to increase consciousness about the issue even in the mainstream. Predictably, it is also creating a strong backlash from certain sections of soci-ety. In fact, the denial of racism as an explicit effort purported by national elites of the post-revolutionary regime (Knight 1990) prevails as a cultural project today (Ceron-Anaya 2019). The conviction that an ostensibly race-less country cannot be racist brushes aside all evidence to the contrary by claiming that these treatments are really classist. While there is no reason to claim that this would be any more ethically acceptable, the empirical evidence also shows that it is simply false: for instance, studies on social mobility still detect residual effects of skin tone after controlling for socioeconomic origins (Monroy- Gómez-Franco and Velez-Grajales 2020).

Instead, it points precisely to the impossibility of unequivocally separat-ing these layers from each other. The superficially straightforward category of 'skin color' is often used as a proxy to point to 'purely racial differences,' but on closer inspection this feature turns out to be a composite made up of many physical and non-physical personal traits bundled together, including—as well as skin pigment, eye color, hair type, body size and face shape—ways of talking, moving and coming across (see also Fanon 1952 on epidermal schemas). Likewise, whereas judging a person's class status presumably relies on their material assets and occupation, most descriptions of the 'wealthy' (or 'poor') rely on financial *and* bodily attributes (see also Nutini 1995 on the characterization of the aristocracy). Both are constructed in parallel. Partly this is because ethnoracial categories need to be understood as permeable and even fluid due to their context dependency and the relationality they rely upon, as do class attributes due to the relational nature of class itself. As has long been understood for class, recent scholarship increasingly highlights the public recognition of 'race' not as a biological concept, but as a social-identity fact that makes sense only in juxtaposition to, and interaction with, an Other (see for instance Wilkerson 2020).

For the same reason, no conclusive judgment can be made as to the prevalence of one type of discrimination over the other; racist and classist prejudice are intimately intertwined. The fact is both are prevalent, and often either is a sufficient, if not necessary, condition for a person to be treated as if both applied. The above testimonies offer a glimpse into the making of "homogenous" social contexts in high socioeconomic level settings, where treatment is adjusted to the place and characteristics of the person at hand. As having friends and contacts from diverse origins helps reduce perceptual biases, the homogenization of spaces is problematic, as it informs judgements and preferences of individuals and their reference groups (Dawtry et al. 2015). Just like social narratives, reference groups are tremendously useful heuristics that help us organize our conceptions of the world. However, availability biases (the tendency to generalize on the basis of available information in our immediate environment) turn counterproductive where information accessible in our proximity differs significantly from other information, and, relatedly, when obtained insights run along lines of difference (Khan 2015). In such cases, segregation by socioeconomic class coincides with separation by color—or, to simplify, each group lives in a world of its own. Participants framed this situation as the coexistence of "the many Mexicos" (#16). It comes about under conditions of segregation, where the overlap between the respective Mexicos steadily decreases, and results in predictive patterns of class based on racialized features (and vice versa).

This is also how, ultimately, inequality feeds racial prejudice (and vice versa). A participant exposed this amalgam of structural discrimination by casually—because it seemed obvious to him—mentioning that "somebody descending from the Sierra Tarahumara could not become president of *Televisa*" (#4). The respective opportunities for an Indigenous person in poverty hailing from the northern mountains and the CEO of Televisa, one of the wealthiest individuals of the country, differ from the outset. They live, quite literally, in different worlds, each in a Mexico of their own, each governed by different laws[10] and life chances, and inhabited by different types of residents.

## Conclusion

In this chapter I have shown that the contemporary myth of mestizaje, which results in an aspiration toward whiteness, coexists with high levels of economic and ethnoracial inequality that are intimately intertwined. I have presented perceptions of members of the Mexican elite to highlight the challenge of disentangling racialized and class-based assumptions in the making of self-image as well as the treatment of others. I have further argued that this situation benefits privilege as it makes its domains easily recognizable at first sight. On the one hand, following criteria of structural racism, discrimination practices are used as a tool to identify whom, where and how to *exclude*. On the other hand, through the use of cultural norms, (spatial) segregation restricts with whom, where, and how to *interact*. Based on the mutual reinforcement of the mechanisms of access control, barriers of entry to these groups are high, which consolidates the identification of each individual with their respective socioeconomic and "cultural" peers. Thus, class-based and racialized behavior cannot be conclusively separated from one another and their codes are often used interchangeably. This results in a social stratification where specific racialized profiles are matched with predetermined economic positions, leading to the cognitive shortcuts described at the outset.

Despite the predominant social narrative of mestizaje that promises equalizing opportunities and results for all Mexicans, differences start even before individuals are born: their household of origin—in relation to both socio-economic and ethnoracial origins—is decisive for the life chances eventually available them. For all the attractiveness of a simplifying myth like mestizaje, in its current understanding it is a collectively harmful system. It separates and divides us as individuals and groups, it confuses us as to who we are, it limits our social mobility and predefines life chances. The problem of widespread racism in Mexico persists because racialized differences are so profoundly normalized on all levels of society that they blind us to the harm this does to all members of society. Instead of cultivating the privilege of being white, it is necessary to create space to coexist, get to know each other and foment tolerance if a less unequal, and more just, society is to be achieved.

## Notes

1 Based on official statistics by the National Statistics Institute INEGI and adjustments for underreporting of top incomes by various researchers available at the time of research (Campos-Vázquez et al. 2014, 2016; del Castillo, 2015; and (Leyva, Bustos, and Romo 2016), I set the threshold for the top 1% of the income distribution at about MXN120.000 monthly per capita. For a more detailed explanation see (Krozer 2018).

2 These amounts are current incomes only, not taking into account material or financial wealth held by the individual or her family, spouses' income, government transfers or other incomes not related to the individual's primary activities.

3 For more information about the project, and the processes of its qualitative data collection and analysis, see (Solís, Güémez and Lorenzo Holm 2019) and discrimination.colmex.mx.

4 Researchers have long pointed out that, biologically, 'race' only accounts for 0.012% of our genetic differences, that is, as human beings, we share over 99%

5 Independent Mexico's foundational myth subjects all Mexicans to the 'mixed-race' identity of 'mestizo', based on the narrative of an allegedly complete merge of indigenous peoples and colonists to form the racially superior 'Bronze race' (Vasconcelos 1925), combining the best of two worlds (Indian and Spanish).

6 By comparison, identification as 'indigenous' triples these amounts, and 'mestizo'—although far less accepted as a category of identification than the founding myth has it—accommodates over half of the population (ibid).

7 In practice they tend to function as triggers mainly when presented in combination with other, *physical* traits, partly because contextual placement is required to 'correctly' socially locate a person wearing traditional indigenous attire: if that person is being perceived as 'white', her treatment would differ compared to if she is not (at worst assuming cultural appropriation or tourism).

8 Inglis (2018) even documents a mutually perceived generosity in his study of caddies and golfers in India.

9 Adler and Perez (1987) note how in Mexico the Spanish were often described as blond and blue-eyed. Presumably most Europeans would describe them as predominantly dark-haired (*'mediterranean'*).

10 Again, this can be read quite literally, since, "when you find yourself in an economically strong position, you can buy justice" (#13A) participants hold, implying dissimilar access to, and kinds of, justice. At the same time, "the issue in Mexico is that often those that have money will degrade those that have less" (#7).

## References

Arceo-Gómez, Eva and Raymundo Campos-Vázquez. 2014. "Race and Marriage in the Labor Market: A Discrimination Correspondence Study in a Developing Country." *The American Economic Review* 104 (5): 376–380.

Barabas, Alicia. 1979. "Colonialismo y racismo en Yucatán: una aproximación histórica y contemporánea." *Revista Mexicana de Ciencias Políticas y Sociales* 97: 105–139.

Campos-Vazquez, Raymundo and Rivas-Herrera, Carolina. 2021. "The Color of Electoral Success: Estimating the Effect of Skin Tone on Winning Elections in Mexico." *Social Science Quarterly* 102 (2): 844–864: https://doi.org/10.1111/ssqu.12933.

Castellanos Guerrero, Alicia. 2018. "Antropología y racismo en México." In *Las Élites de La Ciudad Banca: Discursos Racistas Sobre La Otredad*, edited by Eugenia Iturriaga. Mexico: UNAM. https://www.academia.edu/43394061/Las_%C3%A9lites_de_la_ciudad_banca_discursos_racistas_sobre_la_otredad.

Ceron-Anaya, Hugo. 2019. *Privilege at play. Class, race, gender, and golf in Mexico*. Oxford University Press.

Chavez-Dueñas, Nayeli Y., Hector Y. Adames, and Kurt C. Organista. 2014. "Skin-Color Prejudice and Within-Group Racial Discrimination: Historical and Current Impact on Latino/a Populations." *Hispanic Journal of Behavioral Sciences* 36 (1): 3–26. https://doi.org/10.1177/0739986313511306.

Dawtry, R. J., R. M. Sutton, and C. G. Sibley. 2015. "Why Wealthier People Think People Are Wealthier, and Why It Matters: From Social Sampling to Attitudes to Redistribution." *Psychological Science* 26 (9): 1–12.

Dixon, A.R, and E.E. Telles. 2017. "Skin Color and Colorism: Globalizing White Supremacy." *Annual Review of Sociology* 43: 405–24.

Fanon, Frantz. 1952. *Black skin, white masks*. New York: Grove Press.

Gall, Olivia. 2016. "Hilando fino entre las identidades, el racismo y la xenofobia en México y Brasil." *Desacatos* 51 (May–August): 8–17.

Gaztambide-Fernández, Rubén A. 2015. "Elite Entanglements and the Demand for a Radically Un/Ethical Position: The Case of Wienie Night." *International Journal of Qualitative Studies in Education* 28 (9): 1129–47. https://doi.org/10.1080/09518398.2015.1074752.

Gómez Bruera, Hernán. 2020. *El color del privilegio. El racismo cotidiano en México*. México: Planeta.

Hall, Edward Twitchell, and T. Hall. 1959. *The silent language*. Doubleday.

Inglis, David. 2018. *An invitation to social theory*. John Wiley & Sons.

Iturriaga, Eugenia. 2018. *Las Élites de La Ciudad Banca: Discursos Racistas Sobre La Otredad*. Mexico: UNAM. https://www.academia.edu/43394061/Las_%C3%A9lites_de_la_ciudad_banca_discursos_racistas_sobre_la_otredad.

Khan, Shamus Rahman. 2015. "The Counter-Cyclical Character of the Elite." In *Elites on Trial* (*Research in the Sociology of Organizations, 43*), edited by Glenn Morgan, Paul Hirsch, and Sigrid Quack, (Bradford, UK: Emerald Group Publishing Limited): 81–103: https://doi.org/10.1108/S0733-558X20150000043015.

Knight, Alan. 1990. "Racism, Revolution, and Indigenismo: Mexico, 1910–1940." In *The idea of race in Latin America, 1870–1940*, edited by Richard Graham, 71–113. Austin: University of Texas Press.

Krozer, Alice. 2018. *Inequality in Perspective: Rethinking Inequality Measurement, Minimum Wages, and Elites in Mexico* (PhD Thesis, Centre of Development Studies, University of Cambridge, March 2018): https://doi.org/10.17863/CAM.37302.

Krozer, Alice and Andrea Gómez. 2023. "Not in the Eye of the Beholder: Racialization, Whiteness, and Beauty Standards in Mexico." *Latin American Research Review* 58: 422–39. doi:10.1017/lar.2022.104.

Leal, Alejandra. 2016. "'You Cannot Be Here': The Urban Poor and the Specter of the Indian in Neoliberal Mexico City." *Journal of Latin American and Caribbean Anthropology* 21 (3): 539–559. https://doi.org/10.1111/jlca.12196.

Leyva, Gerardo, Alfredo Bustos, and Ana Miriam Romo. 2016. "Life Satisfaction and Happiness in Mexico: Correlates and Redundancies." In *Handbook of happiness research in Latin America*, edited by Mariano Rojas, 579–611. International Handbooks of Quality-of-Life. Dordrecht: Springer Netherlands. https://doi.org/10.1007/978-94-017-7203-7_32.

Lomnitz-Adler, Claudio. 1993. *Exits from the Labyrinth*. University of California Press.

Mears, Ashley. 2020. *Very Important People: Status and Beauty in the Global Party Circuit*. (New Jersey: Princeton University Press).

Monroy-Gómez-Franco, Luis A., Roberto Vélez-Grajales, and Gastón Yalonetzky. 2022. *Layers of Inequality: Social Mobility, Inequality of Opportunity and Skin Colour in Mexico*. Working paper 03/2018. Centro de Estudios Espinosa Yglesias.

Monroy-Gómez-Franco, Luis, and Roberto Vélez-Grajales. 2020. "Skin Tone Differences in Social Mobility in Mexico: Are We Forgetting Regional Variance?" *Journal of Economics, Race, and Policy* 4 (4): 257–74. https://doi.org/10.1007/s41996-020-00062-1.

Moreno Figueroa, Mónica G. 2016. "El archivo del estudio del racismo en México." *Desacatos* 51 (May–August): 92–107.

Navarrete, Federico. 2017. *Alfabeto Del Racismo Mexicano.* MALPASO. https://hchlibrary.org/Hoopla/14479106.

Nutini, Hugo. 1995. *The wages of conquest: The Mexican aristocracy in the context of western aristocracies.* University of Michigan Press.

Nutini, Hugo. 1997. "Class and Ethnicity in Mexico: Somatic and Racial Considerations." *Ethnology* 36 (3): 227–238.

Oehmichen, Cristina. 2007. "Violencia en las relaciones interétnicas y racismo en la Ciudad de México." *Cultura y Representaciones Sociales* 1 (2): 91–117.

OECD. 2019. *Education at a Glance 2019, OECD Indicators* (OECD Publishing, Paris): https://www.oecd-ilibrary.org/education/education-at-a-glance-2019_f12055c8-en.

Ortiz-Hernández, Luis, Sandra Compeán-Dardón, Elizabeth Verde-Flota, and Maricela Nanet Flores-Martínez. 2011. "Racism and Mental Health among University Students in Mexico City." *Salud Pública de México* 53 (2): 125–33. https://doi.org/10.1590/S0036-36342011000200005.

Oxfam México. 2020. *Mundos paralelos. Big data y desigualdad en la CDMX.* https://oxfammexico.org/wp-content/uploads/2020/07/Oxfam_Big-Data-Y-Desigualdad-CDMX-V04.pdf.

Reis, Elisa, and Mick Moore, eds. 2005. *Elite perceptions of poverty and inequality.* Zed Books Ltd. https://doi.org/10.5040/9781350219878.

Rubin, Rebecca B., Carlos Fernández Collado, Roberto Hernandez-Sampieri. 1992. "A cross-cultural examination of interpersonal communication motives in Mexico and The United States." *International Journal of Intercultural Relations* 16 (2): 145–57. https://doi.org/10.1016/0147-1767(92)90015-M.

Segato, Rita Laura. 2010. "Los Cauces Profundos de La Raza Latinoamericana: Una Relectura Del Mestizaje." *Critica y Emancipacion* 3 (2): 11–44.

Sherman, Rachel. 2017. *Uneasy Street: The anxieties of affluence.* New Jersey: Princeton University Press.

Solís, Patricio, Alice Krozer, Carlos Arroyo and Braulio Güémez. 2019. "Discriminación étnico-racial en México. Una taxonomía de las prácticas."

In *La métrica de lo intangible: del concepto a la medición de la discriminación*, edited by J. Rodríguez Zepeda and T. González Luna, 55–94. Consejo Nacional para Prevenir la Discriminación. https://dds.cepal.org/redesoc/publicacion?id=5051.

Solís, Patricio, Braulio Güémez, and Marcela Avitia. 2020. *Autoadscripción étnico-racial en México. Reporte de la Encuesta Proder # 2* (México: El Colegio de México): https://discriminacion.colmex.mx/.

Solís, Patricio, Braulio Güémez, and Raymundo M. Campos-Vazquez. 2023. *Skin Tone and Inequality of Economic Outcomes in Mexico: A Comparative Analysis Using Optical Colorimeters and Color Palettes.* PRODER Working Paper #8, El Colegio de México.

Tenorio Trillo, Mauricio. 2009. *Historia y celebración: México y sus centenarios.* Mexico City: Editorial Tusquets.

"The World Ultra Wealth Report 2015–2016—Wealth-X Exclusive." 2016. *Wealth-X* (blog). Accessed May 7, 2022. https://www.wealthx.com/report/the-wealth-x-world-ultra-wealth-report-2015-2016/.

Trejo, Guillermo and Melina Altamirano. 2016. "The Mexican Color Hierarchy. How Race and Skin Tone Still Define Life Chances 200 Years after Independence." In *The double bind: The politics of racial and class inequalities in the Americas*, edited by Juliet Hooker and Alvin Tillery, 1–14. Washington: American Political Science Association.

Veblen, Thorstein. 1899. *The theory of the leisure class: An economic study of institutions.* Macmillan.

Wade, Peter. 2014. "Race, Ethnicity, and Technologies of Belonging." *Science, Technology, & Human Values* 39 (4): 587–96. https://doi.org/10.1177/0162243913516807.

Webster, Yehudi. 1993. *The Racialization of America.* St. Martin's Press.

Wilkerson, Isabel. 2020. *Caste: The origins of our discontents.* Random House/Allen Lane.

Winders, Jamie, John P. Jones, and Michael J. Higgins. 2005. "Making Güeras: Selling White Identities on Late-Night Mexican Television." *Gender, Place and Culture* 12 (1): 71–93. https://doi.org/10.1080/09663690500082984.

# INVISIBLE MAYA COMMUNITIES: INDIGENOUS TERRITORY AND THE NATION-STATE IN THE YUCATÁN

José Ángel Koyoc Kú (K'ajlay)
Translated by Ellen Jones

The Yucatán Peninsula is currently undergoing major territorial transformations. However, it is often forgotten that this is not the first time the region has undergone such changes. The Mexican State has played a fundamental role in the relationship between Maya communities and disputed peninsular territories. By detailing the specific histories of Chablekal and Homún, two Maya communities in the state of Yucatán, this article examines how the Mexican State has invisibilized Indigenous communities and their territoriality.

## Defending Territory in the Old North-Eastern Henequen-Producing Region

Chablekal is a Maya community located in the northern part of the municipality of Mérida, which has the administrative status of a precinct. Since 1990, property developers have had their eye on its land with a view to building luxury residential developments and shopping centers. The area has recently acquired commercial value because it is near the highway connecting the state capital to the port of Progreso. As a result, the current ejido[1] commissioners, working hand in hand with officials from institutions like the Agrarian Ombudsman and the National Agrarian Registry, have sold off much of Chablekal's land (see Figure V.1). In order to reclaim their right to the territory, the community set up the Chablekal Residents' Union in 2014. Since the establishment of the Union, residents have reclaimed Misnebalam lands, which take their name from an old henequen-producing hacienda (Indignación 2017, 2019).

For their part, the Maya community of Homún is currently the head of the entire Homún municipality. Since 2017, they have faced the threat of a giant pork factory being built. Construction was begun inside their territory without their consent and without prior consultation—both of which they have a right to under international law. The Yucatecan company Producción Alimentaria Porcina (Pork Food Production) intends to use the mega-factory to raise more than 49,000 pigs and sell their meat for consumption abroad. The farm has faced opposition from part of the community ever since its construction was proposed. The *Kanan Ts'ono'ot* (Guardians of the Cenotes) was set up in 2017, a committee made up of Maya residents of Homún, calling for a consultation process allowing them to exercise their right to free determination. Almost eight hundred people participated in the consultation, in which the residents collectively objected to the building of the mega-factory. Despite the fact that the factory's progress is currently stalled, following an appeal by children living in Homún, there is now a real threat that the pork factory will begin operations (Indignación 2021).

Chablekal and Homún are located in part of the peninsula that has undergone profound transformations over a number of centuries, transformations

Figure V.1.  Location of Homún and Chablekal in the state of Yucatán and in the old north-eastern henequén-producing region.

*Credit*: José Ángel Koyoc Kú (K'ajlay).

that were only possible because the Mexican State has always systematically made Mayan communities invisible by ignoring their relationship with the land. In order to understand Maya communities' territoriality and the way they organize their land, it is important to understand the concept of k'áax. K'áax refers to the parts of the peninsula covered in scrubland; this is sacred land with ritual meaning, where supernatural beings such as the yuumil k'áaxo'ob (forest elders), the báalamo'ob (guardians), and the cháako'ob (rain elders), among others, reside. Cenotes (natural sink holes) located in the k'áax are also an important feature of this land, since they represent a means of communicating with the underground world (García Quintanilla 2000). These "owners" of the scrubland who "dwelled" in cenotes and caves were invoked in 1807 by "eight Indigenous men and four Indigenous women" from Homún to perform a ceremony in thanks for good harvests (Cruz Ramírez 2016, 178–179). This area of scrubland is evidently more than just land for agriculture or forestry; it has held importance for Maya peoples on the peninsula from the precolonial era right up to the present.

This way of understanding the territory has been misunderstood and unrecognized ever since Mexico's emergence as a nation-state. Moreover, in order to appropriate these spaces, successive governments have labelled the territory "wasteland," a term that has been employed by governments of independent republics across Latin America to characterize Indigenous land as empty and uncultivated (Palacio Castañeda 2009, 110). It was used by the Courts of Cádiz in their decrees of November 9, 1812 and January 4, 1813, in order to facilitate the privatization and colonization of Indigenous people's communal land (Güémez Pineda 1994, 267). These laws and decrees were taken up once again by the independent Republic of Yucatán, thus serving in the second half of the nineteenth century to dispossess Indigenous communities in the Yucatán Peninsula of their "communal lands," including communal scrublands and waterways. These are terms used by Indigenous peoples to refer to the natural resources administrated and managed by the organizations known as Indigenous republics (Guëmez Pineda 1994 and Ortiz Yam 2011), in large part in order to oppose their characterization as "wastelands"--uncultivated, empty, and ownerless.

The concept of "wasteland" not only invisibilized the peninsular Mayas' ownership of the forests, it also invisibilized the milpa, the activity that structured the rest of their agricultural production. The nature of the soil and vegetation in Yucatán meant that the land being used for agriculture had to be rotated from time to time, so that although there were large uncultivated spaces at any given time, they were not empty, exactly; rather, they served as areas where wood and medicinal plants could be collected, and where vegetation was allowed to recover so that the land could be sown again in the future. Governments, however, frequently classified these areas as wastelands, or as unproductive, allowing hacienda owners to report them and thus to expand their property or indeed to establish new haciendas. This trend accelerated after the early years of the "Caste War,"[2] giving rise to the large properties that later became henequen haciendas.

At the end of the nineteenth century, both Chablekal and Homún therefore found themselves surrounded by henequen haciendas, having been dispossessed of their communal lands. The henequen region, which was established around the 1880s, is located in the rocky northeast of the peninsula, where the soil is best suited to farming it. Henequen is an agave from whose leaves a fiber can be extracted to make rope. Although it has been farmed since the precolonial era, it wasn't until the end of the nineteenth century that US demand for this "precious" fibre led to thousands of hectares of scrubland in northeast Yucatán being turned over to single crop agave farming. Its production depended on a system of forced labor in which corporal punishment and other kinds of coercive measures were not unusual, leading to conditions in many haciendas that approached de facto slavery (Bellingeri 1999; Cline 1987; García Quintanilla 1986).

The agro-industrial production of henequen led to the Maya people living in the haciendas and surrounding villages gradually leaving corn farming behind and instead taking up grueling jobs on henequen farms—fenced off areas in need of a permanent labor force. In spite of this, the agave monoculture did not wipe out either the milpa workers or the scrubland, as maps of the Misnebalam hacienda, dating back to Porfirio Díaz's time, clearly illustrate (see Figure V.2). For this reason, when the revolutionary regime began to distribute land after the collapse of the Porfiriato, both scrubland and henequen farms passed into the possession of Maya workers. Homún and Chablekal recovered their ownership of the scrubland and waterways during the Revolution thanks to the granting of ejidos, thus taking back possession of areas that had been expropriated, and populating them again with the yuumil k'áaxo'ob, aluxo'ob, and other guardians of the space known as k'áax.

However, post-revolutionary land reform brought with it its own difficulties and contradictions. The revolutionary regime considered two methods by which to return land to those who had been dispossessed of waterways and scrublands following the liberal reform and the June 1856 Lerdo Law. The first of these was restitution. To qualify for this, communities had to reliably document their prior ownership of natural resources that had been expropriated. The second was through land grants, designed for rural workers who could not provide any such documentation or whose documents were deemed insufficient to establish the size and location of the lands that had been seized. Maya-speaking workers received land grants rather than having their land returned to them through a process of restitution, because many communities could not provide the necessary paperwork to prove their ownership of the scrubland expropriated by the hacienda owners, and also because of the time consuming nature of the process of restitution

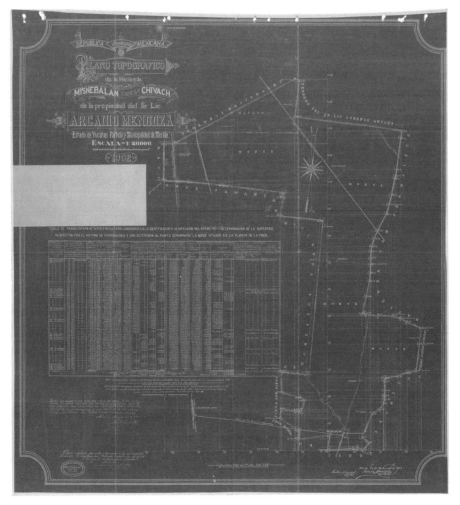

Figure V.2.  Detail of a topographic map of the Misnebalam hacienda.

Note: The area labelled "monte" indicates that the scrublands were not destroyed, or at least not entirely.

Credit: Carlos Miramón, Yucatán, 1902 (MOYB).

(Ortiz Yam 2011, 157–58;Torres Mazuera et al. 2018, 9). The distribution of land through grants allowed for the imposition of a particular kind of territoriality in the postrevolutionary state: the ejido.[3] In the long term, this meant the federalization of natural resources that in previous centuries had been owned, administered, and run by local organizations such as town councils (Aboites 2004, 11).

The reduction of the scrublands to mere agricultural spaces has direct consequences for Chablekal's current struggle to defend the scrubland in its jurisdiction. The Agrarian Ombudsman delegate has denied that the community existed before agrarian reform took place. After the Union sued the ejido to try to prevent the expropriation of ejido scrublands, the delegate gave the following answer in response to the judge's request:

> Regardless of what has been said, I consider it appropriate to inform you that the Agrarian center known as Chablekal, Municipality of Mérida, Yucatán State, was not created in recognition of its status as a community that has owned and occupied the lands since time immemorial, but as a result of the Granting and Expansion of Ejidos intended to benefit groups of rural workers entitled to receive them. For this reason, it was created as an Ejido, and not as an Agrarian Community, which is why nothing alleged by the plaintiffs in their initial appeal applies, nor anything in the brief delivered to this institution, which was duly answered. (quoted in Magaña Canul 2020, 326)

But now it is not only agrarian institutions that have taken it upon themselves to invisibilize Maya communities; environmental institutions have done so too. Homún, for instance, has suffered at the hands of the Ministry for Urban Development and Environment (now the Ministry for Sustainable Development), an institution that depends on the State of Yucatán and which is responsible for authorizing Environmental Impact Statements, a document required by companies if they wish to carry out any kind of construction or project. Eduardo Batllori, the institution's secretary, signed Producción Alimentaria Porcina's Environmental Impact Statement despite the document stating that "no Indigenous communities will be impacted by the development of the project because there is no Indigenous community in the area." The mega-factory is five kilometers from Homún, a community described as "Indigenous" in documents created by the old National Commission for the Development of Indigenous Communities, the Institute for the Development of Yucatec Maya Culture, and the Autonomous University of Yucatán (Velázquez 2020, 188–189).

## Perpetual Invisibilization

Reflecting on how the Mexican state has invisibilized Maya peoples and their territoriality over time helps us recognize that the idea of Maya lands as "empty spaces" continues today, and plays a central role in the current transformation of the Yucatán Peninsula. Since the emergence of the Mexican nation-state, Maya ways of organizing their lands have often been ignored, and with them associated activities such as the milpa, forest management, and the spiritual and ritual practices associated with the land. This is not merely an agrarian issue; environmental institutions have also revealed their ignorance of Indigenous presence, demonstrating that this way of seeing the peninsular territory goes beyond a single institution. The plans for the pork mega-factory in Homún and the dispossession of ejido scrubland in Chablekal indicate that the idea of Indigenous peoples' territory as "empty" space available for colonization or economic exploitation remains strong. The transformations ripping through the peninsula today lead us to wonder how Maya communities can exercise their rights when this imaginary remains so deep-rooted. It is crucial to acknowledge that this type of continuity does nothing but defer Maya peoples' ability to exercise their right to self-determination.

## Notes

1  The ejido came about as a kind of collective land tenancy following the Mexico Revolution.
2  The "Caste War" was an armed conflict that began in 1847 and lasted for over half a century. Rural Maya and mestizo laborers came into conflict with the Yucatán state government and the Mexican national government. One of the long-term consequences of the war was that large swathes of territory in the east of the Peninsula remained under Maya rebel control until the beginning of the twentieth century.
3  An ejido differs from an agrarian community, another kind of collective land tenancy, in the way the land is obtained, which in the case of the ejido is through land grants (Torres Mazuera et al. 2018, 8).

## References

Aboites, Luis. 1998. *El agua de la nación: una historia política de México, (1888–1946)*. Mexico D.F.: Centro de Investigaciones y Estudios Superiores en Antropología Social.

Aboites, Luis. 2004. *Del agua municipal al agua nacional: materiales para una historia de los municipios en México 1901-1945*. Mexico: Centro de Investigaciones y Estudios Superiores en Antropología Social.

Bellingeri, Marco. 1999. "La racionalidad esclavista de la producción henequenera en Yucatán (1880-1914)." In *Para una historia de América Latina III. Los nudos 2*, edited by Alicia Hernández Chávez, Ruggiero Romano, and

Marcello Carmagnani: 221–82. Mexico: Fondo de Cultura Económica, El Colegio de México.

Bracamonte y Sosa, Pedro. 2000. "La jurisdicción cuestionada y el despojo agrario en el Yucatán del siglo XIX." *Revista Mexicana del Caribe* 5 (10): 150–79.

Cline, Howard F. 1987. "El episodio del henequén en Yucatán." *Secuencia* 0 (08), 186. https://doi.org/10.18234/secuencia.v0i08.185.

Cruz Ramírez, Eunice. 2016. "Santos cristianos y rituales indígenas: los curatos del Obispado de Yucatán; entre 1778-1791." Masters thesis, Centro de Investigaciones y Estudios Superiores en Antropología Social, Mérida, Yucatán: http://ciesas.repositorioinstitucional.mx/jspui/handle/1015/327.

García Quintanilla, Alejandra. 1986. *Los tiempos en Yucatán: los hombres, las mujeres y la naturaleza (siglo XIX)*. Mexico D.F.: Claves Latinoamericanas.

García Quintanilla, Alejandra. 2000. "El dilema de Ah Kimsah K'ax, 'el que mata al monte': significados del monte entre los mayas milperos de Yucatán." *Mesoamérica* 21 (39): 255–86.

García Quintanilla, Alejandra, and Tsubasa Okoshi Harada. 2005. "La disputa por la naturaleza: la desaparición de los montes de los mayas yucatecos." *Temas antropológicos: Revista científica de investigaciones regionales* 27 (1), 67–105.

Güémez Pineda, Arturo. 1994. *Liberalismo en tierras del caminante: Yucatán, 1812–1840*. Zamora: El Colegio de Michoacan.

Indignación, Equipo. 2017. "El derecho a la tierra, el territorio y los recursos naturales del pueblo indígena maya de Chablekal, visto desde lo histórico y antropológico." Amicus Curiae memorial presented to the Agrarian Unitarian Tribune of the 34th District in Chablekal, Yucatán. http://indignacion.org.mx/wp-content/uploads/2019/11/Dossier-de-prensa-Uni%C3%B3n-Pobladores-Chablekal-07.11.2019.pdf.

Indignación, Equipo. 2019. "Chablekal: la defensa de los montes del pueblo." Press release. Chablekal, Yucatán. http://indignacion.org.mx/wp-content/uploads/2019/11/Dossier-de-prensa-Uni%C3%B3n-Pobladores-Chablekal-07.11.2019.pdf.

Indignación, Equipo. 2021. "Homún: pueblo maya guardián del agua." Press release. Chablekal, Yucatán. http://indignacion.org.mx/wp-content/uploads/2021/05/FD_Homun_0427.pdf.

Magaña Canul, Rolando. 2019. "¿Luchas indígenas por la tierra en Yucatán? estudio sobre neoliberalismo y apropiación de la identidad maya en la región ex-henequenera." Doctoral thesis, Université Laval, Quebec, Canada.

Ortiz Yam, Inés. 2011. "De milperos a henequeneros: los procesos agrarios en el noreste de Yucatán, 1870–1937." Doctoral thesis, El Colegio de México, Mexico D.F.

Palacio Castañeda, Germán. 2006. *Fiebre de Tierra Caliente. Una Historia Ambiental de Colombia 1850–1930*. Bogotá, Colombia: Universidad Nacional de Colombia, ILSA. https://repositorio.unal.edu.co/handle/unal/57000.

Palacio Castañeda, Germán. 2009. "El papel del derecho en el cambio material y simbólico del paisaje colombiano, 1850-1930." *Pensamiento Jurídico* 25: 91–116.

Torres-Mazuera, Gabriela, Jorge Fernández Mendiburu, and Claudia Gómez Godoy. 2018. "Informe sobre la jurisdicción agraria y los derechos humanos de los pueblos indígenas y campesinos en México." Fundación por el Debido Proceso. www.dplf.org/es/resources/informe-sobre-la-jurisdiccion-agraria-y-los-derechos-humanos-de-los-pueblos-indigenas-y.

Velázquez Solís, Alberto Carlos. 2020. "U tookchajal u lu'umil, u k'áaxil maaya kaaj. Arrebato/defensa de la tierra, el monte del pueblo maya." Doctoral thesis, Centro de Investigaciones y Estudios Superiores en Antropología Social, San Cristóbal de las Casas, Chiapas.http://ciesas.repositorioinstitucional.mx/jspui/handle/1015/1033.

# CHAPTER 9

# Racialized Dispossession in Energy Transition: Indigenous Communities, Communal Lands, and Wind Farms in the Isthmus of Tehuantepec, Mexico

Josefa Sánchez Contreras Translated by Ellen Jones

In the communal lands of the Isthmus of Tehuantepec in the state of Oaxaca, Mexico,[1] a process of racialized dispossession through large scale wind farms is currently underway; the building of this infrastructure has been justified by the need to mitigate climate change and replace the fossil fuel regime at a time when we are experiencing an energy crisis. The case of the Isthmus of Tehuantepec is paradigmatic because it reveals the paradox of the energy transition promoted by companies and governments. This chapter addresses the transition's dependence on mining extraction, its serious impact on biodiversity, and its direct relationship with the privatization of communal lands.

The first part of this chapter is theoretical in nature and gives a global perspective on what is known as the Capitalocene. It argues that management of the climate and energy crisis is laying the foundations of a phenomenon I refer to as energy colonialism; in the light of this claim, it will problematize the link between racialization and accumulation through dispossession, on which energy transition is built.

The second section focuses on the case of the Isthmus of Tehuantepec, analyzing the energy colonialism inherent in the construction of the largest wind farm corridor in Latin America and in open-pit mining projects promoted in the same region, which cause extensive violence against Indigenous communities and specifically against land defenders. This section will focus on the Ikoot, Zapotec, and Zoque Indigenous communities who have a long historical presence in the region, and who, in the twenty-first century, are reviving a series of legal, political, and organizational strategies in order to defend their lands and communal territories from racialized dispossession carried out in the name of energy transition.

## Racialized Dispossession

The twenty-first century has been characterized by an understanding of humanity as a geological force able to alter the planet's climate, among other things. Geologists have been debating the term Anthropocene, which has been rightly associated with the Industrial Revolution, since the end of the eighteenth century. But it was Paul J. Crutzen and Eugene F. Stoermer who presented the idea of the Anthropocene for the first time, in the bulletin of the International Geosphere-Biosphere Program (2010). Before long the term was being used in anthropology, from where it moved into common usage.[2] Various disciplines have proposed that what we are seeing is not only the result of human influence on the environment, but also of a capitalist economic system. As such, this period deserves the name Capitalocene, since the term Anthropocene has a depoliticizing effect, relinquishing responsibility by generalizing and homogenizing the effects of human action on the Earth, insofar as it conceals the fact that not all human beings are responsible for climate change in the same way.[3]

This can be observed in 2015 figures, which show that half of total carbon dioxide emissions (the main greenhouse gas) was the responsibility of just 700 million people, the richest 10% of the population, while half of the human population—some 3,500 million—generated just 10% of greenhouse gas emissions (Riechmann 2021). So, it should be obvious that climate change is profoundly imbricated with economic inequality. The discussion has therefore widened beyond geology and has been taken up in various fields of the humanities and social sciences in attempts to deal with this global emergency. Given this catastrophic prospect, it has become imperative that we look for economic and technological alternatives that can mitigate the climate crisis. Nonetheless, there is a risk that that very imperative is used to justify and heighten dominant relationships and inequality.

For this reason, it is necessary to complicate our analysis by returning to the most important factor influencing global warming: fossil fuels, the reason for the majority of anthropogenic emissions of $CO_2$, especially since the twentieth century, which marked the beginning of industrialized society's profound dependence on the extraction of oil (Sempere 2018). We are witnessing "a double energy crisis, both on the carbon sink side (climate crisis) and on the resource side (peak oil and the end of the era of cheap oil)" (Riechmann, Carpintero and Matarán 2014), which highlights the urgency of reducing greenhouse gas emissions and the need for an energy transition able to replace our dependence on fossil fuels.

In this context, wind energy, classified as a renewable, has enjoyed greater publicity. It is precisely the urgency of an energy transition that has justified the installation of wind farms in various areas despite cultural, political, and even environmental concerns. Wind power is on the agenda of most states that signed the Paris Agreement in 2015 (UNFCCC [United Nations Forum on Forests] 2015), and, importantly, it has opened up another economic sphere of climate crisis management that involves the commodification of wind and the sun as inexhaustible sources of energy.

Energy companies and governments are involved in a wave of investments that supposedly aim to facilitate reaching the 2015 Paris Agreement goal for greenhouse gas reduction. However, in the interests of reaching that goal of decarbonizing the planet, global differences in consumption have not been taken into account, and as a result profound inequalities in access to energy have been covered up. For example, 2015 data show that 10% of the global population used 40% of energy (Riechmann, Carpintero and Matarán, 2018). These figures have not changed significantly between 2015 and the present day.[4] This global tendency turns out to be more unjust when we take into account that the areas consuming the least energy are those currently facing the large-scale installation of wind power infrastructure.

So, it is clear that the dynamics of energy transition are built on the economic relations of accumulation through dispossession, to use David Harvey's terms, which broadly refer to renewed forms of capital accumulation and the total marketization of nature and public goods that accompanied the introduction of neoliberalism.[5]

In other words, the rolling out of wind power infrastructure is based on old capitalist economic relations that exacerbate the process of privatization of communal lands and now of wind, and increase the extraction of minerals and raw materials. This, as we will see in the second section of this chapter with regard to the Isthmus of Tehuantepec (Mexico), generates socio-territorial conflicts and exacerbates violence.

Scientific research has revealed that the infrastructure for the transition to renewable energies depends on fossil fuels for between 80% and 90% of its energy, because of the requirement for minerals such as iron, aluminum, copper, steel, chromium, manganese, tin, nickel, and zinc (Capellán 2019), as well as other less abundant minerals such as lithium and rare compounds. The World Bank has estimated that the global energy transition process over the next 30 years will require the extraction of three thousand million tons of minerals and metals.[6] This dependence on extractivism is an important part of the paradox of these large-scale wind power projects.

The logic of accumulation through dispossession is linked to longstanding colonial relationships, in which the continents of America[7] and Africa[8] are still expected to provide raw materials. Their territories are currently involved in violent disputes over strategic resources necessary for energy transition despite the planned roll out of wind and solar infrastructure there.[9]

On the global scene, energy transition, built on the process of accumulation through dispossession and on colonial relationships, has generated a phenomenon we call energy colonialism. It is worth making clear that, although formally and legally several Latin American and African states are no longer colonies following the processes of independence that took place in the nineteenth and twentieth centuries, in practice they continue to reproduce colonial hierarchies, whether as countries economically dependent on the old metropolis or as settlers on the lands of Indigenous communities or of other nations that find themselves within state borders. For this reason, I use the term colonialism, referring to a long historical process whose key characteristic of domination in cultural, economic, and political spheres remains entrenched, both internally and in relationships with other nations (González Casanova 2006, 188).

Many threads make up this web of colonial relations, which has transformed over time. The conceptual debate is, of course, wide-ranging, and for this reason, I will limit myself here to approaching the phenomenon from the perspective of the term colonialism, taking just one of its characteristics in order to problematize the relationship of domination in which the so-called energy transition is embedded: racialization. In order to understand the process of racialization, we must begin with the fact that race is a historical and social construct that is ontologically empty, the result of complex processes of identifying, distinguishing, and differentiating human beings according to phenotypical, linguistic, regional, and ancestral criteria, among others. Once we have that much clear, racialization can be understood to refer to a kind of hierarchization, to the inequality of access to goods, resources, and services, and an imbalance between "racial groups" (Campos García 2012).

Given this hierarchization, we can surmise that different people experience the Capitalocene and the climate crisis differently, not only in terms of the unequal impacts we generate as humanity, but also in the fact that those who have to give up their territories to save the planet from climate catastrophe, that is Indigenous and Black people, are in the most disadvantaged position in the racial hierarchy. For a reading of global analogies, see, for example, the case of the World Wildlife Fund (WWF), whose conservationist policies have systematically violated the human rights of the native peoples of Africa.[10] We are witnessing new colonialisms that are adjusting to these times of climate emergency and giving way to a process of racialized dispossession, a phenomenon that can be differentiated from accumulation by dispossession, as explained in three points as follows:

1. Racialized dispossession is taking place in the light of a heated debate over the climate and energy crisis, in which social movements, both the defense of Indigenous territories in the global south and demonstrations against climate change in the global north, have forced companies and governments to find ways to address the problem in their agendas. In this context, energy transition has been presented as the great solution, yet we can see that it involves dispossession and violence on Indigenous peoples' land in order to save the planet—a discourse that differs from the one used by twentieth century neoliberalism, of accumulation by

dispossession. In the current context, nature conservation policies and renewable energy projects are participating in racialized dispossession on the justification that it is imperative we save humanity from catastrophe.

2. Racialized dispossession not only takes part in a capitalist order; it also adheres to a racial order that involves taking over Indigenous territories as sites where large-scale infrastructure will be installed, thus supposedly allowing entire countries to mitigate climate change. Mining extractivism is also planned for these territories because they are home to strategic resources necessary for energy transition. All of this is being implemented and decided without dialogue or respect for territorial rights, or Indigenous people's right to self-determination. We are facing an energy transition that violates Indigenous communities, and these violations are reproduced with impunity through a structural racism that has historically been present in the relationship between Indigenous peoples and the state.

3. Racialized dispossession, which justifies itself through the need to mitigate climate change, advocates saving humanity, but a version of humanity that has a privileged position in the racial hierarchy. Meanwhile, it violates the human rights of Indigenous and Black people. It does not challenge the consumption patterns of the global north nor even note the unsustainability of the capitalist way of life, nor question the consumption of the richest 10% of the world's population. Racialized dispossession is once again being carried out on territories that have historically undergone processes of colonization, exacerbating violence and making environmental justice impossible, as is the case in the Isthmus of Tehuantepec, in the state of Oaxaca, Mexico, where large-scale wind farms are being installed.

## Isthmus of Tehuantepec

Mexico has embarked on the path of energy transition. In fifteen of its states, wind farms have been installed with a total output of 8,324 MW according to 2021 figures from the Mexican Wind Power Association (Asociación Mexicana de Energía Eólica).[11] The Isthmus of Tehuantepec, Oaxaca, is the region where most wind infrastructure has been built, as the southern plain is one of the windiest areas on the planet with an average annual wind speed of more than 10 m/s (Zárate 2019).

The Isthmus of Tehuantepec is located in the south of Mexico and forms part of the narrowest stretch of land dividing the Pacific Ocean from the Gulf of Mexico.

Administratively speaking, the isthmus region of Oaxaca is made up of two districts: Juchitán and Tehuantepec, which comprise 41 municipalities and a total population of 595,433 inhabitants (Valencia Núñez 2011), of which approximately 231,952 are Indigenous: Ikoots (Huaves), Angpøn (Zoques), Chontales, Binnizá (Zapotecos), Chinantecos, and Tzotziles; this means that 23 municipalities are recognized as Indigenous municipalities,[12] which is to say that a legal body recognizes their autonomy to appoint authorities based on their Indigenous normative systems.[13]

The Indigenous peoples of the Isthmus inhabit communal[14] and ejido[15] lands. These areas enjoy forms of community organization in which assemblies are the organs of political and legal authority; each agrarian community appoints a communal property commission, and each ejido is represented by an ejidal president. Land tenure is not a minor issue in a country where 50.8% of the national territory is community owned, that is ejido and communal land, which makes up 100 million hectares of Mexico's 196.5 million hectares.[16] The socio-political administrative nature of an Indigenous municipality does not always coincide with the demarcations of communal and ejido lands, although they maintain a deep and long-standing historical relationship that is rarely taken into account. In the Isthmus, however, there is a much greater correspondence between Indigenous people and communal lands.[17]

Among agrarian communities,[18] assemblies are decision-making spaces where a community's rules are established, but they are also political spaces where differences and discrepancies between community members are expressed; in some cases, the assembly is divided and in others even dismantled, mainly because of policies of privatization promoted by the state.

It is in Indigenous municipalities—communal and ejido lands inhabited by the Zapotecs and Ikoots—where the wind farm corridor I have mentioned is being planned and built. The project dates back to 1994, when the first seven wind turbines were built in La Venta (in the Zapotec municipality of Juchitán); this was a small test farm that aimed to measure wind potential and which was run by the Federal Electricity Commission (Comisión Federal de Electricidad). From 2001 to 2004, annual meetings were subsequently held in Oaxaca. Public institutions, banks, local and regional governments, and international development agencies, among others, participated in planning what is now styled the Wind Corridor of the Isthmus of Tehuantepec (Zárate and Fraga 2015, 71–72).

In 2006 the Energy Regulatory Commission (Comisión Reguladora de Energía) initiated the "Open Season for Reserve Transmission Capacity and Transformation of Electrical Energy," which consisted in an open call for a public tender to integrate wind farm projects planned for the Isthmus region into the national electricity grid that turned out to be a mechanism for coordinating work on the design, development, and financing of the transmission infrastructure that would allow energy to be diverted away from those territories (Zárate and Fraga 2015, 71–72).

From then on, wind farms began to be constructed at an accelerated speed all along the Isthmus's southern plain, where the installation of 5,000 wind turbines has been planned (García-Torres 2018), of which, as of 2021, 2,123 have been built in twenty-nine wind farms.[19] The main investors are Spanish companies: Acciona, Iberdrola, Gamesa, Gas Natural, Renovalia Energy, Preneal, and Peñoles, followed by Électricité de France, ENEL in Italy, and City Express in the United States. Two small wind farms belong to Mexican state institutions: one with three wind turbines generating 21.9 GW and belonging to the Institute of Electrical Research (Instituto de Investigaciones Eléctricas) and another with five 42.05 GW turbines that supply energy to various military camps and buildings belonging to the Ministry of National Defense (SEDENA) (Flores Cruz 2015). The wind farms built so far have been installed in Zapotec territory, in the municipalities of Santo Domingo Ingenio, Ixtaltepec, Unión Hidalgo, El Espinal, Ciudad Ixtepec, and Juchitán de Zaragoza. The latter is an agrarian community of 68,112 hectares of communal property, and is where most of the wind infrastructure has been installed.

The arrival of the wind farms has exacerbated the process of privatizing Juchitán's communal lands. This is because companies sought to sign contracts with small landowners,[20] which in turn divided the local population and even provoked violent disputes. In addition, the early wind farms did not carry out Indigenous consultations, which, as has been pointed out, is a violation of the International Labor Organization's Convention 169 (signed by Mexico in 1991), which stipulates the right of Indigenous peoples to free, prior, informed, and culturally appropriate consultation.

In 2014, after several years of social and legal pressure, despite which more than a dozen wind farms had already been installed, the first Indigenous consultation was held for the Eólica del Sur wind farm. However, this consultation was marked by a series of arbitrary decisions and inconsistencies, such as the fact that Indigenous people's participation was limited to a small percentage of the population (only two hundred participants attended, out of a population of 75,000 people). They were provided with limited information, and there was a tense, aggressive atmosphere, and a backdrop of violence against land defenders (Flores Cruz 2015, 31).

Another Indigenous consultation began in 2018, carried out by the Federal Government's Ministry for Energy and the company Électricité de France. It concerned a wind farm project called "gunaa sicarú" ("pretty woman" in Zapotec), which consists of 96 wind turbines with an energy production capacity of 300 MW. Its installation is planned for the communal lands of Juchitán in the agrarian annexes of Unión Hidalgo and La Ventosa.[21] However, the consultation procedure was not carried out in advance; the French company has gone ahead and signed contracts with small landowners before putting the project through an Indigenous consultation. In addition, there have been official legal reports of human rights violations, causing the consultation to be suspended on more than two occasions. A court ruling ordered the suspension of one project in May 2018, having found that it did not comply with ILO Convention 169;[22] despite these allegations, the consultation is forging ahead and the dispute between the Unión Hidalgo Assembly of community members and EDF's wind farm continues, against a backdrop of heightened violence.

For their part, the territory inhabited by the Ikoots people has not seen the construction of wind farms because their communal lands continue to be defended by their assemblies, as political and legal decision-making bodies. The Ikoots inhabit the communal lands of San Mateo del Mar, San Dionisio del Mar, San Francisco del Mar new town, San Francisco del Mar old town, and Santa María del Mar. Despite internal conflicts, the Ikoots people's communal assemblies, together with the Zapotec community of Álvaro Obregón, mounted legal, political, and organizational opposition that prevented the implementation of the "Mareñas Renovables" project, a corporate consortium made up of capital from private companies including Mitsubishi, Fomento Mexicano-FEMSA, the Dutch pension fund PGGM, and Macquarie's Mexican Infrastructure Fund (Flores Cruz 2015, 30). The project proposed the installation of 132 wind turbines on the Santa Teresa bar—the strip of land located between the Pacific Ocean and the Ikoots lagoon complex—and would have a devastating environmental and nutritional impact, damaging the species inhabiting the lagoon and the lives of the communities based in that area.

The arrival of these investments has revealed the direct violence experienced by communal land defenders who have denounced the arbitrary actions taken regarding wind farms, as has been documented by the Observatory for the Protection of Human Rights Defenders[23] and even by the Interamerican Association for Environmental Defense (AIDA) and the Mexican Center of Environmental Law's (CEMDA's) 2012 call to address the irregularities surrounding the construction of wind farms in the Isthmus of Tehuantepec.[24] The most recent instance was expressed in August 2021 in a letter by four UN special rapporteurs sent to the governments of France and Mexico to warn about the possible human rights violations being committed against the Zapotec community by Électricité de France through the installation of its fourth wind farm in the Isthmus of Tehuantepec.[25]

The most high-profile cases of hostility against female land defenders concern three Zapotec women: Guadalupe Ramírez of the Unión Hidalgo Community Assembly, Isabel Jiménez of the Juchiteco People's Popular Assembly (APPJ) (Amnesty International 2014), and Betina Cruz Velázquez of the Assembly of Isthmus Peoples in Defense of Land and Territory (APIDTT). At the same time, we are witnessing an insidious increase in femicidal violence in the region. While these are said to be isolated incidents, my analysis has led me to believe they are linked to dispossession resulting from wind farm construction. It is undoubtedly a complex issue to unravel and one that requires specific research, but so far, two cases directly associated with wind projects have been recorded.[26] Impunity for those who carry out these violent acts is also part of a racialized dispossession that exacerbates dominant relationships in the racial hierarchy where Indigenous peoples are deprived of human rights.

The contrast between the image of the southern Isthmus as a 2,749 MW energy enclave (Mexican Wind Power Association, n.d.) and the image of violence perpetrated against Indigenous peoples and communal territories is even starker when we review the fate of the energy generated by the wind farm corridor. This energy supplies WalMart, Cemex, Femsa, Oxxo, Cruz Azul, Soriana, Nestlé, Nissan, Grupo Modelo, Grupo Bimbo, BBVA Bancomer, and Chedrahui, among others (GeoComunes, n.d.). We have to question this concentration of energy in the hands of companies when thousands of people are left to experience energy poverty, as is clear in the south of the Isthmus where there are 5,200 homes without access to electricity, 2.13% of the total number of inhabited homes. This trend is in line with the figures for the year 2020, in which approximately 32,096 homes in Oaxaca were registered as not having access to electricity, 2.67% of the total number of inhabited homes in the state. Oaxaca is the state with the highest proportion of homes without access to electricity in the country.[27]

This series of acts of racialized, violent dispossession, and inequalities in access to energy, amount to energy colonialism. Part of this phenomenon is the direct relationship between mining extractivism and wind farms in the Isthmus of Tehuantepec. Three mining companies are supplied with energy from wind farms in the region: Minera Autlán with Iberdrola's La Ventosa III wind farm, Industria Peñoles with its Fuerza Eólica del Istmo wind farm (GeoComunes, n.d.), and Grupo México with its El Retiro wind farm.[28] This exposes the fallacy of renewable energy as a way of mitigating climate change and overcoming the energy crisis, as it is both dependent on and also supplies the mining industry, an extractivist sector that is responsible for serious impacts on the environment and which also means energy is not supplied to homes in towns and cities.

The fact that it is the Federal Government's Ministry of Economy that grants communal land concessions to mining companies in the Isthmus region shows the state's complicity in the climate and energy crisis. It is worth pointing out that there are approximately 3 mining concessions in the Isthmus (GeoComunes, n.d.) that have not been able to start operating due to ongoing opposition by Indigenous peoples. One of these concessions is located in the Chimalapas jungle, the historical territory of the Zoque people and the most biodiverse region in Mesoamerica. This concession is for the "Santa Marta" project, which consists of two polygons totaling 6,410 hectares of communal property owned by the Canadian company Minaurum Gold Inc (mineria, n.d. and portalags1, n.d.). The company is interested in extracting gold and copper, two minerals important for the current energy transition. However, its location risks polluting the Ostuta River basin and the Espíritu Santo River, on which the Zoque communities of Chimalapas depend, along with the Zapotec peoples and the Ikoots peoples who live around the lagoons in the southern plains, where the same rivers that begin in Chimalapas flow into the sea.

The dismantling of communal lands is not only a problem of land tenure; it is also a violation of the environment, as there is a deep and long-standing historical relationship between the social ownership of land and the rich biodiversity and Indigenous peoples. It should therefore come as no surprise that 60% of the country's coastline and 70% of the country's forests and extensive biodiversity are located on communal and ejido lands (Registro Agrario Nacional, n.d.). Therefore, if the aim is to mitigate climate change and contain the environmental catastrophe, it is counterintuitive to violate communities, devastate landscapes, and fragment their forms of land tenure.

This is especially the case considering that, for thousands of years, the Indigenous peoples of the Isthmus have ensured a region rich in biodiversity: the Zoque peoples who inhabit the Chimalapas jungle have done so for more than 3,800 years, according to archaeological and linguistic studies; the Zapotecs arrived on the southern plains of the Isthmus in the twelfth century, by which time the Ikoots had arrived by sea to the coastal lagoons. For this reason, we can say that the Indigenous peoples in the Isthmus region have allowed them to establish territoriality and to influence the landscape and even the existence of certain types of flora and fauna.

The process of colonization entailed a violent disruption of this relationship, which brought about a profound change in the way land was used and a reordering based on nascent capitalism's global economy. Faced with this catastrophe, Indigenous peoples fought to secure their existence: one of their strategies was the legal recognition of their lands as communal property; this legal status has for four centuries managed to secure Indigenous ways of life and regions rich in biodiversity.

The defense of rivers against mining extractivism and the defense of wind and communal property are directly associated with the continuing existence of landscapes and biodiversity, as well as with the very survival of Indigenous peoples and human life. Thus, the historical relationship between communal property, Indigenous peoples, and biodiversity is being dismantled with the arrival of wind and mining projects, whose installation is facilitated by the privatization of land, the dismantling of assemblies, and direct violence against Indigenous land defenders.

The fact that 80% of the most biodiverse regions on the planet are located on Indigenous territory[29] exposes the fallacies of an energy transition whose materialization in large-scale wind projects is violating and destroying whole regions, ways of life, and communal societies that have demonstrated their resilience over the course of five centuries. This information also makes it clear that large-scale wind infrastructure is not a viable alternative that will improve the life of the planet and of humanity. On the contrary, it is one of the Capitalocene's false solutions. The building of wind infrastructure constitutes a form of racialized dispossession exacerbated by environmental catastrophe that adheres to the logic of energy colonialism.

**Final Thoughts**

Let's return to the initial discussion and to the twenty-first century, when humanity is revealed to be capable of modifying the planet's climate and is therefore responsible for creating an economic system that has generated a profound energy crisis, beginning with the Industrial Revolution and exacerbated by the twenty-first century's dependence on oil. As I have tried to explain throughout this chapter, this terrifying narrative used to justify the deployment of wind projects is missing some variables that I believe are key to the profound climate imbalance.

Colonialism and accumulation by dispossession. Undoubtedly, both have had an important impact on the energy and climate crisis. For this reason, one scientific camp advocates calling the time we are living in the Capitalocene. But we need to go back a couple of centuries to reveal that colonialism has been a substantial part of this problem, because before the Industrial Revolution humanity had another great impact on the earth, as is evidenced by the great demographic decline on the American continent beginning in 1492, caused by epidemics, genocides, and wars that eliminated 90% of the native population of the continent (it has been estimated that approximately 55 million of the 65 million Indigenous people who lived in the region died during the Conquest and colonization). This led to the abandonment of large tracts of land and inevitably had a major impact on the amount of vegetation and its ability to absorb carbon, thus reducing atmospheric carbon dioxide levels to the extent that it may have contributed to a period of cold weather known as the Little Ice Age.[30]

The same logic of fifteenth- to eighteenth-century colonialism, which resulted in a colossal genocide, is still alive in the twenty-first century, when profound climate crisis means it has taken on the character of energy colonialism. As this chapter has documented, wind projects have been imposed on Indigenous territories through racialized dispossession, seeking to justify themselves as a real alternative to fossil fuels. However, the promise of replacing fossil fuels with renewable wind energy sources is seriously challenged by the biophysical limits of the planet. Antonio Turiel estimates that the maximum amount of energy that renewables could potentially provide is between 30% and 40% of the world's current total consumption (Riechman 2019, 27). Thus, even the dismantling of common lands and dispossession of Indigenous communities for the installation of renewables infrastructure would not be enough to sustain the high rates of energy consumption of a small global elite, let alone ensure that the entire world's population has access to these new energy sources.

Although we all experience the planetary crisis in different ways, we need an energy transition and measures that challenge colonial and capitalist relations if we are to contain the climate catastrophe. If we understand this, it becomes clear that the processes of defense of communal lands and territories led by Indigenous peoples today are possible modes of existence that counter "the eternal renewal of colonialism, which in old and new disguises, shows the same genocidal impulse, the same racist sociability, the same thirst for appropriation of and violence against resources considered infinite, and against people considered inferior and even devoid of humanity," as Boaventura de Sousa Santos (2017, 73) puts it. For this reason, the defense of rivers, mountains, plains, and communal and ejido property trace a horizon of multiple possibilities for resilience and existence.

## Notes

1   This geographic region is located in the southeast of Mexico, the narrowest strip of land separating the Gulf of Mexico from the Pacific Ocean. It is home to the Zoque, Zapotec, Ikoot, Chontal, Popoluca, Nahua, and Chinanteco Indigenous peoples.

2   Helmuth Trischler, "El antropoceno, ¿un concepto geológico o cultural, o ambos?" In Desacatos 54, may–august, 2017, pp. 40–57.

3   What we call climate change is the result of the emission, over the last two centuries, of enormous quantities of gases that exacerbate the greenhouse effect. The signs of climate change are many. The first is a global increase in temperatures, estimated to have been 0.3–0.6°C during the twentieth century, which was warmer than any of the previous ten centuries, and the twelve years between 1995 and 2006 were the hottest since 1850. Taibo, Carlos 2017, En defensa del decrecimiento, 22.

4  Oxfam Intermón, December 2019 report, "Injusticia climática: lo que contaminan los más ricos y pagan los más vulnerables." https://cdn2.hubspot.net/hubfs/426027/ Oxfam-Website/oi-informes/injusticia-climatica-contaminan-ricos-pagan-pobres-oxfam-intermon.pdf

5  David Harvey updates what Karl Marx calls the "so called primitive accumulation of capital," in Chapter 24 of Capital. (Harvey 2007), The New Imperialism, Oxford: Oxford University Press.

6  Map of resistance to the impact and discourse of mining involved in energy transition in the Americas. https://miningwatch.ca/sites/default/files/informe_mapeoderesistencias.pdf

7  The 2019 coup d'état in Bolivia has a complex explanation that I will not dwell on here, but it is worth mentioning that one of things influencing it was the critical debate over lithium. In Chile, the 2019 social unrest was triggered by a rise in fuel prices. The 2021 demonstrations in Colombia were also linked to the increase in fuel prices, as well as to the heightened violence that extractivist megaprojects are provoking on indigenous lands. And, finally, most recently, as I write these lines, a popular rebellion has just taken place in Kazakhstan, the trigger for which has again been an increase in the price of liquefied gas for transport, in a country rich in fossil fuel reserves.

8  In 2021 alone, in Africa, there were six coups, in Sudan, Mali, Guinea, Chad, and Niger, quadrupling the average number of coups over the previous twenty years (1.5 per year) (Naranajo 2021). https://elpais.com/internacional/2021-10-30/seis-golpes-de-estado-este-ano-la-epidemia-putschista-que-recorre-africa.html

9  See the Atlas of Environmental Justice, which documents socio-territorial conflicts in America provoked by extractive projects required for energy transition. https://ejatlas.org/featured/met_america?translate=es. For the case of Africa, see Antonio Turiel's research and his participation in the energy colonialism course: https://www.youtube.com/watch?v=3ZevlKzVvnw&t=457s.

10  The NGO Survival has documented several cases of such violations: https://www.survival.es/conservacion.

11  https://amdee.org/mapas-eolicos.html. The Mexican Wind Power Association (AMDEE) was created in 2005, amalgamating different companies promoting wind power in Mexico with the aim of forming a body of business representatives to mirror similar government and social organizations. Flores Cruz 2015, 4).

12  The data from the population census are from the year 2000, "Regiones Indigenas," available at: https://www.gob.mx/cms/uploads/attachment/file/35735/cdi-regiones-indigenas-mexico.pdf.

13  This is merely an estimate, since at the national level 60% of the Indigenous population lives in indigenous municipalities, while the remaining 40% live in municipalities where they are a minority. Taken from "Regiones Indigenas": https://www.gob.mx/cms/uploads/attachment/file/35735/cdi-regiones-indigenas-mexico.pdf.

14  Their communal character is the result of Indigenous peoples' long history of defending themselves in the face of dispossession by conquistadors and policies of despoilment carried out both by the Spanish Crown over the course of three centuries and by the liberal Mexican state during the twenty-first century. Communal lands are of indigenous origin. They were constituted during the Colonial period and were maintained through different legislation, so that the lands recognized legally by the Spanish monarchy formed the municipalities of the liberal state and even survived under the tutelage of political district leaders during the Porfiriato; therefore the current municipalities have in large part inherited their borders (Michel Aurélia, *Los territorios de la reforma agraria: construcción y deconstrucción de una ciudadanía rural en las comunidades del Istmo oaxaqueño, 1934–1984*).

15  For its part, ejido tenure, according to the definition of the National Agrarian Registry (Registro Agrario Nacional), was a product of the revolutionary process in the twentieth century that brought about agrarian reform, which allowed Indigenous peoples to recover their lands and in other cases to secure them. Ejidos are lands that are subject to a special regime of social property in land tenure; this status is recognized in the constitution and its inheritance is protected in a particular way.

16  National Agrarian Registry (Registro Agrario Nacional), "Nota técnica sobre la Propiedad Social": http://www.ran.gob.mx/ran/indic_bps/NOTA_TECNICA_SOBRE_LA_PROPIEDAD_SOCIAL_v26102017

17  It is difficult to calculate the percentage of social property inhabited by Indigenous people, but in order to form an estimate, we can look at the map of indigenous regions (see https://www.gob.mx/cms/uploads/attachment/file/35735/cdi-regiones-indigenas-mexico.pdf) and the map of communal and ejido land tenure (see http://www.ran.gob.mx/ran/indic_bps/NOTA_TECNICA_SOBRE_LA_PROPIEDAD_SOCIAL_v26102017). This study of indigenous regions relies on the legal and socio-political status of the indigenous municipality, but it is necessary to calculate the percentage of these demarcated lands that are ejidos or communally owned; this is complex, as in several cases the municipal demarcation does not coincide with the division of land. For the moment, it is possible to cross-reference the map of land ownership and the map of indigenous regions to get a general idea; that said, indigenous censuses should be interpreted with a degree of skepticism, since in many cases indigenous identity has been based predominantly on linguistic variables that exclude many people who recognize themselves as part of an indigenous community and people because of their history and territory but who do not speak its language.

18  According to the National Agrarian Registry, an agrarian community ("comunidad agraria") has a constitutionally recognized legal status and its goods and resources receive special legal protection; communal lands are inalienable, imprescriptible, and unseizable, unless they are contributed to civil or mercantile societies. The community, by means of an assembly agreement, may change the ejido regime.

http://www.ran.gob.mx/ran/indic_bps/NOTA_TECNICA_SOBRE_LA_PRO
PIEDAD_SOCIAL_v26102017. The agrarian community of Juchitán reached its
presidential resolution, executed and published in the Official Journal of the
Federation (*Diario Oficial de la Federación*) on Monday July 13, 1964. https://
www.dof.gob.mx/nota_to_imagen_fs.php?%20cod_diario=206395&pagina=3&
seccion=0.

19  According to the research group GeoComunes (http://geocomunes.org/), the
29 parks that currently operate required the installation of 1,564 wind turbines, and
have been developed in an area of 31 thousand hectares.

20  In Mexico, wind energy companies give farmers only 1% and not 4%, as in other
countries. Farmers signed unclear contracts that benefitted them very little. Diana
Manzo, "Contratos sucios y energía limpia." https://www.connectas.org/especiales/
energia-limpia-contratos-sucios/.

21  Agrarian communities are made up of various agrarian annexes or "anexos agrarios."

22  https://www.business-humanrights.org/fr/derni%C3%A8res-actualit%C3%A9s/
m%C3%A9xico-el-parque-e%C3%B3lico-gunaa-sicar%C3%BA-de-edf-en-oaxaca-
registra-acusaciones-de-violaci%C3%B3n-al-derecho-a-la-consulta-ind%C3%
ADgena-la-empresa-responde/

23  "México: Amenazas, señalamiento y estigmatización en contra de miembros de
la comunidad indígena de Unión Hidalgo (Oaxaca)," Organización Mundial contra la Tortura, June 18, 2019. https://www.omct.org/es/humanrightsdefenders/
urgentinterventions/mexico/2019/06/d25388/

24  Aida-americas https://aida-americas.org/en/challenges-deploying-wind-energy-mex
ico-case-isthmus-tehuantepec

25  https://spcommreports.ohchr.org/TMResultsBase

26  The first case was that of a woman whose body was found, along with that of a man,
on January 12, 2020, in a truck belonging to the wind power company Revergy, as is
documented in the interactive map of femicides created by María Salguero https://
www.google.com/maps/d/viewer?mid=174IjBzP-fl_6wpRHg5pkGSj2egE&ll=16.
18076495165269%2C-94.65724173796225&z=9. The second case was the wife of
a wind farm worker; according to field research in the Unión Hidalgo community,
a search for the husband of the murdered woman was underway following labor
disputes in the company. When the worker was not found, his wife was shot; the
case can be found on María Salguero's map: https://www.google.com/maps/d/
viewer?mid=174IjBzP-fl_6wpRHg5pkGSj2egE&ll=16.497572769043423%2C-94.
97749731946982&z=11

27  Of a total 1,125,892 homes in Oaxaca, 1,093,796 have access to electricity, according
to the 2020 population census carried out by the National Institute for Statistics and
Geography (INEGI): https://www.inegi.org.mx/app/tabulados/interactivos/?pxq=
Vivienda_Vivienda_01_4de68d98-e773-43eb-bea7-d239ce35524a&idrt=56&opc=t
https://www.inegi.org.mx/app/tabulados/interactivos/?pxq=Vivienda_Vivienda_04_
1fb94584-4816-4435-a1b7-4689b8d2ee81&idrt=56&opc=t

28  The El Retiro wind farm directs 60% of its energy to Grupo México's mines, 37% to Cinemex, and the rest to its trains. Camimex 2021, 97.

29  Data taken from the NGO Survival: https://www.survival.es/conservacion.

30  These data and studies are taken from scientific research that quantitively surveys evidence of pre-Columbian population size, land use per capita, population decline after 1492, and carbon uptake resulting from abandoned anthropogenic landscapes, and then compares those data with possible natural causes of the reduction in carbon. Koch, Brierley, Maslin, Lewis and Simon 2019.

## References

Amnesty Internacional. 2021. "Sobre llamadas con amenazas a dos empleados del Comité de Defensa Global de Derechos Humanos (Código DH)," July 10.https://www.amnesty.org/fr/wp-content/uploads/sites/8/2021/07/amr410262014fr.pdf.

Campos García, Alejandro. 2012. "Racialización, racialismo y racismo: un discernimiento necesario" *Universidad De La Habana*, No. 273: https://revistas.uh.cu/revuh/article/view/3189.

Flores Cruz, Rosa Marina. 2015. *La disputa por el Istmo de Tehuantepec: las comunidades y el capitalismo verde*. Masters thesis in rural development, Universidad Autónoma Metropolitana, Mexico.

González Casanova, Pablo. 2006. *Colonialismo interno*. Buenos Aires, Argentina: CLACSO.

Harvey, David. 2007. *El nuevo imperialismo*. España: Akal.

Trischler, Helmuth. 2017. El antropoceno, ¿un concepto geológico o cultural, o ambos? *Desacatos* 54 (May–August).

Koch, Alexander, Chris Brierley, Mark M. Maslin, Simon L. Lewis. 2019. "Earth System Impacts of the European Arrival and Great Dying in the Americas After 1492." *Quaternary Science Reviews*, 207: 13–36.

Riechmann, Jorge. 2021. *Informe a la subcomisión de cuaternario*. Madrid, Spain: Árdora Ediciones.

Riechmann, Jorge, Alberto Matarán and Óscar Carpintero. 2018. *Para evitar la barbarie*. Spain: Universidad de Granada.

Riechmann, Jorge, Alberto Matarán and Óscar Carpintero _____. 2014. *Los inciertos pasos desde aquí hasta allá: alternativas socioecológicas y transiciones poscapitalistas*. Spain: Universidad de Granada.

Riechman, Jorge. 2019. *Otro fin del mundo es posible, decían los compañeros. Sobre transiciones ecosociales, colapsos y la imposibilidad de lo necesario*. Spain: MRA Ediciones.

Sousa Santos, Boaventura. 2017. *Justicia entre Saberes: Epistemologías del Sur contra el epistemicidio*. Madrid, Spain: Ediciones Morata S. L.

Sempere, Joaquín. 2018. *Las cenizas de Prometeo*. Barcelona, Spain: Ediciones de pasado y presente.

Taibo, Carlos. 2017. *En defensa del decrecimiento sobre el capitalismo, crisis y barbarie*. Madrid, Spain: Catarata.

Zárate, Ezequiel, and J. Fraga. 2015. "La política eólica mexicana: controversias sociales y ambientales debido a su implantación territorial. Estudio de caso en Oaxaca y Yucatán," Trance, 2015, 71–72.

Zarate, Ezequiel. 2019. "Justice, Social Exclusion and Indigenous Opposition: A Case Study of Wind Energy Development on the Isthmus of Tehuantepec, México." *Energy Research & Social Science* 54.

"Atlas de Justicia Ambiental," last accessed January 22, 2024: https://ejatlas.org/featured/met_america?translate=es.

Capellán Pérez, Íñigo, and Carlos de Castro Carranza. 2019. "Transición a energías renovables y demanda de minerales." *El Ecologista* 102: 32–35. www.ecologistasenaccion.org/133199/transicion-a-energias-renovables-y-demanda-de-minerales/.

Camimex. 2021. Informe de Sustentabilidad. https://camimex.org.mx/application/files/5516/3881/9847 INFORMESUSTENTABILIDAD2021.pdf.

CartoMinMex, Cartografía Mineria. https://e.economia.gob.mx/servicios/cartominmex/). Perhaps the best way to reference it as: "CartoMinMex," Gobierno de México, accessed January 22, 2024, https://portalags1.economia.gob.mx/arcgis/apps/webappviewer/index.html?id=1f22ba130b0e40d888bfc3b7fb5d3b1b.

García-Torres, Miriam. 2018. "El Ibex 35 en guerra contra la vida transnacionales españolas y conflictos socioecológicos en América Latina, un análisis ecofeminista." *Ecologistas en Acción* (January). www.ecologistasenaccion.org/35721/ibex-35-guerra-la-vida/.

Manzo, Diana. n.d. Contratos sucios y energía limpia, Connectas Plataforma Periodística para las Americas www.connectas.org/especiales/energia-limpia-contratos-sucios/.

Michel, Aurélia, Los territorios de la reforma agraria: construcción y deconstrucción de una ciudadanía rural en las comunidades del Istmo oaxaqueño, 1934-1984.

Naranjo, José. 2021. Seis golpes de Estado este año: la epidemia "putschista" que recorre África. *El País*, October 30. https://elpais.com/internacional/2021-10-30/seis-golpes-de-estado-este-ano-la-epidemia-putschista-que-recorre-africa.html.

ONG Survival, n.d. www.survival.es/conservacion.

Organización Mundial contra la Tortura. 2019. June 18. www.omct.org/es/humanrightsdefenders/urgentinterventions/mexico/2019/06/d25388/.

Oxfam intermón, informe diciembre 2019, "Injusticia climática lo que contaminan los más ricos y pagan los mas vulnerables." https://cdn2.hubspot.net/hubfs/426027/Oxfam-Website/oi-informes/injusticia-climatica-contaminan-ricos-pagan-pobres-oxfam-intermon.pdf.

Registro Agrario Nacional. Nota técnica sobre la Propiedad Social. http://www.ran.gob.mx/ran/indic_bps/NOTA_TECNICA_SOBRE_LA_PROPIEDAD_SOCIAL_v26102017.

Regiones Indígenas en México. https://www.gob.mx/cms/uploads/attachment/file/35735/cdi-regiones-indigenas-mexico.pdf.

Salguero, María. n.d. *Yo te nombro: el mapa de los feminicidios en México* (blog). http://mapafeminicidios.blogspot.com/p/inicio.html.

Turiel, Antonio. www.youtube.com/watch?v=3ZevlKzVvnw&t=457s.

UNFCCC. 2015. Paris Agreement, vol. 21932. París. https://unfccc.int/sites/default/files/spanish_paris_agreement.pdf.

Valencia Nuñez, Nashieeli. 2011. Diagnóstico Regional del Istmo de Tehauntepec http://cedoc.inmujeres.gob.mx/ftpg/Oaxaca/OAX_MetaA4_5_2011.pdf.

Velázquez, E. Leonard, Hoffmann Éric, Prévot-Schapira Odile, M.F. 2018. *El Istmo mexicano: una región inasequible, Estado, poderes locales y dinámicas espaciales (siglos XVI-XXI)* La Nación collection. Marseille, France: IRD Éditions. https://books.openedition.org/irdeditions/19263.

# ENVIRONMENTAL RACISM IN MEXICO AND ITS EMOTIONAL EFFECTS: THE CASE OF THE CHACAHUA-PASTORÍA LAGOONS IN THE PACIFIC COAST OF OAXACA

Meztli Yoalli Rodríguez Aguilera

In Mexico, Black and Indigenous communities are disproportionately affected by environmental policies that erase their historical experience of dispossession under the mestizaje ideology of a supposedly raceless nation (see the Introduction to this book). It is precisely the erasure of racism in the country that permits the different forms of racialization, dispossession, and environmental degradation of Black and Indigenous territories. In this essay, I analyze this dynamic through a particular case: the ecocide of the Chacahua-Pastoría lagoons in Oaxaca Mexico, an area designated as Mexico's first National Park in 1937.[1] Based on fieldwork undertaken over a year in 2017 to 2018, the case illustrates how environmental racism operates in the Latin American context and particularly in the context of Mexico's mestizaje ideology by showing the socio-political and economic impact that environmental racism has on the lives of the communities surrounding the lagoon. Less immediately obvious, however, I also argue here that this case of racialized ecocide reveals a previously overlooked yet no less important *emotional* impact for those living around and with the lagoons.

Many studies describe the links between class, race, and exposure to toxicity and pollution (Auyero and Swistun 2009; Bullard 1993; Sun-Hee Park and Pellow 2004; Krauss 2009), some specifically analyzing those links in Latin America and Mexico (Moreno Parra 2019; Masferrer León and Trejo 2019); however, there is a growing field relating environmental racism to the mestizaje ideology, and about environment and affect in Latin America more broadly (Zaragocin 2019; Cabnal 2019; Colectivo de Geografía Crítica del Ecuador 2017). This article contributes to these conversations.

Zapotalito, where I did my fieldwork, is a small community on the Pacific Coast of Oaxaca whose livelihood primarily depends on fishing and, more recently, tourism. The majority of the population self-identifies as Black and Indigenous, but there are also those who self-identify as mestizos.[2] Zapotalito is one of the multiple communities that live around an extensive system of lagoons connected directly to the Pacific Ocean. Once a healthy body of water, the Chacahua-Pastoría Lagoons have undergone environmental degradation since the 2000s due to multiple factors, three of which have been particularly destructive: the construction of breakwaters, a dam, and a lime-oil factory. These three construction projects, built by the state and transnational companies, failed to consider the possible environmental, sociopolitical, economical, and emotional damage to the Indigenous and Black communities who live arounds the lagoons.

The lagoons have started to die as a result. Drying out, polluted, lacking oxygen, their continued degradation also threatens the life of the surrounding communities, who rely on the lagoons for their primary source of income and food. Fishermen and women traditionally go to the lagoons to fish for their families' primary consumption, but also to sell fish to local communities and markets around the coast of Oaxaca. The poverty caused by the increasingly polluted and stagnant water has driven some to migrate to other parts of the country, and others—most of them men—to the United States looking for better economic opportunities. Through this process of ecological dispossession and the economic migration it necessitates, the death of the lagoons is directly connected to the elimination of a Black and Indigenous geography. According to Robert D. Bullard, pioneering theorist of environmental racism, such racism "refers to any environmental policy, practice, or directive that differentially affects or disadvantages (whether intended or unintended) individuals, groups, or communities based on race or color" (Bullard 1993, 5). In the context of Mexico and mestizaje ideology, environmental racism happens when environmental policies and practices disproportionately affect Black and Indigenous populations, just as has been the case at the Chacahua-Pastoría Lagoons.

## The Emotional Impacts of Environmental Racism

While hugely consequential, and indeed my own initial framework for thinking about the lagoons, this political-environmental annihilation is twinned with a more diffuse but no less important emotional impact. While conducting fieldwork, I asked people in the Zapotalito community how they *felt* about the slow death of the lagoons. They named different emotions: sadness, sorrow, anger, frustration, anxiety, melancholia, nostalgia. Previously, I have explored how these emotions are related to the cyclic and complex emotion of grief due to ecological loss and human loss—caused by different forms of violence—or what I call "grieving geographies" (Rodríguez Aguilera, 2021).

Nostalgia is defined by the Cambridge Dictionary as "a feeling of pleasure and sometimes slight sadness at the same time you think about things that happened in the past." Nostalgia was very present in the communities around the Chacahua-Pastoría lagoons, of how the community and the lagoons used to be before the ecocide started. One of the emotional effects that Black and Indigenous communities experience is nostalgia. Nostalgia for the land and the water—before the ecocide—is continuously present in conversations about the lagoons and what the area used to be like before the environmental degradation started. Through nostalgia, there is a direct affective relationship between humans and other-than-humans. It is through nostalgia that grief for the lagoons is also expressed. It is through nostalgia that people around the communities express a longing to go back to a healthy environment, but also back to emotional well-being.

Ricardo, a self-identified Mixteco[3], and another elder and founder of Zapotalito, shared with me, with deep nostalgia, the overabundance of fish in the past:

> Back in the day, we would each go fishing with our panguita[4] and with a hook and a rope, grab the fish in the lagoons, big fish, up to 30–50 kilos each. In the rain season, from June to October, we could never sell shrimp because there was too much, we would fish it with tarraya[5] up to 120–150 kilos.

As explained by Ricardo, the quantity of fish that fishers could catch before the breakwater was closed was vastly different in the nostalgic past. For this reason, many of the fishermen that once dedicated their lives entirely to fishing, primarily for consumption and commercialization, have progressively abandoned this labor and have now shifted to lagoon tourism as a primary source of income.

Federico, an Indigenous Chatino descendant, describes the lagoons before and now:

> Zapotalito was very different. The mangroves were beautiful, the water was clean, with lots of fish and birds. There was everything. I used to fish at that time and there were so many species. But now the number of fish dropped in an incredible way. Before with just a small net, you could get good results and fish a lot of kilos, but today you need a big net and get very little fish. Fishing these days has been severely decreased. (Interview, Zapotalito, May 16, 2018)

Viviana tells me that once she is in the lagoon in her boat, while fishing, she feels calm. While she is in the lagoon, in the middle of the water, she can take moments to think about her life, to have space and time for her own reflection. Raquel, another fisherwoman, told me when I asked her about her relationship with the lagoon, "I spent my whole pregnancy inside the lagoon fishing: there is where my belly grew." Viviana and Raquel have a special bond with the lagoon: their bodies connect to the water; their human bodies—which also contain water—interrelate with the body of water, a lagoon, both as sources of life.

In these testimonies I explore how environmental racism—through the ecocide of the lagoons—affects people not only socioeconomically but also emotionally, creating a sense of sadness and stress due to increasing poverty and lack of food.

## The Racial Ecocide of the Chacahua-Pastoría Lagoons

At the end of September of 2017, I arrived for the first time in Zapotalito, one of the communities surrounding Chacahua-Pastoría Lagoons. A few weeks before, on September 17th, 2017, a 7.1 Richter scale earthquake had its epicenter on the Coast of Oaxaca. It was a powerful earthquake that had multiple damaging and mortal consequences in various regions in the country, including the Chacahua-Pastoría lagoons. Two days after the earthquake, people from Zapotalito woke up to the smell of ammonia. The fishers who usually enter into the lagoon with the sunrise found a horrible sight: the lagoons were covered with a mass of dead fish. People in the community gathered, surprised by the scene. Unfortunately, seeing dead fish in the lagoons and on the shore is very common but never at the volume witnessed after the earthquake. Fishers' families organized and used their fishing equipment to clean the lagoons. Tons of fish were thrown away. The local government only helped with buses to transport the waste. Local families were concerned about the situation since fishing is the primary living for the communities. Some people even decided not to throw away all the fish since it would mean having no food for themselves and their families. According to local people, the explanation for the phenomenon is as follows: All the toxic gases and pollution in the lagoons' subsoil were removed with the earthquake and came to the surface of the water, killing the fish and many other animals, including shrimps and mussels. Recent scientific studies (Guajardo-Panes et al. 2020) have demonstrated the high levels of pollution and low quality of water in the Pastoría side of the lagoons, which is in close proximity to the Zapotalito community.

In 1962, the Federal government, through the *Secretaría de Comunicaciones y Transportes,* built a breakwater to "stabilize" the lagoon system. Later, in the 1990s, the government built the Ricardo Flores Magón dam in a community close to Zapotalito. The reason was supposedly to provide water for irrigation, since the region is a high producer of papaya, lime, sesame seed, and coconut, amongst other crops. The dam retained water from the Río Verde (Green River), a big river on the Coast of Oaxaca that is also at risk of disappearing. As a result of all these governmental initiatives, the water that initially nourished the Chacahua-Pastoría lagoon Magon stopped flowing. To combat this, Comité de Pueblos Unidos en Defensa del Río (COPUDEVER), a local organization composed of Black, Indigenous, and mestizo people defending the Río Verde, has used a range of juridical approaches to protect local ecosystems, even though the government has tried on multiple occasions to get transnational capital invested into the region to create hydroelectric projects that would have a significant effect on the natural environment.

To add into the environmental degradation, in the early 2000s, the government, through the Comisión Nacional de Acuacultura y Pesca (CONAGUA), built more breakwaters in Cerro Hermoso, which is a community next to Zapotalito and directly connected to the Pacific Ocean. The state project´s goal was to "stabilize" the water flow in between the ocean and the lagoons, but the breakwaters permanently disconnected the ocean from the Chacahua-Pastoría lagoons, causing the lagoons to become an isolated body of water with no access to oxygen needed for its life. Another important factor that is affecting the lagoons is a transnational lime-oil factory situated in a community close to Zapotalito. This factory brings waste directly to the lagoons through the canals that were built originally to irrigate crops in the region. The US-owned factory called *Primus Citrus* produces large quantities of lime oil every day for the manufacture of cleaners and detergents. According to the official report *Racismo Ambiental-Institucional en México. El caso de las comunidades del sistema lagunar Chacahua-Pastoría en Oaxaca* (COPERA 2018), presented to the Interamerican Commission of Human Rights, the Mexican government gave legal permission to the factory two decades ago to operate in the region. The production of lime oil demands the extraction of juice from thousands of limes through a chemical process. The waste from this process is dumped around the factory. According to local residents, the highly acidic waste goes directly into a canal that is connected to the lagoons, which severely pollutes them. The fact that there is transnational capital involved in the environmental degradation of the lagoons reflects the imbrication of State and capitalism through the exploitation of nature and its effects on local racialized populations.

Local communities had warned government officials who oversaw building the breakwaters about the risks and possible consequences and had come up with alternative proposals. However, according to the local fishermen that I interviewed, they were not heard because they were not deemed "experts." The fishermen said that the people in charge of the breakwaters told them they had no university degrees nor were they engineers who knew about the subject. This is a clear example of how epistemic violence happens, in which Black and Indigenous epistemologies based on experience and ancestral knowledge are ignored or undervalued. Additionally, over the past 15 years, local communities have organized in different ways including protests and visits to the regional, state and federal government to demand a solution to the ecocide but the answer up to now has been silence or temporary solutions that don't work. In other words, these catastrophic environmental policies are part of a colonial continuum of erasure and dispossession of racialized Black and Indigenous territories in the country.

Most recently, in May 2021, the lagoon was briefly re-connected with the Pacific Ocean in Cerro Hermoso, which brought hope to the communities. However, it came with another tragedy when a local child drowned in the water stream, which brought more grief and sadness to the communities. The lagoon and the ocean disconnected once again after some weeks. The reason, according to the local people, was that this was only a "temporary solution" achieved by dredging the sand between the ocean and the lagoons. According to the communities, what is necessary for the permanent re-connection of the lagoons is the removal of the breakwaters located in Cerro Hermoso, which continue to divert the water stream from the lagoons. The lack of response, listening, and prioritization of a Black and Indigenous territory and water in the country, indicates, again, how environmental racism operates in Mexico.

## Conclusion

In this interlude, I have argued that the ecocide of the Chacahua-Pastoría lagoons in Oaxaca, Mexico is an example of environmental racism in Latin America that has not only socioeconomic impacts, but also profound emotional ones. Dispossession can happen through different strategies such as pollution, tourism, and toxicity, however, dispossession can also have an emotional effect: dispossession of life and joy. The exposure to toxicity and pollution in the lagoon's water also generates health problems and puts people's lives at risk. Black and Indigenous communities are sustained primarily by the Chacahua-Pastoría lagoons not only through fishing for market or more recently tourism, but for their everyday food. If the lagoons die, the communities around the lagoons will no longer be able to live there and sustain themselves. The communities surrounding this body of water have made multiple local, national, and even international efforts to bring attention to this ecocide. However, these efforts have been met by silence and a lack of response from the government: a continuation of a colonial project of dispossession of the local Black and Indigenous population by the government on the other through toxicity and pollution created by the decisions of the state and transnational capital which center on exploitation of natural resources and sacred lands.

Black and Indigenous local people suffer disproportionately from the consequences of environmental racism in a country that only recognized its Afro-descendant population for the first time in 2019, and which continues to dispossess ancestral lands and waters deeply connected to their well-being as communities.

## Notes

1  On July 9th of 1937, President Lázaro Cárdenas declared the "*Sistema Lagunar Chacahua-Pastoría*" a National Park, the first one ever declared in the country.
2  Data collected during my fieldwork, there is no official current numbers.
3  Mixteco is an Indigenous group in Mexico.
4  The diminutive of panga, a modest-size boat use for fishing.
5  A rounded net used for fishing in the shallow water.

## References

Rodríguez Aguilera, Meztli Yoalli. 2021. "Grieving Geographies, Mourning Waters: Life, Death, and Environmental Gendered Racialized Struggles in Mexico." Feminist Anthropology 3 (1): 1–16.

Auyero, Javier, and Débora Alejandra Swistun. 2009. *Flammable: Environmental Suffering in an Argentine Shantytown*. Oxford, New York: Oxford University Press.

Bullard, Robert D. 1993. "The Threat of Environmental Racism." *Natural Resources & Environmental* Vol. 7, No. 3, Facility Siting (Winter): 23–26, 55–56.

Cabnal, Lorena. 2019. "El Relato de Las Violencias Desde Mi Territorio Cuerpo-Tierra." In *En Tiempos de Muerte: Cuerpos, Rebeldías, Resistencias IV*, coordinated by Xochitl Solano and Rosalba Icaza, 113–26. Mexico and Argentina: Editorial Retos, CLACSO, Institute of Social Studies, Erasmus University Rotterdam.

Colectivo de Geografía Crítica del Ecuador. 2017. "Geografiando Para La Resistencia." *Journal of Latin American Geography* 16 (1): 172–77.

COPERA. 2018. "Racismo Ambiental/Institucional En México. El Caso de Las Comunidades Del Sistema Lagunar Chacahua-Pastoría En Oaxaca." Human Rights Report. Unpublished manuscript. Colectivo Para Eliminar el Racismo en México.

Guajardo-Panes, Rafael, Finlandia Barbosa-Moreno, Gabriel Díaz-Padilla, and Ignacio Sánchez-Cohen. 2020. "Cálculo de Un Índice de Calidad Del Agua En Un Cuerpo de Agua: Estudio de Caso Lagunas Chacahua y Pastoría, Oaxaca." *RINDERESU. Revista Internacional de Desarrollo Regional Sustentable* 5 (2): 650–69.

Krauss, Celeste. 2009. "Mothering at the Crossroads. African American Women and the Emergence of the Movement Against Environmental Racism." In *Environmental Justice in the New Millenium. Global Perspectives on Race, Ethnicity and Human Rights*, edited by Filomina Chioma Steady, 65–89. United States of America: Palgrave Macmillan.

Masferrer León, Cristina V., and Leopoldo Trejo, eds. 2019. *Diversidades en Crisis. Transformaciones Socioambientales en Regiones Indígenas y Afromexicanas en Oaxaca*. Mexico City: INAH.

Moreno Parra, María. 2019. "Racismo Ambiental: Muerte Lenta y Despojo de Territorio Ancestral Afroecuatoriano En Esmeraldas." *Íconos-Revista de Ciencias Sociales* 64: 89–109.

Sun-Hee Park, Lisa, and David N. Pellow. 2004. "Racial Formation, Environmental Racism, and the Emergence of Silicon Valley." *Ethnicities* 4 (3): 403–24.

Zaragocin, Sofia. 2019. "La Geopolítica Del Útero: Hacia Una Geopolítica Feminista Decolonial En Espacios de Muerte Lenta." In *Cuerpos, Territorios y Feminismos. Compilación Latinoamericana de Teorías, Metodologías y Prácticas Políticas.*, edited by Delma Tania Cruz, Manuel Bayón Jiménez, and Colectivo Miradas Críticas del Territorio desde el Feminismo, 81–97. Mexico: Abya Yala, Instituto de Estudios Ecologistas del Tercer Mundo, Bajo Tierra Ediciones and Libertad Bajo Palabra.

# CHAPTER 10

# Reconfiguring Methodologies for the Study of Textiles: Weaving and Wearing the Huipil in Villa Hidalgo Yalálag

Ariadna Solis Translated by Ellen Jones

When we visited[1] Bertha Felipe, an 85-year-old weaver from the Yalálag community,[2] she asked us: "le'ben llenhe gún be urash?" The question was directed at me: she was asking if I was the one who wanted to dress as a Yalaltecan woman.[3] I begin this essay with her question because the conversations we had with the female weavers in my community prompted the critical methodology proposed in this essay. By this I do not mean it is my intention to "give voice" to the weavers; on the contrary, I acknowledge their presence in this work as my interlocutors and speak based on my experience with them, and in light of the possibilities and specific problems we established through studying textiles produced by our community. So, the emphasis on methodology in the study of the making and wearing of lhall xha or huipil dresses in my community stems from collective concerns about the epistemic extractivism to which the world's various indigenous nations have historically been subject.

And so, while I was learning how huipiles are produced, the logics of their meaning, and how they are used by Yalaltecan women, I had to rethink how we approach textiles (and more generally objects from indigenous communities) and how the knowledge and practices that develop around them are presented. By reconfiguring the methodologies used to work with objects that belong to our histories and communities, we have an opportunity to rethink the racism on which academic discussions have been based, discussions that leave out the practices, affect, knowledge, and memories of various agents who have been considered "objects of study" rather than knowledgeable interlocutors.

It was thus that I perceived the need to reconfigure the methodology used in this chapter if I was to approach this work in all its specificity—work that is imbricated with the construction of a particular notion of communality, and which shapes research paths that are profoundly anti-racist and anti-capitalist. This includes the wearing of the huipil and the key role of the body in the very construction of community life; in other words, how we express our belonging and our presence through the way we dress.

I mention this because I am interested in acknowledging the different threads that must be woven in order to achieve this knowledge, specifically for a researcher who, like me, is part of the community.[4] Not only is it not possible to separate the acts of understanding and wearing a huipil in the community of Yalálag; these actions also acquire more complex nuances for indigenous researchers who build knowledge around their own communities.

In positioning myself as an indigenous researcher, I follow proposals made by Linda Tuhiwai Smith, taking care to make clear that for me it's not about romanticizing an identity but rather about claiming "a genealogical, cultural, and political set of experiences" (Tuhuwai Smith 2012, 12). I recognize, as do the woman who will appear in this chapter, "the ways in which scientific research is implicated in the worst excesses of colonialism" (Tuhiwai Smith 2012, 1). As a consequence, by taking up Tuhiwai's methodological approach, in this chapter I seek to understand research as "a place that reveals" Western interests and ways of knowing and the modes of resistance used by otherness. In this sense, this chapter intends to begin with the question: who benefits from research into a particular object? What purpose does it serve? In the case of textiles, the discussion around their commercialization in recent years has been particularly important, and although they are an object of study in their own right, so are the forms of community support that allowed these cracks in the community economy and in the formation of communality.

When embarking on the study of the lhall xha or Yalaltecan huipil dress, it was fundamental to do so principally through the memories, knowledge, and repertoires of the women who live in the community of Yalálag and who make and wear these garments every day. I understand "knowledge" as the concrete experience of these women in the making and wearing of huipiles, and I understand "repertoires," following Diana Taylor's formulation of the concept, as the embodied practices that respond to other forms of knowledge creation related to the body, memory, and presence (Taylor 2009, 110). Repertoires are ways of safeguarding collective memory, a notion that will help us understand the urgency of redirecting methodology towards the activation of bodily knowledge, instead of focusing exclusively on the technical, formal, and symbolic knowledge associated with these garments.

The research on which this chapter is based was carried out in the Zapotec spoken in Yalálag and principally through conversations with elderly women in the community who weave and wear these garments.[5] For my part, working with and in Zapotec allowed me to recover and restructure my personal history in this context. Tuhiwai explains this gesture using the notions of "re-writing" and "re-righting" our position in history (Tuhiwai Smith 2012, 6). This ties in with Silvia Rivera Cusicanqui's proposed methodology, which involves "decolonizing gestures," such as the reactivation of indigenous languages, in order to subvert the way that knowledge has been produced.

Weaving, both as a practice and as an image, helps explain what Rivera Cusicanqui defines as the web of experiences and actions that make it possible to weave a community:

> The notion of women's identity resembles weaving. Rather than establishing the ownership and jurisdictional authority of a nation—or community, or indigenous autonomous region—women weave the fabric of interculturality through their practices: as producers, traders, weavers, ritual makers, creators of languages and symbols able to seduce the "other" and establish pacts of reciprocity and coexistence among people who differ from one another. (Rivera Cusicanqui, 2010, 72)

In Yalálag Zapotec,[6] we can understand this identity as "be'ne urash."[7] This term acknowledges a kind of belonging that does not work in the same way as identification with a nation-state, nor as the idea of ethnic identity (Gutiérrez Chong 2012).[8] In fact, to call ourselves be'ne urash is a way of opposing the ethnic identities that are inserted into the discourse of the multicultural nation.

Indeed, the discourse of identity promotes a largely uncritical understanding of the ethnic as something primordial that sustains the formation of a national identity. It is a selective and racist rescuing of the past that favors the integration of indigenous peoples into the nation-state project, and which presupposes clothing, language, and customs as essential signs of indigenous identity. "Bilha" is another word that, contrary to this way of determining ethnic identities, brings a specific community into view, made up of women linked by affective ties over time. It is used to refer to sisters and female cousins and friends, without referring to the hierarchies and obligations imposed by the patriarchal family. It is a word used to name the women who are dearest and closest to us, and it allows me to describe the closeness I have experienced with the weavers (it is in fact a term they themselves have used to refer to "us" as a group). Although it might seem similar to be'ne urash, bilha has a more affective character, which is why it has prompted much of the methodology used in this chapter. So, the information contained here has been used with the consent of the women who were my interlocutors, and I have left out what they preferred to be omitted in order to avoid conflict with the community. For this reason, I want to emphasize that by calling my female interlocutors in this chapter bilha, I am trying to demonstrate a point made by Rivera Cusicanqui: that the affective tie has the power to produce communality and the responsibilities and obligations we assume when we create that tie. For that reason, when skin is described as a place of knowledge, this is not a metaphor but rather an act of recognizing "that the body has its own modes of knowing" and that "the hand knows" (Rivera Cusicanqui 2019), which in turn demands that we reconfigure our modes of listening and producing knowledge, or of being part of and present in our communities, while at the same time confronting the plunder of natural, economic, cultural, and epistemic resources.

With these observations I want to acknowledge the different logics of meaning making that are at play in the making and wearing of huipiles for and in community life. By organizing and transmitting their knowledge, and by dressing themselves in garments with particular meaning (in our case, huipiles), community members generate embodied commitments or, in Diana Taylor's words, a politics of presence (Taylor 2009) that plays a fundamental role in sustaining community life not only in Yalálag but also outside it. We can therefore understand why weaving, along with clothing, plays a key role in the community of Yalálag that goes beyond that of commercialization. Having said this, I will now explain the directions the concerns around the huipil have taken in light of the textile collections and Yalálag community photographic archives. In order to do this, I examined archival records and collections. I was accompanied by women from the community, which allowed for interchange and dialogue about the ethical and political implications of studying and representing them. Many of the women who collaborated in this research were introduced to me by aunts or by female cousins and friends who live in the community.[9] This meant they welcomed me into their homes and together we created an affective tie which, for me, is the backbone of an anti-extractivist methodology.[10] Indeed, in this chapter the affective approach is also intended to be a response to a common practice among those seeking knowledge in indigenous communities, in which, rather than constructing knowledge together, knowledge is extracted and then presented outside the community. So, the affective ties that were jointly created and imbued with the responsibility to create both material and immaterial common goods for the community itself, led to what I have called "an archive return," which was an excuse for building meaningful and reciprocal long-term relationships. The starting point for this approach was to visit textile and photographic collections where I found objects that people in Yalálag, or at least the weavers I was working with, did not know existed. I photographed all the objects I found in these collections so that the weavers, my mother, and I could analyze the pieces together (Tuck and Yang 2014, 226–231). The collections we consulted were the Oaxaca Textile Museum, the ethnographic collection at the National Museum of Anthropology, and the textile collection at the National Institute of Indigenous Peoples.

Using this methodology, I worked with six community weavers: Bertha Felipe, Apolonia Morales Limeta, Eufemia Lonche Tomás, Marga Aceves, Viviana Cano,[11] and Aurora Tizo, among whom only Eufemia Lonche, Marga Aceves, and Aurora Tizo are currently engaged in textile work. All of them have consented to share their knowledge with me and know that this information will be published. Moreover, they have a copy of the completed research, as well as a copy of all the material gathered in the archives and collections. This not only allowed me to analyze the pieces with them; it also prompted them to take their own critical look at the way textiles have been collected and preserved in the archives: as forms of symbolic and economic capital whose logic of accumulation and of the exhibition of fetishized objects permits the mechanics of dispossession, exoticization, and institutional racism by contributing to representation of Yalaltecan women as other in photographs circulating both inside and outside those spaces.

The process of analysis was based on audio and video interviews and photographs.[12] The "archive return"[13] took place through the exchange of images in the collections, which led to a joint selection of some of the photographs and, in some cases (including Eufemia Lonche and Inés López Cano), learning techniques involved in making a huipil using a backstrap loom.[14]

We articulated the work around two thematic axes, approached on three hermeneutic levels: field practice, textile archives, and photographic collections. First, we gave a technical and formal account of the huipil, including the evolution of its production and use. This information was mainly condensed into bilingual diagrams of elements of textile practice in Yalálag that note the Zapotec names for the garment and the elements required to make it. These will be held as archive material for future generations. To complement the study of the garment, we also analyzed two photograph collections containing images of women wearing the huipil in question: Julio de la Fuente's photograph collection[15] and Citlali Fabián's documentary project,[16] selected because they are the best known within the Yalálag community itself. By considering these two forms of representation through the textile and photograph collections, the aim was to analyze the formation of a visual imaginary at different moments in time and in different materials in order to account for how a "legitimate" story was constructed around the garment that contrasts with the story told by the women who make and wear it. This was the pillar of our methodology, which allowed us to continue the transformation of this object in two ways: on the one hand, through "official" state archives, museums, and private collections, and on the other hand, through the oral, visual, and bodily memories of the Zapotec women, articulated through a study of archives, objects, and images.

Secondly, I was interested in acknowledging the community networks that textile practice involves, and the different route knowledge production takes when the strategies of dialogue and collaboration are reconfigured to involve interlocutors who have historically been outside of institutions of epistemo-logical production such as academia or museums. I have therefore sought to use the discussion around communality as a strategy for thinking about practices that can reconfigure the study of indigenous community objects, basing their study on the political potential of their use by the communities themselves. In this sense, rather than a "representative" sample of textiles or of women who wear huipiles, the images we selected together express a set of collective concerns about the garment, its place in collections and exhibi-tions, and the way it has been used in the representation of Yalaltecan women in photographs.

## The Yalálag Huipil

In the community of Yalálag, it is elderly women who preserve the knowledge of weaving or gub'yelhe and whose bodies keep huipil use alive by wearing them every day. In Yalálag, weaving is an exclusively female skill, and the lhall xha or huipil[17] is just one of the textiles worn by female community members. Today, the complete outfit comprises seven pieces.[18] Starting from the top, these include a black wool duxlú—a headpiece also known as a tlacoyal,[19] Yalálag crosses, worn as earrings, and a necklace[20] of red and gold beads and a silver, or occasionally gold, cross around the neck. Covering most of the body is a huipil woven on a backstrap loom from white cotton; this garment does not always have the characteristics described here—there are variations in color, shape, and design. Previously they extended right down below the knees and had elbow-length sleeves, so the length of the fabric varied depend-ing on who was wearing them. Weavers use Zapotec words for elbows, arms, or hands to describe different sizes. An adult huipil is usually nine elbows in length, a measurement that in Zapotec is known as ga'llit. Underneath the huipil is a xtap, a wrap-around underskirt or slip, also made on a backstrap loom.[21] This garment is fitted to the body in a particular way: one of its edges is always lined up with the right-hand side of the person wearing it and tied with a belt or baidún, which can either be made just of cloth or combined with a xpac, or zoyate palm belt, in the shape of a flattened cylinder. When the belt is made up of these two elements it is known as a pak nhen baidún, a sash or zoyate. It not only holds the xtap in place but also supports the waists of women doing heavy work in the fields or at home (it is also used after women give birth). These days, female attire is completed with a pair of san-dals known as yelh in Zapotec, which are made of leather, velvet, and rubber.

The "traditional" huipil is a piece made from two long pieces of symmetrical white cotton, woven on a backstrap loom,[22] which are obtained by cutting an approximately four-meter-long piece of woven fabric in half. There are two possible types of weave, each producing a different texture: they can be made with a simple, plain or flat weave, but there are also huipiles made with a weave called sab bchadj in Zapotec,[23] also known as gauze, a technique that allows for the production of a fine, light, lace-like fabric (Lechuga 1982, 32).

The above is a formal description of the huipil, made the way the weavers showed my mother and me how to dress. When we visited the homes of Eufemia Lonche, Aurora Tizo, Marga Aceves, and Inés López Cano, they explained production techniques and different levels of formality among the items. As we mentioned in the introduction, it's important to note that these women agreed to show us the techniques for making huipiles because we are part of the community.[24] Eufemia, in particular, reminded us of the importance of mutual aid that benefits the community at large. This is why they welcomed us into their homes with particular affection, because these forms of cooperation and mutual aid always have future generations in mind. Mutual aid creates and sustains community ties that go beyond the family and a particular generation of community members. For this reason, a central element of my methodology in this chapter involves recounting the community networks I have had to navigate—this allows me to understand and shape knowledge relating to the practice of weaving in the light of the idea of communality. The way I obtained this information is rooted in these encounters, inextricably linked to the commitment I make to my community. For this very reason I must stress that when transmitting this knowledge, I have sought to confine myself to the limits imposed by my interlocutors, despite the implicit conflict with the demands of academia, which urged me to construct, step by step, a detailed technical account. By undertaking this task on these terms, I have sought to respond to the urgency of generating strategies that allow us to understand and preserve our knowledge without replicating extractivist forms of knowledge creation around and within indigenous communities.

In the case of this chapter, this mainly involved tackling the question through the materiality of the huipil and its presence on the body. This meant it was important to find a way of weaving the technical, formal, and stylistic story together with the social story, with communal life and the role of women in sustaining it. Unlike many, especially older, women, who taught us to dress, to put on our underskirt and tie the baidún, and who have resisted pressure to dress differently, the community's younger women, who, like myself, are scattered among regions far from the Oaxacan sierra, no longer use the huipil on a daily basis but rather, for various reasons, tend to use it on special occasions such as festivities. One of the reasons for this is that when we wear this garment in non-community contexts, we make ourselves visible as racialized women. Although this experience—making ourselves visible as indigenous women—is complex, part of our resistance as Yalaltecan women has been to *wear* our collective identity: to wear the memory of our community on our bodies is a way of reminding ourselves that we exist through the community and in deep reciprocity with it.

In this context it is worth raising a question to which I have already alluded but which is rarely tackled: who wears the "traditional" huipil in Mexico?[25] A "traditional" huipil in my community can cost as much as 8000 pesos (around USD 400), or even more if it includes characteristics considered "authentic" according to the largely malign discourses that regulate the commercialization of huipiles in non-community circles. Anyone who wears a "traditional" huipil in Mexico, or at least a Yalálag huipil, is therefore displaying that they have the financial means to acquire one. Here I want to stress that these garments circulate differently within communities themselves: usually, if you are not wearing your own huipil, you are wearing one borrowed from an aunt, a cousin, your mother, a friend, or, ideally, one your grandmother gave you once it no longer fitted her, or one she left when she passed away (assuming the huipil was not buried with her). In the past, there were people who could lend or rent you the embroidered strips that decorate the huipil, because in truth it is very expensive to wear a "traditional" huipil, known in the community of Yalálag as a "party" huipil or "gala" huipil. So, although it is possible to find huipiles circulating "outside" the community, they are produced mainly for community members who now live elsewhere. As Yalaltecan women, we know that wearing our community's clothing is principally part of an "everyday" struggle in which the ways we articulate our resistance are negotiated. We also know that the acts of weaving, embroidering, and wearing clothing are charged with material and technical but also symbolic and visual potential, capable of sustaining community life. Here I want to return to the question posed by Bertha Felipe, one of the Yalálag weavers, when I sought her out to talk about her work and her use of the huipil. Bertha asked if it was me who wanted to dress like a Yalaltecan woman. By asking me this question, Bertha reminded me that knowing about and wearing the huipil are fundamental ways of resisting and of reclaiming the ways of life and community memory that have been forgotten. "What should we wear?" is a question we indigenous women ask ourselves every day, in order to assure our survival without forgetting our predecessors, all the while rejecting the folklorification and depoliticization of our collective identities.

### Du yichj du lhall'lhe llaklhenlé nheto: Strategies for Communal Thinking

¿Kelh tuzen nhakllo, nhe'?

Are we not one?

Eufemia Lonche

The care and responsibility on which community life is built are exemplified in a memory Eufemia Lonche shared with us. She told us that when she was orphaned as a child, the woman who would later become her mother-in-law took her into her home and taught her the weaving trade. This sense of community responsibility also appeared in tales told by my grandmother; she, like Eufemia Lonche, was orphaned very young and it was a woman from the community who, by teaching her about textiles (in this case sewing and making clothes) put into practice this repertoire of care that exists outside the logic of individual gain. It is no coincidence that these two stories were connected by the practice of textile making and the agency of women, outside of commercial interests per se. All the weavers insisted that weaving, while it was an important source of income, was by no means their main occupation, of which they had many: they also help tend to the land, care for domestic animals such as hens, pigs, and turkeys, and cultivate fruit trees. In this sense, reproduction was at the center of their activities. They also prepare food to sell, either occasionally or regularly, in Yalálag itself and to send to communities of Yalaltecans on the outskirts of Oaxaca City and Mexico City. Most of their time is devoted to care work and to making visible concrete ways of safeguarding community knowledge and sustaining life in material ways, not only in the highland community but also in migrant communities outside of Yalálag itself. The care, the food, the organizing of celebrations, their work tending the land, and their textiles: all these are repertoires of communal action carried out by women's bodies.

## Communal Repertoires

As mentioned above, textile practice has ongoing meaning for the Yalaltecan community in terms of sustaining community life. Although this is particularly palpable at celebrations and at difficult moments such as burials or periods of illness, there are different levels that must be untangled if we are to thoroughly understand how communality is continually being updated in a situated way. It strikes me that one mistake many discussions of communality make is to talk about the term as though it were disconnected from the concrete territories where specific practices related to the construction of community life are carried out. In our interaction with the weavers, during which we analyzed images and recalled anecdotes, often about celebrations but mainly about their work sustaining community life, we identified at least three repertoires that, although not the only ones, are useful to understand the complexity of the community network of women in Yalálag. It is this network we are trying to reconstruct, but without simplifying it, as often happens when the notion of communality is used without situating these practices properly. By using the term, I do not seek to position my argument within the framework of discussions around communality currently taking place in Mexico and Latin America more broadly, but rather to untangle the specificities I see in my own community and which sustain life through a complex network of daily actions that I define as repertoires of communality.

The first of these repertoires I want to mention is known as tequio in Spanish, although the Zapotec term offers nuances that are important to highlight: llin lhao refers to work that is obligatory for everyone in the community—tasks or duties that are assigned during regular assemblies. Those who live far from the community and cannot complete their tequio pay an annual fee, which is voluntary. In our case, we have paid two days of work, which amounts to six hundred pesos (around USD 30) a year. Assemblies are how the community has come to be governed and is where tasks are decided, the community's needs are discussed, and duties are delegated. Assemblies are also when community projects are proposed, and then approved or rejected by the community itself. While my own research, because it involves working with elderly women and is affective in nature, did not need to be approved by the assembly, other proposed projects, such as those involving children and the community in general have, however, had to pass through this filter; some have been rejected and others are now in process.[26]

The second repertoire can be denoted by the Zapotec expression "ke yoitello," which can be translated as "that which is communal" or "that which is for everyone." Ke yoitello might refer to roads, death, churches, or the cemetery. Although it is used mainly to describe spaces, in recent years this word has lost its meaning in people's concrete reality. The weavers, because of the nature of their work, work outside in the sun. This is only possible on the patios or in the corridors characteristic of traditional Yalálag buildings, which have wide corridors and patios around which the rooms of a house are arranged. These houses used to lead directly onto public throughways that encouraged community members to share spaces and get to know one another, as well as facilitating the weaving of pieces of cloths up to four meters long. This architecture and its associated dynamics have changed in recent years as a result of migration and remittances sent back from afar, among other factors. As a result, community spaces of mutual recognition and care have been shut down. With it, weaving's status as an activity that, although not strictly public, was always available to anyone moving through those spaces, has been lost.

The term wzon, on the other hand, allows me to explain a dynamic we encounter every time we visit the elderly women in the community. Although there is no term in Spanish that precisely captures the meaning of this repertoire, it has a certain similarity to what anthropology has described as reciprocity. However, in Zapotec, the term denotes a type of commitment not necessarily implied in "reciprocity," because wzon refers to work or knowledge that is shared, but the reciprocity of which applies across generations. It is mainly used to refer to work involved with mourning or celebration. However, this intergenerational commitment also appears when we indigenous researchers want to do work in our communities. The degree of our participation in community activities is important, as well as obligatory. For us, as women who participate in community life, it is also about "giving back" rather than extracting knowledge. This resonates with the methodologies proposed by other indigenous researchers, such as Leanne Simpson, who refers to a deep local reciprocity (Klein 2013) that involves respect, meaningful and authentic relationships, and a responsibility for the impact academic or investigative work can have at a community level. So the emphasis, when it comes to rethinking methodologies for the study of textiles and more generally of objects belonging to indigenous communities, should be on reinforcing the protective and caring relationships on which community dynamics are based, not on the "discovery" or "recovery" of the techniques, symbols, or iconographic meanings of those objects. This methodological principle makes clear that those techniques, symbols, and meanings lack significance outside those community dynamics, and alerts us to the fact that their extraction, by reinscribing them in discussions in other contexts, often contributes to the crystallization of diverse indigenous identities and thus their exoticization and commercialization.

This last repertoire can be explained using the example of a very particular experience: when we introduced ourselves to Eufemia Lonche, she immediately brought two moments up in conversation: first, she reminded us that she had whisked pozontle[27] at my mother's wedding. In Yalálag, it is understood that when a woman helps out at another woman's celebration or a funeral, she can expect that, in turn, when she requires help, those same women will come without being asked. Older women are the first to arrive and the last to leave when it comes to activating this repertoire. The second moment Eufemia recalled was when she and her husband were going through a crisis. During that time, my grandparents (my mother's parents) lent them their land so they could sow and harvest food until they emerged from economic hardship. This was done without my grandparents expecting anything in return, but knowing that the repertoire known as wzon was being activated. The fact that Eufemia had those two moments at the front of her mind shows how wzon can be activated even down the generations, and this is something that seems to me to have been gradually forgotten by the community's younger generations.

On the basis of this "consciousness of the other" and "deep reciprocity," characteristic of what is known in Zapotec as wzon and which rarely exists within individualist, neoliberal logic, I would like to return to the concept of communality located specifically in this community and closely connected to textile practice.[28] In this way, communality appears as a phenomenon we can situate and sketch out based on observations made in the community and thanks to the memories of the women with whom I spoke for this project. When we approach textile practice on the basis of the repertoires at play in the making and wearing of textiles in Yalálag, we glimpse everyday forms that make it possible to subvert the sense and direction of projects of domination and colonization. This is not only because it provides access to a way of knowing that in itself has the potential to care for and protect the body and community life, but also because it forms part of the resistance that is exercised through these other modes of seeing and being in the world.

I understand textile practice as a form of resistance not necessarily linked to identity struggles; nor do I see it as a romanticized practice, but rather as a space of "everyday" struggles where means of articulation are negotiated and a specific community of women is produced. To make and wear a huipil in Yalálag is one way of articulating and of resisting, but also of belonging and of engaging in communality. Thus, the "everyday" and the extraordinary appear "as forms of the same unit of historical time" (Chatterjee 1997, 209). In this sense, textile practice in indigenous communities cannot be understood except in connection to the cultivation of land, the production and commercialization of textiles, and as intrinsic to personal use, because it is there that we can find various kinds of autonomy. The relationship between textiles and the body is indispensable, so much so that the former are produced with and for the body. What is more, we must not forget that it is elderly women who have sustained the everyday use of this garment.

## Conclusions

As Eufemia told us about the process of creating huipiles, while the pieces were being analyzed and the results returned, stories of her obligations to community life began to emerge. Specifically, I would like to mention that in October 2018 a member of the community who lived in Yalálag died while the traditional tamales for Day of the Dead were being prepared. Like many of the women resident in the community, Eufemia always made bean tamales to place on the altars of the dead. After attending this funeral, my mother and I bumped into her on her way back from the cemetery, and we took the opportunity to say goodbye, because it was our last day in the community before our next visit in December 2018. We were not surprised to find that, in addition to those she had shared out among her loved ones, she had already put aside some tamales for my mother and me. When we tried to kindly reject the gift she had so generously prepared for us, Eufemia used the expression "kelh tuzen nhakllo, nhe'?" which in Spanish could be translated (notwithstanding losses) as "are we not one?" This expression, my mother explained to me, is used when someone enters someone else's closest circle of affection. Although in legal terms it refers to the family, in reality what happens when this Zapotec expression is uttered is a taking stock of the community that is formed when affective ties are re-structured through listening and spending time together. In my case this was enhanced through my work with the weavers on huipiles. Studying and analyzing the cultural heritage, images, and photographs together created a kind of community across two generations that had seemed distant not only spatially and temporally but also epistemically. While the "excuse" was the study of the huipil, the central weight of my research was a profound criticism of academia's extractivist dynamics and the pressing need to reconstruct networks of solidarity in contexts where migration, dispossession, and racist violence have shaped how we relate to our belongings. For this reason, many of us women have decided to abandon our traditional clothing, and for this reason we need to create strategies for approaching our histories with care, respect, and affection.

As an indigenous researcher, I believe my ethical and political commitments to my community are clearer now, because the memory of my community and my belonging in it are at stake, and also because I know the effects of research that has not been returned to the community. However, this points to challenges that need to be worked through more carefully. How can we create an engaged way of knowing, a process of being with, of walking and talking with others, with all the problems, complications, and contradictions this involves (Taylor 2017, 11)? How can we create ethical methodologies to produce knowledge and images in a collective way? The repertoire of wzon, which played a central role in the methodology of this research, was activated thanks to the incorporation of knowledge from both parties, which is to say, knowledge that was shared in a reciprocal manner. What I have called "archive return," in conjunction with the incorporation of knowledge that emerged during our discussions in Zapotec, was woven while we analyzed the pieces in the textile collections, the official photographs and those taken by the community. But the key to the writing of this chapter has been the work that was based on the knowledge and memories of the weavers themselves.

For this reason, I'd like to close by quoting the words of the Unión de Mujeres Yalaltecas (Yalaltecan Women's Union) in 1970: the goal is not "to be an object of study but rather an object of actions in which studies converge into a reflection that can improve our own living conditions and which is based on our own reality" (Vásquez Vásquez 2021, 136).

## Notes

1   I will sometimes use the first-person plural to acknowledge the role of my mother, Genoveva Bautista, in accompanying, translating, and interpreting for the Zapotec-speaking weavers and myself, a non-Zapotec speaker. As part of this process, we decided to jointly undertake the task of re-learning about our history.

2   In 1877 Yalálag changed its name from San Juan Yalálag to Villa Hidalgo Yalálag. In this chapter I will refer to it simply as Yalálag, its everyday Hispanicized name. The town of Yalálag has 1844 inhabitants according to the 2010 census carried out by INEGI. It is situated in the municipality of Villa Hidalgo, east of the capital of the State of Oaxaca. The community is mainly Spanish speaking, but it is also possible to find speakers of Zapotec and Mixe.

3   Although the closest literal translation of "be urash" in Bertha Felipe's question is "paisana" or fellow countrywoman, I use the identity marker "yalalteca" here. To use the term "paisana" in Spanish would be to overlook a communal meaning that is not limited by place of birth.

4   It should be noted that the community of Yalálag, like many other Indigenous communities, usually makes certain demands of the researchers among them. Since commitments both to family and to society are at stake, our actions have repercussions for members of our families, possibly for generations. For this reason, the level of responsibility when undertaking the study of certain topics tends to be more immediate and has degrees of complexity that differ from those faced by researchers "outside" the community.

5   Most of the older women in the community of Yalálag do not speak Spanish, although they understand it perfectly. This means I am at a disadvantage communication-wise.

6   The Zapotec mentioned throughout this chapter is the dill wlhall [diʃuraɪʃ] variant, or southeastern highland Zapotec. It is worth mentioning that to date there is no grammar or dictionary of Yalálag Zapotec that allows us to establish a common framework for its writing or reading or to determine unequivocal meaning.

7   See third footnote of this chapter.

8   Rita Segato describes this phenomenon more clearly as "political transnational identities" (Segato 2007, 62–66).

9   The women themselves gave me further names of women who accompanied them in their work or who also carried it out. This methodology is described in the social sciences as snowball sampling, but I prefer to think of these references as affective ties that are sustained in the community in the long term.

10  I use this term to name the profit-making extraction of knowledge, techniques, iconographies, and images of Indigenous communities and subjects, often to the benefit of those (companies, businesses) outside the community (Grosfoguel 2016, 33–45).

11  Vivian Can Ure is the name with which she was introduced to us and how she is known in the Geminiana Cano Alejo community. While this research was being edited, and before the results were returned to the weavers, Viviana Cano passed away on October 9, 2019 at the age of 86. The archive return in this specific case was therefore delivered to her closest daughter, Inés López Cano, with whom the methodology proposed in this chapter will continue.

12  I invoke the "refusal to research" that Eve Tuck and K. Wayne Yang propose in their third axiom, where they maintain that there are types of knowledge that academia

"does not deserve" to possess. In this sense, I respect the limits imposed by the subjects of knowledge tackled in this research, who are the community's weavers (Tuck and Yang 2014, 224). This is why, although the nature of the research meant that details of manufacturing were recorded, they will not be discussed in this chapter.

13  During our fieldwork, the textile archives, built as "official" public and private archives, were contrasted with the weavers' own knowledge. The process then consisted of "returning" the images to them, so I created a register of all the pieces found in the collections and gave them copies of the archive material and of the process of documentation. I did a first selection of photographs of textile objects in the collections, hoping they would prompt stories, memories, and knowledge from the weavers, as well as allowing us to understand the logic of their production. With this dynamic we tried at first to approach the production of the huipil through the weavers' own experiences in order to understand the logics to which they respond and the ways they have structured an imaginary around this garment.

14  The manual learning experience I will incorporate into this epistemic exercise will allow me to gain textile know-how; learning about textiles happens not through the verbalization of knowledge but rather by putting it into practice.

15  Julio Antonio de la Fuente Chicoséin (1905–1970) was a photographer, graphic artist, anthropologist and Mexican Indigenist who spent much of his life documenting and carrying out ethnographic work in various Indigenous communities in Mexico, especially with the Yalálag Zapotecs. His collection of photographs of this community, which dates from the early twentieth century, is the largest among official archives and the best known by the community.

16  Citlali Fabián is a photographer from the Yalálag community.

17  Huipiles are items of women's clothing that have been used since the classical period by Maya cultures and since the postclassical period by Nahua cultures. They are garments that cover the torso right down to the knees, composed of two or more lengths of cloth joined at the edges (Rieff Anawalt 2005, 17).

18  A complete illustration with the Zapotec names can be consulted at the following link. This study was carried out by the Dill Yel Nbán collective, to which I belong, and was made possible thanks to the present study. The project also produced a glossary of textile-related terms in Zapotec: https://drive.google.com/drive/u/1/folders/17g5WmFkXfCw_Vna_4KaKpMV99fBdTFCm.

19  Previously this was made entirely in the community, from the threadwork to the finish. Now the wool is acquired ready-prepared from Teotitlán del Valle and is worked on in the community. Alba Cano is one of the people who currently safeguards the knowledge of how to produce these pieces.

20  Previously these beads were made of coral and gold, which we can take as a reflection of the wealth and level of trade communication the community had. These days pieces of painted plastic are used.

21  The huipil's xtap (wrap-around underskirt or slip) is made with two long pieces of cloth, approximately four meters in length, joined horizontally to achieve the width

of the skirt. The clothes are made with white cotton and cotton dyed with the bark of holm oak or prairie acacia. The measurements of the pieces can vary, but the most common is four meters long by a meter wide for an adult.

22 Generally speaking, the backstrap loom is a tool that allows the warp of the fabric (the threads that will make up the length of the cloth) to be held tight so that the weft can be interwoven at a right angle. It is made of two sticks or warp beams to which the ends of the warp are fixed. The upper warp beam is tied with a cord to a fixed point (in Yalálag this is usually a tree or the column of a house) and the lower warp beam is held across the weaver's hips using a leather strap. In this way the weight of the weaver's body pulls the threads taut (Lechuga 1982, 26–31).

23 Here, and in other passages in this chapter, we use Zapotec terms where we cannot find an adequate translation into Spanish.

24 A common denominator in the community of women weavers in Yalálag is that they do not share information about how huipiles are made with people who are not from the community. This distrust is a response to cultural extractivism.

25 The term "traditional" refers here to huipiles made on a backstrap loom that are hand embroidered, sometimes with handmade thread and natural dyes.

26 In methodological terms it would be interesting for "external" researchers to have to pass through all these filters, which are often overlooked, whether due to ignorance or negligence, when research processes are being developed. Their methodological approaches would have to be constructed based on a principle of care and ethical responsibility, and their proposals would have to "contribute" something to the community instead of being limited to extracting information in order to gain symbolic and cultural capital from the academic institutions into which their research is inserted.

27 A cacao and corn-based drink made for festivities and special occasions. It is foamed using a hand whisk and drunk cold.

28 Two key sources on the topic of community feminisms are Tzul Tzul (2016, 20) and Cabnal (2010, 10–25).

## References

Cabnal, Lorena Cabnal, "Acercamiento a la construcción del pensamiento epistémico de las mujeres indígenas feministas comunitarias de Abya Yala," in *Feminismos diversos: el feminismo comunitario*, edited by Lorena Cabnal (Nicaragua: ACSUR-Las Segovias, 2010).

Chatterjee, Partha. "La nación y sus campesinos," in *Debates poscoloniales: Una introducción a los estudios de la subalternidad*, edited by Silvia Rivera Cusicanqui y Rossana Barragán (La Paz: Editorial Historias, Ediciones Aruwiyiri, Sephis, 1997), 209.

Grosfoguel, Ramón. "Del extractivismo económico al extractivismo epistémico." *Revista internacional de comunicación y desarrollo* 4 (2016), 33–45.

Gutiérrez Chong, Natividad. *Mitos nacionalistas e identidades étnicas. Los intelectuales indígenas y el estado mexicano*. Mexico: Instituto de Investigaciones Sociales, UNAM, 2012.

Klein, Naomi. 'Dancing the World into Being: A Conversation with Idle No More's Leanne Simpson." *Yes Magazin*, March 6, 2013. Available at: https://www.yesmagazine.org/social-justice/2013/03/06/dancing-the-world-into-being-a-conversation-with-idle-no-more-leanne-simpson.

Lechuga, Ruth. *Las técnicas textiles en el México indígena* Mexico: FONART, 1982.

Rieff Anawalt, Patricia. "Atuendos del México Antiguo": Textiles del México de ayer y hoy. *Arqueología Mexicana* 19 (2005): 17.

Rivera Cusicanqui, Silvia. *Ch'ixinakax utxiwa. Una reflexión sobre prácticas y discursos descolonizadores*. Tinta limón, 2010.

Rivera Cusicanqui, Silvia. "Tenemos que producir pensamiento a partir de lo cotidiano," interview with Kattalin Barber, *Feminismo Poscolonial*, February 17, 2019, https://bit.ly/2JilB6y.

Segato, Rita. *La nación y sus otros. Raza, etnicidad y diversidad religiosa en tiempos de políticas de la identidad*. Buenos Aires: Prometeo Libros, 2007.

Taylor, Diana. "¡Presente! La política de la presencia." *Investigación Teatral* 8, no. 12 (2017), 11–34.

Taylor, Diana "Performance e historia." *Revista Apuntes* 131 (2009).

Tuhiwai Smith, Linda. *Decolonizing Methodologies: Research and Indigenous Peoples*. London: Zed Books, 2012.

Tuck, Eve and K. Wayne Yang, "R-words: Refusing Research," in Humanizing Research: Decolonizing qualitative inquiry with youth and communities, edited by D. Paris and M.T. Winn (Thousand Oaks: Sage Publications, 2014).

Tzul Teatro, Gladys. "La producción comunal de la autoridad indígena, breve esbozo para Guatemala." In *El apantle. Revista de estudios comunitarios* 2 (2016).

Vásquez Vásquez, Yunitza. *Hacedoras de memoria y políticas de resistencia. La lucha de las mujeres por el derecho a la libre determinación y autonomía en Villa Hidalgo Yalálag, Oaxaca*. Undergraduate thesis, 2021: UAM-I.

# THE COMMUNAL DYNAMICS OF TEXTILE IDENTITY: #MYTLAHUIBLOUSE

Tajëëw B. Díaz Robles Translated by Ellen Jones

**Määy—Good Morning**

It's market day in Tlahuitoltepec. People start arriving early—mostly women but a few men too—on foot or in pickup trucks, to sell some of their harvest. Only after celebrations or on very cold, wet days is the market ever small—usually there's an abundance of seasonal produce here. You hear Mixe being spoken as people do their shopping. It's how older women give their prices: "makoxk pes, mäjk pes," while younger people say: "five pesos, ten pesos, three tamales or tortillas spread with beans for ten pesos." In addition to local produce, there are groceries brought in from the state capital, Oaxaca, mostly by local traders. At the bottom of the market, you hear more Spanish. There's also an area where you can buy clothes, American clothes, clothes in bulk—in recent years there are a number of clothes stalls whose prices vary from 30 to 200–300 pesos for a decent jacket, while other stalls sell gabanes, a kind of woollen poncho, usually woven on a foot loom. You can also find the community's characteristic wide, traditional skirts and of course Tlahui blouses, which many women are wearing, both young and old, because market day is also a day to get your glad rags on.

## My Tlahui Blouse

Tlahuitoltepec is a Mixe community in the Sierra Norte of the state of Oaxaca. It's known for being home to one of the state's longest standing musical education projects, the Centro de Capacitación Musical y Desarrollo de la Cultura Mixe (Center for Musical Training and the Development of Mixe Culture). In 2015, Tlahui made it into the news because its traditional blouse was plagiarized by a French brand. The story goes something like this.

We learned via social media that the designer Isabel Marant had begun selling a Tlahui blouse, and later realized she also had a skirt, jacket, trousers and tunic bearing patterns that are characteristic of our community's blouse. All these items formed part of her low-cost spring-summer line and they each had a name: Vicky, Viola, April, as well, of course, as labels bearing the brand name "Isabel Marant." In June 2015, a couple of months after the news began to circulate, the community leaders spoke out against what they considered to be an act of plagiarism, because nowhere in the marketing materials could they find a reference to the community where the patterns originated.

## Xëëw—Celebration

At Tlahuitoltepec's village celebrations there are always at least three philharmonic bands, comprising around 150 musicians, both men and women. Forty years ago, the first Mixe women began to read music and play instruments. There are currently two women's philharmonic bands. A huge amount of community work goes into making this music available—there is a whole communal structure ensuring the bands are fed and that the events taking place during the festivities are organized. During calenda processions, on the first day of festivities, those who have been selected to look after the bands in their homes are formally presented. This responsibility, borne once in each person's lifetime in the community, is called the Festivities Commission or the Captaincy (Kaptän). The women wear their Tlahui garb, skirt, blouse, sash, rebozo and huaraches. There are skirts in every color and blouses in many different patterns. These days there are even huaraches with Tlahui embroidery on them. The official uniform of the Tlahuitoltepec Philharmonic Band is Tlahui traditional dress—for both women and men, wearing textiles is part of their community identity.

## Appropriation by Dispossession

David Harvey proposes the concept of "accumulation by dispossession," referring to the perpetuation and proliferation of the accumulation practices Marx considered to be "original" or "primitive" during the rise of capitalism. In practice, these involve the commodification and privatization of land and the forced displacement of rural populations, as well as the conversion of different kinds of property rights (communal, collective, state, etc.) into exclusively private property rights.

Building on this idea, I propose that the *plagiarism* and/or appropriation of the Tlahui blouse and its pattern by Isabel Marant and Antik Batik (another French fashion brand that also copied Tlahui textiles, in their Bartra collection in 2014) comprises the changing of various forms of collective-communal property rights into private property, given that before the act of plagiarism occurred the embroidery was considered part of a collective cultural identity. It was a textile bearing patterns that identify a specific community and which are reproduced communally. This isn't to deny that the patterns were elaborated by specific people nor that there was local commercialization, but these people create and produce in a defined community context and the clothes they make circulate in a market that clearly identifies their origin. Which is to say, in the words of Tlahuitoltepec's community leaders in their June 2015 statement, Marant and Antik Batik have committed "the appropriation of cultural heritage."

Harvey's "accumulation by dispossession" involves privatization and commodification, for example in the form of biopiracy and the commodification through tourism of cultural forms, history, and intellectual creativity. Although Harvey takes music as his example, the ideas could perfectly well be applied to textiles. By 2019, several cases of textile plagiarism had been documented in different parts of Mexico, by both Mexican and foreign brands, as had similar cases in Indigenous villages and communities in other countries.

In Oaxaca we have a clear example of the commodification of culture through tourism: Guelaguetza, the annual Indigenous cultural festival, confirms that the prevailing economic model's mechanisms of dispossession are effective and that Indigenous towns and communities themselves can and do form part of that logic. In this sense, what those brands did with the Tlahui blouse was to turn it into a commodity, to remove a common good from its communal logic.

Similarly, the Maya Kaqchikel researcher Aura Cumes identifies this act as the consequence of a process of colonization in which not only "are Indigenous populations excluded or marginalized, we are also turned into subjects available for plundering."

## The Community's Response

In 2015 the community leaders issued a statement about what was known of the situation so far. In the statement they denounced the act of plagiarism and demanded reparations for the damage—reparations which, in this case, were never said to involve financial compensation. Their main demands were:

1) public recognition of the plagiarism
2) that the production of the items in question be halted
3) that the named designer visit the community and learn about the local context in which the blouses are made

Articles published in the wake of the press conference emphasized that the Tlahuitoltepec community would sue the designer Isabel Marant for plagiarism. But nowhere does the statement talk of legal action; instead, it demands public recognition of the plagiarism.

The response from the Tlahuitoltepec community can be considered counterhegemonic in the face of an economic system that tolerates cultural dispossession and the commodification of goods understood to be communal. Indigenous populations around the world are part of the tolerated margins of states and of the prevailing economic system, because, as collectives, they are not completely integrated into that system, although individuals are gradually being incorporated. The way Indigenous peoples resist as collectives is based on the logic of their own political, territorial, and social rights; in that sense, to speak out as a community about an act of plagiarism, of cultural dispossession, without making financial demands, is to defy commercial logic, because we would usually expect a plagiarism claim to include monetary compensation as part of the reparations for the damage.

## Liv Tyler

In April 2015 an English online magazine published an article about the actress Liv Tyler, in which she appeared wearing a dress that, it was clear to me, bore Tlahui embroidery. But the magazine specified that the dress was by Isabel Marant. Some months later, a local Oaxacan newspaper used a photo of the same actress in the same dress in order to discuss the act of plagiarism, and the photo caption stated that Liv Tyler was wearing a Tlahui blouse. Comparing these two different approaches, I, at least, felt sure that that the latter's reference to the community amounted to reparations for the damage done.

## The Communal Dynamics of Textile Identity

In my community, it is mainly the women who embroider. The embroidery itself has changed over the course of the years, but recent iterations are still identifiable as part of a continuum, as the characteristic Tlahui textile. In several conversations, different women have told me that previously, when they travelled to the city of Oaxaca and saw someone in a Tlahui blouse, it was a sign that you had met a fellow member of the community, that that person was certain to be from Tlahuitoltepec. Now it's common to see not only the classic colors but also new colors and embroidery worn by people who are not from Tlahuitoltepec. Whether this is a good or bad thing is not for me to decide, but what I can say is that it has brought about a transformation in the dynamics of production and trade. The cost of the blouses has increased, and the embroidery has diversified to a great variety of clothing, including accessories and shoes.

In 2018 the Museo Textil de Oaxaca (Oaxaca Textile Museum) and the municipality of Tlahuitoltepec organized a temporary exhibition in the Museo Comunitario (Community Museum), showcasing blouses from different communities that had all been made on sewing machines. Nicholas Johnson, an anthropologist and an expert in textiles, has demonstrated on various occasions that though the sewing machine arrived just over a hundred years ago in the Sierra Norte of Oaxaca, thanks to the use of this new technology people began to create clothes that are today considered part of our culture, and that those clothes have no less value as part of our identity than clothing made on a backstrap loom. The backstrap loom is still used in Tlahuitoltepec, mainly to make gabanes. The exhibition "Ja kipy ja ujts miti' pëjtëp" (Flowering Trees) was opened as part of a community patron saint celebration; women who had at some point in their lives embroidered textiles were invited to the opening. One grandmother brought with her a blouse she had embroidered herself, to show the others and to demonstrate her worry that the blouses made today aren't of the same quality. "These days the machines do all the needlework," she said, suggesting that it's not the same. Indeed, it's not the same, as there is now greater access to tools to help embroider clothing, but what has remained constant is the fact that it is still women's work. That said, there are also men who do it, who have joined the centers of family production due to the current high demand for embroidery.

During the month that the exhibition lasted, children, teenagers, and adults from the community were able to see a blouse that was part of the Museo Textil de Oaxaca's cultural heritage, a blouse from Tlahuitoltepec made around the beginning of 1970. It was, let's say, the star of the exhibition. I learned many things about the business of the cloth and thread, about the community's first sewing machines, about cotton production, and about the church's role in reviving the use of the Tlahui traditional garb. This last move was so successful that one of the community's primary schools has it as its official school uniform. Every Monday you can see the girls arrive at school in their green skirts and embroidered blouses.

Embroidery provided several women in their sixties, seventies, and eighties with an additional source of income that, in certain cases, allowed them to provide better living conditions for their children. A grandmother spoke of how she wasn't necessarily paid in money; exchanges were also made with other kinds of goods, such as firewood, food, poultry, etc. There weren't many women who embroidered blouses—it was more common to learn to embroider the wide skirts bearing designs that represent ears of wheat.

Thanks to the publicity of the plagiarism case, the blouses became more widely known, and some women who previously only sold their wares locally were invited to craft fairs. Those women who already had access to those sales channels now have even more avenues open to them. The impact of the media attention gradually became tangible, both in the demand for clothing and in the increase in its price. Many family workshops grew and took on new hands. In 2012 I was aware of only one social media page that sold items, including blouses, with Tlahuitoltepec embroidery; in 2019 I can count at least sixteen digital platforms where either the embroiderers themselves or their family members who live in the city are selling more or less directly. These platforms are in addition to increasingly popular collaborative design pages: designers who travel to the communities and buy embroidery or establish collaborative relationships, whether just or unjust, with the embroiderers.

## Kutunk—Authority

For as long as I can remember, women have worn their Tlahui garb to carry out the responsibilities conferred on them—when they're given some community task, on 1 or 15 January, say, or 1 November. Being given this responsibility, taking up that baton, is an important moment for which you dress elegantly. Over the last ten years I've seen how the Tlahui garb has come to be an important part of women's public service. Recently, men too have opted to wear embroidered shirts, but the women of Tlahuitoltepec—the Xaam Të'ëxy—have always stood out because at public events, whether communal or not, they always wear their Xaam Nïxuy.

In the prevailing economic system, the mechanisms for plundering Indigenous communities are increasingly diverse and as violent as ever. If one designer can claim to have been inspired by Tlahui's textiles, another can go so far as to sue for authorship of them, because the legal mechanisms are not clear, nor does the current legal framework accommodate things that are considered to have been collectively created and owned. While these mechanisms of symbolic dispossession continue to be consolidated and to find a degree of validation in comments claiming, for instance, that we ought to be pleased such a famous designer "noticed our clothing," the Tlahui embroiderers operate increasingly often according to the supply and demand logic of the market outside the community. That logic has a direct impact on the way they work, but it has also allowed the women to increase their buying power.

**Milena Ang** is Assistant Professor in the Department of Political and Social Sciences at Universitat Pompeu Fabra, Barcelona. Her research interests include democratization, transitional justice, and inequality in the Mexican criminal justice system. Milena holds a BA in Political Science from CIDE in Mexico City (2008) and a PhD in Political Science from the University of Chicago (2017).

**Tania Islas Weinstein** is an Assistant Professor in the Political Science Department at McGill University. She studies the ways in which art and aesthetics shape the way people experience the world as politically significant and the ways in which identities become essentialized and politically mobilized, as well as interpretive theories and methods. She earned her BA in Political Science from the Centro de Investigación y Docencia Económicas (CIDE) and her MA and PhD from the University of Chicago.

**Ellen Jones** is a writer, editor, and literary translator from Spanish. Her recent and forthcoming translations include *Cubanthropy* by Iván de la Nuez (Seven Stories Press, 2023), *The Remains* by Ave Barrera (Charco Press, 2023), and *Nancy* by Bruno Lloret (Two Lines Press, 2021). Her monograph, *Literature in Motion: Translating Multilingualism Across the Americas* is published by Columbia University Press (2022). Her short fiction has appeared in *Slug* and *The London Magazine*.

**Jumko Ogata-Aguilar** is a writer and antiracism educator from Xalapa, Veracruz. She studied an undergraduate degree in Latin American studies at UNAM in Mexico City. She writes fiction, essays and film criticism and has been published by the British Council in Mexico, *la Revista de la Universidad* and *Vogue Mexico*, and is currently a columnist for Coolhuntermx.

**Eugenia Iturriaga** is Professor of Anthropological Sciences at the Universidad Autónoma de Yucatán. She has published numerous scholarly articles and books, including her much applauded book, *Las élites de la ciudad blanca: discursos racistas sobre la otredad*.

**Mónica G. Moreno Figueroa** is a Black-mestiza, Mexican-British, Associate Professor in Sociology at the University of Cambridge. She is also a Fellow in Social Sciences at Downing College, Cambridge. Her research focusses on the intersectional lived experience of 'race' and racism in Mexico and Latin America; antiracism; feminist theory, intersectionality, and racism. Since 2010, alongside Emiko Saldívar and Judith Bautista, Mónica has co-led the Collective for the Elimination of Racism in Mexico, COPERA, a non-profit organization where activists and scholars work towards the elimination of racism in Mexico.

**Perla Valero** is a doctoral candidate in Latin American Studies at the National Autonomous University of Mexico (UNAM) where she currently teaches at the Faculties of Philosophy and Political Science.

**Patricio Solís** is Professor-Researcher at the Center for Sociological Studies at El Colegio de México, where he studies inequality, social mobility, and racial/ethnic discrimination in Mexico. He is the principal investigator of the Proyecto sobre Discriminación Etnico-Racial en México (PRODER).

**Braulio Güémez** is a PhD student in the Department of Sociology at Duke University. His research interests are centered around racial stratification across the Americas using quantitative methods.

**Máximo Ernesto Jaramillo-Molina** is an Associate Professor at CUCSH, University of Guadalajara, Mexico, where he studies attitudes to redistributive justice, the legitimacy of inequality, social policies, fiscal justice and the measurement of poverty and inequality. He is also a researcher and founder of the Institute of Studies on Inequality (INDESIG) and Senior Fellow by the Atlantic Fellows for Social and Economic Equity (AFSEE) at the London School of Economics.

**Yásnaya Elena A. Gil** is an Ayuujk linguist, writer, translator, and human-rights activist. Born in Ayutla Mixe, Oaxaca, she collaborates for a variety of outlets in Mexico, including *Letras Libres* and *Nexos*, as well as in international publications, like *El País*. Her edited book *Ää: Manifiestos sobre la diversidad lingüística* was published in 2020 by Editorial Almadía.

**Alejandra Leal** is Professor of Anthropology at Mexico's National Autonomous University and an affiliated researcher to the Program on "Cities, Management, Territory and Environment" at the same university. She holds a doctorate in anthropology from Columbia University.

**Alfonso Forssell Méndez** is a writer and independent researcher in cultural studies. He has an MSc in Sociology of Media and Communication from Lund University, Sweden. His line of work, published in specialized and general spaces, pursues a materialist perspective to analyze how cultural practices relate to wider systems of power in Mexico, such as class and race.

**Itza Amanda Varela Huerta** is an Assistant Professor in the Department of Education at the Autonomous Metropolitan University Xochimilco (UAM-X). She was previously a professor at the Interdisciplinary Program of Gender Studies at the Colegio de México and a postdoctoral researcher at the Centro de Investigaciones y Estudios Superiores (CIESAS) in Social Anthropology in the city of Oaxaca. She holds a PhD in Social Sciences from the UAM-X and an MA in Latin American Studies from the UNAM.

**Hugo Ceron-Anaya** is an Associate Professor of Sociology at Lehigh University. Dr. Ceron-Anaya's work has appeared in a wide range of academic journals. His first book, *Privilege at Play: Class, Race, Gender, and Golf in Mexico* (Oxford University Press, 2019), was awarded the "2020 Outstanding Book Award" by the North American Society for the Sociology of Sports.

**Alice Krozer** is Assistant Professor at the Centro de Estudios Sociológicos at El Colegio de México. Dr. Krozer holds a PhD in Development Studies from University of Cambridge. In addition to publishing in academic venues, Dr. Krozer writes avidly for the popular press and hosts the "Inequalities" series of FutureFramedTV.

**José Ángel Koyoc Kú** holds a BA in History from the Universidad Autónoma de Yucatán (UADY) and a MA in History from Centro de Investigaciones y Estudios Superiores en Antropología Social–Sede Peninsular (CIESAS). He is an activist and an independent historian for the Equipo Indignación, Promoción y Defensa de los Derechos Humanos and a founding member of the public history Project K'ajlay.

**Josefa Sánchez Contreras** is a PhD candidate of Mesoamerican studies from UNAM, where she also obtained a MA degree in. Latin American Studies. She writes about energy colonialism and community and Indigenous movements in Latin America, tracing agrarian conflicts and communal resistance to extractive projects.

**Meztli Yoalli Rodríguez Aguilera** was born and raised in Puebla, Mexico. She is an Assistant Professor of Latin American and Latino Studies at **DePaul University**. She holds a PhD in Latin American Studies with an emphasis in Social Anthropology at the University of Texas, Austin. She is part of the Decolonial Feminist Network in Mexico.

**Ariadna Solis** is a Yalalteca woman, second generation migrant. She is a political scientist and art historian from the National Autonomous University of Mexico. She is part of the Dill Yel Nbán collective, whose work focuses on the investigation, transmission and dissemination of the Zapotec language and culture.

**Tajëëw B. Díaz Robles** holds an MA in Social Anthropology and is a member of the Colmix collective. Her work is primarily on the normative systems of Indigenous communities in Oaxaca, textile identity, and digital activism in Indigenous languages.

# Acknowledgments

The authors would like to thank the following sources for allowing a translated reprint of the following chapters.

Interlude 1: "Race is an illusion" by Jumko Ogata-Aguilar was originally published in the September 2020 issue of the *Revista de la Universidad* magazine. The original title is "La raza es una ilusión." The original article can be found in the following link: https://www.revistadelauniversidad.mx/articles/d59cd971-a224-4ef3-b220-e08bc6866048/la-raza-es-una-ilusion.

Interlude 2: "What is disgust for? Antiblack Racism in Mexico" by Mónica G. Moreno Figueroa was originally published in the September 2020 issue of the *Revista de la Universidad* magazine. The original title is "¿De qué sirve el asco? Racismo antinegro en México." The original article can be found in the following link: https://www.revistadelauniversidad.mx/articles/1d9d5638-d8fb-46b1-a0bc-b74715ec5994/de-que-sirve-el-asco-racismo-antinegro-en-mexico.

Interlude 3: "Mirrors for Gold: The Paradoxes of Inclusion" by Yásnaya Elena A. Gil was originally published on the website of Revista Gatopardo on July 9th, 2020.The original title of the article is: "Espejitos po roro: las paradojas de la inclusion" and can be found in the following link: www.gatopardo.com/opinion/yasnaya-gil-espejitos-por-oro-el-abuso.

Interlude 7: "The Communal Dynamics of Textile Identity: #MyTlahuiBlouse" by Tajëëw B. Díaz Robles was originally published in the September 2020 issue of the *Revista de la Universidad* magazine. The original title is "Dinámicas comunitarias de la identidad textil #MiBlusadeTlahui." The original article can be found in the following link: https://www.revistadelauniversidad.mx/articles/9697b7cd-80bb-44b3-95d3-571d5d3c32d5/dinamicas-comunitarias-de-la-identidad-textil.

Chapter 10: "Reconfiguring Methodologies for the Study of Textiles: Weaving and Wearing the Huipil in Villa Hidalgo Yalálag," by Ariadna Solis was originally published in *H-ART. Revista de historia, teoría y crítica de arte*, number 7 (2020): 69–89: https://doi.org/10.25025/hart07.2020.05. The original title of the article is "Reconfigurando las metodologías para el estudio de nuestro textiles: tejer y vestir el huipil en Villa Hidalgo Yalálag."

The editors would also like to thank Paula López Caballero, Jonny Bunning, and Jan Dutkiewicz for their insightful feedback on the Introduction, as well as Haley Aguilar and Guadalupe Cruz Orozco for the research support provided. Finally, they would also like to thank the Race and Capitalism Project for providing the funds to cover the cost of all the translations. They also want to thank the Project's director, Dr. Michael Dawson for the support, encouragement, and enthusiasm, which were crucial to getting the manuscript published.